THE IRISH QUESTION
1840–1921

by the same author

THE IRISH FREE STATE
ITS GOVERNMENT AND POLITICS

THE GOVERNMENT OF NORTHERN IRELAND
A STUDY IN DEVOLUTION

SOUTH AFRICA 1906–1961
THE PRICE OF MAGNANIMITY

THE IRISH QUESTION

1840–1921

*A Commentary on Anglo-Irish Relations and on
Social and Political Forces in Ireland in
The Age of Reform and Revolution*

by

NICHOLAS MANSERGH

M.A., D. LITT.

---

*My mind is upon Erin,
Upon Loch Lene, upon Linny,
Upon the land where the Ulstermen are,
Upon gentle Munster and upon Meath*

COLUMCILLE, GREETING TO IRELAND
TRANS. KUNO MEYER

NEW AND REVISED EDITION

LONDON: GEORGE ALLEN & UNWIN LTD

ST. BONAVENTURE LIBRARY
ST. BONAVENTURE, N. Y.

DA
951
.M3
1965a

NEW AND REVISED EDITION
UNDER THE TITLE *The Irish Question*
FIRST PUBLISHED IN 1965

*This book is copyright under the Berne Convention.
Apart from any fair dealing for the purposes of private
study, research, criticism or review, as permitted under
the Copyright Act, 1956, no portion may be reproduced
by any process without written permission. Inquiries
should be made to the publishers*

This Revised Edition © George Allen & Unwin Ltd., 1965

FIRST PUBLISHED IN 1940
UNDER THE TITLE *Ireland in The Age of Reform
and Revolution*

PRINTED IN GREAT BRITAIN
in 11-point Fournier Type
BY UNWIN BROTHERS LTD
WOKING AND LONDON

400361

AUG 6 '30

MAR 6 1931

TO DIANA

CONTENTS

INTRODUCTION

A generation ago it was frequently remarked that the Irish question had never passed into history because it had never passed out of politics. That is no longer true. Anglo-Irish relations, though liable to be a source of recurring friction while the Border remains, are not now the subject of unending and embittered political controversy either in England or in Ireland. For that the Anglo-Irish Treaty, 1921, was chiefly responsible. By transforming the character of Anglo-Irish relations, it removed the major cause of conflict. The petition for a reform of the constitution of the United Kingdom of Great Britain and Ireland, so persistently pressed for so many years at Westminster by Irish Nationalist Members had therein found its answer—though not as the result of Parliamentary debate and henceforward the pattern of Anglo-Irish relations was determined by negotiations between two sovereign States. The Irish Question as it was understood in Victorian England had passed into history.

This book aims at throwing light on the nature of Anglo-Irish relations in that long, last phase of the Union, which opened when Repeal became the declared goal of Irish nationalist endeavour and closed when that goal was finally attained. It is intended, however, not to provide a history of Anglo-Irish relations 1840–1921, but rather to offer a commentary upon some of the more important aspects of them. It is the case that the problems of which the book treats have been suggested by the period it covers, but it is the problems, not the period, with which it is at root concerned. This happens to be in accord with Lord Acton's injunction that one should study problems not periods, but it was in fact an approach suggested by less abstract considerations. There are already in existence some few chronicles covering this highly significant period in English as well as in Irish history, but in them the recording of events has precluded much in the way of critical analysis of the interaction of short-term policies and underlying causes. Here the emphasis is otherwise. It is the principal purpose of this book to explore some questions that possess enduring historical significance and in so doing to illuminate the background to policies, whose merits are often disputed with insufficient awareness of the practical preoccupations and the theoretical preconceptions of those by whom they were first formulated. This book is, therefore, essentially an essay, or rather a series of essays, in political and historical analysis. As such it is inevitably selective, but not, I hope, arbitrary in its choice of topics.

The time has perhaps come when it is necessary, as it was not when this book was published in its earlier form, to emphasize the importance of the task. The Irish Question was the most significant problem in *politics* which confronted English democracy in the late nineteenth and early twentieth centuries. It failed to provide a solution. Why? Was the Question not in fact susceptible of a democratic solution? Or alternatively was it one which a democracy was ill-fitted to resolve? Or was it because the Irish social system and her economic circumstances worked against or even precluded an otherwise seemingly natural political solution? Or because Irish intransigence made it unattainable? Or was it because English statesmanship was insular and unimaginative? To these questions many categoric but few convincing answers have been given. This book is written in the belief that a reappraisal of contemporary evidence of a kind that may serve to place in perspective the growth and gradual development of those forces which were to prove dominant in moulding the future history of Ireland, affords a fruitful approach to an assessment of the nature of the Irish question and to an understanding of the difficulties of resolving it peacefully. For the history of nineteenth-century Ireland is more than a prologue to the events of the twentieth and has a character of its own, which is all too often distorted by those who, neglecting all else, confine their attention to the signposts which point to the developments of a later age. Irish history would be a simpler, but a less rewarding subject, were it indeed the case that all the signposts pointed one way.

Gibbon in his *Autobiography* confessed that he shrank in terror from the prospect of writing a history of England under the Stuarts, because in such a history 'every character is a problem, and every reader a friend or an enemy', and the author was supposed 'to hoist the flag of party' and then having done so was 'devoted to damnation by the adverse faction'. The terrors which determined Gibbon to seek a more congenial field, may be thought fanciful by comparison with those which await the writer, who ventures in a critical spirit into the field of modern Irish history. It is a field some parts of which at least, it may well be for this reason, have remained almost unexplored and if I may not claim indulgence for courage (or temerity), perhaps some allowance may reasonably be made for the difficulties in assessing evidence on topics subjected to varying and controversial analyses over a con-

siderable period of time. 'Where to find the absolute truth', reflected
Alexis de Tocqueville in July 1835, after some hours spent discussing
the state of Ireland, first with the Catholic priest and then with the
Protestant rector of a small distressed parish near Tuam in Co. Galway.[1] Historians, and not least Irish historians, are, however, less
aspiring. They would be well content with relative truth, and in the
search for that more modest goal, the observations of travellers from
other countries and the commentaries, especially of some distinguished
European observers of the nineteenth-century Irish scene, may serve,
even where factual precision is lacking, to widen the view and to
prompt some critical enquiry into large, but often neglected topics.
Of course these visitors, experienced and eminent men though many
of them were, neither discarded their preconceptions nor assumed a
mantle of impartiality when they embarked upon their Irish travels.
It was, however, because of, rather than in spite of this limitation that
they looked on Ireland's past and present problems as at once a part
and an outcome of European history and, in so doing, they not only
shed some new light upon them, but asked questions of lasting and
fundamental significance. They, at least, did not think that the signposts all pointed one way.

This book is based upon an earlier work, *Ireland in the Age of
Reform and Revolution*, published in 1940. Since that time there have
been many specialist studies treating of episodes or events of great and
sometimes dramatic moment, which both individually and collectively
have contributed much to the extension and enrichment of our
knowledge of nineteenth-century Irish history. In so far as is consistent
with the design of the book, full account is taken of what may be
not unfairly described as the revolution[2] that has taken place in
modern Irish historical studies and thinking in the last quarter
of a century. It is, moreover, a revolution whose force is by no means
spent. In the course of rewriting I have also made use on particular
points of the evidence to be found in certain collections of private
papers, notably the Gladstone and the Campbell-Bannerman papers in
the British Museum, the Carnarvon papers at the Public Record Office,
the Asquith papers in the Bodleian Library at Oxford, the Redmond

[1] Alexis de Tocqueville, *Journeys to England and Ireland*, edited by J. P. Mayer
(London, 1958), p. 173. For the record of his conversations see pp. 160–73.
[2] *Irish Historical Studies*, the Journal of the Irish Historical Society and the Ulster
Society for Irish Historical Studies, which were founded in Dublin and Belfast respectively in 1936 to promote the scientific study of Irish history, has been an important,
possibly determining, factor in bringing it about.

papers in the National Library in Dublin and the archives of the State Department, Washington. This has meant a book very considerably enlarged, new in the greater part of its content, but retaining the design and purposes of its predecessor.

The book belongs, in that last sense, to its own time. This, I think, is as it must and should be. But the lapse of nearly a quarter of a century since the earlier work was published has caused me to make revisions more personal in kind. My own reflections and research on Anglo-Irish history in the intervening years have led me to develop the argument or extend the enquiry in respect of topics, which seem to me to have acquired enhanced interest with the passage of time. I have also qualified assertions which seem to me now to have been too strongly phrased and modified, or altogether removed, exuberances of style which now appear to me no longer tolerable. 'I had too much fondness for my productions to judge of them at first,' wrote Alexander Pope in the preface to his Collected Works first published in 1716,[1] 'and too much judgment to be pleased with them at last.' In this Pope was speaking for many authors.

My thanks remain to Professor, now Senator, George O'Brien, D.Litt. of University College, Dublin; to Mr R. B. McCallum, now Master of Pembroke College, Oxford; to Dr G. D. Ramsay, Fellow of St Edmund Hall, Oxford, with whom I had many discussions on the comparative validity of the essentially political and the economic interpretation of nineteenth-century Irish history, which I still remember with pleasure and profit; and the late Miss Olive Armstrong, Lecturer in Political Science at Trinity College, Dublin, for criticism, comment and advice in the preparation of the earlier edition of this book. My greatest debt remains to my wife, who has read both editions in proof and prepared the indices for each of them.

N. MANSERGH
St John's College,
Cambridge.
July, 1964

---

[1] *The Works of Alexander Pope, Esquire; with explanatory Notes and Additions never before printed,* was first published in Ireland in M,D,CC,XL by A. Bradley and T. Moore, Booksellers in Dame-Street, and it is from this edition (p. 8) that my quotation is taken.

ACKNOWLEDGEMENTS

The extracts from *Karl Marx and Friedrich Engels: Correspondence 1846–95* and from *Marx, Letters to Dr Kugelmann* are reprinted by kind permission of Martin Lawrence Limited and the extracts from W. B. Yeats's *Collected Poems*, and from his *Last Poems* by kind permission of Messrs. Macmillan. I am indebted to the Trustees of the British Museum for leave to consult the Gladstone and the Campbell-Bannerman papers, to the Public Record Office and to the National Library, Dublin, respectively for permission to use the Carnavon and the Redmond papers, to Mr Mark Bonham-Carter for allowing me to study the Asquith papers in the Bodleian Library at Oxford and to the State Department, Washington, for giving me access to material in their archives.

PART I
IRELAND UNDER THE UNION:
THE OPINIONS OF
SOME CONTEMPORARY OBSERVERS

CHAPTER I

THE STATE OF IRELAND
IN THE EARLY YEARS OF THE UNION

CONTEMPORARY OBSERVATIONS
AND SOME REFLECTIONS UPON THEM

The most terrible thing is that there is nothing terrible.
TURGENEV

———————

When Queen Victoria ascended the throne, England was already
confronted with the consequences of the greatest failure in its history.
The passing centuries had witnessed the attempts of Englishmen to
conquer Ireland. The task that seemed more than half accomplished by
the ruthless efficiency of the predatory barons, who owed allegiance to
the great Angevin king, was nearly all undone two centuries later when
the feckless Richard of Bordeaux was trapped among the Wicklow
hills. It was resumed with force and finesse by the Tudors, who saw in
Ireland at once a menace to their security and an outlet for the super-
abundant vitality of Renaissance England. A generation ambitious 'to
seek new worlds, for gold, for praise, for glory' undertook, among
more distant but scarcely more hazardous enterprises, the colonization
of Ireland. The names of the Planters, or Undertakers as they were
known, reflected the brilliance of an heroic age. Edmund Spenser was
among them and while living at Kilcolman castle under the Ballyhoura
hills he added two cantos to *The Faerie Queen*. Nearby, in the demesne
of Doneraile 'among the coolly shade of the green alders', he walked
conversing with Philip Sidney and with Walter Raleigh[1]—that 'tall
handsome bold man' who was 'damnable proud' and who may indeed
be thought of as the prototype of all Elizabethan planters. Raleigh
acquired some 40,000 acres of Munster land, but despite still vivid
tradition in Youghal, he lived but briefly in his house beside St Mary's

[1] Cf. Elizabeth Bowen, *Bowen's Court. The story of an Anglo-Irish family from the time
of Cromwell to the present day* (London, 1942), pp. 3–4.

Church and, regrettable as it may seem, neither planted the first Irish potatoes in its garden[1] nor was dowsed with water under the mulberry tree by a housekeeper, who thought he was on fire, when he was smoking tobacco.[2] But it was the case that all his vast estates, after years of neglect, were bought by a more businesslike adventurer, Richard Boyle, the Great Earl of Cork, for a mere £1,000.[3] In this there was something symbolic. The reputation of the Elizabethan settlers, won for the most part in other fields, remains; but their Irish enterprise, lacking all sustained sense of purpose, proved deservedly transient. And so in succeeding centuries the sombre tale of Plantation, of rebellion, of Cromwellian violence, of civil and religious war, of the penal Code, mocked the illusion of a final Elizabethan settlement.

The English invasions of Ireland were unending because the conquest was never complete. And all the while through the long years of adversity, pressure from without was consolidating within a core of resistance to the invader, which depended in the last resort, not upon destructible material forces, but upon a slowly maturing and finally indestructible conviction that Ireland should and would be free. Resistance and rebellion were always unavailing, for a poverty-stricken and ill-disciplined people, whose distaste for compromise left them disunited in many crises, could not hope successfully to challenge the resources of an island power whose heritage was the dominion of the sea. Yet in as much as manifestations of the will to resist kept alive the spirit of resistance, they were not barren of result. While the sporadic rebellions were wasteful of lives that could ill be spared, it may well be that nationalist historians are right in saying that, by such sacrifices alone, was Ireland enabled to nourish a tradition so vivid, so emotional, so fanatical as to resist the miasmata of failure and despair. As Napoleon had fanned to flame nationalism in conquered Germany and in Italy, so, too, the English rulers of Ireland, having failed while yet there was time to take the measures necessary to conciliate a not-

---

[1] Milton Waldman in his biography, *Sir Walter Raleigh* (London, 1950, New Edition), p. 45 despairs of controverting a legend that has persisted almost unquestioned from the seventeenth century until now. So do I—but *magna est veritas et praevalebit*!

[2] An illustration by Alfred Croquis (D. Maclise, R.A.) in *The Reliques of Father Prout* (coll. and arranged by Oliver Yorke, London, 1860) combines something of both stories in that it shows Raleigh directing the planting of the first potato in Ireland with smoke rising in a small cloud from his pipe.

[3] The tomb of the Great Earl, one of the most splendid and elaborate pieces of late Renaissance sculpture in Ireland, is in St Mary's Church at Youghal: Raleigh's body is buried in the Tower of London, his head having been given to his widow after his execution.

unfriendly people, were confronted at the last by an Irish ideal which, alien to their outlook yet fostered by their misrule, was to prove a source of strength more resilient, because it was more single-minded, than any which a great Empire could command.

At the accession of Queen Victoria the catastrophic climax of British rule in Ireland lay in the distant future, yet its coming was not hidden from the sight of the observant. Nassau William Senior, the first Professor of Political Economy at the University of Oxford, a man so remarkable for his qualities of mind and judgement that Count Cavour acclaimed him '*l'ésprit le plus éclairé de la Grande-Bretagne*', was moved to discard his customary restraint in language and in the use of imagery and to write on a visit to Ireland in 1843: 'When Irish questions, or rather the *Irish Question* (for there is but one), has been forced on our attention, we have felt, like a dreamer in a nightmare, oppressed by the consciousness that some great evil was rapidly advancing—that mere exertion on our part would avert it, but that we had not the power to will that exertion.'[1] It was psychologically a revealing reaction to the state of Ireland after some forty years' of government under the Union.

THE STATE OF IRELAND: THE TESTIMONY OF TRAVELLERS AND COMMISSIONERS

The condition of Ireland in the middle years of the nineteenth century, or at least all of it outside Ulster, dismayed and distressed those who saw it—from Italian nationalists to Communist Internationalists, to Frenchmen, Germans, Americans and by no means least, to Englishmen, whether economists, officials or more ordinary voyagers. Some of them left records of their impressions and of these one of the most substantial and more rewarding was written by Gustave de la Bonninière de Beaumont, a scion of the lesser nobility in France, the lifelong friend of Alexis de Tocqueville, the companion of his American journeys of political exploration and finally his literary executor.

De Beaumont was brought up on the small family farm of the Château de la Borde by the valley of the Sarthe and there the life of the countryside pursued its accustomed ways. De Tocqueville, who stayed with the de Beaumonts, received impressions there which he felt threw

[1] *Journals, Conversations and Essays relating to Ireland* (London, 1868), 2 Vols., Vol. I, p. 19. Nassau Senior was descended from Spanish creoles who became British in the Bahamas and were first known as El Señor.

new light on the human heart. 'These "brave gens",' he wrote,[1] 'calm
of imagination and tranquil of heart, find pleasure where I should
never have been able to imagine that any existed. They take the liveliest
interest in the growth of a tree, in the raising of a crop, in the hatching
of a brood. They continue interested in such things for years and desire
nothing more, while men who have shaken the world have often died
of chagrin at being unable to do more.' Such simple, inherited interests
served de Beaumont well in the writing of his observations on Ireland
and if, by comparison with de Tocqueville, who visited the country
but once and alone in 1835 and recorded his impressions for the most
part in dialogue form,[2] de Beaumont's narrative lacks something in
directness and in purposefulness of enquiry, it compensates by its
descriptions and understanding of rural conditions.

De Beaumont had travelled widely, both in the New World and the
Old, when he came to write of the state of the Ireland of pre-famine
years; and he did so with a vividness that still strikes a chill of horror
to the heart. In an opening, carrying overtones of the challenging
aphorism with which Rousseau had prepared his readers for the
political doctrine of Le Contrat Social, his imagination finds an exci-
ting, and possibly for readers in this more prosaic age, a disturbing,
outlet. 'L'Irlande a été,' he begins,[3] 'par un destin fatal jetée sur
l'Océan auprès de l'Angleterre, à qui elle semble enchaînée par les mêmes
liens qui unissent l'esclave au maître.' But thereafter de Beaumont's
descriptions of life in pre-Famine Ireland, enlivened, if not perhaps
always enriched, by some flights of style and fancy, offer vivid,
illuminating and often penetrating commentaries on what he saw.

M. de Beaumont was most affected by the poverty that was apparent
in Ireland wherever he travelled, save only in Ulster. The country itself,
despite its beauty and the richness of its soil, seemed to him impoverished because of continuous mist and rain blowing across from the
Atlantic. It was the victim of its climate; and while 'ces montagnes
élégantes, ces grands lacs, ces praieries éternelles, ces collines aussi
fraîches que les vallées'[4] delighted the traveller with their beauty in the
bright sunlight, M. de Beaumont saw them nearly always half hidden
under leaden skies. The countryside, too, in most parts, having been

[1] G. W. Pierson, Tocqueville and Beaumont in America (New York, 1938), p. 21.
[2] Alexis de Tocqueville, Journeys to England and Ireland, edited by J. P. Mayer (London, 1958).
[3] L'Irlande Sociale, Politique et Réligieuse (Paris, 1839) 2 Vols., Vol. I, p. 187. The book is prefaced by a lengthy historical introduction.
[4] Op. cit., Vol. I, p. 189.

despoiled of trees, was bleak and so on a spring day it failed to give
that impression of renewed vitality for which the traveller had looked.

But if a countryside, whose charm may elude those who do not
know and love it well, depressed this French aristocrat, with memories
of his home by the sunlit, wooded valleys of the Sarthe, it aroused in
him emotions in full accord with those prompted by the sight of the
condition of the people themselves. 'I have seen the Indian in his
forests and the negro in his irons', wrote M. de Beaumont, 'and I
believed, in pitying their plight, that I saw the lowest ebb of human
misery; but I did not then know the degree of poverty to be found in
Ireland. Like the Indian, the Irishman is poor and naked; but he lives
in the midst of a society which enjoys luxury and honours wealth. . . .
The Indian retains a certain independence which has its attraction and a
dignity of its own. Poverty-stricken and hungry he may be, but he is
free in his desert places; and the feeling that he enjoys this liberty
blunts the edge of his sufferings. But the Irishman undergoes the same
deprivations without enjoying the same liberty, he is subjected to
regulations: he dies of hunger. He is governed by laws; a sad condition,
which combines the vices of civilization with those of primitive life.
Today the Irishman enjoys neither the freedom of the savage nor the
bread of servitude'.[1]

The language of one generation rarely carries conviction to the
men of another and M. de Beaumont's description, with its but half-
dissipated illusions about the happiness of the 'splendid savages' so
dear to the Romantics, so seductive to French travellers in the New
World from the Marquis de Lafayette to Alexis de Tocqueville
himself, might inspire little confidence, were it not that the accumulation of personal impressions and the factual evidence as to the dreadful
poverty of Ireland at this time are alike, and as it were, independently
irrefutable. De Tocqueville's notes on the conditions he observed on
his journey to the south by Carlow and Waterford to Kilkenny, and
on to the south-west by Mitchelstown to Cork, precisely recorded in
relation to area, at least explain why de Beaumont was stirred to write
in such terms, while his account of what he saw in a Dublin poor-house[2]
—brief, factual and quite horrible—brings a sharper and more painful
realization of the depths to which Irish misery could sink at this time
than any of the more eloquently phrased generalizations of his friend.
Nassau Senior, who was assuredly little disposed to exaggeration,

[1] Op. cit., Vol. I, pp. 204–5.
[2] *Journeys*, pp. 129–30, 136, 158 and pp. 121–2 for his account of his poor-house visit.

wrote of 'a population more unhappy in itself, and the cause of more
unhappiness to all who have to deal with it, than any other civilized
and free community in existence',[1] whilst the Report of the Commission appointed in 1843 by Peel to enquire into Irish agrarian problems
with Lord Devon as Chairman and with a wholly landlord membership,
remarked upon the 'patient endurance which the labouring classes have
generally exhibited under sufferings greater, we believe, than the people
of any other country in Europe have to sustain'.[2]

M. de Beaumont shared this opinion and considered that the
wretched condition of the Irish people could scarcely be compared
with that of any other country. Elsewhere the traveller might see some,
even a majority of the population, destitute, but nowhere else was
there to be found a whole nation of poor. To understand the social
state of such a country it was necessary to recall only 'ses misères et ses
souffrances; l'histoire des pauvres est celle de l'Irlande'. In order to
appreciate the measure of Irish poverty all preconceived ideas as to the
distinction between rich and poor must be put aside. In other countries
only those who were unemployed or who begged were considered
poor, but in Ireland farm labourers and even small farmers suffered a
degree of poverty such as was almost unknown elsewhere.[3] And the
wretchedness of the Irish people did not lessen with time; it was permanent because its cause was permanent, and famine, its most dread
manifestation, constituted a recurring climax.

The Irish countryside itself affords many contrasts between wealth
and poverty. The rich grass lands of Meath give way to the barren
beauty of the west, the Golden Vein where feed the cattle for which
Ireland is famed and the wide plains of Tipperary are bounded on the
north by hills and bog and by the Galtee mountains on the south,
while out to the west lies the windswept, rocky soil of the County
Clare. M. de Beaumont looking out over the Lakes of Killarney from
Muckross Abbey saw on the one side uncultivated fields, marshy wastes
studded with patches of heather, with here and there a stunted fir tree,
and on the other at the foot of a range of mountains, rich and smiling

---

[1] Op. cit., Vol. 1, p. 23.
[2] Report from H.M. Commissioners of Inquiry into the State of the Law and Practice in
Respect to the Occupation of Land in Ireland (Dublin, Alexander Thom for HMSO,
1845), p. 12.
[3] de Tocqueville on his journey from Kilkenny to Mitchelstown found relays of
children importuning passers-by almost all the way. He assumed from the houses that they
must be the children of beggars. He was assured this was not so—that the houses were
the homes of small farmers. Journeys, p. 158.

fields, woods of an almost tropical vegetation, a countryside at once fertile and extraordinarily beautiful. And he felt that the contrast between richness and poverty presented there reflected something characteristic of Ireland, not only of its countryside but also of the people who dwelt in it. The contrasts of nature were equalled by contrasts in the state of man. 'In Ireland the traveller', he noted, 'sees magnificent castles and wretched cabins: but no house which stands midway between the palaces of the great and the hovels of the indigent, for in this country there are only rich and poor.'[1]

M. de Beaumont believed the violent contrasts in living conditions in Ireland to be the outcome of a process, which had acquired momentum through the centuries, and by which rich and poor pursued their separate ways, the one leading to great wealth, the other to abject poverty. As the wealth of the one class increased, so the resources of the other diminished, till by the middle years of the nineteenth century, the country was inhabited by an aristocracy small in number living in great luxury, and the great majority of the people living in the lowest depth of poverty.

The oversimplified history and the epigrammatic distinctions, in which de Beaumont delighted, suggest a society in which the divisions were even more rigid and the contrasts even more pronounced than was in fact the case. When he writes that the incomes of landowners sometimes reached sums 'dont l'énormité nous paraît presque chimérique', when he describes the magnificent clothing of the rich in this impoverished island, their splendid castles, their huge demesnes, their mountains and fields, their woods and lakes and notes how the luxury of their life and the ostentation of their wealth stood out against the misery of the people, is he not allowing a natural emotion to influence judgement? The condition of Ireland was deplorable, the contrast between wealth and poverty in the opinion of the time as well as of later generations inexcusable, yet none the less it is also the case as de Tocqueville had occasion to note more than once, that the resources of many landlords were quite unequal to their responsibilities and to the state they sought or felt obliged to maintain. Nor is it to be doubted that the wealth of the greater Anglo-Irish landlords was equalled, and indeed generally much surpassed, by that of the land-owning classes and the new industrial élites in other countries,[2] that the magnificence of their

---

[1] Op. cit., Vol. I, p. 198.
[2] Arthur Young in his *Travels in Ireland* in 1777 remarked that 'There is a very good society in Dublin in a Parliament winter; a great round of dinners and parties. . . . The

ST. BONAVENTURE LIBRARY
ST. BONAVENTURE, N. Y.

country houses, which were in all too many instances indifferently designed, straggling buildings, composed of a central block with 'wings' added at various periods as capital allowed or pretension dictated, could scarcely bear comparison with the 'stately homes' of England, and still less with the Châteaux of the Loire. The 'luxury', too, of the lives of the Anglo-Irish landlords is frequently exaggerated. If abundance of food and wine—Father Mathew's Temperance movement was to gain few adherents among the ruling classes—be accounted luxury then the indictment is valid, but if by luxury is to be understood, not somewhat primitive pleasures, but the refinements of civilization in the art of life, then the charge must be disallowed. 'The *savoir-vivre* is but moderately advanced in Dublin', wrote John Gamble, an Army surgeon in 1810 and we know Dublin contrasted favourably with the provinces in this respect.

On the other side, too, M. de Beaumont compares the conditions of the people with those of the Indians in America. But he does not compare them with those of the factory workers in England and France, where even the children toiled in the coal mines some eighteen hours a day, with those of the Ruthenian peasant under his Magyar lord, with those of the Sicilians under Bourbon tyranny; or with those of the Spaniard toiling for the welfare of the high-bred nobles of Castile. Only a contemporary observer could have determined with finality what such a comparison would have revealed, but it is, to say the least, doubtful whether conditions were worse in Ireland than in Central Europe, in Spain or in the two Sicilies.[1] The point, though it deserves to be considered, little blunts the edge of criticism, for was it not the proud boast of Englishmen that they excelled all others in the art of government and that their country had acquired a standard of civilization unknown to the peoples of central and southern Europe? The

style of living may be guessed from the fortunes of the resident nobility and great commoners; there are about thirty that possess incomes from seven to twenty thousand pounds a year'. The standard of living among the wealthy impressed him as differing in nothing from that in England. C. Maxwell, *Dublin Under the Georges* (Revised edition, London, 1956), p. 314.

[1] While there is much valuable information about agricultural conditions in, for example, B. H. Slicher van Bath, *The Agrarian History of Western Europe A.D. 500–1850* (London, 1963), it is difficult, perhaps impossible, to secure reliable statistical evidence of rural conditions in the former Habsburg Empire or in Spain, or the two Sicilies of a kind to make comparisons worth while. *Labour in Agriculture*, by L. E. Howard (Oxford, 1935), published under the auspices of the Royal Institute of International Affairs, was in many respects a pioneer work but it gave an account of agricultural conditions only since 1919.

boast, which was not on the whole ill-founded, seems strangely in-substantial when it is found necessary to compare the consequences of British rule in Ireland with those of the rule of the most backward and tyrannical governments in Europe.

There are other and more personal considerations to be borne in mind. Travellers, and by tradition especially Gallic travellers, are tempted to generalize from what they themselves have seen. M. de Beaumont travelled much in the West and he was a witness to the ravages of famine in Connaught in 1835 and 1837. They made a deep and dreadful impression upon him. But in the West in general, and Connaught in particular, living conditions were worse than elsewhere in Ireland. The *Census* of 1841,[1] showed that the pressure of population upon resources was greater in Connaught than in any other province. Some 30 per cent of all the uncultivated land in the country was in that province, nearly 2,000,000 of its 4,392,043 acres being uncultivated, 78 per cent of its people were dependent upon agriculture and, more densely populated than either Munster or Leinster, Connaught had 386 people to the square mile of *arable* land as against 335 per square mile of arable in Ireland as a whole.[2] The proportion of very small holdings was greater than in any of the other provinces since Ulster, though more densely populated and having also a high proportion of very small holdings, possessed a diversified economy, which qualified both its dependence on agriculture and the pressure of population on the land.

De Beaumont recognized the distinctive character of Connaught; he wrote of it as '*le type de la vieille Irlande*' which, it appeared, '*la nature ait pris à cœur de lo distinguer des autres provinces*' and he noted that there was no part of the country where recollection of war and con-quest was more lively or where '*l'Anglais et le protestant ne sont détestés d'une haine plus religieuse et plus nationale*'.[3] De Tocqueville

---

[1] *Report of the Commissioners appointed to take the Census of Ireland for the year 1841* (Dublin, Alexander Thom for H M S O), Parl. Papers, 1843, xxiv.

[2] *Census Report* p. xiii and *Tables of Rural Economy* pp. 452–3. See also and generally E. R. R. Green's contribution on 'Agriculture' in *The Great Famine* edited by R. Dudley Edwards and T. Desmond Williams and published for the Irish Committee of Historial Sciences, Dublin, 1956, pp. 89–128. There is some discrepancy between the figures given by Dr Green on p. 89 and those given above. Dr Green, using the same census sources, states that 43 per cent of the uncultivated land in the country was in Connaught, which would appear to be an overstatement, and that the number of people per square mile of arable in Ireland as a whole was only 217, which would seem to be an understatement.

[3] Op. cit., Vol. I, pp. 193–4.

passing through Ennis seated on the top of the diligence was told by
his companion, an old man, of 'the fate of a great many families and a
great deal of land, passing through the times of Cromwell and of
William III with a terrifying exactitude of local memory'.[1] To the
West of the Shannon and along that 'stony sea-board, far and foreign'
recollection of the harsh Cromwellian alternatives of 'Hell or Connaught' indeed remained, and for long after de Tocqueville and de
Beaumont's time, even though in London clubs it was thought that it
might be more civilized to forget about them. But de Beaumont,
sympathetic, understanding and appalled by the consequences of
forcible transplantation still apparent to him two centuries later, would
seem to have allowed his impressions of that one province to have
imposed something of a stereotype upon his conclusions on the state
of the country as a whole outside Ulster. Or to put the point—and it is
one of some importance—rather differently, and perhaps more exactly,
he would seem to have taken insufficient account of the gradations in
the conditions, which we know existed, between the comparatively
fertile and less densely populated south and east and the comparatively
infertile and more thickly populated west and which were an important
element in the social and economic condition of Ireland at the time.
The Devon Commission gave graphic illustrations of these differences
in plates published with their Report, showing standards in house-
accommodation, in education (in terms of reading and writing) and the
amount of capital invested in livestock in the counties of Ireland. The
highest proportion of fourth class accommodation—and to qualify for
it housing conditions had to be on a level lower than would seem en-
durable by human beings in Irish climatic conditions—was all in the
Western counties, Roscommon, Sligo, Galway, Limerick, Cork,
Clare, Mayo and Kerry and included all the counties of Connaught.
In terms of literacy Galway and heavily populated Mayo came on their
own at the bottom of the list, as they did also in terms of property
invested in livestock. The contrast here was very marked, Meath at the
top of the list with £155 invested in livestock per 100 acres, had more
than twice as much as either Mayo or Galway with £69 and £67
respectively.

While the gradations in living conditions between counties and
provinces were thus appreciable and deserving of note, the division
between rich and poor in the Ireland of the Union, of which de Beaumont wrote, remained the dominant social reality. It was not only

[1] *Journeys*, p. 174.

great; it was also unbridgeable. This was only partly and questionably because, as de Beaumont maintained, it was wider than any to be found in other countries and far more, because of psychological mistrust verging in many areas on open hostility between rich and poor, and deriving at root from differences in origin and religion.

The Devon Commission remarked upon the existence and consequences of the mistrust between rich and poor, between landlord and tenant and they had no doubts about the unhappy consequences that flowed from it. 'The foundation of almost all the evils by which the social condition of Ireland is disturbed,' its authors observed, 'is to be traced to those feelings of mutual distrust, which too often separate the classes of landlord and tenant, and prevent all united exertion for the common benefit.'[1] 'Here', de Tocqueville was told by the Director General of the National Schools, a government official, 'we have all the evils of an aristocracy and none of its advantages. There is no moral tie between rich and poor; the differences of political opinion and religious belief and the actual distance that they live apart, make them strangers one to the other, one could almost say enemies.'[2] This mistrust or enmity extended, indeed, beyond the landlords and tenants to people and government. Of this Dr Doyle, Bishop of Kildare and Leighlin, gave a telling illustration—and incidentally also of the problems confronting the taking of a Census in Ireland in the early nineteenth century. 'The Catholics', the Bishop wrote[3] with a characteristic flourish, 'have ever been unwilling to make known their numbers to any agent of the Government. Having too often experienced from it what they deemed treachery or injustice, they naturally distrusted whomsoever approached them in its name. Ignorant of its views in computing the number of its slaves, these latter rather feared they were to be decimated or banished, as if in the time of Cromwell, to some bog or desert if found too numerous, than that any measures were to be adopted for the improvement of their condition.' A German traveller commented upon the scale of the violence bred by this canker of mistrust, eating away the fabric that ordinarily keeps societies at peace. 'We had now', wrote J. G. Kohl[4] of his experiences in 1843 'entered the notorious county of Tipperary, in which more murders and assaults are committed in one year than in the whole kingdom of

[1] P. 44.
[2] *Journeys*, p. 124.
[3] Quoted in K. H. Connell, *The Population of Ireland 1750–1845* (Oxford, 1950), p. 2. See also Chap. I for discussion of the reliability of the Census returns for 1841.
[4] J. G. Kohl, *Ireland, Scotland and England* (London, 1844), p. 110.

Saxony in five.' A chance encounter and a simple but misguided enquiry of the driver of a donkey cart[1] in the main street of Cahir, evoked a response so vehement and menacing as to convince the robust, hard-living German that the mistrust verging into violence might easily be extended to strangers.

'There is an upper class and a lower class. The middle class evidently does not exist, or else is confined to the towns as in the Middle Ages.' So de Tocqueville noted[2] and this absence of a middle class, apparent to all who visited Ireland, certainly underlined the gap between rich and poor and probably, by providing no social intermediary grouping, accentuated mistrust between them. Indeed, in de Beaumont's diagnosis of the manifold ills of the Irish social system, the growth of the *bourgeoisie* was assumed to be an essential preliminary condition to the application of any effective remedy; whilst Nassau Senior, at least equally aware of the gap and the consequent imbalance in the Irish social system, was concerned first with systematic analysis of causes and then with remedies that were practicable. A middle class, he was at some pains to emphasize, could not be quite simply wished into existence.

The evils that afflicted Ireland, Nassau Senior thought, like all other causes of national misery or happiness might be divided into two classes, those which were *material* and those which were *moral*. The material evils he thought were want of capital and want of small proprietors; the moral evils—'Insecurity, Ignorance and Indolence'. He did not think the material evils necessarily inconsistent with the substantial welfare of the people, though he was emphatic that without capital there could not be a middle class, for a middle class 'is the creature of capital'. But where, as in Ireland, there was little capital and therefore few small proprietors, society was divided into the very rich and the very poor, with scarcely any intermediate class. The land consequently was parcelled out into small holdings, because tenants without capital could cultivate them alone. In turn this subdivision made landlords unwilling or unable to employ capital, not least because to achieve results they would require the assistance and co-operation of many tenants, who were only too likely to entertain the suspicion that what was beneficial to the landlord must be mischievous for them.[3] All this

[1] Kohl asked him which way was he going—the sort of open question which country-men at all times view with not unreasonable suspicion.
[2] *Journeys*, p. 137.
[3] Op. cit., Vol. I, pp. 23–4.

was in sharp contrast to the situation in England and even in Ulster—
which he argued must be thought of as a different country because
with few exceptions the state of the population there was 'not merely
dissimilar but opposed'[1] to that in the rest of Ireland—and persuaded
him that the underlying weakness of the Union settlement lay in the
establishment of a single government to legislate for two countries,
whose social organizations were so sharply contrasted. 'It is frequently
overlooked', he wrote,[2] 'that the people of England and of Ireland—
meaning here, by Ireland, the provinces of Munster, Connaught,
some parts of Leinster, and the whole county of Donegal—are among
the most dissimilar nations in Europe. One is chiefly Protestant, the
other is chiefly Roman Catholic; one is principally manufacturing and
commercial, the other almost wholly agricultural; one lives chiefly in
towns, the other in the country. The population of the one is laborious,
but prodigal; . . . that of the other is indolent and idle, but parsi-
monious. . . . The one country possesses a large middle-class, the other is
divided between landlords and peasants: in the one the proprietors of
the soil are connected by origin, by interest and by feeling, with those
who occupy it; in the other, they are, in many cases, strangers, and, in
almost as many, enemies. In the one, public sympathy is with the law;
in the other, it is with those that break it. In England crime is infamous;
in Ireland it is popular.'

This imposing catalogue (which is here abbreviated considerably) of
national differences comprised some that were lasting, others that were
incidental and transient. Nassau Senior, who for all his air of academic impartiality was rather apt to ensure that the 'Irish dogs'
got the worst of it, concluded that to give similar treatment to countries
not merely different but contrasted was 'prescribing the same regimen
to the weak and to the strong, to the excitable and to the apathetic, to
the sound and to the diseased'.[3] The remedy he prescribed, however,
was political and economic reform conceded to Ireland by a paternal
government, not as his own diagnosis might rather suggest—a grant
of self-government. But Nassau Senior recognized the incompatibility
of despotic government in Ireland, side by side with constitutional
government in England. In consequence he recommended that while
Parliament should resolutely refuse to legislate for Ireland as if she
were a distinct state, yet the democratic element there should be
allowed to prevail to an extent which would be inadvisable 'if we looked

[1] Op. cit., Vol. I, p. 22. [2] Ibid., pp. 211–13.
[3] Ibid., p. 213.

merely to its immediate results; we must allow the people an amount of free action, which we know they will abuse, because worse evils even than that abuse will be produced if we restrain it'.[1]

Nassau Senior's enlightened advice was not of a kind that governments are generally disposed to follow save under extreme pressure. The democratization of Irish government in O'Connell's day might well have produced in time benefits to England, which would have been less substantial only than those conferred on Ireland. But none-the-less it was a remedy, however far-sighted, that had little to recommend it in the eyes of the English Government. For on the most favourable reckoning such a process would take long to achieve results and would therefore, apart from all other considerations, accord ill with the exigencies of party warfare. Moreover, while Englishmen who knew nothing of Ireland fully endorsed Nassau Senior's opinion that the Irish people 'agitate for the sake of agitation and select for their avowed object an unattainable end because it is unattainable—because its mischief cannot be tested by experience or its stimulus by possession', yet unlike him they did not sense, that even if the demand for Repeal were dismissed as a chimera, none the less the social and economic conditions of the people might lead to a catastrophe, such as would for ever tarnish the reputation of English government.

LAND TENURE; THE SYSTEM AND ITS ECONOMIC AND SOCIAL CONSEQUENCES

Statesmen, commissioners, travellers of every nationality and outlook who visited Ireland in the years before the Famine came to regard the system of land tenure as the chief cause of Irish distress, however much responsibility for its evil consequences might be attributed to different sources. The visitor to Ireland in this period was confronted with the sight of rural distress as it had intensified with a growing population and a declining agriculture since the end of the Napoleonic wars. On most estates there was a mass of small farmers. At the bottom of the scale were the cottiers, who cultivated a small plot of land, paying their rent in labour; at the top the Anglo-Irish landlords, of whom it was reckoned that one-third were absentees at the time of the Union. During the long Napoleonic Wars, when the price of corn was high, comparative prosperity encouraged both the subdivision of farms and the fixing of rents on a scale that could not be maintained when the

[1] Ibid., p. 215.

price of corn declined. Since the tenant did not enjoy security of tenure the landlord, finding the conversion of arable into pasture a profitable expedient, at any rate in some of the eastern counties after 1815, planned to consolidate his estates by getting rid of the smaller tenants. In economic terms this was often a condition of improvement; in social terms it was no solution for anyone except the landlord. With the use of steamboats the cattle trade developed, but it did not give employment. Since an evicted tenant usually had no capital, hardships ensued which appalled outside observers. They were accentuated by the rapid growth in population, which between 1800 and 1841 rose from an estimated 5,000,000 to 8,175,000. Since the tenants had no alternative means of livelihood, those that were not evicted subdivided farms sometimes with the encouragement, but often with only the reluctant acquiescence of the landlord, until the estates were covered with multitudes of destitute families. In a country, observed Nassau Senior,[1] 'where the three only alternatives are—the occupation of land, beggary, or famine—where there is nothing to repress competition, and everything to inflame it'—the struggle for land is 'like the struggle to buy bread in a besieged town, or to buy water in an African caravan'. In 1841 the Census showed there were some 600,000 holdings under fifteen acres and less than 130,000 over fifteen acres in extent.[2] Nearly 50 per cent of all holdings were under five acres.[3]

The small and still more the very small farms supported the families settled on them with a standard of life little above subsistence level, even in good years, thanks chiefly to pigs and potatoes. The German, Kohl, had never seen so many pigs in any other country 'except perhaps in Walachia; but the Walachian pigs, feeding in the woods, are a much wilder race than the Irish pigs, which are literally the inmates of their master's home . . . What the horse is to the Arab, or the dog to the Greenlander, the pig is to an Irishman.' And why? '"The pig it is must pay the rent", is a speech you may hear repeated hundreds of times!'[4] It was its importance that accounted for its favoured treatment. Even, indeed most of all, in the impoverished West it had to be tended and cared for. Kohl saw thousands of cabins 'in which not a trace of a window is to be seen; nothing but a little square hole in front, which doubles the duty of door, window and chimney' and through this one

[1] Op. cit., Vol. I, p. 29.
[2] *Tables of Rural Economy*, pp. 454–5.
[3] See also Connell, op. cit., Chap. VI on *Subdivision and Consolidation;* and Green op. cit.
[4] Kohl, op. cit., p. 25.

B

aperture 'light, smoke, pigs, and children, all must pass in and out'.[1]
De Tocqueville had seen them also and in the East as well as in the
West. 'Most of the dwellings in the country seem very poor,' he noted
as he journeyed from Dublin to Carlow, 'a large number of them
wretched to the last degree. Mud walls; thatched roofs; one room; no
chimney; smoke comes out of the door; a pig lies in the middle of the
room.'[2] And of what he saw in the West he noted impressionistically:
'The pig in the house. The dung hill. The bare heads and feet. Describe and paint that . . .'[3] The same association was presumably in the
mind of Sir Walter Scott in 1825, a year after a visit to Ireland, which
had been in the nature of a triumphal procession, when he noted in his
Journal[4] that the poverty of the Irish was not exaggerated, 'it is on the
extreme verge of human misery; their cottages would scarce serve for
pig-styes, even in Scotland . . .' Scott also noticed in 1824 that, while
the Irish had for their food 'only potatoes, and too few of them' yet
'the men look stout and healthy, the women buxom and well-coloured'.
This was a tribute, and no doubt a just one, to the nutritive value of
Ireland's staple food, the potato.[5] It was the potato and pigs, and more
especially the potato alone, that made possible the subdivision of farms
on a scale, which in turn enabled the Ireland of the early nineteenth
century to support a population twice as large as that of the partly
industrialized country of the later half of the twentieth century. It also
opened the road to calamity. Ordinarily the potato, cultivated in Ireland by methods of trenching, manuring and earthing, which bore an
exact resemblance to those used by the Peruvian Indians of the Andes,[6]
produced a prolific crop. But that, if anything, accentuated the degree of
dependence on a single crop, which in turn meant that its failure at any
given time would deprive the majority of the people of their one staple
food.

The small-holder had little inducement and less opportunity to
improve his lot or safeguard his future. The reason for this was suc-
cinctly given by the Secretary of the Poor Law Commission in answer
to an enquiry by Nassau Senior and in the presence of de Tocqueville,
who recorded the conversation. 'To what', Senior asked John Revons,

[1] Kohl, op. cit., p. 48.
[2] *Journeys*, p. 129.
[3] Ibid., p. 161.
[4] *The Journal of Sir Walter Scott* (Edinburgh, 1890), 2 Vols., Vol. 1, pp. 1 and 2.
[5] Its place in Irish history has been examined in an interesting if controversial work by
R. N. Salaman, *The Influence of the Potato on the Course of Irish History* (Dublin, 1943).
[6] Slicher van Bath, *The Agrarian History of Western Europe*, p. 269.

'do you chiefly attribute the poverty of Ireland?' And Revons, a young Radical, replied, 'To the system by which the landlords take advantage of the intense competition between the labourers to demand excessive rents for their farmlands. From the moment the farmer starts making a profit, the landlord raises the rent. The result is that the farmer is afraid to make improvements, lest the landlord should raise his rent by an amount greater than the value of the improvements and is simply concerned to keep alive.'[1] A generation later John Stuart Mill in some telling sentences expressed the same opinion, 'Almost alone amongst mankind the cottier is in this condition', he wrote[2] 'that he can scarcely be either better or worse off by any act of his own. If he were industrious or prudent, nobody but his landlord would gain; if he is lazy and intemperate, it is at his landlord's expense. A situation more devoid of motives to either labour or self-command, imagination itself cannot conceive. The inducements of free beings are taken away, and those of a slave not substituted. He has nothing to hope, and nothing to fear, except being dispossessed of his holding, and against this he protects himself by the *ultima ratio* of a defensive civil war.'

Certainly the peasant fought tenaciously for the meagre measure of subsistence that the land afforded. Middle-class sentimentalists, entertaining the illusion that the impoverished victims of injustice and tyranny are ordinarily paragons of virtue and patterns of goodness, were horrified at the measures taken by him to retain his land. Not so M. de Beaumont. With him profound sympathy with the lot of Irishmen was not permitted to blunt the edge of judgement. For M. de Beaumont understood well that the moral reactions to oppression might be no less terrible than its material consequences and might prove far more difficult to eradicate. That the Irishman was generous, easily inspired to enthusiasm, full of vitality and charm, M. de Beaumont gladly conceded. But he observed, too, some less pleasing traits. The Irishman was slothful, deceitful, intemperate, easily moved to violence; he had an unconquerable aversion to the truth; he was continually affirming 'upon my honour, upon my word', which the Frenchman not unhappily described as a '*locution familière à ceux qui ne disent point la vérité*'.[3] M. de Beaumont conceded that the peasant was lazy, because circumstances made him so. The issue for him was not a choice

---

[1] *Journals*, p. 118. The conversation took place in London on June 7, 1835.
[2] J. S. Mill, *Chapters and Speeches on the Irish Land Question* (London, 1870), pp. 77–8.
[3] Op. cit., Vol. I, p. 351.

between a wretched existence, which was the fruit of his own indolence and a life of comfort earned by hard work; in any event he would be wretched, so he considered merely whether he would be a little more or a little less unhappy and decided the slight accession of comfort that alone was possible was not worth the extra work involved.[1] Yet he thought many Irishmen, who were wretched, increased their misery by their idleness. A little work would have alleviated their lot, but nothing seemed to stir them from their apathy. De Tocqueville, on the other hand, finding five or six young men full of health and strength lying nonchalantly by the banks of a brook near Tuam, restrained his indignation at such indolence amid such poverty, with the reflection that he now understood enough of Irish conditions to realize that there was 'a ceaseless lack of employment'.[2] Nassau Senior expressed another view, and one closer to de Beaumont's, when he said that, while the Irish worked well for a master, 'they are negligent taskmasters to themselves'.

M. de Beaumont attributed to the Irishman some terrible characteristics. 'Violent and vindictive,' he wrote, 'the Irishman displays the most ferocious cruelty in his acts of vengeance ... The evicted tenant ... takes terrible reprisals and the punishment he invents in his savage fury cannot be contemplated without horror. Often in his anger he is as unjust as he is cruel and he takes revenge on persons quite innocent of the misfortunes he has experienced.'[3] De Beaumont recognized that these traits in the Irish character were not natural to Irishmen, but had been brought into unhappy prominence by the course of Irish history. '*L'Irlande a subi le régime du despotisme: l'Irlande doit être corrompue; le despotisme a été long, la corruption doit être immense*'.[4] The Irish peasant was not by nature ruthless, but only or chiefly because he believed that by his actions he was averting or avenging wrong.

Illegal organizations, threatening violent action or taking planned revenge, were endemic in Ireland since the late eighteenth century and to many, who condemned their methods, they appeared to offer the protection against injustice, which the law should have, but did not afford. De Tocqueville enquired of the Catholic Bishop of Carlow in July 1835, and with reference to the best known of them, whether there were many Whiteboys or Whitefeet in the county. The Bishop replied that there were few in Carlow, but many recently in surrounding counties. And he proceeded to tell how a local priest discovering a

---

[1] Op. cit., Vol. I, pp. 356–7.   [2] *Journeys*, p. 161.
[3] Ibid., p. 351.   [4] Ibid., p. 353.

gang of Whitefeet reproached them severely. Their leader, the Bishop recalled, had replied as follows: 'The law does nothing for us. We must save ourselves. We have a little land which we need for ourselves and our families to live on, and they drive us out of it. To whom should we address ourselves? We ask for work at eightpence a day and we are refused. To whom should we address ourselves? Emancipation has done nothing for us. Mr O'Connell and the rich Catholics go to Parliament. We die of starvation just the same.'[1]

The circumstances and conditions which explained the continued existence of the Whiteboy associations did not pass unnoticed in England. Poulett Scrope, a geologist who entered Parliament and contributed so much to the written debate of public issues that he earned the soubriquet of 'Pamphlet Scrope' in the House of Commons, interested himself in Irish problems, wrote not less than seventeen pamphlets on them in a period of about five years and addressed a public letter to Lord Melbourne as Prime Minister in 1834,[2] which he had reprinted and readdressed to Sir Robert Peel in 1844, explaining in turn to each of them, in terms echoed later by John Stuart Mill,[3] why the Irish peasants placed their faith in illegal associations and actions. He wrote:

The peasantry of Ireland do more or less obtain from the Whitefoot associations that essential protection to their existence which the established law of the country refuses to afford. The Whitefoot system is the practical and effective check upon the ejectment system. It cannot be denied that but for the salutary terror inspired by the Whitefoot the clearance of estates (which in the over-peopled districts of Ireland is considered, justly or not, to be the only mode of improving or even of saving them) would proceed with a rapidity and to an extent that must occasion the most horrible sufferings to hundreds and thousands of the ejected tenantry.

[1] *Journeys*, pp. 131–2. For an account by a land agent of the activities of another illegal organization, the Ribbonmen, in Tipperary and neighbouring counties, see W. S. Trench, *Realities of Irish Life* (London, 1868), Chap. IV and generally. Trench was land agent at various times to the Marquis of Lansdowne, the Marquis of Bath, Lord Digby and others of lesser standing. His book was widely read and much praised in England, but more critically received in Ireland, partly because it was felt that the author insufficiently resisted the temptation to make a good anecdote even better.

[2] This extract from the letter is quoted in E. L. Woodward, *The Age of Reform* (Oxford, 1938), p. 319. Poulett Scrope, like the present author, migrated from Pembroke College, Oxford to St John's College, Cambridge, but any consequent sense of affinity does not extend to the writing of pamphlets on public issues.

[3] Op. cit., p. 78.

De Beaumont and Poulett Scrope were right in seeing in the passionate resentment of the dispossessed and their resolve to protect by any means what little remained to them, the root cause of the violence and of the outrages against man and beast that characterized some phases of the land war. As the provocation to a people long deprived of education and security had been great, so too, the retribution was often fearful. There are phases in the history of Ireland in the eighteenth and nineteenth centuries, which find their only commentary in the lines of Aeschylus:

> Lo! sin by sin and sorrow dogged by sorrow
> And who the end can know?

M. de Beaumont described the Anglo-Irish landlords as '*une mauvaise aristocratie*'. De Tocqueville, who recorded no meeting with a member of the land-owning class, in his reflections and even more by implication, reached a conclusion no less unfavourable. They were, it may be accepted, a bad aristocracy not so much because as a class they were deficient in good qualities, but because they were the instruments, later in some measure the victims, of the intolerable and unworkable system to which they were the heirs. Even absentee landlords, content to be mere rent-receivers, parasites on the wealth of a country they rarely, if ever, visited, were in part at least encouraged in their negligent irresponsibility by history and circumstances. The Devon Commission, not admittedly a disinterested body, in recognizing 'the great extent of misery' that followed ill-considered evictions, maintained, probably not unreasonably, that the 'sweeping charges' of cruelty brought against Irish landlords generally were much exaggerated.

The landowners of Ireland possessed much the same political outlook as the mill owners and manufacturers of England. The inhumanity of both alike was due chiefly to callousness and indifference, not to vindictive cruelty. It was the outlook of the governing class of their day. The enclosures of landlords in Tudor England were bitterly denounced by the first Reformers. But where Latimer had preached with fiery eloquence from the text in Isaiah:[1] 'Woe unto them that join house to house, that lay field to field, till there be no place, that they may be placed alone in the midst of the earth', the Church of the nineteenth century was silent. The age of morality had been superseded by the age of economics.

[1] Isaiah, v. 8.

Not all the landlords were either Anglo-Irish or absentee or indifferent. There was in fact a great variety in personality and outlook among the estimated 10,000 members[1] of this idiosyncratic class in the pre-Famine period and the stereotyped figure of the landlord is usually as facile and as misleading as that of the peasant. There were even reforming landlords—but they were not generally popular. They were apt, in some areas virtually bound, to conclude that improved conditions meant larger holdings, which in turn meant consolidation or at the least, objection to further sub-division and squatting. 'It was', wrote a land agent, with some exaggeration but more truth, 'the careless, spendthrift, good for nothing landlord, who hunts and shoots and drinks and runs into debt, who even exacts the most exorbitant rents from his tenants, provided only that he does not interfere with their time-honoured customs of sub-dividing, squatting, conacre, and reckless marriages, who might live in peace and careless indolence on his estate in high favour with the surrounding peasantry . . .'[2]

Again, while the landlords as a class were generally assailed or condemned, it is still worth noting that those who passed judgement upon them were not all disinterested, or without preconceptions. Irish hostility had immediate cause and was at once understood. The Irish peasants desired in the long term ownership of land, from which in the past their fore-fathers had in many cases been forcibly dispossessed and, in the meantime, they struggled for reform of the worst abuses of the system. Chief among these abuses, as may be seen from the evidence submitted to the Devon Commission, were uncertainty of tenure which the Commission reported 'is said to paralyse all exertion, and to place a fatal impediment in the way of improvement';[3] rents unreasonably fixed or inequitably raised, sometimes with the deliberate intention of preparing the way for ejection for failure to pay them; and the lack of compensation for improvement. What profited it a tenant to improve his farm, if an improvement might open the way to an increase in rent, with no recompense to him when his tenure expired, but a bigger rent for a landlord, who in accord with a not unfamiliar practice in the south-west, might advertise the holding for auction to the highest bidder? These were injustices to be redressed. But it was not reform of the existing land system, but its abolition that

[1] See R. D. Collison Black, *Economic Thought and the Irish Question 1817–1870* (Cambridge, 1960), p. 5 fn. 2. The category of 'landed proprietor' did not appear in the Census of 1841; in 1861, 8412 were recorded under it, but this was considered an underestimate.
[2] W. S. Trench, op. cit., pp. 47–8.   [3] P. 16.

was the Irish goal. This did not encourage peasants or politicians to see anything good even when it might exist. They were concerned to end the system over and above the evils in it and that being so, their objections and denunciations were ultimately on a matter of principle, not practice. They did not want good landlords in place of bad ones; they wanted no landlords.

For most English critics the angle of approach was quite otherwise, but the end not so very different for the landlords. They thought, or preferred to think, that reforms of the abuses in the system of land tenure would solve the Irish land problem. Thus Nassau Senior, restating an opinion generally entertained, remarked that the feeling in Ireland is 'not against the landlord, but against the absentee'[1] and John Bright in 1849 recorded his opinion that Irish discontents were due 'to an absentee aristocracy and an alien Church'. If this were indeed so, then land reform and Church disestablishment would remove them and the Union itself would survive, not merely unimpaired, but presumably strengthened. The landlords, their fecklessness, rapacity, absenteeism and their ascendancy Church, on this view, provoked the demand for Repeal of the Union and blame and responsibility for Irish discontent rested with them and, by implication, not with the British government which had brought the Union into existence and now, albeit in practice at one remove, administered its affairs.

How much truth was there in this view? Among landlords none were more severely or apparently more justly condemned than the absentees. Undoubtedly they discredited the system. Yet Nassau Senior implies that the principal resentment against absentees was felt not by their tenants, but by their fellow-landlords. They were, he notes, objects of jealousy to resident proprietors, as men enjoying many of the advantages of property without its dangers and its troubles.[2] Evidently jocular observations about absentees, refusing to be intimidated by the shooting of their agents, had a wry flavour for landlords, who stood themselves in the firing line should trouble arise on their estates.[3] On the other hand, evidence given by tenants or their

[1] Op. cit., Vol. I, p. 163.
[2] Ibid., p. 163.
[3] 'If you think you can intimidate me by shooting my agent, you are mistaken' was the phrase actually used by the eccentric and miserly Lord Clanricarde in a message to the tenants on his estates at Portumna in the eighties. There is a character sketch of him in T. P. O'Connor, *Memoirs of an Old Parliamentarian* (London, 1929), 2 Vols., Vol. II, pp. 120–25 ,where it is recorded that one of his agents was in fact assassinated as he was driving to church by the side of his wife. See also L. P. Curtis, *Coercion and Conciliation in Ireland 1880–1892* (Princeton, 1963), pp. 255–6.

spokesmen before the Devon Commission suggested that generalizations even about absentees were without universal application, no doubt because absentee landlords often had more capital than resident proprietors and this enabled them to spend more on improvements and might make them less exacting in fixing rents. One witness, a farmer and land agent at Kanturk, went so far as to tell the Commission that 'the farmers of the country would rather have a farm from an absentee than a resident proprietor', on the ground that absentees could generally afford to let at lower leases.[1] Elsewhere it was remarked that there was little to choose in respect of quality of management, between resident and absentee proprietors and that with the latter a tenant had to watch his step less carefully.[2] Sir John Gray, the proprietor of *The Freeman's Journal*, many years after the Famine, also questioned the view that as a class the absentees were necessarily the worst landlords. In the course of a detailed and highly critical analysis of the land system he observed that it happened 'that as a rule the great properties of the absentee proprietors were not the worst managed properties'.[3] In its social context the indictment against them stands; in economic terms the harm done would seem to have been chiefly in respect of a drain of capital from a community, where there was a desperate shortage of it. But as a whole, consideration of the role of absentees draws attention firstly to a fundamental, but still insufficiently considered, factor in the Irish land system—lack of adequate capital at every level and secondly to the absurdity of suggesting with Bright that the ending of absenteeism would effect a transformation in the system of a kind to reconcile the Irish peasant to it. On the contrary the idea was itself an illustration of well-intentioned and not unfamiliar nineteenth-century liberal misconceptions about the nature of the Irish problem.

THE ECONOMISTS: DOCTRINE AND DIAGNOSES

The relative share of responsibility for the state of Ireland to be attributed to the Ascendancy and to the British Government respectively has been variously assessed. De Beaumont, for example, exonerated the British Government of immediate and direct responsibility on the

[1] *Devon Commission. Minutes of Evidence.* 773. 90.
[2] Ibid., Part II, p. 485. See also p. 562.
[3] *Freeman's Journal,* October 22, 1869, p. 4. The report of his speech occupied eight columns.

ground that British rule in Ireland was not absolute, but rather was
dependent on the administrative machine ensconced in Dublin Castle.
David Ricardo, the classical economist, went further asserting that
'Ireland is an oppressed country—not oppressed by England, but by
the aristocracy which rules with a rod of iron within it; England could
redress many of her wrongs but stands in awe of the faction which
governs.'[1] Such contentions, however, possess no great validity.
Under the Union the British Government was responsible for the good
government of Ireland; indeed by forcing through that Act it had
deliberately and of its own volition assumed that responsibility. If its
agents in Dublin disregarded its instructions, that was no reason for an
abdication of authority. On the contrary, it was an occasion for its
unsparing exercise.[2] The truth indeed is far simpler. The British Government was passive, more landlord than the landlords, Dr Hammond
observed,[3] simply because that was its fully considered policy. Legislation enacted by the British Parliament after the Napoleonic Wars
facilitated the process of eviction. Why? Because the peasant was viewed
in the philosophy of that time as an incubus on society, his survival
as a barrier to social and economic progress. For this reason the tenant
farmers of England were being converted into labourers and it was
thought well to facilitate a similar process in Ireland. The motive was
not malevolent; it was economic. Writing to Ricardo in January 1822,
Trower observed: 'It appears to me, that no permanent or substantial
good can be done till all *small farms* and small tenancies, are got rid of.
These are the curse of Ireland.'[4] And Ricardo replied that while he
thought it desirable that small farms and tenancies should be got rid of,
he believed that Ireland's first need was a good and properly administered system of law, which by encouraging an inflow of capital from
England and the accumulation of capital in Ireland, would lead by
natural economic processes to the consolidation of smaller holdings
into larger farms.[5] But at best this would take a long time and in the

[1] Letter to Hutches Trower, July 24, 1823, reprinted in *The Works and Correspondence of David Ricardo* edited by P. Sraffa (Cambridge, 1951–55), 10 Vols., Vol. IX, p. 314.
[2] R. B. McDowell, *The Irish Administration 1801–1914* (London, 1964), provides the first authoritative study of the administration of Ireland under the Union and it is clear from what he has written that, while the administration was decentralized in a haphazard and little considered way, and while the Dublin Castle régime remained strongly entrenched after the Union, in all major issues of policy the British Government through the Chief Secretary had, and customarily exercised, the decisive voice.
[3] J. L. Hammond, *Gladstone and the Irish Nation* (London, 1938), p. 13.
[4] *The Works of David Ricardo*, Vol. IX, p. 145.
[5] Ibid., p. 153.

meantime the impoverished cottiers and small-holders remained well-nigh destitute. What could be done in the situation as it actually existed? There was no helpful answer.

Orthodox economy of the day, the theory of Ricardo, of the Utilitarians, affirmed that measures of positive relief to improve the lot of the poor were outside the proper function of government. Thus, Sir George Cornewall Lewis, in a letter written in 1838 to the Chancellor of the Exchequer, rejected on grounds of *principle* any suggestion that Irish agriculture, and the community dependent on it, should be assisted by constructive effort on the part of the Government. He wrote: 'A Government can only, as it seems to me, attempt to accelerate the improvement of the soil by *indirect* means. In this as in most other cases connected with the *material* part of civilization, its functions are simply negative; it can do no more than remove obstacles to amelioration and suffer a society to proceed unchecked in its natural career of advancement.'[1] This belief, responsible for the long-endured miseries of the early Industrial Revolution and of hours of work in factories and mines in the Black Country that now seem incredible, prevented the subsidizing of Irish agriculturalists in any form.[2] In the England of the heyday of the industrial revolution, such an economic doctrine left open the way both for the amassing of great wealth and untold suffering; in Ireland where agriculture, not industry, constituted the all-important source of livelihood, it precluded positive reform and in so doing, it marked out the road that led to famine, death and emigration on a vast scale. For Irish society, alas, there was no 'natural career of advancement'!

There remained, therefore, the landlords. But in an economic context, lack of capital gravely limited their capacity to improve their estates, in cases where they might otherwise have done so. De Tocqueville realized that this was so and Nassau Senior put the point with characteristic force and conciseness. 'The English public' he wrote, 'seem to believe that it is the fault of an Irish landlord, that the tenants and cottiers on his estate are not as comfortable as the farmers and labourers of Yorkshire. They forget the capital of the Yorkshireman.'[3]

---

[1] Quoted in Hammond, op. cit., p. 17.

[2] O'Connell himself was deeply influenced by the teachings of classical economists. His reactions to proposals for positive economic action had much in common with those of Cornewall Lewis. This is brought out clearly in Sean O'Faolain's biography entitled, *King of the Beggars: A life of Daniel O'Connell, the Irish liberator, in a study of the rise of the modern Irish democracy (1775–1847)*, (London, 1938).

[3] Op. cit., Vol. I, pp. 161–2.

There was another limiting factor and that was the pressure of population, with the consequent multiplication of small holdings. Was improvement possible if the holdings continued to multiply or even to exist? The classical economists thought not. They were, however, no friends of the landlords,[1] Ricardo, for example, contrasting Irish landlords most unfavourably with English, denouncing their rapacity, their outlook—'considering the people as being of a different race who are habituated to all species of oppression'[2]—and their indifference to the sufferings they caused. This dislike led the classical economists into certain apparent inconsistencies. They deplored sub-division of holdings as uneconomic, they advocated consolidation, yet some at least among them denounced landlord attempts at consolidation. This inconsistency evoked the wrath of Nassau Senior. 'To produce this prosperity, and to maintain it,' he wrote, 'they [the Irish landlords] must eject and consolidate. This disgusts the English public. With a perverseness which, if it were not the result of ignorance, would be intolerable, and if it be the result of *wilful* ignorance is inexcusable— they execrate the landlord for his harshness if he be vigilant, and for the wretchedness of his tenants if he be careless.'[3] Senior himself believed in consolidation made practicable by large scale and rapid emigration; others among the classical economists favoured a variety of means for making provision for the large number of those (in their view) necessarily to be dispossessed. But faith in large holdings and capitalist farming implied no confidence in the existing landlords. If the classical economists regarded the Irish peasant, especially in his existing numbers, as an incubus to be removed in the interests of better economics, they thought of the existing Anglo-Irish landlords as another, to be replaced by more purposeful, up-to-date and less rapacious capitalist farmers. John Stuart Mill demolished a growing mountain of unreality, when he described the introduction of capitalist farming into Ireland generally as 'wholly impracticable' and reminded the orthodox that 'the people are there, and the problem is not how to improve the country, but how it can be improved by and for its present inhabitants'.[4]

It is hard to see how the country could have been improved, given the landlords' lack of capital (and outlook) and the numbers settled

[1] On this see Collison Black, op. cit., pp. 21–4.
[2] See letter to Trower, July 24, 1923, reprinted in *The Works and Correspondence of David Ricardo*, Vol. IX, p. 314, and from which a quotation has been made above, p. 42.
[3] Op. cit., Vol. I, p. 162.
[4] Quoted in Collison Black, op. cit., p. 31. Mill was writing in 1846.

on the land, without state intervention. If this were indeed so, then it was not the landlords, as Ricardo so insistently argued, but the classical economists who carried the greater responsibility for the inaction that led to catastrophe. Therein lies the importance of Professor Collison Black's study of *Economic Thought and the Irish Question 1817–1870*. There is, as Professor Black is the first to recognize, great difficulty in assessing precisely the influence of economic thought upon economic policy at any time—how far, for example, the one is the consequence or alternatively the inspiration of the other. But in so far as the influence of economic doctrine was substantial, possibly even decisive at this time, then and to that extent, the classical economists were responsible for discouraging remedial action by the government, which had the power, the resources and the capacity—none of which the landlords possessed—to make that action effective. They pointed to landlord vices with an accusing finger, but in fact a very considerable share of responsibility for ultimate disaster in Ireland may have rested with these high minded publicists of laissez-faire economics. Or so, at least, it may appear to an age in which there is a predisposition to weigh the influence of ideas or concepts, more heavily than the human factor, in the determination of the historical process.

There is a stage, however, in the argument at which a certain scepticism may be allowed to creep in. Behind the economists, as the final arbiters of action or inaction, stood the Government. Its members, whether representative of the dominant landed, or the newer commercial classes, had their own preoccupations and interests. The kingdom for the administration of whose affairs they were responsible was a United Kingdom. Principles of government introduced for one part of that United Kingdom could hardly be confined to that part. Having enacted Union, there was extreme aversion to practising separation. Ireland might socially and economically be altogether distinct, as de Beaumont and Nassau Senior among many others, recognized. But politically it was not and therein lay the heart of the matter. Legislation or action which seemed appropriate to Irish needs was not enacted, nor was the possibility of its enactment seriously weighed, when the principles behind it were such that self-evidently they could not be confined to Ireland. State intervention on land or invasion of property rights in Ireland opened the way to state intervention or invasion of property rights in England. And the economists, radical in other respects, were at one with the governing classes in regarding property as sacrosanct. The fear of the possible repercussions of action in Ireland on society

and interests in England was an all-important consideration, which
would of necessity have applied, irrespective of the doctrines of economists, so long as opinion in Parliament was resolutely opposed to
intervention by the state in principle and so long as the great majority
of its members were men of substantial property. Ireland was not a
distinct political entity; it was dangerous to legislate for it as if it were.

The supposed predominance of economic doctrine, though not its
importance, may give rise to doubts on other grounds. Isaac Butt, the
Conservative, Protestant, nationalist who later founded the first Home
Rule Movement gave expression to them. Ireland, he wrote in a pamphlet published during the Famine,[1] had been deprived by the Union
of all separate power of action. She could not, as in the days of her
own Parliament, call upon her own resources or pledge her own credit
in the event of a great national disaster. She had to look to England and
was she not entitled, in so looking, for that measure of state assistance,
which 'any portion of a Nation, visited with such a calamity, has a right
to expect from the Governing power? If Cornwall had been visited
with the scenes that have desolated Cork, would Cornwall have been
thought disentitled to immediate aid on a national scale on the ground
of a separate identity with a separate responsibility?' But Irish property
on the other hand was expected to carry the burden of Irish poverty,
to which at that time it was clearly unequal. The deliberations of the
Cabinet, Butt alleged, were 'too much influenced by the fear of offending powerful British interests' and 'give too much weight to those
interests, and too little to the safety of the Irish people'. There was
certainly some truth in this, but if one asks further, why in time of
famine such interests were so tenderly considered, the answer lies little
in lack of humanity, to some extent certainly in deference to economic
views, but most of all, it may be suspected, to lack of awareness and
imaginative sympathy. Why was there not only a famine, which with
the failure of the potato crop could hardly have been altogether avoided,
but a great famine? An important part of the answer lies surely in the
failure of English statesmen, once Union was a fact, to act and think
and move throughout its confines, as though it were one kingdom and
to sense themselves the magnitude of the problems that afflicted the
Irish part of it. 'The really great evil', so the editors of *The Great Famine* justly conclude, 'lay in the totality of that social order which made
such a famine possible and which could tolerate, to the extent it did,

[1] Isaac Butt, *The Famine in the Land*, 1847, quoted in P. S. O'Hegarty, *A History of
Ireland Under the Union* (London, 1952), pp. 318–19.

the sufferings and hardship caused by the failure of the potato crop'.[1] It was this formidable fact which English statesmen as a class were so reluctant to face and so slow to comprehend.

'If the Devil himself had exercised all his ingenuity to invent a scheme which should destroy the country', remarked the Polish Count Strzelecki fresh from his humanitarian labours for famine relief in the West to John Bright in Dublin on September 7, 1849[2], 'he could not have contrived anything more effectual than the principles and practices upon which landed property has been held and managed in Ireland.' The landlords were at the heart of the system; they were at once its exploiters and also in some measure its victims. As 'une mauvaise aristocratie' they go down in history, even though many landlords made what retribution lay in their power in the years of famine, even though the destiny of their class at the last was unhappy. Those landlords, whom de Beaumont observed, in their arrogance and wealth and luxury, were only some twenty years later associated by Engels with debt and the bankruptcy court, and early in the new century their great estates were divided up. Today the traveller visiting Ireland a century or more after de Beaumont will see tangible and melancholy reminders of that phase of Irish history, which de Beaumont observed and in which landlordism was the dominant feature of the Irish social system. Most of all will this be so in Connaught, where among the lakes and mountains that have made Connemara a delight to tourists and the inspiration of a school of modern Irish painting, the traveller will see on every side fragments of stone walls, that were once part of cottages made desolate forever in the famine years and will be told something and may learn more of the history of great estates, not least of the greatest owned by 'Humanity Dick' Martin, friend of the Prince Regent, noted duellist, founder of the Royal Society for the Prevention of Cruelty to Animals;—of how it extended to some 200,000 acres with a private road running through it all the forty odd miles from Richard Martin's neo-Gothic castle at Ballynahinch to Galway City and with innumerable tenants, sub-tenants, cottiers and squatters seeking a living from small, mostly barren holdings and of how it

---

[1] *Edwards and Williams*, op. cit., p. XV.

[2] *The Diaries of John Bright*, edited by R. A. J. Walling (London, 1930), p. 105. Count Strzelecki (Bright misspelt the name Straletski) remembered and honoured in Ireland for his relief work, left a more substantial memorial in Australia where he went as an explorer, in the form of a mountain called after the Polish patriot Kosciuszko at whose fall freedom shrieked. His claim that the summit was the highest in Australia, once disputed, is now generally recognized.

passed to his son in 1834, of his son's remission of rents in the famine years, of his early death from famine fever following a visit to Clifden poor-house to see his tenants, who had been moved there and at the last, of the sale of the estate under the provisions of the Encumbered Estates Act for a comparatively trifling sum. In other parts the visitor today will find himself in a country of peasant proprietors and small farms, with here and there great rusty gates breaking the monotonous length of some crumbling demesne wall, which open on to a grass-grown drive. Far back from the road enveloped in ivy, may lie the blackened ruins of some country house recalling the elegance, the culture, the idiosyncratic and often self-destroying extravagances of a vanished order.[1] 'Of a truth', cried the prophet Isaiah, 'many houses shall be desolate, even great and fair, without inhabitant.' They are—or were until after 1945 when many of them were repaired and re-occupied, some by a new wave of English settlers unable to reconcile themselves to the rigours of life in a welfare state, others by emigrants from Europe, chiefly from Germany and Holland, seeking opportunities in a land more comfortably remote from the ideological frontiers of the Cold War than their own and others again by hoteliers drawn by Ireland's developing tourist trade.[2]

STATESMEN: THEIR NEGLECT AND INDIFFERENCE

In Ireland the indictment against England is regarded as political in character. The vindictive suppression of rebellion looms larger than the continuance of economic distress. Yet in retrospect the failure to make possible some tolerable standard of living for the mass of the Irish people seems the less pardonable. The Irish have rarely compared their political treatment with that of other subject nationalities or of minorities in Europe. Yet in fact the suppression of La Vendée was as brutal, probably more so, than that of Ireland in '98, certainly the crushing of revolt in Spain, in Italy, in Hungary in the nineteenth century was more savage in character than that of contemporary re-

[1] The Marquesses of Sligo, of whom de Tocqueville heard much and little that was favourable, owned estates of 114,900 acres (as stated in *Who was Who 1897–1915*) and enjoyed an income estimated at £40,000 a year. One of them developed an acquisitive taste for the antiquities of Greece, and paid British sailors to bring them to his house at Westport in County Mayo. So it was that a portico of Westport House was supported by pillars from the site of the tomb of Agamemnon. The Government prosecuted the Marquis for bribing British sailors. The pillars were sold to the British Museum in 1910. They were replaced at Westport House by concrete substitutes.
[2] Ballynahinch Castle was no exception. It became an American owned luxury hotel.

pression in Ireland. But the poverty of the country after centuries of
English rule and the sense of continuing oppression that went with it,
was an admission of failure in a field where achievement was surely
practicable. Save only in Ulster where, as de Beaumont and others
observed, higher living standards due to industrial development and a
more equitable land practice, allowed of a measure of social advance
and cohesion not to be found elsewhere, the conditions of life in Ireland excited only expressions of dismay, of pity and of horror from
those who saw them. Why, and this at the last is the most surprising
fact of all, did they not stir British public opinion and British statesmen
to concern and to remedial action? Fears of Irish economic competition,
of disturbing vested interests in Ireland and, by force of example,
thereafter in England, political preconceptions and economic principles,
all have been advanced by way of explanation. And there was some
measure of truth in most, if not in all of them. But at a deeper level
an explanation may be offered that is at once more general and more
simple. The inertia and indifference of English opinion and government in respect of the state of Ireland is to be attributed chiefly to
ignorance. Sir Jonah Barrington, who considered the Irish people to
have been 'as little known, as they have been grossly defamed',[1]
observed that a visit to Ireland appealed to the ordinary Englishman's
sense of adventure since he knew as little of it as he did of Kamchatka.
'The principal cause of misgovernment, particularly of the misgovernment which irritates rather than injures', wrote Nassau Senior, on this
point in full agreement with Barrington, 'is ignorance.' English people
did not understand the feelings of Irishmen simply because there was
no contact between the two peoples. 'The great majority of the Members of each House—that is to say, of the two Assemblies which govern
Ireland—know less of that country', remarked the same author, 'than
they know of Belgium or of Switzerland.'[2] And he added that the
inhabitants of the North and South knew little of one another—as
indeed they do to this day.

What was the cause of this ignorance of Irish problems and of the
Irish outlook? It was certainly not from lack of official information.
Between 1810 and 1833 Parliament appointed 114 commissions and 60
select committees to investigate Irish affairs, in addition to the long
hours spent in debate in the House. This accumulation of evidence

---

[1] Sir Jonah Barrington, *Historic Memoirs of Ireland* (London, 1833), 2 Vols, Vol. I,
p. 62.
[2] Op. cit., Vol. I, p. 130.

continued thereafter most notably with the appointment of the Devon
Commission of Inquiry into the Occupation of Land, whose report of
forty-four pages, with three volumes of evidence amounting in all to
not far short of four thousand pages, was published in 1845.[1] Dr R. B.
McDowell has suggested that in these years some of the best work done
by the state was the collection, through parliamentary and royal commissions, of a mass of information about Irish conditions. But such
information, however illuminating for the historian, served no valuable
contemporary purpose unless action was taken upon it. It was not.
Before much of this clinical material could be used, writes Dr Mc-
Dowell,[2] 'the catastrophe occurred'. In so far as this suggests that
given time, it would have been effectively used his judgement may
well be over-sanguine. What was wanting was a sense of urgency and
since the lack of it derived from a lack of intimate, personal knowledge
of the country on the part of its rulers, it was not something that time
in itself would have remedied. If one asks why nothing very much
was done before the Famine to redress analysed and catalogued evils,
the first and possibly the most important part of the answer may be
found in the fact that very few people ever visited Ireland. Between
reading analyses of distressful conditions and seeing them there is a
great gulf fixed. Where the one may prompt discussion, the other alone
is likely to stimulate timely action.

Why did not more English people visit Ireland? A Mr Grant, who
went there in 1844 and who wrote with delightful naïveté of the country and its inhabitants, considered the scarcity of English travellers was
to be attributed to indifference or unwillingness and not to the difficulties of travel. On the contrary Her Majesty's Mail packets crossing
from Liverpool to Kingstown were both cheap and comfortable.
'The passage-money is one pound, which includes the usual half-
crown to the steward', writes Mr Grant, and he proceeds with enthusiasm[3], 'a finer set of vessels than these government packets never
quitted any English or other port. They are of a large size, and are
fitted up in a style of comfort which calls forth the admiration of all
who travel by them. But their greatest recommendation is their sailing
capabilities. Not only can they perform the voyage in eleven or twelve

---

[1] *Report from Her Majesty's Commissioners of Inquiry into the State of the Law and
Practice in respect to the Occupation of Land in Ireland.* Parl. Papers 1845, xix–xxii.

[2] R. B. McDowell, 'Ireland on the Eve of the Famine' in *The Great Famine*, p. 7.

[3] Quoted from James Grant's *Impressions of Ireland and the Irish* (London, 1844), 2
Vols., Vol. II, p. 92.

hours, but they sail so steadily, that in ordinary weather, persons seldom experience sea-sickness in performing the voyage.'

In Ireland itself Mr Grant was agreeably surprised by the travelling facilities and the moderation of the charges—but then he was certainly an accommodating visitor. The Dublin to Drogheda railway was at this time the only railway of any length, so Mr Grant for the most part travelled by coach at a speed averaging nine miles an hour. His one complaint was a familiar one—the number and importunity of the beggars, who swarmed around the coach. The immense crowd of mendicants gave a vivid impression of Irish poverty and at first 'the circumstance of so many fellow-creatures . . . importunately soliciting charity from you, is far from agreeable; but as you proceed on your journey, the novelty of the thing wears away, and you feel less disturbed by their appearance and importunities'.[1]

But Mr Grant, a man of easy temperament and kindly disposition, looked on Ireland with the eager, unprejudiced, if superficial, gaze of a traveller, resolved not to be discouraged by what he sees in another land. His approach was not common among his fellow-countrymen. The inducements to visit Ireland seemed, especially to the more sophisticated among them, quite incommensurate with the trouble involved. 'Ireland', wrote Nassau Senior in 1844, 'is not on the road to any other place; and the greater part of it is not, at present, an inviting country to travel in. There are scarcely any railroads—the climate is wet and ungenial—the inns are generally bad—the greater part of the inland scenery is uninteresting, and almost all the moral objects are painful. Until it has been greatly altered, nothing but necessity will make it frequented by those who belong to happier countries.'[2] Therefore, he concluded, in gloomy surmise, English ignorance of Ireland 'does not seem likely to diminish'.

More important, however, than the ignorance of the many was the ignorance or at the least the lack of first-hand knowledge on the part of the few, who determined the pattern of nineteenth-century government and politics. They did not visit Ireland. There were, of course, honourable exceptions, the two most notable members of the

---

[1] James Grant, *Impressions of Ireland and the Irish*, pp. 102–4. This description may be compared with that of Arthur Young who noted on June 23, 1776: 'Before I conclude with Dublin I shall only remark, that walking in the streets there, from the narrowness and populousness of the principal thoroughfares, as well as from the dirt and wretchedness of the *canaille*, is a most disgusting and uneasy exercise.' *A Tour of Ireland*, edited by Constantia Maxwell (Cambridge, 1925), p. 6.

[2] Op. cit., Vol. I, p. 131.

Manchester School, Richard Cobden and John Bright, high among them. Cobden, who had a cousin who was Church of Ireland Rector in Tipperary, went there many times, but contributed less than he might otherwise have done to debate and discussion on Irish problems, because he developed an antipathy to Daniel O'Connell so disturbing that he 'never shook hands with him or faced his smile without a feeling of insecurity'.[1] Cobden's conclusions on Irish problems, formulated against his background of personal knowledge were all, however, that 'the Liberator' could have desired. They were, negatively, the removal of the 'landlord spirit', which he considered the great obstacle to all progress and positively, the giving of 'Ireland to the Irish' both in Church and State. John Bright, rather less uncompromising in his views but more sympathetic in personality, having briefly visited Ireland as a young man in 1832, undertook a fact-finding expedition in 1849. 'Be assured', wrote Cobden when he learned of his plans, 'you have done the right thing in going there. It is a duty that ought to be similarly fulfilled by all of us.'[2] Certainly Bright's travels throughout the countryside, studying the causes and seeing at first hand the dread aftermath of famine,[3] heightened his sense of the urgency of Irish problems. For the next thirty years he remained an outstanding champion of redress in Ireland and not all the acrimony that followed upon his repudiation of Home Rule in 1886 effaced the recollection of earlier years, when he was esteemed among Irishmen, as were few others, as a reformer of understanding and of high integrity. The pity was that his mission was undertaken after and not before the Famine.

The visits of Cobden and Bright were of moment; but the failures of Gladstone to visit Ireland as he had planned in the summer of 1845 and of Disraeli, again as he had planned, in the autumn of 1876, may have been of historic significance. Gladstone had just resigned from Peel's administration on a point of conscience so fine that, after lengthy exposition of his reasons for it in a letter to his Prime Minister, Sir Robert was left complaining, not perhaps altogether unreasonably, that he really had 'great difficulty sometimes in exactly comprehending what he means'. The occasion was the Government's recommendation of an increased grant to the Roman Catholic seminary at Maynooth, for which Gladstone voted in the House of Commons, but on account of which he felt he could not remain in the Cabinet, because the prin-

---

[1] John Morley, *The Life of Richard Cobden* (London, 1881), 2 Vols., Vol. II, p. 27.
[2] Ibid, p. 50.
[3] Some of his impressions are recorded in his *Diaries*, pp. 97–107.

ciple of the grant conflicted with views he had earlier expressed in his book on State and Church.[1] The upshot of this curious political episode was that Gladstone, out of office on an issue of Irish policy and without immediate cause, was psychologically prepared to study Irish problems at first hand for the first time and to champion redress of Irish grievances. The visit was planned, the arrangements completed and then at the last moment all was cancelled, because one of the many crises in the life of his sister Helen compelled Gladstone to travel to her in Baden-Baden.[2] So it was that he was destined to visit Ireland but once and that briefly,[3] when Anglo-Irish relations had once again hardened in an uncompromising mould and the chance of making a deep and immediately favourable impression on English opinion had long since passed.

While Gladstone thus visited Ireland but once and late in life, his great rival Disraeli never went there at all. As Disraeli's biographer allows, these are facts which would be incredible, if they were not true and one can but reflect uneasily on the consequences that may have flowed from trivial causes. For Disraeli also planned to visit Ireland— for the first time—on his first vacation after becoming Prime Minister early in 1874. In his case it was not an eccentric sister, but a traditional ailment, that frustrated his design. He was to have gone to stay with the Viceroy on October 24th and to have proceeded thence to Killarney, Cork, Waterford, Derry, the Giant's Causeway and Belfast but, to quote his own words, he 'fell into the gout and that very badly' so that it was thought inadvisable that he should travel. 'The attack', notes his biographer in a strange judgement[4] 'came in time to prevent him committing a great imprudence.' Certainly apart from considerations of health, his colleagues were disposed to deem the visit ill-advised, Lord Derby being especially discouraging. What, he enquired, could Disraeli usefully say when he was in Ireland? Every question

[1] In our own time Gladstone's resignation has been held up as an example for Ministers to study and as a model of honourable political practice for them to follow. This is admirable—unless indeed it be thought that the explanation of Gladstone's action was that he was looking for an opportunity to resign and he found one that might appear at once highly creditable to him and not altogether implausible to others.

[2] For an account of the circumstances of Gladstone's resignation see John Morley, *Life of Gladstone* (London, 1903), 3 Vols., Vol. I, pp. 277–9, Sir Philip Magnus, *Gladstone. A Biography* (London, 1954), pp. 68–70 and Woodward, *The Age of Reform*, p. 336.

For the reasons for the postponement of the Irish visit see Magnus p. 71 and Morley Vol. I, p. 281. Morley walks delicately and does not mention why it was cancelled.

[3] See below, p. 122.

[4] G. E. Buckle in W. F. Monypenny and Buckle, *The Life of Benjamin Disraeli* (London, 1910–20), 6 Vols., Vol. V, pp. 345–7.

past, present or future was a party question. The moderates were feeble. He could concede nothing he was asked to concede. He could not even 'be decently civil to Catholics without offending Protestants and vice versa'. It does not seem to have occurred to Lord Derby at the time, or later to Disraeli's biographer, that a Prime Minister, who had never visited one of the countries comprising the Union of Great Britain and Ireland, might have something important to learn by so doing, and be neglecting a self-evident duty by not. And Lord Salisbury followed his example, professing himself, when invited to go to Belfast, unable to face a crossing of the Irish Sea, even though he had earlier visited South Africa, Australia and New Zealand![1]

So it was that the rulers of Ireland rarely, if ever, visited it, never saw its miseries, never experienced themselves the people's sense of injustice, nor comprehended their resentment at remedies concocted by those, who had not troubled to acquire first-hand knowledge of the disease. For that reports, however numerous or however well drafted, offered no sufficient compensation. Nassau Senior understood that this was so. He had the perception, which so many English statesmen seemingly lacked, to recognize the evil consequences of their own complacent neglect. Even more, he had a remedy. If Englishmen would not willingly visit Ireland, and, as we have seen, he conceded there was no natural inducement for them to do so, then the necessity must be imposed upon them. That necessity would be created by the holding of a Parliamentary session in Dublin, if not regularly, at least from time to time. The session would attract many besides members of Parliament and they would not confine themselves to the capital, but disperse throughout the countryside. Irish questions, 'in consequence, would be no longer left to be discussed by only the Irish Members'.[2] And by way of additional inducement Nassau Senior dwelt upon the attractions of the Irish capital. 'The situation of Dublin', he wrote, 'is far more agreeable than that of London—indeed than that of any English town; except perhaps Plymouth—and the climate in autumn is delightful.'

Statesmen rarely incline favourably to the advice of professors and Nassau Senior entertained little hope that his would be heeded. The country he described with academic detachment was unhappy and he

---

[1] It is clear that he felt the strain of travel in a somewhat unusual degree. See Lady Gwendolen Cecil, *Life of Robert, 3rd Marquess of Salisbury* (London, 1921–32), 4 Vols., Vol. I, pp. 25–35.
[2] Op. cit., Vol. I, p. 131.

knew that this was not only because the people were desperately poor, though indeed the majority, as was soon to be most terribly shown, lived close to the starvation line, but because remedy and reform seemed hopeless. What oppressed him most profoundly was the feeling 'that there were means by which the existing misery might be relieved and the approaching dangers averted: but that the prejudices and passions of England and Scotland rendered it useless to suggest them because they made it impossible to apply them'. It may be that not even first-hand knowledge would have tempered such sentiments sufficiently; it is certain nothing else could.

CHAPTER II

EUROPEAN AND IRISH NATIONALISMS: THE VIEWS OF ITALIAN NATIONALISTS ON THE NATURE OF THE IRISH QUESTION

One's country, before all, is the consciousness of country.
MAZZINI
To the Young Men of Italy (1859)

———————

IRELAND: THE OLD WORLD AND THE NEW

As Alexis de Tocqueville crossed the Place du Palais-Bourbon on February 24, 1848, after leaving the Chamber of Deputies where all was confusion, he saw Gustave de Beaumont and Camille Barrot. 'Both of them', he noted, 'wore their hats crushed down over their eyes; their clothes were covered with dust, their cheeks looked hollow, their eyes weary: never were two men in triumph so suggestive of men about to be hanged.' De Tocqueville ran up to de Beaumont and asked him what was happening. De Beamont whispered in reply that the King had abdicated in his presence, and had taken to flight.[1] The year of Revolution had begun. From the Seine to the Vistula, from the Elbe to the Danube, to the shores of the Adriatic, and over the length and breadth of Italy, Liberals and Nationalists received the signal from Paris and united to overthrow the old order in Europe.

'When France sneezes', said Metternich, 'all Europe catches cold.' But England did not and Englishmen reflected, and may still reflect, with pardonable satisfaction upon their immunity from infection. At home indeed, despite Chartist agitation, 1848 was a year of prosperity and peace; in the Empire overseas it witnessed in Nova Scotia the practical application for the first time of Lord Durham's recommended system of responsible government for colonial territories and, most gratifying, it made plain to all the world the contrast between the

[1] *The Recollections of Alexis de Tocqueville.* Trans. by A. T. de Mattos and edited by J. P. Mayer (London, 1948), p. 48.

stability of British institutions and the instability of those of its principal continental rivals. Only one thing remained to diminish a sense of well-merited self-congratulation—and that, as so often earlier and later, was the state of Ireland. Though members of the House of Commons might prefer to contemplate happier things, John Bright, for one, was not prepared to allow them to do so undisturbed. In a famous passage in a speech on April 2, 1849, he said: 'Hon Gentlemen turn with triumph to neighbouring countries, and speak in glowing terms of our glorious constitution. True, that abroad thrones and dynasties have been overturned, whilst in England peace has reigned undisturbed. But take all the lives that have been lost in the last twelve months in Europe amidst the convulsions that have occurred—take all the cessation of trade, the destruction of industry, all the crushing of hopes and hearts, and they will not compare for an instant with the agonies which have been endured by the population of Ireland under your glorious constitution.'[1] Disraeli, who disassociated himself from the sentiments and deprecated the reformist conclusions of Bright's speech, none the less praised it for qualities of thought and style be-fitting the dignity and the best traditions of the House.[2] But something more than that was needed if the condition of Ireland were to be remedied before it provoked some final breach, bringing Union to a disastrous end in unfriendly separation.

To change the English temper towards Ireland, to shake fundamental views of property or economics, to overcome all the prejudices that estrange men divided by race, religion and history, to interest Parliament in duties to which it was indifferent, this was a task in which no man could hope to succeed if his mind never moved outside the English orbit. In these words Dr Hammond defines the task with which English statesmanship was confronted in Ireland and the conditions of its achievement—conditions which, in his view, Gladstone alone really fulfilled. Unlike the majority of his contemporaries, Gladstone both understood the character of Irish problems and possessed the courage to advocate solutions certain to be unpopular and misinter-preted in England. It was a case in which comprehension was even more remarkable than the action which followed from it. For as John Stuart Mill and de Beaumont were well aware, there were no people less fitted to understand Irish problems than the English. Ireland had

---

[1] Hansard's *Parliamentary Debates*, April 2, 1849, Vol. CIV, col. 180. The whole of his long speech repays study.
[2] Ibid., coll. 190–1.

so long been in subjection harsh enough to embitter, yet not complete
enough finally to subdue, that English statesmen were no longer
capable of seeing her problems and her discontents in perspective.
From the prevalent, apathetic, insular approach common to English
statesmen, Gladstone's stands out in sharp relief. He looked at Ireland
through the eyes of a European. He had travelled widely, he had learned
what Europe thought of English rule in Ireland. A chance meeting on
his way to Baden-Baden[1] in 1845 with Guizot, who like him brought
great qualities of mind into the service of the State, had a profound
influence on Gladstone's thinking about Ireland. He wrote to Guizot
twenty-seven years later:

'It is very unlikely that you should remember a visit I paid you, I
think at Passy in the autumn of 1845. . . . The Maynooth Act had just
been passed. Its author, I think, meant it to be final. I had myself
regarded it as seminal. And you in congratulating me upon it, . . .
said we should have the sympathies of Europe in the work of giving
Ireland justice—a remark which evidently included more than the
measure just passed, and which I ever after saved and pondered. It
helped me on towards what has since been done.'[2] Clearly, as Gladstone's most recent biographer remarks, the conversation registered 'a
minor but distinct earthquake shock' on Gladstone's mind.[3]

What Gladstone did and still more what he tried to do for Ireland
was the fruit of his European sense. In the Irish question, says Dr
Hammond in that remarkable book, of which this is the principal
theme,[4] Gladstone the European came into conflict with the firm and
fixed ideas of the English ruling class. The Home Rule struggle was 'a
battle between men moving within the circle of an island mind and a
man who lived in the wisdom of the ages', a man who was deeply
religious, a man who was steeped in the learning and literature of
Greece. It was the duty of Englishmen, Gladstone once told the House
of Commons, to remove Irish grievances 'so that instead of hearing
in every corner of Europe the most painful commentaries on the policy
of England towards Ireland we may be able to look our fellow Europeans in the face'. If there is some over-simplification in Dr Hammond's
analysis, and in particular underestimate of the influence of developing
relations between Britain and her colonies—it was not liberal

---

[1] See above, p. 53.
[2] Quoted in Morley, *Life of Gladstone*, Vol. II, p. 240.
[3] Magnus, op. cit., p. 71.
[4] *Gladstone and the Irish Nation*, pp. 738–9.

European essays in constitution making, but imperial precedents in Canada, that Gladstone had in mind by 1882 as providing a model for the reform of Irish government—it is none the less in substance clearly correct. Europe provided the urge to action, even if the Empire supplied the pattern of it.

Like Gladstone, his enigmatic rival, Disraeli, also appreciated the European background to the Irish Question. By race, by tradition, by intellect, he was indeed the better qualified to do so. In his 'Young England' days Disraeli's analysis of Irish problems was chiefly remarkable for its sympathetic insight, but when he became the leader of the Tories, surrounded by colleagues sprung from and representative of the land-owning classes, he cast off the Irish remnants of his inconvenient radical clothes. Like Gladstone, a European outlook enabled him to see the Irish Question in broad perspective, but unlike Gladstone he had not the zeal and perhaps not even the assurance to run counter to the cherished convictions of Englishmen on so controversial a subject. His approach, accordingly, was essentially political, in the sense that it was conceived in terms of party politics, and his tone betrayed his lack of preoccupation. Certainly, he assured the House of Commons in April 1849 after listening to Bright's impassioned appeal, misconceptions between the two islands that prevented co-operation should be removed, but once that were done, he affected to be sanguine enough to believe that 'Ireland will be like the patriarch, after his struggle with the mystic wrestler. Until the setting of the sun he thought he was striving against an oppressor, but at last he found that, instead of an oppressor, he was struggling against a guardian angel.'[1] The hope was unfounded, the expression of it lacking in feeling to the point of tastelessness on the morrow of the famine but perhaps, indeed, only an Englishman by birth and creed could have challenged his fellow countrymen, as Bright had done and as Gladstone was to do on a grander scale in 1886,[2] on an issue that touched their emotions and their interests so closely. Disraeli was the leader of the Tories, but not a member of the ruling class and he had not those particular qualifications.

While Englishmen, apart from Gladstone, were little interested in the European implications of the problem of Anglo-Irish relations there was by contrast much interest in Europe in the nature of them. What, asked Europeans, was the fundamental character of the Irish

[1] P. Guedalla, *The Queen and Mr Gladstone* (London, 1933), 2 Vols, Vol. II, p. 177
[2] Vide Hammond, op. cit., pp. 33–4.

question? Was it a national question? Was Ireland rightly to be numbered with the resurgent nationalities of Europe? Or was it in essence
a social and economic question, at the root of which lay an iniquitous
land system in the present and the enforced suppression of industries
and trading restrictions in the past? Or was it a combination of the
two? And if it were, wherein was to be found the driving force behind
Irish demands? In the field of political nationalism or in that of social
reform? All these were questions which English statesmen could not
wholly evade, for policies were necessarily determined in the light at
least of the implicit answers given to them. But they were little debated
in Parliament, partly no doubt because they were uncongenial, but
partly also because Englishmen were not interested in the abstractions
of politics. They seemed to them fit subject matter for fruitless and
interminable debate by continental theorists, for whom they continued to have a vast contempt.

It cannot be said that Irishmen either were as interested in the
theoretical debates on nationalism and social reform as might be
supposed. Domestic distress and geographical isolation account for
this, even if they do not sufficiently explain it. Certainly European
observers showed themselves—and it is at once a matter of some interest and moment alike—more conscious of the broad political significance of the historical process in Ireland, than were Irishmen themselves. Italians and Magyars, Czechs and Poles were more preoccupied
with the question of whether Ireland was to be numbered as one among
the suppressed nationalities of Europe, than Irishmen for their part
showed awareness of Ireland's position, as one engaged with the
historic nations of Europe in a struggle to regain her liberty and
separate identity. In nineteenth-century Ireland there was no one who
used the analogy of the Slav or Czech struggle for independence as,
for example, Havlitcheck used the nationalist movement under
O'Connell to inspire his compatriots at Prague.[1] The articles, in *le
Journal de Prague*, in which this gifted journalist popularized the name
of 'Repeal' and which led in time to the foundation of a Czech 'Repeal
Club', as an association of intellectual nationalists, afford an illustration
of this contrast between the European attitude to nationalism, as part
of a cosmopolitan political movement and the Irish tendency to regard
it as an individual particularist revolt. Even the Young Ireland Movement, psychologically predisposed though its leaders were to the

[1] E. Denis, *La Bohême depuis la Montagne-Blanche* (Paris, 1903), 2 Vols., Vol. II,
pp. 227–9.

revolutionary, liberal-national ideals of contemporary Europe, sought none the less to rekindle Irish nationalism not from without but from within. It was to Irish history, not European movements, that they looked for inspiration and example, and it was through a fresh understanding of Ireland's past that they hoped to stir the young men of their day to continue the struggle for Irish liberties. And so it is not perhaps surprising that in the decades which followed the execution of Tone and the failure of the United Irishmen, the Irish people seem to have been but little moved by the revolts against imperial dominion in partitioned Poland, in Italy, in Hungary and in the Balkans. It was in the streets of Paris, not in the streets of Dublin, that the crowds came out in 1831 singing the refrain from *La Varsovie:*

> *Pour nos vieux frères d'armes*
> *N'aurez vous que des larmes?*
> *Frères, c'était de sang que nous versions pour vous!*

in protest against the Czar's brutal suppression of the Poles. When early in the twentieth century Arthur Griffith defined the aims of Irish nationalism by comparison with Magyar achievement, he unfolded a fresh field of vision to the majority of his readers. *The Resurrection of Hungary*[1] enabled Irishmen to understand, what Tone and Mitchel had long since understood, that Irish nationalism could reinforce its strength and broaden its inspiration from the varied expressions of the nationalist movement in Europe.

In the later nineteenth century there was another factor drawing Irish eyes away from Europe and towards the West. In the seventeenth and eighteenth centuries the Irish exiles went to Europe: in the nineteenth they went chiefly to the United States of America. In time of need these exiles or their descendants could be relied upon to supply arms, dollars, and for two or more generations after the Famine which was the cause of their going, fanatical hatred of England. But from Europe none of these things were likely to come. For Irishmen the year of revolution was in this respect a year of disillusion. Old and Young Ireland were at one in welcoming the overthrow of the July Monarchy, as the barricades once more went up in the Paris streets in February 1848. John O'Connell, the Liberator's son, who was in Paris in these stirring days wrote to Ledru-Rollin hailing the revolution as 'the really sublime spectacle presented to the world'; *The Pilot* also voicing the sentiments

[1] A. Griffith, *The Resurrection of Hungary: A Parallel for Ireland* (Dublin, 1904).

of 'Old Ireland' called upon Irishmen to emulate the 'most glorious revolution recorded and consecrated in history' while *The Nation* for Young Ireland in conscious cultivation of the language of the Revolution expressed a conviction that in this new dawn Old Irelanders like Young Irelanders were 'animated by the same noble spirit of fraternity and forgiveness'.[1] If the spirit indeed existed, it did not last long, chiefly because of the alarm of Old Ireland, in the person of John O'Connell, at the revolutionary republican overtones to Mitchel's utterances though it did produce, albeit without O'Connell's co-operation, an address to the people of France to be presented by a delegation, sent to Paris for the purpose and including, in deference to the temper of the times, a working-class representative.[2] It was an emotional gesture, but who could say that in the new wave of revolutionary sentiment it might not have practical consequences? The British Government, at any rate, did not discount such a possibility and was resolved to take no chances with the result that Lamartine, Foreign Minister of the Second Republic, soon learned that the romance of revolution must needs be restrained by the realities of power. England, the most liberal of the Great Powers, had given informal recognition to the new French republic, but formal recognition was withheld and made conditional upon further experience of republican behaviour. Was the Second Republic about to display the missionary zeal of the First? Was it about to challenge the established order outside its own frontiers? Was it going to interfere in the domestic affairs of other states?

The British Government, disturbed by public statements, displaying sympathy with Ireland, had enquiry made of Lamartine. He was altogether reassuring. He could never, he told the British representative in Paris, consider Irish nationality 'in any sense except as identical with English nationality'. But to a deputation of Irish residents in Paris Lamartine struck a different note. He eulogized Daniel O'Connell and Ireland and, what was more, he accepted, so it was reported, an Irish flag from the deputation 'as a symbol of French sympathy with Irish nationalism'. The British Government, once more through their representative, Lord Normanby, demanded an explanation. Lamartine said he had received no flag, but the British insisted, and Lamartine agreed to a published assurance that the Second Republic recognized

---

[1] See Dr Kevin B. Nowlan in *The Political Background*, Chapter III, p. 190, in Edwards and Williams, *The Great Famine*, from which these quotations are reprinted.
[2] Ibid., pp. 191–2.

no flag in the British Isles other than that of the United Kingdom. When, therefore, the delegation arrived from Dublin, not revolutionary ardour, but considerations of diplomatic prudence, determined the character of their reception. Lamartine told Lord Normanby in advance of the substance of his proposed remarks and he earned the subsequent thanks of Lord Palmerston for the judicious utterance he made. John Mitchel said all that needed to be said—'We are well pleased that M. Lamartine has let us know distinctly we must rely on ourselves'.[1] It was a lesson that was not forgotten.

To sense a conflict between Irish affinities with the Old World and the New would be unrealistic. There was none. But as the nature of the affinity in each case differed, so too emphasis varied according to time and circumstance. To Irishmen of the sixteenth, seventeenth and eighteenth centuries there rested in Europe, not only the supreme authority of the Church, not only the continuing source of Western culture, but also the forces that might restore Irish liberties. For Irishmen of the later nineteenth and early twentieth century the links of Church and culture remained unimpaired at the least, and possibly strengthened, but the prospect of aid had diminished to vanishing point, except in the event of major war. So much the events of 1848 alone had made clear and accordingly Irish nationalists generally and physical force advocates in particular, were bound in this respect to look no longer to Europe, but to the Irish exiles and their revolutionary societies in the New World. To that extent the balance of Irish relations with Europe and America had perceptibly shifted.

It may not be altogether fanciful in this context to see something symbolic in the contrast between the European sympathies of the founder of the first Home Rule movement, the agreeable, convivial and largely ineffectual Isaac Butt, and the United States oriented outlook of his ruthless and realistic successor, Charles Stewart Parnell. Butt,[2] a Protestant, conservative by temperament and in his early years also by party allegiance, held the chair of Political Economy, founded in 1836 by Archbishop Whately, in the University of Dublin, before he entered Parliament. Among the more substantial of his

---

[1] *The Political Background*, pp. 192–4. Dr Nowlan has written an account of these events, based upon an examination of British and French Foreign Office archives, and other sources.

[2] T. de V. White has written his biography under a title—*The Road of Excess* (Dublin, 1946)—that has its appropriateness, but is apt to mystify. David Thornley's *Isaac Butt and Home Rule* (London, 1964), is a study of the origins of Home Rule and of the first Home Rule Movement.

writings was a two-volume history of Italy from 1814. Though Butt refrained from direct association of Irish with Italian nationalism, the work concluded with sentiments that might have seemed assured of general acclaim in his native land. They read:[1]

. . . there are elements in the life of nations that are indestructible as that life itself—there are passions and feelings which the lapse of centuries cannot suppress, . . . The Italian was not yet reconciled to the ascendency of the German—the contest that had marshalled the bands of patriotism on the field of Legnano was bequeathed to a remote generation. In the new subjugation which the Treaty of Vienna imposed on Italy, another page of her history is opened—but a page still to be written over with the records of the undying struggle against the dominion of the stranger.

The book, published in 1860 and therefore most happily timed in terms of topical interest, also coincided with mounting Irish hostility to Italian Nationalist claims to the Papal states. Money was collected and an expeditionary force organized to assist Papal resistance to the unification of Italy. Garibaldi, in England a national hero, in Ireland was Anti-Christ. Butt, however, had some compensation for ambivalent reactions at home in warm appreciation of his work in England, not least from Lord Palmerston, who wrote with enthusiasm of 'the elements of healthful independence and of well-regulated liberty, of manly energy, and of steady determination to be free', that had developed in Italy 'to the surprise and admiration of mankind'.[2]

Parnell, by contrast, thought little, if at all, of Italian or any other European nationalism; his interest and concern was to retain the support of Irish-Americans, including not least those who favoured physical force. Though not without moments of uncertainty, as after the Kilmainham treaty and still more after the defeat of the first Home Rule Bill in 1886, he was in this successful and it was a condition of success at home. 'Without American support', wrote a contemporary, 'Mr Parnell ceases to be a power . . .' And after the Chicago Convention of the Irish National League of America in August 1886, when Parnell's continuing faith in parliamentary methods was by no means universal, another commented: 'Here was a great gathering of Irish-American citizens, men who had differences . . .—but at the name of

---

[1] Isaac Butt, *The History of Italy from the Abdication of Napoleon I*, 2 Vols. (London, 1860), Vol. II, pp. 534–5.
[2] Quoted in White, op. cit., pp. 179–80.

Parnell, those differences disappeared. . . . It is one of the most marvellous things which, I think, have occurred in the history of our
country—the marvellous allegiance of the Irish race throughout the
world to their leader'.[1] In brief the Irish of the diaspora were a major
factor in Irish politics; Europe, with the one and very important
exception of the Vatican, had ceased to be.

Comparative and growing Irish detachment from continental in-
fluences, little if at all diminishes interest in European interpretations
of the nature of the Irish question. An attempt to survey so wide a
field in its entirety would be outside the scope of this study and indeed
might not prove particularly rewarding, but a selective approach may
none the less throw some light on the problems of that phase of Irish
history, which reached its climax in the overthrow of the Union. And
if, in this and the succeeding chapter, attention is confined to the observations of Italian nationalists and of the apostles of modern communism upon Irish problems, it is not because the commentary they
supply is necessarily more searching or more profound than that of
other observers, but rather because, being concerned with fundamental
issues the conclusions at which they arrive have the sharpness that
provokes disagreement and further reflection.

Both Italian and Marxist were alike in that they misjudged the relative strength of the political forces in the Ireland of their day. That in
itself in one respect may serve to make their commentaries the more
instructive, since it emphasizes the danger of interpreting Irish history
in the light of subsequent events. Anglo-Irish relations had no *inevitable* solution as the land question had no *inevitable* outcome. What
has been done has been achieved by the conscious will of Irishmen: it
has not been the product of some rigid ordinance of history. And if the
opinions of European observers serve merely to remind us that, even
in the second half of the nineteenth century, the force that was to
dominate Ireland's political future was not yet unmistakably identi-
fiable, then they may be read not without profit, inasmuch as their
external judgements may help to place a period in the wider historical setting, so essential to its understanding.

THE ITALIAN AND IRISH NATIONAL MOVEMENTS

In 1848 it seemed to Italian patriots as though the great moment in the
Italian Risorgimento had come, that 'the hour of Austria had struck'.

[1] Conor Cruise O'Brien, *Parnell and his party 1880–90* (Oxford, 1957), pp. 195–6.

C

'Italia Una!' now the war-cry rang
From Alp to Etna; and her dreams were done
And she herself had wakened into life
And stood full armed and free . . .

On May 8, 1848, Angelo Brofferio, leader of the Radicals, speaking in the first Piedmontese Chamber of Deputies in the Carignano Palace at Turin, urged immediate war upon Austria. A peroration in which he recalled to deputies the precepts of Daniel O'Connell is a stirring example of demagogic oratory in Italy.

Too many injuries have we to avenge, too many accounts to settle, too many insults to wipe out, and too much cause for boasting has our last retreat given to Austria, for us not to seek with all our power to prove to the foreigner, who watches us and laughs, that the bells of the Sicilian Vespers and the trumpet of the Lombard League and the devouring flames of Pietro Micca, are not the symbols of an ancient pride but the glories of the present! (prolonged applause). Pursue this policy of useless delay and what will you find in Lombardy? Leave the Bohemians to sack it, the Bavarians to burn it, and the blood-thirsty Croat to dye its soil with Italian blood, and when the hour of victory sounds, you will reconquer cities destroyed, a devastated countryside, and a people wasted with misery—you will build it again, but you will build upon ruin and ashes! When O'Connell, the great apostle of Irish liberty, rose against the oppression of Britain, 'three things I urge upon you,' he said, 'sons of Ireland: agitate, agitate, agitate! And I, O Italians, urge three things upon you: audacity, audacity, audacity!' (Clamorous and prolonged applause.)[1]

It is in a context and on an occasion such as this that one would expect to find a reference to the Irish nationalist movement, though an Irish speaker might prefer to invoke other names than that of O'Connell when advocating a policy of 'audacity'. But in Italy O'Connell's reputation remained unchallenged. G. M. Trevelyan wrote: 'O'Connell's methods in Ireland and Cobden's in England were quoted by Mazzinians and Moderates alike, as models of organization to be imitated in Italian national affairs.'[2] The address of Tommaseo, prepared to welcome Cobden on his visit to Venice, is typical. 'England [sic] alone has

---

[1] Quoted in A. J. Whyte, *The Political Life and Letters of Cavour, 1848–61* (London, 1930), pp. 19–20.
[2] *Manin and the Venetian Revolution of 1848* (London, 1923), p. 52.

given the world the spectacle of an advocate [O'Connell] more powerful than warrior or sovereign, who incites and restrains millions by his voice alone; a friar [Father Mathew] who by his voice alone regenerates through temperance tens of thousands of men of different religions; a private citizen [Cobden] who makes the greatest of living statesmen his disciple, subjugates wrong-headed opinion . . . who while obeying the law gives orders to the law.' The tribute to England, two-thirds undeserved, expressed by implication the prevailing view that Ireland's efforts were directed to the securing of good government and that the claim to distinct nationality was at the least subordinate to it.

Such casual allusions recall the half realist, half romantic attitude towards Ireland with which Italians of that time were very familiar. Lacking in any intrinsic significance, they yet serve to place in perspective the more considered opinions of two of the most famous of all Italian nationalists, Cavour and Mazzini. These opinions were formulated between 1842–65 and for the most part at least twenty years before Home Rule became the declared policy of the Nationalist Party and half a century before the birth of the Sinn Féin movement. Cavour surveyed the Ireland of O'Connell; Mazzini, a country whose vitality was sapped by famine, whose resources were diminished by emigration, whose political leadership was deficient and uncertain,[1] a country at the ebb tide of its fortunes. Yet the contrast in material conditions appears to have influenced the substance of their judgment scarcely at all.

The majority of the great Italian patriots of the Risorgimento were 'anglophile' in sentiment. In the long years of exile Italian nationalists found in London a welcome, such as they could find in no other capital of Europe. Cavour, that most practical of statesmen, dreamed for one brief moment that English troops might fight on the plains of Lombardy for the independence of Italy. And even if, in the event, it was Louis Napoleon who was the victor of Magenta and Solferino, Italian sentiment still cherished English friendship. That sentiment was not mistaken; for Englishmen felt genuine affection for peoples 'struggling to be free'—so long as their struggles did not threaten 'the integrity of the United Kingdom'. In the opinion of Italian statesmen, there may be detected, therefore, a disposition to interpret contemporary Ireland in a manner not unduly displeasing to their English friends. This was supplemented by antagonism between Italian and Irish Nationalists,

[1] On Irish politics at this time see J. H. Whyte, *The Independent Irish Party 1850–9* (Oxford, 1958).

divided as they were over the future of the temporal dominions of the Papacy. On this issue Irish Catholic opinion took uncompromisingly and consistently what was in Italy the unpopular, the anti-nationalist side. When the London Committee of the Reform League, an Anglo-Irish body, espoused the cause of Garibaldi, it introduced a source of division with Irish members, which contributed decisively to the demise of the League in 1867. And as late as the General Election of 1880, when Parnell was fighting for the leadership of the Irish party and was widely considered to represent dangerously radical if not revolutionary forces, his candidature in Cork City was condemned at a meeting of the Bishop and Catholic clergy of Cork, Canon Cullinane later alleging that 'one of Mr Parnell's followers boasted that he ate meat on Good Friday and that he was the follower of Garibaldi the assassin'.[1] These things represented views which Italians, at least, while engaged in a life and death struggle for a united and independent nation, were not disposed to discount or disregard. Yet when every allowance is made for the shadow cast by differences on the Roman question, it remains remarkable that men so different in temperament, so antagonistic in outlook, as Mazzini and Cavour should find themselves in substantial agreement in their assessment of the nature of Irish nationalism.

COUNT CAVOUR ON IRELAND

In the years 1842–43 Cavour spent eight months in France and England. During that time his able and acquisitive intellect was engaged in assimilating the political and social structure of the lands he visited. Soon he became interested in the Irish question. He wrote about it on his return to Piedmont, in a letter to Auguste de la Rive dated August 24, 1843.[2] After giving some account of events in Italy, he proceeded, 'However, as I find I have some spare time, I have allowed myself to be dominated by the fury with which all these idiotic articles upon Ireland, appearing daily in the papers of all colours and countries, inspires me; and I set myself to write an article upon this question. . . .' He proceeded to indicate the character of the article which indeed was destined to reach the dimensions of 'a small book'. 'My opinions', he wrote, 'are opposed to those current on the Continent: they will, I

---

[1] Quoted in C. C. O'Brien, *Parnell and his party*, p. 27.
[2] This letter is quoted in A. J. Whyte, *The Early Life and Letters of Cavour, 1810–1848* (Oxford, 1925), pp. 287–8.

believe, displease everybody except you and a few reasonable people like you. I wish at all costs to maintain the Union, first in the interest of Ireland herself, then in that of England, and finally in the interest of material and intellectual civilization. The motive on which I oppose the plans of O'Connell will as much displease one side as my opinion of the opportuneness of these plans will displease the other.'

The article on Ireland duly appeared in the *Bibliothèque Universelle de Genève* early in 1844. It attracted considerable attention, was quoted from in the House of Commons and has twice been translated into English.[1]

In the years that elapsed between Catholic Emancipation and the Repeal of the Corn Laws, European papers made Ireland an habitual theme for discussion. Usually brief on the affairs of England, as Cavour observed, they filled their columns with reports of the smallest meetings in favour of the repeal of the Union. 'From the hopes, the ill-concealed joy of certain journals, of certain political parties, when they speak of Ireland it is clear that they delight in the prospect that this crisis threatens with a violent catastrophe the ancient edifice of the British constitution.' The reason was the quite simple one that public opinion on the Continent was as a whole hostile to England. 'Extreme parties, opposed in all besides, agree in their violent hatred of that country. Moderate parties love it in theory, but in reality they feel towards it little instinctive sympathy. . . . From St Petersburg to Madrid, in Germany as in Italy, the enemies of progress, and the partisans of political revolutions alike regard England as their most formidable foe.'

Cavour did not share the general antipathy. He associated himself with those 'few isolated men, superior to the passions of the crowd' who 'cherish towards England the esteem and interest which may well be inspired by one of the greatest nations that have done honour to humanity'. But he did not allow his admiration for England to make him insensible to the wrongs or indifferent to the cause of those evils in Ireland whose 'oppressive reality cannot be denied'. His brief review of Irish history before the Union in the opening chapters of the book is unsparing in its denunciation of the then existing system of government. The penal laws at first inspired by religious fanaticism lost by degrees their primitive character and became in the hands of those who applied them a means of social domination. During the greater part of

---

[1] The extracts that follow are taken from the translation by W. Hodgson entitled, *Thoughts on Ireland: Its Present and Its Future* (London and Manchester, 1868). The book first appeared in English in 1845.

the eighteenth century the Irish peasant was reduced to a state of slavery worse than that of the negroes in the Antilles. 'During this period', Cavour concluded, 'Ireland presents the saddest spectacle to be found in any civilized society—complete and absolute oppression of the poor by the rich, of him who labours by him who possesses, organized by the law, and maintained by the ministers of justice.' It was this social domination that aroused his most bitter condemnation, for he observed that religious persecution was unfortunately not exceptional in that age, the injustices inflicted on Irish Catholics being matched or even surpassed by those inflicted on the Huguenots after the Repeal of the Edict of Nantes.

Cavour regarded the Act of Union as an 'irreproachably just', economic and political settlement of Anglo-Irish relations. He wrote: 'We must distinguish the merits of this measure in itself from the means employed for its accomplishment. There can be but one voice in condemning to infamy those who made traffic of the independence of their country, who bartered their rights and their political influence against gold and places, who sold their vote and sanctioned an act which their conscience disapproved. But must we equally condemn the government which purchased those corrupt men? I would not hesitate to do this if by a fatal error, public opinion in ages past and even in our own, had not in some measure sanctioned on the part of government a morality different from that which private persons recognize; if it had not, in all times, treated with excessive indulgence the immoral acts which have brought about great political results.'

Then Cavour proceeded to maintain that the Union had achieved 'great political results' for the United Kingdom; he argued that the repeal of the Union would be damaging to Ireland's interests. 'Europe, in general,' he wrote, 'has applauded the conduct of O'Connell, and has seemingly agreed with him in believing that the legislative independence of Ireland is the only effectual remedy for the evils of that country. . . . I regard this notion as erroneous and as fatal to the improvement of the condition of the Irish people.' Cavour reached this conclusion after analysing the question of repeal under five headings: Taxation; Commerce and Industry; Public Works; Emigration and Poor Rates; and the Reform of Territorial Property. On all these counts Cavour decided that Ireland's material gain lay in the maintenance of the Union, not so much because of what it had achieved, but because of what it might achieve. If the Melbourne Ministry had been as powerful in England as in Ireland, if it could have commanded a majority in the House sufficient to compel the Lords to adopt remedial measures for Ireland, then all that country's ills would have been on the way to cure; for political reforms would have made possible the enact- ment of those social reforms which alone could restore conditions of repose and prosperity. So Cavour argued, but later experience made that 'if' loom large indeed, for it showed that reformist policies in Ireland were unlikely to command the support of a majority of the electorate of the United Kingdom as a whole.

Yet it is probable that on the broad view Cavour was right. England was entering upon the heyday of her industrial supremacy. For the next half century she was to remain unchallenged as the foremost industrial and commercial nation in the world. Had Ireland been pre- pared frankly and fully to renounce her nationalist claims, and to devote the energies dissipated, on this line of argument, on the political field, to the development of her material resources, then it is possible, even probable, that England would have recognized her claim to participate in the fruits of industrial expansion and that as a consequence, Ireland would have attained a far greater degree of prosperity by the end of the century than in fact she did. Political acquiescence in Union and the sense of stability and security which might have ensued, might rea- sonably have been expected to encourage an inflow of capital for de- velopment, thus helping to meet Ireland's greatest need. There was a price to be paid, the sacrifice of a belief in a distinct national identity. It was a great one indeed. But what if, as Cavour by implication as- sumed, this claim to a distinct nationality were no more than an illusion fostered by centuries of injustice and oppression? Then indeed the realist had but one path to pursue—to remedy those injustices, to reform the existing Irish economy, particularly the land system, and to foster co-operation between the various parts of the British Isles on the basis of unity, equality and of a common participation in a com- mon benefit.

There is no evidence that O'Connell and his contemporaries realized as clearly as Cavour the choice that might lie before Ireland—material prosperity, or years of bitterness and frustration devoted to the realiza- tion of the national principle. It is certain that the majority of Irish nationalists reckoned material prosperity to weigh lightly in the balance against national independence. Cavour wrote as a spectator, who analysed an intricate question with lucidity and without discernible bias, but always in the light of a cold, unemotional reason. 'His purely economic handling of the question', commented Mr Whyte, 'and his failure to attach any weight to the claims of national sentiment is typical of his outlook at this time.'[1] Even in Piedmont, Italians mistrusted this liberal intellectual and landowner, whose 'heart is in his brain, whose sentiment is the slave of reason' and who concealed beneath a cold exterior of practical materialism a patriotism so devoted, as made him one day the architect of a united Italy, the sober-minded hero of a national movement, whose romantic qualities excited the imagination of the world. And if in his essay on Ireland Cavour neglected what history has shown to be most significant, it was partly because, feeling 'so far from the scene of action,' it seemed reckless to attempt to weigh imponderables. So he confined himself to the material aspect of Ireland and based his conclusion on the facts at his disposal.

Count Cavour's opinions on outstanding events have not lost their interest and a few may illustrate the quality of his judgement.

On the Act of Union:

Britain committed an enormous fault in not granting to the Catholics emancipation as a consequence of the Act of Union.

On the Reform Bill of 1832:

Parliamentary Reform cannot, any more than emancipation, dry up the springs of popular agitation in Ireland. Lord Grey erred in regarding it as the proper boundary of the reforming Party.

On the economy of Ireland in 1842:

Ireland is a country (except in the North) exclusively agricultural. This is ordinarily a condition eminently favourable to the maintenance of order and of peace; but here it is otherwise. The land to which the Irish are attached by an insurmountable necessity belongs almost wholly to a foreign race, which has for them neither sympathy nor affection, with which they are not united by the multitude of moral ties that everywhere else exist between the owners and cultivators of the soil.

On the Anglo-Irish aristocracy:

While I acknowledge the very important place which the aristocracy has held, and still holds, in the British constitution, I utterly reject the

[1] *The Early Life and Letters of Cavour*, pp. 289–92.

claim of the Irish aristocracy to be regarded as on a similar footing. How can two things so widely different be likened to one another? . . . The two aristocracies have assuredly no more in common that a sound and vigorous arm has with its fellow which gangrene has blighted.

His judgement upon the disastrous effects of absentee landlordism was the sharper because his own experience led him to lay great stress on the moral and material value of a resident aristocracy.

It is difficult to estimate with justice the value which a wealthy or even a well-to-do family living in the midst of a poor and ignorant peasantry can exercise. . . . It is so easy for an enlightened and well disposed land-owner to win the affection and respect of all those about him, that he can, without very much effort, acquire a moral influence more powerful and effective than all the material influence exercised by the possessors of the soil under the feudal system. If ever the majority of landowners consent to devote themselves for some years to the betterment of their estates without neglecting the lot of those who cultivate them: if these same proprietors strive to spread around them healthy knowledge and good principles, the social hierarchy will rebuild itself upon much sounder bases than those which 1789 destroyed.[1]

Cavour, in this as in many other respects a typical representative of nineteenth-century liberalism, had unbounded faith in education. Rightly he diagnosed that education constituted the fundamental social need of the Ireland of his day. With equal firmness he maintained that such education should not be clerical. 'While I honour the sincere faith of the Catholic clergy, their zealous charity, their boundless devotion', he wrote, 'yet I do not recognize in them the qualities necessary to direct successfully popular instruction. Their profound ignorance, their numerous prejudices, their exaggerated political notions render them unfit to fulfil the task of primary teachers.'

To his denunciation of the absentee landlords of Ireland, Cavour added the further observation that 'all these evils are aggravated by the presence of a Protestant clergy who divide with the rich proprietors the fruit of the toil of the devotedly Catholic population in the midst of which they live'. But at the same time Cavour's view of the importance of a properly constituted hierarchy of the land led him to fear the revival

[1] From an article in the *Bibliothèque Universelle de Genève*, September 1843: quoted in Whyte, ibid., pp. 290–1.

of a Dublin Parliament on the ground that it might 'despoil landowners' instead of reforming the system and so provoke civil war.

In conclusion, it is of interest to recall Cavour's estimate of Daniel O'Connell. In 1843 he wrote: 'Though O'Connell at times uses the language of a thorough democrat he is at heart, as regards the laws of property, friendly to the aristocratic system.' And just after the meeting on Tara Hill in 1843, Cavour, unimpressed by appearances, wrote: 'O'Connell's conduct proves clearly that he is audacious only in proportion to the patience of his adversaries.'[1] It is not a far cry from this verdict on O'Connell to that of Young Ireland on the 'rosewater revolutionary' and the opinion of Cavour recalls the substance—though not indeed the vigorous expression—of that famous sketch, in which John Mitchel portrayed 'a man of giant proportions in body and in mind; with no profound learning, indeed, even in his own profession of the law, but with a vast and varied knowledge of human nature, in all its strength, and especially in all its weakness; with a voice like thunder and earthquake, yet musical and soft at will, as the song of birds; ... with profound and spontaneous natural feeling ... yet withal, a boundless fund of masterly affectation and consummate histrionism —hating and loving heartily, outrageous in his merriment, and passionate in his lamentation, he had the power to make other man hate or love, laugh or weep at his good pleasure—in so much that Daniel O'Connell, by virtue of being more intensely Irish . . . than other Irishmen, led and swayed his people by a kind of divine, or else diabolic right.'

He led them, as I believe, all wrong for forty years. He was a lawyer; and never could come to the point of denying and defying all British law. He was a Catholic, sincere and devout; and would not see that the Church had ever been the enemy of Irish Freedom. He was an aristocrat, by position and by taste; and the name of a Republic was odious to him.[2]

Mitchel's brilliant, malicious portrait reminds us that Cavour judged O'Connell's policy in the light of his own experience of the nationalist movement in Italy, and it is not surprising that an Italian patriot, who had grown up in an atmosphere of conspiracy and violence, should

---

[1] Noted in Thayer, *The Life and Times of Cavour* (London and New York, 1911), 2 Vols., Vol. I, p. 64.

[2] John Mitchel, *Jail Journal*, ed. by Arthur Griffith (Dublin, 1913), p. xxxv.

pronounce a similar verdict. For Cavour knew that Italy could win her independence only by force of arms; he realized too that conflict with the Church for possession of the temporal dominions was inevitable. In Italy a middle course was impossible. 'Between the dagger of the Carbonari and the chocolate of the Jesuit', said Charles Albert the King of Sardinia, 'I know no peace.' And if it seemed to Cavour, as it seemed to Mitchel, that O'Connell in pursuing a policy of moderation, blunted the force of the nationalist movement; and if furthermore it seemed to Cavour, not without reason, that O'Connell's policy was favoured by the vast majority of the Irish people, then the reasons for his conclusion that Ireland desired good government rather than national government became clear enough. And such reasons, it should be added, whatever view may be taken of their validity, did not imply a condemnation of O'Connell's leadership. But they did serve to place a European interpretation upon that distinction which O'Connell drew between *national separation*, which he considered undesirable and *national independence*, which he resolved to restore by effecting the Repeal of the Union.

MAZZINI ON IRELAND

The life of Joseph Mazzini was characterized by a devotion to the cause of nationality of an intensity unsurpassed in the annals of Europe. Yet his life, though crowned with notable achievements, was clouded by frustration. He wrote, he slaved, he conspired for the cause of Italian liberty at a time when Italian despair was blackest and Italian divisions seemed eternal. Admired by all the world in 1848–49 as the unyielding triumvir of the short-lived Roman Republic yet he lived on, an unsparing critic of the United Italy for whose creation he had sacrificed all. For Mazzini was rigid, uncompromising, and it must be confessed, a bitter doctrinaire. Italian unity must be won by the methods he advocated and in accordance with the principles he held with such unswerving tenacity, if Mazzini was to co-operate. He would not acknowledge the Italian monarchy, even though an Italy, free and united at last, owed so much to the House of Savoy. Yet despite his faults his strength of purpose was a source of inspiration to nationalists in every land. One recalls that on November 19, 1853, when John Mitchel heard the first rumours of impending war in the Crimea, he thought how the news 'would refresh many a weary exile', and he saw before him, in vision, Giuseppe Mazzini, 'with his lofty brow and pensive eye,

shadowed by many a doleful memory, of the murdered Menotte . . . of
the youthful brothers Bandiera . . . and the noble struggle of those last
of Romans in fatal '48 . . . but now Mazzini looks up again with hope.
. . . O, Triumvir, is this dawning hope also to fade in another evening
of despair? Is this to end but in another Romiorno expedition? Another
Carbonaro conspiracy? Another Roman carnage? Mazzini knows not;
but one thing he knows—if the neck of this foul European 'peace' be
once broken, the cypress branch of young Italy will be reared again
and the resolute watchword *Ora e sempre* shall ring along the Appenine.'
Like Mazzini, Mitchel too believed that a European war would bring
nearer the hour of national resurgence.

> You that Mitchel's prayer have heard,
> 'Send war in our time, O Lord'.[1]

It is at first sight surprising to discover that Mazzini, the doctrinaire
republican, held opinions similar to those of Cavour the pragmatic
monarchist on the national movement in Ireland. In 1847 Mazzini
founded a People's International League to resume the work of Young
Europe. Some Repealers complained to the League that it had omitted
Ireland from the list of the nationalities of the future. Mazzini drafted
an answer. He argued that the Irish demand was essentially one for
better government only; and while he had every sympathy with their
'just consciousness of human dignity, claiming its long violated rights'
with their 'wish to have rulers, educators, not masters', with their
'protests against legislation grounded on distrust and hostility', he yet
maintained that the Irish claim was not a national claim. He believed
that the nationalist movement was not likely to be permanent, and he
refused to see in it any elements of true nationality because the Irish
'did not plead for any distinct principle of life or system of legislation,
derived from native peculiarities, and contrasting radically with English
wants and wishes', nor claimed for their country any 'high special
function' to discharge in the interests of humanity. The spectacle of the
great Irish Exodus after the Famine appalled him. 'They come and tell
us', he said, 'that it is a well ordered state of society in which, for lack
of a few potatoes, thousands, and even millions are reduced to starvation.'[2] But sympathy did not alter his judgement.

Twenty years later Mazzini's views on Ireland had not changed, nor
had his sympathy diminished. 'I am feeling', he wrote, 'between the

[1] W. B. Yeats, *Last Poems and Plays* (London, 1940), 'Under Ben Bulben'.
[2] Bolton King, *Mazzini* (London, 1902), pp. 106–7.

unhappy and the ferocious about the Fenians condemned. Today, I think, is the Queen's birthday. Does she read a newspaper? Cannot she find a womanly feeling in her heart and ask the Cabinet to commute the punishment? In point of fact the killing of these men will prove an absolute fault [sic]. Burke will be the Robert Emmet of 1867. A feeling of revenge will rekindle the energy of the discouraged Fenians. The dream will become, through martyrdom, a sort of religion. But that is not my ground. It is the legal murder re-enacted against a *thought*, a thought which ought to be refuted, destroyed by thought only. Burke and others are genuine believers in Irish nationality. I think they are philosophically and politically wrong; but are we to refute a philosophical error with hanging?' After their reprieve he wrote, 'You have been spared the infamy of Burke's execution. I am glad of it. I have weakness for England and did not like the shame for her.'[1]

It would be easy to say of Mazzini's conclusions on Irish nationality that history has proved them mistaken. That indeed is substantially true. But none the less Mazzini's observations are enlightening. He doubted the reality of Nationalism in Ireland chiefly because of deficiencies in respect of the two things which in Ireland are commonly held to provide its most distinctive qualities—endurance and mission. The first—lack of endurance—was deduced from purely contemporary and therefore transient conditions. Mazzini surveyed the Ireland of the post-famine years, an Ireland depressed and divided, whose resources spiritual as well as material were diminished by the steady drain of emigration. But the second—the inability by one of the greatest of nationalist thinkers to discover the elements of true nationality in the Irish movement on the ground of its lack of a distinctive mission— cannot be so lightly discounted. Was Mazzini justified in claiming that the Irish people did not stand for 'any distinct principle of life'? And if this contention be admitted, was he right in questioning the reality of nationality on this ground alone?

The answer to all these questions is implicit in Mazzini's political philosophy, a philosophy whose principles have a continuing relevance in our age, which has neglected to its cost the distinction between true and false nationality.[2] The duty of man, duty to the State, and duty to

---

[1] Bolton King, op. cit., pp. 199–200.

[2] For appreciations of Mazzini's political thought see Bolton King, op. cit., Gaetano Salvemini, *Mazzini* (London, 1936), especially Chap. 9, and C. E. Vaughan, *Studies in the History of Political Philosophy* (Manchester, 1925), 2 Vols., Vol. II, pp. 251–325; and for Mazzini's own writings see *The Duties of Man and other Essays* (London, 1907), and *The Life and Writings of Joseph Mazzini* (London, 1891), 6 Volumes.

the world was the foundation of Mazzini's thought. Nationality exists as the means whereby the individual in serving his country may serve humanity. 'Nationality', he wrote,[1] 'is sacred to me because I see in it the instrument of labour for the good and progress of all men.' And again, 'Countries are the workshops of humanity: a nation is a living task, her life is not her own, but a force and a function in the universal providential scheme'.

What then are the essential marks of nationality? Mazzini disposed of the argument that race is the true basis of nationality. There is not a single spot in Europe where an unmixed race can be detected. 'France, the most powerful nationality of the modern world is a mixture of Germans, Celts, Romans.' He recognized the influence of geography, 'nationalities appear to me to have been traced long ago by the finger of Providence on the map of Europe'; and he noted with pardonable satisfaction that God had stretched around Italy her 'sublime and irrefutable boundaries'.[2] But he was too clear-sighted to regard a transcendental interpretation of geography as the final definition of nationality. Geography, history, race and language might have a formative influence on nationality, but they did not in themselves constitute its true foundation. That was to be found 'in the will of the people' who desire to be a nation; and *provided* that behind the desire there lies a moral purpose, then they have a right to be one. Mazzini was not alone in maintaining that nationality must have a democratic basis—the will of the people—but he was the first to claim that this basis is insufficient, unless there is a moral aim to justify it. 'In questions of nationality, as in every other question, the end alone is sovereign'; and a true nation must have a moral intention, its clear and understood mission to accomplish for itself and humanity. The struggle of a community for a selfish materialistic end is not consistent with the principle of nationality. For the moral end is supreme; and it is only in homage to the moral law that a nation finds its 'baptism and consecration'. 'National life and international life should be two manifestations of the same principle, the love of good.'

The distinctive principles of Mazzini's thought on Nationality explain the ground on which he withheld his benediction from the Irish national movement. He could detect in it no distinct principle of life, nor any high 'special function', which Ireland sought to fulfil in the interests of humanity. Now Mazzini's principle that nationality has a

[1] Quoted Bolton King, op. cit., see also Mazzini, *Life and Writings*, Vol. III, p. 33.
[2] *The Duties of Man*, p. 53.

moral function to fulfil may be thought to deserve every emphasis; and only too often, in Ireland, as in other nations, the purpose of nationality was forgotten in the immediate struggle for independence. Thomas Davis had seen the danger, and it may well be that historians of later times will attribute some of the troubles of the post-Treaty period in Ireland to the neglect of the longer and the deeper view.

But when Mazzini elaborated his principle of the moral purpose of nationality, in order to propound a theory that every nation has a distinct and recognizable service to render to humanity, then he was on very uncertain ground. It is all very well to write in general terms:— 'Special interests, special aptitudes, and before all special functions, a special mission to fulfil, a special work to be done in the cause of the advancement of humanity seem to me the true, infallible characteristic of nationalities', but to descend to a particular definition of these 'missions' is a thankless task indeed. Mazzini, with characteristic courage, attempted it. England's functions were 'industry and colonies'; Russia's 'the civilization of Asia'; Poland's 'the Slav initiative'; Germany's distinctive characteristic was 'thought', France's was action, Italy's thought in union with action. 'While the German walks the earth with his sight lost in the depths of heaven, and the Frenchman's eye rarely looks aloft but scours the earth's surface with its restless penetrating glance, the Genius that guards the destinies of Italy has ever been wont to pass swiftly from the ideal to real, seeking from of old how earth and heaven may be joined together.'[1] Today one would hardly describe the 'missions' and characteristics of the nations in just these words. The Soviet might indeed be gratified to learn that the 'civilization of Asia' was its appointed task, but Mussolini, nauseated by 'the putrefying corpse of liberty'[2] appeared to emphasize rather different aspects of the Italian character and Hitler displayed an un-mistakable aversion to the 'German who walks with his sight lost in the depths of heaven'. Time changes so much of what might at one moment appear to be a fundamental natural characteristic, that the belief in a special mission pushed beyond a certain point becomes absurd. Signor Croce writing[3] of the 'missions' assigned to Italy after 1870 declared that 'nations, like individuals, have no other mission save that of living their lives as human beings, that is as idealists, acting in

---

[1] Bolton King, op. cit., pp. 306–7 and generally Chap. XVII on *Nationality* and also Gaetano Salvemini, p. 51 and Chap. 9 generally.

[2] These were his own words.

[3] *A History of Italy, 1871–1915* (Oxford, 1929), p. 4.

accordance with the conditions and opportunities which present themselves'. For it is clear that a belief in the 'mission' of a nation can be no
more than a myth, and like all myths it will sometimes point in the right
direction and sometimes in the wrong; at times it will encourage, at
times it will discourage; on some occasions it will do good, and on
others it will do harm. But it has no historical reality. That is not to say
that nations have no distinctive contribution to make, but that such
contributions are usually incidental and certainly indefinable.

'What did Mazzini say?' Douglas Hyde in an address to the Irish
National Literary Society on November 25, 1892,[1] which foreshadowed
the foundation of the Gaelic League a year later, asked himself this
question. And he answered—'That we ought to be content as an integral
part of the United Kingdom because we have lost the notes of nationality, our language and customs.' Hyde did not blame Mazzini. He
thought the Irish position was anomalous and open to misunderstanding; that the Irish people had, or were in danger of losing, their distinct identity because they were increasingly forgetful of their own past.
That, in Hyde's view, was the only true source of their life and their
national personality; 'in anglicizing ourselves wholesale we have
thrown away with a light heart the best claim which we have upon the
world's recognition of us as a separate nationality'. And in another
passage Hyde remarked upon how curious it was that 'Irish sentiment
sticks in this half-way house—how it continues to apparently hate the
English, and at the same time continues to imitate them; how it
continues to clamour for recognition as a distinct nationality, and at the
same time throws away with both hands what would make it so'. Hyde,
and the protagonists of the Gaelic revival, had their remedy. In
Gaelicization was the true national self to be found or restored.[2] But
until that was accomplished, until the Irish people were once again
back, so to speak, in their own home and out of their nineteenth-
century half-way house, Hyde was understanding of, even though he
did not share, Mazzini's doubts.

Hyde was speaking of national identity in terms of history, language
and custom. Without necessarily accepting these criteria as in themselves sufficient or indeed indispensable, it will be recalled that Mazzini
had said rather more. He had spoken also and further in terms of

---

[1] Douglas Hyde, *The Revival of Irish Literature and other addresses* (London, 1894)
p. 119. An extract from the address is reprinted in E. Curtis and R. B. McDowell,
Irish Historical Documents 1172–1922, pp. 310–13.
[2] See below, Chap. VIII.

mission and function. In these respects, it may perhaps be accepted that Mazzini tested Irish nationalism by standards of no historical validity. If the recognition of 'some high special function' is the final condition of true nationality, then Mazzini judged Irish nationalism by a standard that has been asked of few nations.

But because much of Mazzini's analysis of Irish nationalism was deduced from unreal or mistaken premises, it is not to be assumed that he had little worth while to say. On the contrary, in underlining the three essential characteristics of true nationality, he reminded the world of some things of which it cannot be too often reminded. First was his assertion that nationality was not an end in itself, but that its justification was to be found only in the moral purpose which it fulfilled. Secondly, and even more relevant in later times, was his conviction that a nation cannot live to itself alone. Humanity is one, and all the nations owe a duty to it.[1] 'There exists in Europe a harmony of needs and wishes, a common thought, a universal mind, which directs the nations by convergent paths to the same goal.' A nation that stands aloof is a selfish nation; a patriotism that despises other countries is a poor counterfeit patriotism; a nation that lives to itself alone forgets the moral foundation of its nationality. There was a period in Ireland before the Second World War, when rejection of all things 'foreign' was in danger of being regarded as the hall-mark of patriotism, when men strangely unmindful of Ireland's European tradition, dating from noble contributions to the culture and religion of the Europe of the Dark Ages, hailed cultural and political isolation as the pathway to national salvation.

Finally, there is Mazzini's doctrine that 'nationality can be founded only for and upon and by the people'. Nationality must be democratic. Consequently the expansion of a nation at the cost of others is but a perversion of true nationalism. 'I hate the monopolist, usurping nation that sees its own strength only in the weakness and poverty of others. It is a poor stunted people whose foreign policy is one of aggrandizement and selfishness whether it seeks them basely or buys glory at other persons' expense.'

The significance of Mazzini's political teaching cannot disguise the limitations of his doctrinaire outlook. He was single-minded with the blighting single-mindedness of the fanatic. His contribution on Irish nationalism may be taken as an instance of that lack of imaginative sympathy, which ultimately made co-operation with his Italian com-

[1] On this point see *The Duties of Man*, Chaps. V and VII.

patriots impossible. But it were wrong indeed to think that 'the pale, frail Genoese whose face was scarred with the sorrows of his country' had no message for a nation that after long adversity regained her freedom. So to conclude, some aphorisms from his writings not inappropriate to later times and circumstances may be recalled.

Where the citizen does not know that he must give lustre to his country, not borrow lustre from it, that country may be strong but never happy.

Flattery will never save a country, nor proud words make us less abject.

The honour of a country depends much more upon removing its faults than on boasting of its qualities.

Great thoughts make great peoples.

. . . after many centuries of slavery, a nation can only be regenerated through virtue or through death![1]

[1] See Bolton King, op. cit., pp. 301–2; Mazzini, *Faith and the Future* (reprinted with *The Duties of Man*), p. 178, and *Life and Writings*, Vol. I, p. 121.

CHAPTER III

THE COMMUNIST INTERNATIONAL AND
THE IRISH QUESTION

The voice I heard was the voice of all generations
Acclaiming new faiths, horrible, beautiful faiths.
DOROTHY WELLESLEY, on *Lenin*

—————

Karl Marx and the Communist International are not esteemed in
Ireland. Leaders of every shade of political opinion, spokesmen of
every, and not least, the working class, survivors of the old establishment and members of the new élite, Ulster Unionists and new republican nationalists, in accord on no other topic, are all at one in their
denunciation of Communism. A correspondent sent by *The Daily
Worker* to survey the Irish scene in 1950 reported that it 'required a
considerable amount of courage to be a Socialist in Ireland' and that
there appeared little or no 'hope of improvement'. Partly no doubt for
this reason what Marx and later Communists thought of Ireland remains virtually unknown. Yet Marx and Engels were much interested
in the Irish Question and their attitude towards it is brought out in
some detail in the Marx–Engels correspondence and to a lesser extent
in Marx's letters to Dr Kugelmann, both of which have been translated into English. The publication of the correspondence under the
auspices of the Marx–Engels–Lenin Institute was approved by Lenin.
'In this correspondence', he wrote, 'it is not merely that Marx and
Engels here stand out before the reader in striking relief and in all their
greatness. The extremely rich theoretical content of Marxism also is
unfolded most vividly' since in these letters 'Marx and Engels prompted
by the most diverse occurrences in various countries, at different historical moments would discuss what was most fundamental in the
formulation of questions concerning the *political* tasks of the working-

class'.[1] One of the 'various countries' whose politics are interpreted in the light of the Marxist dialectic is Ireland.

It has been justly observed that no work on Marx can expect to be received with anywhere near the same detachment as a book on the Ammassalik Eskimo or a treatise on the internal constitution of the stars; and in the briefer compass of a chapter, it is clearly not possible to present the reader with a statement unbiased in every respect. For though Marx and Engels had no decisive influence on events during their lifetime, they became later the acknowledged prophets of a creed which confronted the established order of society with the most uncompromising challenge in history. In consequence their work has been the subject of so much interpretation by their followers and so much denunciation by their opponents that the original meaning is apt to be overlaid or obscured by later commentaries. Yet the opinions of Marx and Engels as first expressed on the Ireland of nearly a century ago deserve to be studied, if only because they impress upon the reader the importance of placing the economic factor in Irish history in proper perspective. That indeed may well be the most lasting contribution to historical understanding of letters, in which succeeding phases in the growth and crystallization of Marxist opinion are recorded and doubtful points discussed with more candour than, for example, in the articles on Ireland, which Marx contributed to the American Press. For the letters not only set out in some detail Marxist conclusions on Irish politics but, at least as important, something of the way in which they were reached.

THE MARXIST APPROACH TO IRELAND

An extract from Engels furnishes an appropriate point of departure. He wrote:

It was seen that *all* past history, with the exception of its primitive stages, was the history of class struggles; that these warring classes of society are always the products of the modes of production and of exchange—in a word, of the *economic* conditions of their time; that the economic structure of society always furnishes the real basis, starting from which we can alone work out the ultimate explanation of the whole superstructure of juridical and political institutions as well

[1] Karl Marx and Friedrich Engels, *Correspondence 1846–95; A Selection with Commentary and Notes* (first published in English, 1934); Karl Marx, *Letters to Dr Kugelmann* (first published in English, 1934).

as of the religious, philosophical, and other ideas of a given historical period.[1]

It was an understanding of this guiding principle which, according to Marx and Engels, made self-evident that the coming of Socialism was inevitable. It was 'the necessary outcome of a struggle between historically developed classes—the proletariat and the bourgeoisie'. As the character of the struggle was predetermined, so also it had its logical, inevitable outcome in the victory of the proletariat. Admittedly capitalists might for a time secure partial victories, but the Marxist assumption was that despite such set-backs, the establishment of the Communist society was the ultimate certainty. For this reason politics were to be regarded as a manifestation of the conflict of classes. That alone was fundamental, unchanging.

It was with the eyes of protagonists in the conflict that Marx and Engels regarded Ireland. Their interest was fostered by two considerations, the one of particular, and the other of general, application. The former was inspired by a belief that Irish discontents might be used as a lever to overthrow the strongly entrenched capitalist system in Great Britain and the latter by the recognition that proletarians must learn to unite first nationally, before they could hope to act internationally. Marx argued that a series of conflicts, such as those which occurred in Paris in the early months of 1848, would progressively weaken the bourgeoisie and so hasten the day of the Communist triumph. It was therefore the duty of Communists to organize national revolution, in order to prepare for later international working-class co-operation, and they could fulfil this task with the comforting assurance that the logic of history had predetermined the triumph of their cause. This was as well for their peace of mind, because in fact they were paving the way for Hitler as surely as for Lenin.

MARX, NATIONALITY AND THE CLASS WAR

Marx, though without sympathy for nationalist aspirations, considered that at times they might be turned to advantage. In his letters there happens to be no direct reference to Irish nationality as such, but his attitude to the struggles of suppressed nationalities to re-establish their

[1] Friedrich Engels, *Socialism Utopian and Scientific* (English translation, London, 1892), p. 41. See also Bertrand Russell, *Freedom and Organization 1814–1914* (London, 1937), pp. 217–18 and Chapter XVIII generally.

historic identities is made clear enough in a commentary upon the revolutions of 1848. He wrote:

Thus ended for the present, and most likely for ever, the attempts of the Slavonians of Germany to recover an independent national existence. Scattered remnants of numerous nations, whose . . . nationality and political vitality had long been extinguished, and who in consequence had been obliged, for almost a thousand years, to follow in the wake of a mightier nation, their conqueror, the same as the Welsh in England, the Basques in Spain . . . these dying nationalities, the Bohemians, Carinthians, Dalmatians, etc., had tried to profit by the universal confusion of 1848, in order to restore their political *status quo* of A D 800. The history of a thousand years ought to have shown them that such a retrogression was impossible; that if all the territory east of the Elbe and Saale had at one time been occupied by kindred Slavonians, this fact merely proved the historical tendency, and at the same time the physical and intellectual power of the German nation to subdue, absorb, and assimilate its ancient eastern neighbours: that this tendency of absorption on the part of the Germans had always been, and still was, one of the mightiest means by which the civilization of Western Europe had been spread in the east of that continent . . . and that, therefore, the natural and inevitable fate of these dying nations was to allow this process of dissolution and absorption by their stronger neighbours to complete itself. Certainly this is no very flattering prospect for the national ambition of the Panslavistic dreamers . . . but can they expect that history would retrograde a thousand years in order to please a few phthisical bodies of men . . .?[1]

Though Irishmen were not specifically numbered with those Marx termed 'pluralistic dreamers', it may be inferred, from this contemptuous and very Teutonic dismissal of Panslavism, that their national aspirations would have been no differently regarded. A belief in the economic interpretation of history in any event relegates nationality to the level of a secondary or superficial phenomenon.[2]

The Marxist creed of the class war deriving from a conviction of predestined conflict, inevitably fostered a spirit of hatred. Socialists like Robert Owen in England and Saint Simon in France, who aspired

---

[1] From Karl Marx, *Revolution and Counter-Revolution, or Germany in 1848* (London, 1896). As quoted in Bertrand Russell, op. cit., pp. 245–6.
[2] cf. Bertrand Russell's critical account of Marxist thought, op. cit., pp. 217–53.

to reform the evils of capitalism by an appeal to man's benevolence, were dismissed as Utopian dreamers. For Marx—and it may possibly be remembered to his credit—believed that no reliance might be placed on men's, and particularly on capitalists', sense of justice. Consequently, if the need for a radical change in the economic structure of society be once admitted, then as a realist he was driven to conclude that such reform could be effected only by the ruthless application of revolutionary methods. But the sympathy that might be felt for a man, irresistibly impelled by logic to an unwelcome conclusion, is sensibly diminished by the belief that the doctrine of class war was by no means repellent to his nature. For indeed, there were few who found Marx a pleasant colleague. Bitter, unforgiving, autocratic, insanely jealous, his treatment of fellow Communists, like Bakunin, is more repellent than his unrelenting hostility to the world outside the then small band of the elect. The editor of the Marx–Engels correspondence refers with satisfaction to the letters dealing with the strategy and tactics of the proletarian party, since they show how 'Marx and Engels fought for and carried through the policy of revolutionary Marxism, a thoroughgoing series of characteristic examples of their struggles against all varieties of opportunism and class conciliation, examples of the fight on two fronts'. They do indeed. But it is a hard creed that condemns the orthodox to believe that class-conciliation is crime; it is absurd for him who sows the seeds of hate to hope to garner a harvest of fraternal love.

ENGELS ON IRELAND

Friedrich Engels had been converted to Communism before he met Marx. Hess gave the following account of his conversion in 1843: 'Engels came to see me on his way from Berlin. We discussed the questions of the day, and he, a revolutionist of the Year One, parted from me a convinced Communist. Thus did I spread devastation.'[1] Thirteen years later, Engels, on his return from a visit to Ireland, sent Marx a long letter, with much vivacious and pointed comment on conditions there.

Engels to Marx
Manchester, May 23, 1856.
In our tour in Ireland we came from Dublin to Galway on the west coast, then twenty miles north inland, then to Limerick, down the

[1] Quoted in Bertrand Russell, op. cit., p. 208.

Shannon to Tarbert, Tralee, Killarney and back to Dublin. A total of about four to five hundred English miles in the country itself, so that we have seen about two-thirds of the whole country. With the exception of Dublin, which bears the same relation to London as Düsseldorf does to Berlin and has quite the character of a small one-time capital, all English-built too, the whole country, and especially the towns, has exactly the appearance of France or Northern Italy. Gendarmes, priests, lawyers, bureaucrats, squires in pleasant profusion and a total absence of any and every industry, so that it would be difficult to understand what all these parasitic growths found to live on if the misery of the peasants did not supply the other half of the picture. 'Strong measures' are visible in every corner of the country, the government meddles with everything, of so-called self-government there is not a trace. Ireland may be regarded as the first English colony and as one which because of its proximity is still governed exactly in the old way, and here one can already observe that the so-called liberty of English citizens is based on the oppression of the colonies. I have never seen so many gendarmes in any country, and the drink-sodden expression of the Prussian gendarme is developed to its highest perfection here among the constabulary, who are armed with carbines, bayonets and handcuffs.

Characteristic of this country are its ruins, the oldest from the fifth and sixth centuries, the latest from the nineteenth—with every intervening period. The most ancient are all churches; after 1100, churches and castles; after 1800 the houses of peasants. The whole of the west, but especially in the neighbourhood of Galway, is covered with these ruined peasant houses, most of which have only been deserted since 1846. I never thought that famine could have such tangible reality. Whole villages are devastated, and there among them lie the splendid parks of the lesser landlords, who are almost the only people still living there, mostly lawyers. Famine, emigration and clearances together have accomplished this. There are not even cattle to be seen in the fields. The land is an utter desert which nobody wants. In County Clare, south of Galway, it is rather better, here there are at least some cattle, and the hills toward Limerick are excellently cultivated, mostly by Scottish farmers, the ruins have been cleared away and the country has a bourgeois appearance. In the south-west there are a lot of mountains and bogs but also wonderfully rich forest growth, beyond that again fine pastures, especially in Tipperary, and towards Dublin land which is, one can see, gradually coming into the hands of big farmers.

The country has been completely ruined by the English wars of conquest from 1100 to 1850 (for in reality both the wars and the state of siege lasted as long as that). It is a fact that most of the ruins were produced by destruction during the wars. The people itself has got its peculiar character from this, and despite all their Irish nationalist fanaticism the fellows feel that they are no longer at home in their own country. Ireland for the Saxon! That is now being realized. The Irishman knows he cannot compete with the Englishman, who comes with means in every respect superior; emigration will go on until the predominantly, indeed almost exclusively, Celtic character of the population is all to hell. How often have the Irish started to try and achieve something, and every time they have been crushed, politically and industrially! By consistent oppression they have been artificially converted into an utterly demoralized nation and now fulfil the notorious function of supplying England, America, Australia, etc., with prostitutes, casual labourers, pimps, thieves, swindlers, beggars and other rabble. This demoralized character persists in the aristocracy too. The landowners, who everywhere else have taken on bourgeois qualities, are here completely demoralized. Their country seats are surrounded by enormous, wonderfully beautiful parks, but all around is waste land, and where the money is supposed to come from it is impossible to see. These fellows ought to be shot. Of mixed blood, mostly tall, strong, handsome chaps, they all wear enormous moustaches under colossal Roman noses, give themselves the sham military airs of retired colonels, travel around the country after all sorts of pleasures, and if one makes an inquiry, they haven't a penny, are laden with debts, and live in dread of the Encumbered Estates Court.[1]

How much of this letter is description and how much deliberate distortion is not altogether easy to determine. Assuredly Engels painted conditions at their worst in order to contrast the ills of the present with the blessings of the Marxist society of the future. But in the Ireland of 1856 he may have found the disintegration and misery of those post-famine years sufficed his purpose, with no more needed than some heightening of colours.

MARX ON ANGLO-IRISH POLITICS

While Engels provided a description of conditions in Ireland, Marx confined himself to an interpretation of the *politics* of the Irish question.

[1] *Marx–Engels, Selected Correspondence, 1846–95*, pp. 92–4.

His opinion did not remain static. At first he believed the separation of Ireland from England impossible, but in 1867 he wrote to Engels to say that he no longer thought so. This change of view was prompted by what Marx chose to regard as a new, though not conscious, direction in British policy in Ireland.

What the English do not yet know is that since 1846 the economic content and therefore also the political aim of English domination in Ireland have entered into an entirely new phase, and that, precisely because of this, Fenianism is characterized by a socialistic tendency (in a negative sense, directed against the appropriation of the soil) and by the fact that it is a lower orders movement. What can be more ridiculous than to confuse the barbarities of Elizabeth or Cromwell—who wanted to supplant the Irish by English colonists (in the Roman sense)—with the present system, which wants to supplant them by sheep, oxen and pigs! The system of 1801–46, with its rackrents and middlemen, collapsed in 1846. . . . Hence from then onwards systematic consolidation of farms. The Encumbered Estates Act, which turned a mass of previously enriched middlemen into landlords, hastened the process. The *clearing of the estate of Ireland* is now the one idea of English rule in Ireland. The *stupid* English government in London itself knows nothing, of course, of this immense change since 1846. But the Irish know it.[1]

Earlier in the month Marx had illustrated his theme by referring to the number and the nature of the evictions that were being carried out. In a letter to Engels he instanced the fact that 'the Irish Viceroy, Lord Abicorn' (this is *roughly* the name)[2] had recently 'cleared' his estate of thousands by forcible evictions and that among the evicted were well-to-do farmers whose improvements and capital investments were confiscated, as evidence of a form of expropriation which was taking place in Ireland and was unknown elsewhere since, so he affirmed, the Prussians in West Prussia bought out and the Russians confiscated only for political reasons. The change in land policy, which Marx believed evictions of this kind and on this scale represented, led him to conclude that the political separation of England and Ireland had become inevitable, although he felt that after separation there might come federation.

[1] Letter dated November 30, 1867. Ibid., pp. 228–30.
[2] Lord Abercorn. Letter dated November 2, 1867. Ibid., p. 228.

The issue that interested Marx and Engels was not, however, the future government of Ireland, on which Marx's views changed with almost casual frequency, but the policy to be pursued by the English workers. How were they to turn the Irish question to the ultimate advantage of the proletariat? On this Marx commented, on November 30, 1867:

In my opinion they [the English workers] must make the *repeal of the Union* . . . into an article of their *pronunziamento*. This is the only *legal* and therefore only possible form of Irish emancipation which can be admitted in the programme of an *English* Party. Experience must show later whether a purely personal union can continue to subsist between the two countries. I half think it can if it takes place in time.

He then proceeded to draft a programme of reform for Ireland which was to be carried through with the assistance of the English working class. The three points in this programme were:

(1) Self-government for Ireland.
(2) An agrarian revolution. With the best will in the world the English cannot accomplish this for them, but they can give them the legal means of accomplishing it for themselves.
(3) *Protective tariffs against England.*[1]

It was scarcely a programme likely to arouse enthusiasm in the English working classes, least of all perhaps the contemplated concession to Ireland of the right to levy protective tariffs against British goods. But in 1867 Marx believed that the ascendancy class in Ireland could be overthrown by the efforts of the English working class. Two years later he realized his mistake. The English working class was probably unable, and certainly unwilling, to devote its efforts to the task. It was therefore necessary to look elsewhere.

Engels in the course of his travels in Ireland seems by a rather different process of thought to have reached a conclusion identical with that of Marx. They both disapproved of the outrages and agrarian murders in Ireland. While Marx was active in promoting agitation for the release of the Fenian prisoners, he expressly condemned 'terrorist' manifestations, such as the blowing up of Clerkenwell prison, on the ground that it was bad policy: Engels describes the movement 'in the

[1] Ibid., pp. 228–30.

first place violent and in second place anti-English' as something 'unheard of in English conditions and really amazing' and his revolutionary expectations were heightened by the sympathy manifested for the Fenians by some of the London proletariat. But he was outspoken in his repudiation of the 'Bakunistic, braggart, aimless propaganda through action' and insisted that Communism should not be made answerable for such 'donkey tricks'.[1]

The interest of Marx and Engels in the Irish Question was none-the-less deepened by a growing belief that events in Ireland might at the last assist, and indeed might even occasion, the outbreak of the general social revolution, for whose coming they conspired and planned with such zealous intensity. As a first step it seemed a matter of cardinal importance that the working classes in England and in Ireland should be united in a bond of sympathy. But the task presented exceptional difficulties and indeed provides a practical illustration of one of the weak links in the Marxist argument. It was easy to proclaim with the Communist Manifesto, 'Proletarians of all nations, unite!'; it was not difficult to produce valid reasons why they should unite, but it was an illusion to suppose, as Marx supposed, that the self-interest of the proletariat was, or is, necessarily a force sufficient to over-ride a historic sense of national difference or still less antagonism. Such sentiment, amounting in this particular instance to a deep-rooted prejudice, in fact altogether precluded the possibility that the English working-class would assist the cause of Irish independence. As early as 1856 Engels had realized how profound was the aversion of the English industrial worker for Irish competitors with their lower standards of living. Later he was to meet this distaste even on the Council of the International and was enabled to defeat a proposal to subject the Irish sections to a British Federal Council only in the teeth of violent opposition.[2]

Marx also came to learn from experience something of the difficulties of Anglo-Irish working-class unity. In 1869 he wrote to Kugelmann: 'Every one of its movements in England itself is crippled by the disunion with the Irish, who form a very important section of the working class in England.'[3] But while acknowledging the antagonism between the English and Irish working classes and recognizing that 'the revolutionary fire of the Celtic workers does not harmonize with the

[1] Gustav Mayer, *Friedrich Engels, A Biography* (London, 1936), p. 191.
[2] Ibid.
[3] *Letters to Dr Kugelmann*, November 29, 1869, p. 96.

restrained force but slowness of the Anglo-Saxons',[1] he continued to insist that union must be achieved, if the capitalist régime in the United Kingdom was to be overthrown. And he believed it would be, through compulsion of economic forces. Subsequent history has revealed this characteristic doctrinal assumption to have been indifferently founded in fact.

IRELAND AND THE PROLETARIAN REVOLUTION

Why did the question of Anglo-Irish working-class relations assume such prominence in the Marx–Engels correspondence in the years immediately succeeding 1867? The answer is the enactment in that year of the Second Reform Bill. The Act gave the vote to the urban working classes, and Engels hoped that this extension of the suffrage would lead to the rise of a revolutionary workers' party and even that revolutionary conditions would soon appear. The election of 1868 when the workers voted *en masse* for the first time showed his hopes to be illusory. He pronounced the election to be 'a desperate proof of the incapacity of the English proletariat' and complained to Marx that 'any parvenu swell got the votes of the workers'. Engels' biographer records that he was furious at this disappointment, and adds, 'Since the extension of the suffrage did not move the English workers to independent action, the Irish Question gained a new significance for him: and Marx's hypothesis seemed more and more attractive—that the fall of the landed oligarchy and the revival of the revolutionary spirit in England must start in and be prompted by Ireland.'[2]

In this way we come to the concluding phase in the thinking of Marx and Engels about the Irish Question. At the outset it was the English working-class that was to overthrow aristocratic and bourgeois ascendancy in Ireland as the first step to its overthrow in England or, as Lenin put it later, 'at first Marx thought that Ireland would not be liberated by the national movement of the oppressed nation, but by the working-class movement of the oppressor nation'.[3]

But after 1868 Marx conceived of the fall of the landed oligarchy in Ireland, as a stepping-stone to the outbreak of the revolutionary move-

[1] From the resolution drafted in 1869 by Marx and adopted by the International Workingmen's Association. Reprinted in *A Handbook of Marxism:* ed. Emile Burns (London, 1935), pp. 194–6.

[2] Gustav Mayer, op. cit., p. 192.

[3] V. I. Lenin, *Collected Works* (Moscow, 1960–), 21 Vols. in progress, Vol. XX, p. 440 Translation of 4th edition prepared by the Institute of Marxism–Leninism.

ment in England. Thus while the goal remained identical, the means to be employed profoundly differed. For it was recognized that the election of 1868 presented, not a chance verdict that might soon be reversed, but the deliberate choice of the English working class. Engels admitted that this class had benefited from the increase in British trade and began to fear that 'in this most *bourgeois* of all nations' 'a *bourgeois* aristocracy and a *bourgeois* proletariat' might one day arise 'beside the existing *bourgeoisie*'. But no such prospect loomed on the Irish horizon.

Letters from Marx and Engels record these successive modifications in their thinking about Ireland between 1867–70. On April 6, 1868, Marx wrote to Kugelmann:[1]

The Irish question is dominant here just now. Of course it is only being exploited by Gladstone and Co. in order to get them into office, principally as an election cry for the forthcoming elections, which will be held on household suffrage. At the moment this turn of affairs is harmful for the workers' party; for the intriguers among the workers who want to get into the next parliament, like Odger and Potter, now have a new excuse for joining with the bourgeois Liberals.

On November 29, 1869, Engels in a letter to Marx, discussed the significance of the return at the Tipperary by-election of O'Donovan Rossa, then a well-known Fenian prisoner and one at whose graveside in Glasnevin, Patrick Pearse was to deliver his most famous oration some forty-five years later.

The election in Tipperary is an event. It forces the Fenians out of empty conspiracy and the fabrication of small *coups* into a path of action which, even if legal in appearance, is still far more revolutionary than what they have been doing since the failure of their insurrection. In fact, they are adopting the methods of the French workers and that is an enormous advance. If only the thing is carried on as intended. The terror which this new turn has produced among the philistines, and which is now being screeched throughout the whole Liberal press, is the best proof that this time the nail has been hit on the head. Typical is the *Solicitors' Journal*, which remarks with horror that the election of a political prisoner is *without precedent* in the realm of Britain! So much the worse—where is there a country *except* England in which such

[1] *Marx–Engels Correspondence,* p. 277.

a case is not a common event! The worthy Gladstone must be horribly annoyed.

But you really ought to look at *The Times* now. *Three* leaders in eight days in which either it is demanded of the Government or the Government itself demands that an end be put to the excesses of the Irish Nationalist press.

I am very eager to hear about your debate to-morrow evening and its result, about which there can be no doubt. It would be very fine to get Odger into a hole. . . . For the rest, if the English workers cannot take an example from the peasants of Tipperary they are in a bad way. . . .[1]

The debate, to which Engels refers, appears to have been a lively affair. It arose out of a discussion on '*the attitude of the British Ministry to the Irish Amnesty question*', which had taken place on November 18, 1869. On this occasion Marx made a speech 'of about three-quarters of an hour, much cheered', and then proposed certain resolutions on Gladstone's Irish policy.[2] It was resolved, *inter alia:*

that on his reply to the Irish demands for the release of the imprisoned Irish patriots—a reply contained in his letter to Mr O'Shea, Mr Gladstone deliberately insults the Irish nation;

that his whole proceedings with reference to the Irish Amnesty Question are the true and genuine offspring of that *policy of conquest* by the fiery denunciation of which Mr Gladstone ousted his Tory colleagues from office;

that the *General Council* of the International Workingmen's Association express their admiration of the spirited, firm, high-souled manner in which the Irish people carry on their Amnesty movement.

The adjourned debate on this resolution was described in a letter from Marx to Engels, dated November 26, 1869.[3]

The meeting last Tuesday was very fiery, heated and violent. Mr Muddlehead or whatever in the hell the fellow is called[4]—a Chartist and old friend of Harney's—had brought along Odger and Applegarth as a precaution. On the other side Weston and Lucraft were absent

[1] *Marx–Engels Correspondence,* pp. 274–6.   [2] Ibid., pp. 265–6.
[3] Ibid., p. 276.   [4] Mottershead.

because they had gone to an Irish ball. *Reynolds* had published my resolutions in its Saturday issue, together with a summary of my speech . . . which was put right on the front page, after the first leading article. This seems to have scared the people who are making love to Gladstone. Hence the appearance of Odger and a long rambling speech from Muddershead, who got knocked on the head damned heavily by Milner (an Irishman himself). Applegarth was sitting next me and therefore did not dare to speak against the resolution, indeed he spoke *for* it, obviously with an uneasy conscience. *Odger* said that if the resolutions were forced to a vote he would be obliged to vote for them, but unanimity would surely be better, could be reached with a few small modifications, etc. To this, as *he* is the one I particularly want to put into a hole, I replied that *he* should bring forward his amendments next Tuesday! At our last meeting, although many of our most reliable members were absent, we should have got the resolution through with *only one* vote against. Next Tuesday we shall be in full force.

And of the final discussion Marx reported to Engels on December 4th:[1]

The resolutions unanimously carried, despite Odger's persistent *verbal* amendments. I only gave way to him on one point: to omit the word 'deliberate' before 'insults' in paragraph one. I did this on the pretence that everything a Prime Minister did publicly must be presumed *eo ipso* to be *deliberate*. The real reason was that I knew that if once we got the essential point of paragraph one conceded all further opposition would be useless. . . . With the exception of Mottershead, who came out as John Bull, and Odger, who was as much of a diplomat as ever, the English delegates behaved splendidly.

A general debate on the relation of the English working class to the Irish Question was to follow.

It may be mentioned that Marx's vindictive desire to get Odger and Applegarth 'into a hole' was prompted by their moderation and reluctance to accept a Marxist doctrine of violence in its undiluted form. They were both leading members of the 'new model' trade unionism. 'Odger and Applegarth', Marx once wrote, 'are both possessed with a mania for compromise and a thirst for respectability!' Yet Marx's opinions whether on colleagues or on opponents should be treated

[1] *Marx–Engels Correspondence*, pp. 276–7.

with reserve. Odger, it is fitting to recall, appears in a more sympathetic light at a meeting as memorable as that which Marx described. The speaker was John Stuart Mill, then a candidate for Parliament, but one who displayed little regard for the conventional reticences expected of such persons by an English electorate. Having noted in his *Representative Government* that the Conservative Party was by the law of its composition the stupidest party, Mill observed in a pamphlet that the English working classes, though differing from those of some other countries in being ashamed of it, were yet generally liars. At a meeting chiefly composed of the working classes, Mill was asked whether he had written and published this opinion. He at once answered, 'I did'. Scarcely were the words out of his mouth when vehement applause resounded through the meeting. The first working man who spoke after the incident was Odger, and as Mill records in his *Autobiography*, he said that the working classes had no desire not to be told of their faults; they wanted friends, not flatterers.[1]

On November 29, 1869, that is after the initiation, but before the conclusion of the debate, Marx wrote to Kugelmann, explaining that his support of the Fenian prisoners had an object other than that of speaking out loudly for the Irish oppressed. It was to convince the English working class that it could not hope to overthrow the ruling classes unless and until the national demands of Ireland were conceded. This letter[2] is an elaboration of Marxist thinking on Ireland in this later phase.

Marx to Kugelmann

London, November 29, 1869.

You will probably have seen in the *Volksstaat* the resolution against Gladstone which I proposed on the question of the Irish amnesty. I have now attacked Gladstone—and it has attracted attention here—just as I formerly attacked Palmerston. The demagogic refugees here love to fall upon the Continental despots from a safe distance. That sort of thing only attracts me, when it happens *vultu instantis tyranni*.

Nevertheless both my coming out on this Irish Amnesty question and my further proposal to the General Council to discuss the relation of the English working class to Ireland and to pass resolutions on it, have of course other objects besides that of speaking out loudly and decidedly for the oppressed Irish against their oppressors.

[1] This account is taken from J. S. Mill, *Autobiography* (London, 1873), pp. 283–5.
[2] *Marx–Engels Correspondence*, pp. 278–9.

D

I have become more and more convinced—and the only question is to bring this conviction home to the English working class—that it can never do anything decisive here in England until it separates its policy with regard to Ireland in the most definite way from the policy of the ruling classes, until it not only makes common cause with the Irish, but actually takes the initiative in dissolving the Union established in 1801 and replacing it by a free federal relationship. And, indeed, this must be done, not as a matter of sympathy with Ireland, but as a demand made in the interests of the English proletariat. If not, the English people will remain tied to the leading-strings of the ruling classes, because it must join with them in a common front against Ireland. Every one of its movements in England itself is crippled by the disunion with the Irish, who form a very important section of the working class in England. *The primary condition* of emancipation here —the overthrow of the English landed oligarchy—remains impossible because its position here cannot be stormed so long as it maintains its strongly entrenched outposts in Ireland. But there, once affairs are in the hands of the Irish people itself, once it is made its own legislator and ruler, once it becomes autonomous, the abolition of the landed aristocracy (to a large extent the *same persons* as the English landlords) will be infinitely easier than here, because in Ireland it is not merely a simple economic question, but at the same time a *national* question, since the landlords there are not like those in England, the traditional dignitaries and representatives, but are the mortally hated oppressors of a nation. And not only does England's internal social development remain crippled by her present relation with Ireland; her foreign policy, and particularly her policy with regard to Russia and America, suffers the same fate.

Marx developed this theme in subsequent letters. He wrote to Engels,

quite apart from all phrases about 'international' and 'humane' justice for Ireland—which are to be taken for granted on the International Council—*it is in the direct and absolute interest of the English working-class to get rid of their present connection with Ireland.* And this is my most complete conviction for reasons which in part I cannot tell the English workers themselves. For a long time I believed it would be possible to overthrow the Irish regime by English working-class ascendancy. I always expressed this point of view in the *New York Tribune.* Deeper study has now convinced me of the opposite. The

English working class will *never accomplish anything* before it has got rid of Ireland. The lever must be applied in Ireland. That is why the Irish question is so important for the social movement in general.

Marx detected three important factors in the contemporary Irish movement which, he thought, might enhance the prospects of proletarian revolution. They were:

(i) Opposition to lawyers and trading politicians and blarney.
(ii) Opposition to the dictates of the priests who (the *superior ones*) are traitors as in O'Connell's time.
(iii) The agricultural labouring class beginning to come out against the farming class at the last meetings.

But Engels, writing at almost the same time from Manchester, candidly admitted the profound distaste for the Communists' doctrine that existed in Ireland. He warned Marx on December 9, 1869:[1]

. . . Ireland still remains the Holy Isle whose aspirations must on no account be mixed with the profane class-struggles of the rest of the sinful world. This is no doubt partly honest madness on the part of the people, but it is equally certain that it is also partly a calculation on the side of the leaders to maintain their domination over the peasant. Added to this, a nation of peasants always has to take its literary representatives from the bourgeoisie of the towns and their intelligentsia.... But to these gentry the whole labour movement is pure heresy and the Irish peasant must not on any account know that the Socialist workers are his sole allies in Europe.

A last pronouncement of Marx upon the Irish Question appeared in a letter to Meyer and Vogt in the United States, dated April 9, 1870. This shows that Marx's opinions had further crystallized. He wrote:[2]

After occupying myself with the Irish Question for many years I have come to the conclusion that the decisive blow against the English ruling classes (and it will be decisive for the workers' movement all over the world) cannot be delivered *in England but only in Ireland*. . . .

Ireland is the bulwark of the English *landed aristocracy*. The exploita-

[1] *Marx–Engels Correspondence*, p. 280.   [2] Ibid., pp. 288–90.

tion of this country is not only one of the main sources of their material wealth, it is their greatest *moral* strength. They, in fact, represent the *domination of England over Ireland.* Ireland is therefore the great means by which the English aristocracy maintains *its domination in England* itself.

If, on the other hand, the English army and police were withdrawn to-morrow, you would at once have an agrarian revolution in Ireland. But the overthrow of the English aristocracy in Ireland involves and has as a necessary consequence its overthrow in England. And this would fulfil the prerequisite for the proletarian revolution in England. The destruction of the landed aristocracy in Ireland is an infinitely easier operation than in England itself, because the *land question* has hitherto been the *exclusive* form of the social question in Ireland, because it is a question of existence, *of life and death,* for the immense majority of the Irish people, and because it is at the same time inseparable from the *national* question. Quite apart from the passionate character of the Irish and the fact that they are more revolutionary than the English.

. . . England now possesses a working class population *divided* into two *hostile* camps, English proletarians and Irish proletarians. The ordinary English worker hates the Irish worker as a competitor who lowers his standard of life. In relation to the Irish worker he feels himself a member of the *ruling* nation and so turns himself into a tool of the aristocrats and capitalists *against Ireland,* thus strengthening their domination *over himself.* . . . The Irishman pays him back with interest in his own coin. He regards the English worker as both sharing in the guilt for the English domination in Ireland and at the same time serving as its stupid tool.

The antagonism is artificially kept alive and intensified by the press, the pulpit, the comic papers, in short by all the means at the disposal of the ruling classes. It is the secret of the impotence of the English working class, despite their organization. It is the secret by which the capitalist class maintains its power.

. . . to hasten the social revolution in England is the most important object of the International Workingmen's Association. The sole means of hastening it is to make Ireland independent.

Hence the task of the 'International' is everywhere to put the conflict between England and Ireland in the foreground, and everywhere to side openly with Ireland. The special task of the Central Council in

London is to awaken a consciousness in the English workers that for them *the national emancipation of Ireland* is no question of abstract justice or human sympathy but the first condition of *their own emancipation.*

SOME REFLECTIONS ON THE MARXIST INTERPRETATION OF THE IRISH QUESTION

If one accepts without qualification the assumptions of dialectical materialism, then the nature of the conclusions to be deduced from any particular political questions are predetermined. If the materialist conception of history is true, if as Engels said in his classic definition of that conception, 'the final causes of all social changes and political revolutions are to be sought not in men's brains, not in man's better insight into eternal truth and justice, but in changes in the modes of production and exchange', and if, that is to say, these 'final causes are to be sought not in the *philosophy* but in the *economics* of each particular epoch', then one is bound to conclude that political motive forces are no more than a superficial manifestation of a fundamental economic struggle. Marx and Engels interpreted the forces at work in the Ireland of their day in accordance with this presumption. They assumed that 'political' and 'religious' controversies, however acute they might appear, were in fact not fundamental. So it was that questions that loomed large in the eyes of contemporary politicians were for the most part dismissed out of hand or quite differently regarded in the Communist commentary.

The Marxist interpretation of Irish history derives from, and in the last analysis depends upon the validity of the materialist conception of history as a whole. But that is not to say that there is nothing to be learnt from a critical survey of the Marxist approach to a particular problem. On the contrary such an examination provides a useful criterion by which to judge the validity of the Marxist assumptions as a whole. Moreover, it may be suggested that Ireland, because of the complex forces which have moulded its history, and because of the highly particularized character of its politics, does furnish a subject of more than ordinary interest. The merit of the Marxist approach may be tested by a question: to what extent has the Marxist analysis of Irish politics or of Anglo-Irish relations proved accurate?

It may be acknowledged that the letters of Marx provide a needed corrective to the hitherto dominant school of Irish history. The emphasis that was long placed upon political history in nineteenth-century form only too frequently resulted in a neglect of some underlying factors. In this way the economic motive until recently has been ignored almost entirely, whereas in fact such a motive played a significant, though not, it would seem, a decisive role, in Irish history between the Union and the Treaty. Of this two illustrations may be given. The question of the Repeal of the Union, whether in the form of Home Rule or otherwise, was in essence a political issue, that is to say a question of government—by what authority was Ireland to be governed? But associated with it were social and economic questions of great, if not as great, significance. The answer given to the question of who was to govern Ireland was also likely to determine, either immediately or in the long run, the ownership of land in Ireland. Not for nothing was the first Home Rule Bill linked with one more Irish Land Bill. Gladstone may have been, as is often alleged, tactically unwise in thus complicating the issue, but that was not because he saw less clearly, but rather because he saw more clearly into the consequences even of a limited transfer of power to a Dublin Parliament. There was the more generally neglected question of protective tariffs. The one Marxist historian of nineteenth-century Ireland goes so far as to write[1] it was 'a matter of historical notoriety that the Irish demand for protection prevented an alliance between British and Irish Radicals during the years of O'Connell's Repeal movement; that it precipitated the break between the British business classes and the Liberal Party at the time of the first Home Rule Bill and entrapped Parnell into his damning alliance with the Tories;[2] that it formed an insurmountable obstacle to any compromise between Protestant Ulster and the South, where it figured prominently in the Sinn Féin programme. . . .' Even though none of these things are 'matters of historical notoriety' all of them have their importance and most of them will be considered in later chapters. If there seems little or no justification for Mr Strauss's allusion to the 'subterranean domination of respectable Irish politics by the tariff question' there is assuredly sufficient cause shown particularly in 1885–6 and in 1917 for detailed analyses of its influence on Anglo-Irish relations. The Irish, like other nationalities, were resolved to establish their economic identity as a necessary support and counterpart of their independent political identity and certain consequences followed from that resolve.

[1] E. Strauss, *Irish Nationalism and British Democracy* (London, 1952), p. 280.
[2] See below. pp. 142–5.

For his part Marx was misled by his conviction that economic conflicts are always conflicts between classes, whereas frequently they are betweeen nations or political groups. It is true, that in Ireland there was a possibility in the years following the Famine, that Irish nationalism might be diverted to a struggle for economic power, but its realization was averted in part at least by the emergence of the Ulster Question in its most acute form. Thenceforward a distinct economic motive force animated, though it did not inspire, Ulster's resistance to Home Rule. As a result the economic causation of events in Ireland in the later years of the Union operated within its sphere of influence, chiefly as a force dividing the nation, not horizontally into classes as the disciple of dialectical materialism would expect, but vertically into groups, thus exposing the fallacy of the Marxist dogma that economic conflicts are invariably class conflicts. But again this does not diminish but rather enhances the need for a clear study of the economic motive in Irish history.

The limitations of the Marxist commentary become more apparent when Marx's Irish policy is considered. Subsequent history has shown his analysis to be mistaken alike in principle and in detail. Thus while he appreciated the significance of the land question, pointing out 'that it had hitherto been the exclusive form of the social question in Ireland', he inferred from this that the 'land question was inseparable from the national question'. In fact the virtual solution of the land question by Wyndham's Act in 1903 proved but the prelude to a decisive forward movement in national sentiment. It is clear, therefore, that the land question was not an integral and necessary part of the nationalist movement, however much it contributed for a period to its driving force. Here indeed Marx was making a miscalculation similar to that of Balfour when he planned to 'kill Home Rule by kindness'. They both started from the assumption that Ireland's discontents derived from an economic source, and history has shown the Marxist analysis and conservative statesmanship alike to have been misconceived.

The antipathy between the English and Irish working classes is well known, but it is an illusion to suppose, as Marx and Engels supposed, that every one of the movements of the English working class 'was crippled by disunion with the Irish', and that the 'English working class will never accomplish anything until it gets rid of the Irish'. In fact such a division had its own importance, but to use it to explain the reluctance of English and Irish working classes to adopt a revolutionary programme is *prima facie* absurd. It is a more serious criticism of the

Marxist analysis that it should ignore the problem of Ulster. Because the division between North and South, between Protestant and Catholic, between Orangeman and Nationalist was not a class division, Marx regarded the whole question as superficial. Dialectical materialism conceived that the final causes of all *political* revolutions are to be found in the *economics* of each particular epoch. But the Ulster question was not susceptible of an exclusively *economic* explanation. It is true that on occasions, as when great emphasis was placed on the issue of fiscal independence at the Irish Convention in 1917, divergence of economic interest between North and South did play a distinct and not insignificant part. But it was never a directing force. And in any case this economic conflict was in no sense a class conflict, but rather an indication of the more fundamental, social, religious and cultural differences dividing the North from the South. There has been, and to this day there exists as between Northern Ireland and the Republic of Ireland, an external economic conflict of limited dimensions, but there is not and there has not been an internal class conflict of such importance as might tend to override the traditional sectarian strife in the North. So Marx was mistaken not merely in the assumption that economic conflicts are always class conflicts, but also in the belief that economic motives were necessarily of greater historical moment than political, national or religious sentiment. Even though the Ulster Question did not assume its outwardly intransigent character until after the First Home Rule Bill of 1886, no one save a theorist observing Ireland from the narrow window of rigid dogma could have overlooked its potential significance. Yet Marx confined himself in these letters to a single reference to Ulster. Writing on April 6, 1868, to Dr Kugelmann he demonstrated his almost total lack of comprehension of the forces at work, remarking:

. . . once the Irish Church is dead, the Protestant Irish tenants in the province of Ulster will unite with the Catholic tenants in the three other provinces of Ireland and join their movement, whereas up to the present landlordism has been able to exploit this religious hostility.

The Irish policy, which Marx submitted to the International, may be thought of on a broader field as one more and indeed a conclusive indication of his failure to understand the relative strength of the forces which were to mould the future course of Anglo-Irish relations. In the 1869 Resolution, Marx enunciated it in these terms:

If England is the fortress of European landlordism and capitalism, then the point at which a strong blow can be struck at official England is *Ireland*. Above all, Ireland is the fortress of English landlordism. If it falls in Ireland then it will inevitably fall in England also. In Ireland this operation is a hundred times easier because the economic struggle is concentrated there exclusively around landed property. This struggle is there also a *national* one and the people of Ireland are more revolutionary and embittered than is England. . . .

In this way the viewpoint of the International Working-men's Association is very clear. Its first task is the speeding on of the Social Revolution in England. For this end the decisive blow must be struck in Ireland.

. . . the *essential preliminary condition of the emancipation of the English Working Class* is the turning of the present *compulsory union*, that is slavery, of Ireland with England into an *equal and free union*, if that is possible, or *into full separation* if this is inevitable.[1]

This policy, the theme of all the later Marxist correspondence on Ireland, is at least logical. The English social system was most vulnerable in Ireland, therefore it would be sound strategy to attack it at its weakest point, and if that attack were successful then the collapse of the ruling class in England must soon follow. The Marxist hypothesis— that the overthrow of the landed oligarchy and the revival of the revolutionary spirit in England must start in and be prompted by Ireland —was inspired by the belief that the revolutionary movement in Ireland was but a particular manifestation of the universal class war. Engels might warn, as we have seen, that 'Ireland still remained the Holy Isle whose aspirations must on no account be mixed up with the profane class struggles of the rest of the sinful world', but any misgivings as to the implications of this in terms of the validity of the Marxist interpretation were silenced by allusions to 'honest madness' or the wiles of 'capitalist intellectuals'. But in fact it was true that Ireland, or to be more precise the politically conscious minority in Ireland, showed itself willing to sacrifice even economic prosperity on the short term, in order to realize her national aspirations. But it was not prepared to sacrifice national aspirations for possible economic advantage. National sentiment, in this way, was shown to be the fundamental motive force. In other words the Irish Question was, as Marx never understood, a *political* question. From this miscalculation

[1] Quoted in Emile Burns, op. cit., pp. 195–6. See above pp. 92–3.

springs his curious misconception as to the extent to which the English social system would be affected by the overthrow of the landed oligarchy in Ireland. Today the Anglo-Irish aristocrats, whom Engels so happily caricatured, the 'tall handsome men with their enormous moustaches under colossal Roman noses', with their sham military airs, their pleasures and their debts, live no longer in their country seats surrounded by 'wonderfully beautiful parks', but have become little more than a memory in the land whose destinies they once controlled, and the Union has been replaced by a national government, enjoying a political freedom fuller than that which Marx foresaw. Yet the day of social revolution in England has been seemingly neither hastened nor delayed in any material respect by those events in Irish history.

In what way then was Marx's detailed reasoning at fault? He had always maintained with perfect justice that the overthrow of the landed aristocracy would be infinitely easier in Ireland than in England 'because in Ireland it is not merely a simple economic question', but at the same time a *national* question, since the landlords were not like those in England the traditional dignitaries and representatives, 'but the mortally hated oppressors of a nation'. Count Cavour, it will be remembered,[1] had put the same point more tellingly in speaking of two aristocracies which had 'no more in common than a sound and vigorous arm has with its fellow which gangrene has blighted' and there is no need to question its general validity. But, since on Marx's own admission the relation between the aristocracy and the other classes in Ireland differed so profoundly from the relations between the aristocracy and the other classes in England, what reasons were there to suppose that the fate of the former should materially affect the fortunes of the latter? Further, might it not be argued that the destruction of the Irish landlords would strengthen the position of the English aristocracy by ending an unpopular association—by cutting off the limb that was diseased? But this was a possibility Marx could not entertain and his ideas of historical causation, in this context derived from a determined application of the theory of class war to Anglo-Irish relations in defiance of historical evidence already at his disposal, were mistaken because he failed—and one always returns to this point—to allow for the dominantly political character of the Irish Question.

Hitherto no distinction has been drawn between the attitude of Marx and that of Engels to Ireland, since their conclusions were in all vital

[1] See above, p. 73.

respects identical. But the evidence of the letters alone would suggest that Engels understood Ireland and the character of its people to an extent to which Marx could not pretend. Engels' comments are direct, critical, outspoken, but they betray a genuine interest in Irish affairs. Where Marx writes of little but the use that can be made of Ireland for furthering the cause of proletarian revolution, Engels, though equally devoted to that overriding Communist aim, does not regard Ireland and her aspirations with the same cold-blooded detachment. His descriptions of the countryside, though fanciful at times, are not lacking in insight. He planned a history of Ireland, and papers which were found after his death showed that he had completed some parts of it. He considered that Ireland's 'ill luck' began millions of years ago, when the island's coal deposits were washed away, and she was condemned 'as if by Nature's decree' to be a farming country situated beside a great industrial land. He asked himself, too, the long-recurring question, was Ireland destined by its climate for agriculture or cattle-rearing or both? He came down in favour of a balanced farming system; 'compared with England, Ireland is more suitable for cattle-rearing,' but compared with France, England is the more suitable. Are we to conclude, he enquired, 'that the whole of England should be changed into cattle ranches, and the whole of the agricultural population sent into the factory towns or shipped to America (except for a few cattle ranchers) to make room for cattle which are to be sent to France in exchange for silks and wines'? His affection for Ireland is expressed in his description of the Irish climate; 'the weather, like the inhabitants, is full of violent contrasts: the sky is like an Irish woman's face, rain and sunshine succeed each other suddenly and unexpectedly, and there is none of the humdrum greyness of England'.[1] But theoretic preconceptions, not actual observation of conditions, determined the character of Communist policies.

THE VERDICT OF LENIN

Lenin, whose views on Irish developments in the early twentieth century are considered later,[2] wrote in February 1914:

The policy of Marx and Engels in the Irish Question serves as a splendid example, which is of *immense practical* importance to this day of

---

[1] Quoted in Gustav Mayer, op. cit., pp. 195–6.
[2] See below, pp. 241–2 and 272–4.

the attitude the proletariat of the oppressing nations should adopt towards national movements. It serves as a warning against that 'servile
haste' with which the philistines of all countries, colours and languages,
hurry to declare as 'utopian' the idea of changing the frontiers of states
that have been established by the violence and privileges of the landlords and bourgeoisie of one nation.[1]

As a model for Communist policy elsewhere, the Marxist interpretation
of the Irish Question remained of enduring interest. It was for this
reason that Lenin was so concerned to defend the validity of Marx's
interpretation against all criticism and even to justify those expectations, which had been manifestly falsified by events. Marx, as we have
seen, though opposed to federalism in principle, had advocated a
federal solution of the Irish Question, provided that Ireland should be
liberated, not by a Repeal of the Union enacted by Parliament, but by
revolutionary action originating in Ireland and supported by the
English working class. Such a prospect, always very remote, had no
chance of realization by 1914. Yet Lenin would not acknowledge that
Marx's hopes were built on a foundation of sand. Federalism brought
about by Marxist methods and resulting in proletarian government
throughout the British Isles was in Lenin's view the 'ideal solution' of
Anglo-Irish difficulties. He admitted that the chances of it were lessening with time, not because the Marxist premises were mistaken, but
because 'both the Irish people and the English proletariat proved to be
weak'[2]–the familiar explanation that shirks the issue. Marx miscalculated the reactions of the English working class; he simply did not
understand the conservative, the fanatical character and the emotional
side of Irish nationalism, with the result that the Communist tactics
were suited to a situation which in fact did not exist. It was inaccurate
observation, which was responsible for Marx's miscalculations and
Lenin's special pleading will carry conviction only to the converted.

More important, however, than the tactical approach is the theoretic
interpretation of the Irish role in the coming proletarian revolution.
Why was Ireland of such interest to Communist leaders from Marx to
Lenin? What is the lasting significance of their writings on Ireland?
The interest of Marx and Lenin in Ireland, a country which neither of
them ever visited, was not aroused by sympathy with nationalist ideals.
So far as subjective considerations influenced their highly abstract

---

[1] *The Right of Nations to Self-Determination: Collected Works*, Vol. XX, p. 442.
[2] Ibid.

analysis of the Irish Question it was sympathy with the proletariat, with the 'men of no property' who were thought of as the predestined victors in the class war. But other and more far-reaching factors dominated their thought. In the last half century before the collapse of the Union, Ireland by her proximity, and still more by her relation to Great Britain acquired a remarkable significance for the Marxist. Politically and socially the Irish people were discontented. The political system and the social systems derived their authority from the same source. The end of British rule in Ireland would accordingly bring about the breakdown of British 'capitalist' society. Though the interdependence of politics and the social order diminished rapidly after the Land Act of 1903, yet Lenin still maintained on the eve of the First World War, that the fall of the Liberal Government on Irish issues would prove the prelude to a Communist revolution brought about by events in Ireland. If, so the argument may be summarized, the Irish were assisted in their fight for political freedom by the English working class, then the triumph of the proletariat in Ireland would inevitably pave the way for the final overthrow of capitalist democracy in Great Britain. Since England in turn was the 'bulwark of European capitalism', then revolution in England would be the decisive step forward in the history of World Revolution. Such was the sequence of cause and consequence, all of which, according to Lenin following Marx, were in the last analysis dependent upon the course of events in Ireland. And such were the circumstances, which have given the Irish Question its vicarious significance in Communist literature.

The interest of the Marxist commentary on Ireland is therefore twofold. On the one hand it is a most instructive illustration of the long view and the wide vision that has inspired the programme of revolutionary Communism, and it throws into relief as well that inflexibility of mind, which is the most serious disadvantage of an ideological approach to political problems. On the other hand the Communist interpretation of the Irish Question, a question highly particularized in its history and development, and in some respects unique in its form and expression, has an enduring interest, because it affords an admirable opportunity of testing the historical validity of the precepts of dialectical materialism as a whole. The distinctiveness of the Irish Question makes it impossible that the accuracy of the Communist doctrine should be finally judged by its application in this one instance, but equally it is an instance that cannot well be ignored. The commentary of Marx is the offspring of the materialist conception of history and it must be viewed in relation to its philosophic background. But the truth of that conception may be tested by reference to particular problems and its inability to furnish a satisfying explanation of Anglo-Irish relations renders the more suspect its ultimate validity. Furthermore, the fundamental doctrine of the class-war is challenged by the evidence of recent Irish history, which by suggesting that economic conflicts between communities are at least as important as economic conflicts between classes and which, by showing that religious and national loyalties may exact an allegiance which overrides sectional interests, exposes an intrinsic weakness in the materialist assessment of the fundamental forces at work.

The last word may be allowed to lie with Lenin. He wrote in 1915:

. . . in 1869 Marx demanded the separation of Ireland, not in order to split but to achieve subsequent free alliance between Ireland and Britain, not in order to secure 'justice for Ireland', but in the interests of the revolutionary struggle of the British proletariat. . . .[1]

[1] V. I. Lenin, *The Revolutionary Proletariat and the Right of Nations to Self-Determination*, reprinted in V. I. Lenin, *On Britain*, A compilation. (Moscow, n.d.), p. 252.

PART II
REFORM
ENGLISH STATESMEN:
AND THE REPEAL OF THE UNION

CHAPTER IV

THE LIBERAL CONVERSION TO HOME RULE

And what he greatly thought he nobly dared.
POPE

Mr Gladstone has reserved for his closing days a conspiracy against the honour of Britain and the welfare of Ireland more startlingly base and nefarious than any of those numerous designs and plots which, during the last quarter of a century, have occupied his imagination. . . .

LORD RANDOLPH CHURCHILL.
June 20, 1886.

————————————

Hitherto the circumstances of Ireland have been viewed chiefly through the eyes of contemporary thinkers and statesmen, who were concerned less with personalities, political programmes or immediate problems, than with the principles, which should determine her future government and her place in the society of European states. In consequence their commentaries upon the condition of Ireland were apt to derive their character, as much from the philosophy of the individual commentator, as from a precise observation of the country. This has its admitted disadvantages, but they are in part at least counterbalanced by the advantages of a more detached and distant view. Traditionally the onlooker sees the most of the game, and, even if he does not watch it very closely or for very long, he may acquire, whatever may have been his particular preconceptions, a sharp impression of the run of the play.

Cavour, Mazzini, Marx, Engels, and, to a lesser extent, de Beaumont, considered the principles governing the Irish struggle in a way that was rarely considered by English statesmen or Irish leaders in the nineteenth century. They asked themselves, as we have seen,[1] certain fundamental questions which may be conveniently restated here. Is the Irish movement a national movement? Or is it merely a demand for

[1] See above, pp. 59–60.

better government, which has assumed national pretensions through exacerbation with the injustices, the ineptitudes and the inefficiencies of the Union system? If it claims to be a national movement then how far is the Irish claim to distinct nationality justified? How far are these political claims the superficial manifestation of a fundamental economic struggle? These are far-reaching questions to which continental observers addressed themselves and to which they attempted to formulate answers. They are questions on which there was little clear thinking nearer home. To the Irish many of them appeared otiose; to the British most of them were uncomfortable.

The reactions of English statesmen to Irish problems, by contrast with those of the more didactic Europeans, suggested at once a more limited view and a more flexible approach. Englishmen did not consider the questions, which absorbed the attention of other observers, largely because they did not feel that such questions were important. To them it seemed of little practical advantage to know whether the Irish claim was for national or for good government or whether, if the claim for treatment as a distinct nationality were advanced, that claim was susceptible of philosophic justification or not. Victorian England, permeated with the political philosophy of Burke, was not interested in the 'rights' of Irishmen and relegated the whole question to the safer plane of expediency. To them appeals to 'natural rights' were as unrealistic and as dangerous as the generalizations of the Gironde on the Rights of Man. The result was unhappy, because each people was speaking in a language, which the other did not wholly understand. English statesmen were ignorant, not only of Irish affairs, but of the Irish outlook. They did not grasp the significance of that underlying affinity between the Irish and the continental mind and so attributed to Irish perversity, what was at least in part an emanation from the continental conception of the supremacy of symbols and abstract ideals in politics. In the later years of the Union, English statesmen were prepared to do much to ease the economic conditions of Ireland. Many of them were prepared to reform her system of government, some of them recognized the necessity for a grant of self-government, but only Gladstone at the last spoke as though he understood how large the symbols of sovereignty, and especially of an Irish parliament sitting in Dublin once again,[1] loomed in Irish minds.

It was because Gladstone possessed, or rather acquired through

---

[1] On this point see his speech April 8, 1886, introducing the first Home Rule Bill. Hansard's *Parl. Deb.* 3rd series, Vol. CCCIV, coll. 1054–5.

European channels, this insight into the Irish mind, that he was the one English statesman of this epoch to make a positive contribution, so ambitious in character as to hold out hope of a final settlement of the Irish Question. By the Home Rule proposals of 1886 he transformed for good or for evil the existing conception of Anglo-Irish relations; and by the dynamic force of his own personality compelled an un-willing English electorate to regard Ireland as the all-important poli-tical issue of the day. By this achievement he influenced, sometimes indirectly, but more often directly, the actions of English statesmen for the next half century. Home Rule provided the motive force even of those policies, which were designed to render it superfluous. There-fore what Gladstone said in 1886 remained a matter of continuing political significance.

In his speech on the first reading of the first Home Rule Bill, Glad-stone dwelt upon the fundamental considerations which had prompted his dramatic initiative. In so doing he refused in the face of much criticism to admit that Home Rule was the least of likely evils—rather, he argued, it was a good in itself. These were his words:[1]

We stand face to face with what is termed Irish nationality. Irish nationality vents itself in the demand for local autonomy, or separate and complete self-government in Irish, not in Imperial, affairs. Is this an evil in itself? Is this a thing that we should view with horror or apprehension? . . . Sir, I hold that it is not. . . . I hold that there is such a thing as local patriotism, which in itself, is not bad, but good. . . . I do not believe that local patriotism is an evil. I believe it is stronger in Ireland even than in Scotland. Englishmen are eminently English, Scotchmen are profoundly Scotch and if I read Irish history aright, misfortune and calamity have wedded her sons to her soil. The Irish-man is more profoundly Irish, but it does not follow, that because his local patriotism is keen, he is incapable of Imperial patriotism. . . .

I ask you to show to Europe and to America that we, too, can face political problems which America 20 years ago faced, and which many countries in Europe have been called upon to face. . . . I ask that in our own case we should practise, with firm and fearless hand, what we have so often preached—the doctrine which we have so often inculcated upon others—namely that the concession of local self-government is not the way to sap or impair, but the way to strengthen and consoli-date unity. I ask that we should learn to rely less upon merely written

[1] Hansard's *Parl. Deb.* 3rd series, Vol. CCCIV, coll. 1081–5.

stipulations, and more upon those better stipulations which are written on the heart and mind of man. I ask that we should apply to Ireland that happy experience which we have gained in England and in Scotland, where the course of generations has now taught us . . . that the best and surest foundation we can find to build upon is the foundation afforded by the affections, the convictions, and the will of the nation.'

Irishmen may have entertained some reservations about some of the premises from which Gladstone derived a very welcome conclusion, but in England criticism in mounting and ultimately in fatal volume was directed against the conclusion itself. Was this inevitable, irre-) spective of political circumstances? Or did the misjudgements and impetuosity of an old man render fruitless his last, and some may think, his finest labour?

'MY MISSION IS TO PACIFY IRELAND'

In an election address of 1812, Sir Samuel Romilly explained to the electors of Bristol what he considered to be the principles of a sound Whig:

He ought to be a Man firmly attached to those principles of our Constitution which were established at the Revolution. . . . He should justly appreciate and be ready at all times to maintain the liberty of the press and the trial by jury which are the great securities for all our other liberties. He should be a sincere friend of peace. . . . He should be an enemy to that influence of the Crown and of the Ministers of the Crown which has been so fatally exercised in the House of Commons, and consequently a friend to Parliamentary Reform. He should be a constant advocate for economy in the public expenditure and a determined enemy to corruption and peculation. He should be ready, when he sees abuses arising from any of our present institutions, to enquire into the causes of them, and to suggest a remedy, notwithstanding the reproach of being an innovator. Above all he should be a man incapable of being severed from his duty by the threats of power, the allurements of the great, the temptations of private interest or even the seduction of popular favour.[1]

[1] Quoted in H. W. Carless Davis, *The Age of Grey and Peel* (Oxford, 1929), pp. 267–8.

This portrait of a Whig, old-fashioned and a trifle self-righteous though it be, does present an ideal to which Gladstone himself would hardly have hesitated to subscribe. He was a friend of peace, a constant advocate of economy, he opposed the undue influence of the officers of the Crown, not least in Dublin Castle, where it most notably survived and it was because he saw abuses arising 'from our present institutions' that he advocated the remedy of Home Rule, notwithstanding the politically fatal 'reproach of being an innovator'. And neither defeat in the Commons, followed by defeat in the country, nor even the partial disintegration of his party, caused him to modify a policy in order to further his private political interest[1]—or to regain popular favour. But, in his impassioned advocacy of Home Rule, Gladstone displayed one quality, or defect, foreign to this portrait of a Whig. He was stirred by emotion, and as his most recent biographer has observed[2] this messianic mood was wholly alien to the Whig temperament. Romilly's description suggests a man too sagacious to be passionate, whereas Gladstone in his later Irish policies may be thought too passionate to be sagacious.

Gladstone's conversion to Home Rule was, however, a more gradual process than is allowed by those who profess to see in it the outcome of a zealot's unreasoning impulse or alternatively, and contradictorily, the throw of a political gambler. Long before 1886 he had been extraordinarily conscious of Ireland. In 1845 he wrote from Germany, 'I cannot trace the line of my own future life, but I hope and pray it may not always be where it is . . . Ireland, Ireland! that cloud in the west, that coming storm, the minister of God's retribution upon cruel and inveterate and but half-atoned injustice'.[3] Nor was his choice of words fortuitous. Gladstone believed that in the end there was retribution for unredressed injustice; that such retribution was visited as surely upon nations as upon mortal men; that atonement was required as much of the one as of the other and that in respect of English injustice to Ireland full atonement had yet to be made.[4] He believed it was the supreme responsibility of his later years to ensure that it was. Early in 1868

---

[1] In writing this I have taken account of the view that throughout Gladstone was preoccupied only with the furthering of his own political interests. I do not subscribe to it.

[2] Magnus, op. cit., p. 192.

[3] To Mrs Gladstone: Morley, *The Life of William Ewart Gladstone* (London, 1903), 3 Vols., Vol. I, p. 383.

[4] Gladstone was not alone among his contemporaries in entertaining these views. John Bright, as is implicit in many, and explicit in some, of his speeches on Empire as well as on Ireland, also and notably, subscribed to them. See below p. 119.

Gladstone wrote to his sister, that he was aware he could not expect to 'live politically to see the Irish question settled', but that he had taken up that question in the name of 'the God of truth and justice'.[1] His Irish critics, however, merely noted for future reference that he had taken it up the year after the Fenian rising.

Gladstone, like Cobden and Bright before him, felt at first that atonement to Irish-Ireland might be made by depriving Anglo-Ireland of its privileges and its pre-eminence. In the election of 1867 he voiced his sentiments at Wigan in a stirring peroration in which he likened the Anglo-Irish ascendancy to:

Some tall tree of noxious growth, lifting its head to Heaven and poisoning the atmosphere of the land so far as its shadow can extend. It is still there, gentlemen, but now at last the day has come when, as we hope, the axe has been laid to the root [Loud Cheers]. It is deeply cut round and round. It nods and quivers from top to base [Cheers]. There lacks, gentlemen, but one stroke more—the stroke of these Elections [Loud Cheers]. It will then, once for all, topple to its fall, and on that day the heart of Ireland will leap for joy, and the mind and conscience of England and Scotland will repose with thankful satisfaction upon the thought that something has been done towards the discharge of national duty, and towards deepening and widening the foundations of public strength, security, and peace [Loud and prolonged applause].[2]

The stroke of the elections was duly and successfully delivered and it was on the afternoon of December 1, 1868, when Gladstone was in his shirt sleeves wielding an axe, that a telegraph messenger arrived with the news that he had been charged with the formation of his first Cabinet. He remarked, 'Very significant' and at once resumed his work. But after a few minutes the blows ceased and Gladstone resting on the handle of his axe looked up and with deep earnestness in his voice exclaimed, 'My mission is to pacify Ireland'. He then resumed his chopping and did not stop till the tree was felled.[3]

GLADSTONE'S EARLY AND LIMITED INTERPRETATION OF HIS MISSION

Gladstone, like other well-intentioned English liberals, entertained some large illusions about what the fulfilment of his mission of paci-

---

[1] Quoted in Magnus, op. cit., p. 192.   [2] Ibid., p. 193.
[3] Morley, *Life of Gladstone*, Vol. II, p. 252.

fication might entail. This was not to be wondered at. When Gladstone formed his Government in 1868, writes Sir Philip Magnus, 'he had no experience and no real knowledge of the Irish problem, and his ignorance was shared by the whole of his Cabinet and by the mass of the British people'.[1] Nothing indeed is more revealing in this respect than that Gladstone hoped that his self-appointed mission might be accomplished within a year or two of his taking office, after which he might retire to Hawarden and devote himself to religion.[2] Those oratorical flourishes in his Wigan speech about the strokes that would topple the noxious tree of Protestant ascendancy implied, indeed, that with Bright, he believed that the British people might atone for past injustice and ensure future co-operation in Ireland by what for them would be the painless, even satisfying, elimination of the privileges of a settler aristocracy, which had outlived its usefulness. But at this period there is no evidence that Gladstone was aware that the problem might go deeper—that it might lie in the existence of an Irish nationality, confronting an English nationality and challenging some of its most deeply cherished convictions. The resolution of any such conflict would allow of no quick or painless solution.

Gladstone's early actions confirm this interpretation. He struck his blows at the toppling tree. Contrary to his earlier and published views, he concluded that the Church of Ireland should be disestablished and in March 1868 he declared that the Irish Church 'as a state church, must cease to exist'.[3] In this he had the fervent and understanding support of John Bright, who in the debate in the House on April 1st on Gladstone's disestablishment resolutions declared that England and Scotland were 'eager to make atonement for past crimes and past errors' and that it now depended upon the Imperial Parliament 'whether that atonement shall at length be made'.[4] Gladstone further believed, as no one else is likely to have done, that the dignitaries of that Church might be led by the same process of reason, that had persuaded him to change his views, to acquiesce amicably in the disestablishment of their own Church. In this he was, not surprisingly, disappointed. But despite denunciations of Gladstone's sacreligious assault upon the Church from the pulpit[5] and at Diocesan conferences in Ireland and

---

[1] Op. cit., p. 196.　　　　　　　[2] Ibid.

[3] Quoted in Woodward, op. cit., p. 346.

[4] Thorold Rogers, *Speeches by the Right Hon. John Bright, M.P.* (London, 1869), p. 223.

[5] For reflections more considered and, be it added, unusually temperate and also understanding of consequences, see the text of the Sermon preached by the Very Reverend

even a self-imposed exile after disestablishment by some Church of Ireland clergy, this breach of the Act of Union, which under Article 5 had united the Churches of England and Ireland into one Protestant Espicopal Church, was finally effected, after hard practical negotiations, which in their last phase prompted Gladstone to write to Lord Granville of 'this woful huckerstering affair'.[1]

After the Church came the land. For three months in 1869 Gladstone studied this most testing and complex of social issues. Not surprisingly the Cabinet was divided upon the scope of reform. 'The contest, so to call it, among us upon Irish Land', wrote Gladstone to Granville on December 27, 1869,[2] 'has been no more than that twofold contest which is the best foundation of hope, and the only, or rather the indispensable condition, of success in difficult questions: first, rivalry in the desire to bring out fully, and from their root the difficulties of the subject, and secondly, a like rivalry in the endeavour to overcome them by patience and goodwill. No members of the Cabinet have shown more of the second, than those who have most keenly felt the first. . . .' Gladstone also observed that 'the end of our measure is to give peace and security to Ireland, and through Ireland to the Empire'.[3] But the final provisions of the 1870 Land Act hardly warranted such spacious language. The principle of the Act was protection for tenants without infringement of property rights. Gladstone himself was prepared to go no further; it was hard indeed to persuade some members of his Cabinet to go so far. And so it was that while the tenants were safeguarded under the Act against the worst forms of eviction, they had to wait another eleven years before they secured fixity of tenure and fair rents. In the meantime they were left to face the long years of agricultural depression after 1875 with no provision for a downward adjustment of rents. Gladstone's first essay in land legislation was far from being a blow that would topple the Ascendancy tree. But among its more important consequences may be numbered the education of Gladstone in the intricacies of the social question in its distinctive Irish form.

It was education at one remove, for by 1870 Gladstone had still not visited Ireland. This, however, by no means discouraged him from

Dr W. C. Magee, Dean of Cork, at the opening of the Church Congress in Dublin, September 1868. Dr Magee was later Archbishop of York.

[1] *The Political Correspondence of Mr Gladstone and Lord Granville 1868–1876*. Edited by Agatha Ramm (London, Royal Historical Society, Camden Third Series Volumes) LXXXI-LXXXII, *89*. This correspondence is a valuable source of information about Gladstone's views on both disestablishment and land reform in Ireland in these years.

[2] Ibid. *180*.   [3] Ibid.

admonishing the Queen upon the importance of royal residence in Ireland. He felt such residence would be at once beneficial for Anglo-Irish relations and for the Prince of Wales, who seemed to him to lack sufficient worthwhile occupation. In a letter of December 3, 1870, to Lord Granville Gladstone outlined his proposals, prefaced by a disquisition upon manhood and duty.[1] The Prince, Gladstone surmised, had 'that average stock of energy, which enables men to do that which they cannot well avoid doing, or that which is made ready to their hands: but he has not that rare supply of it, which enables a man to make duty, and so to win honour and confidence. When this negative position as to duty is combined with the highest activity of the appliances and stimulants of pleasure, the position is, for the formation of character, the most dangerous in which a human being can be placed; and perhaps, all things considered, we ought to be thankful even that matters are no worse than they are. But the outlook for ten, twenty, thirty, forty years hence is a very melancholy one.'

To relieve this forbidding prospect Gladstone thought the Lord Lieutenancy in Ireland might be abolished, the Chief Secretary assuming full responsibility for the Government of Ireland and the Prince of Wales installed as a permanent Viceroy residing in Dublin during a large part of the year. Such an arrangement in Gladstone's opinion would have had a double advantage. It would have 'not only salutary, but also very powerful effects on the popular mind in Ireland' and 'meanwhile the Prince would obtain a very valuable political Education'. On neither count, however, was the Queen impressed. She told Gladstone at an audience on June 25, 1871, that it was a stupid waste of time to try to connect the Royal Family with Ireland, since 'Scotland and England deserved it much more'[2] and, as almost anyone but Gladstone might have expected, she strongly resented the tenor of his observations about the Prince of Wales. Gladstone did not abandon his efforts for another year, but the task of royal persuasion was one for which he was supremely ill-equipped. Yet in the context of Anglo-Irish relations Gladstone's proposal had possibly rather more to recommend it than the general reflections in which it was embedded might suggest, even though Gladstone was seemingly unaware of the growing hostility in Ireland to the Crown since the Famine. In the context, however, of the Prince's future it may perhaps be questioned whether six months' residence each year in the Vice-Regal Lodge in

[1] Ramm, op. cit., Vol. I, *383.*
[2] Magnus, op. cit., p. 209.

Phoenix Park would have encouraged a 'worthy and manly mode of life' in quite the way Gladstone supposed.

In 1877 Gladstone, out of office, at long last visited Ireland. He spent three weeks there. 'He was feasted', writes John Morley,[1] 'by the provost of Trinity, in spite of disestablishment, and he had a friendly conversation with Cardinal Cullen, in spite of Vaticanism.' And, of one so well remembered for the timber he felled, it deserves also to be recorded that, while in Ireland, he planted a tree. It was on Lord Monck's estate (as it then was) in Enniskerry and the tree flourishes to this day, though it is said that Lord Monck considered uprooting it, when later he parted from Gladstone on Home Rule.[2] But Gladstone's visit had seemingly little influence on his thinking about Ireland; at the age of sixty-eight, even for him the impressionable years were gone.

When Gladstone returned to office in 1880 his mission of pacification remained almost as far, and to outward seeming even farther, from fulfilment than when he voiced his sanguine purpose twelve years earlier. The Church question might be deemed disposed of: but land and politics remained. The land problem was intensified partly and as is so often the case, by ameliorative, but insufficient measures of reform, coupled with the disastrous fall in agricultural prices, due to the competition of cheap New World imports; while the political problem approached a climacteric with the organization of the Irish Home Rule Party as an oath-bound phalanx of parliamentary members behind Charles Stewart Parnell, the Anglo-Irish landlord, later to be described by Gladstone as 'the most remarkable man I ever met'. Temperamentally, however, the two were ill-fitted to understand each other and the measure of Parnell's misunderstanding, illustrated by his dismissal of Gladstone as 'this masquerading knight-errant, this pretending champion of the rights of every nation except the Irish nation', may well have been the greater, as it was certainly the costlier. When after five troubled years the Government fell in June 1885, what was remembered was not a Land Act which opened the way to peasant ownership, but violent and foreclosed debate in the Commons, Gladstonian denunciation of Home Rulers 'marching through plunder to the disintegration of the Empire', Gladstonian warnings that in dealing with them the 'resources of civilization were not exhausted', murder in

---

[1] *Gladstone*, Vol. II, p. 571.

[2] Neither Morley nor Magnus mention the planting of a tree, and it is to Mr Eoin O'Mahony that I am indebted for my knowledge of it. Lord Monck had been the first Governor-General of the Dominion of Canada.

Phoenix Park, and the strange episode which began when the Liberal Government perpetuated 'England's cruel wrong'.[1]

Before this wrong all other wrongs of Ireland do grow pale,
For they've clapped the pride of Erin's Isle into could Kilmainham jail.
It was the tyrant Gladstone, and he said unto himself
'I nivir will be aisy till Parnell is on the shelf.
So make the warrant out in haste and take it by the mail,
And we'll clap the pride of Erin's Isle in could Kilmainham jail'.
So Buckshot[2] took the warrant and he buttoned up his coat
And tuk the train to Holyhead to catch the Kingstown boat.

THE IMMEDIATE CIRCUMSTANCES OF HIS CONVERSION

Gladstone's Government was brought down by a combination of Tories and Nationalists on June 9, 1885. 'Some of us said', recalled James Bryce, 'as we walked away from the House under the dawning light of that memorable 9th of June, "This means Home Rule".'[3] The Liberal administration was succeeded by a minority Conservative Government under Lord Salisbury, which lasted seven months. This Government, dependent on the Irish vote, was anxious to retain the goodwill of Parnell. So Lord Spencer's system of 'firm government', enforced after the Phoenix Park murders, came to an abrupt end, in accord with assurances given by Lord Randolph Churchill to Parnell before the vote of June 9th[4] and in its place Ireland enjoyed the spectacle of a Conservative Government, sponsoring the first State-assisted scheme of Land Purchase.[5] The compliance of the Conservatives confirmed Parnell in his contemptuous belief that English parties could always be bought—with votes. In August he declared that the Irish in the new Parliament would have 'a platform with only one plank, and that one plank National Independence'. The English Press was loud in denunciation, but both Lord Salisbury and Lord Randolph Churchill maintained a discreet reserve. Gladstone, too, kept his door open, but of his former colleagues both Hartington, on behalf of the

---

[1] Quoted in St John Ervine, *Parnell* (London, 1925), p. 183.
[2] Known in England as the Right Hon. W. E. Forster. He acquired his Irish pseudonym by recommending the use of buckshot for dispersing illegal gatherings.
[3] H. A. L. Fisher, *James Bryce* (London, 1927), 2 Vols., Vol. I, p. 200.
[4] Cf. C. C. O'Brien, op. cit., p. 97.
[5] Lord Ashbourne's Act.

Whigs, and Chamberlain, on behalf of the Radicals, sternly rebuked Parnell.[1] Both the silence and the condemnation carried a significance not to be lost on the Irish leader.

The conversion of the Tories from a policy of 'resolute government', to one of concession in Ireland, made a startling impresssion among the rank and file of the Tory party. Joseph Chamberlain, who approved the new policy, none the less denounced that 'astounding tergiversation' of ministers and declared that 'a strategic movement of this kind, executed in opposition to the notorious convictions of the men who effected it, carried out for party purposes and for party purposes alone, is the most flagrant instance of political dishonesty this country has ever known'.[2] Lord Hartington added in weighty and more restrained language that the Government had dealt a heavy blow 'both at political morality and at the cause of order in Ireland'. But for Parnell the victory was complete. The moral reputation of English parties was not among his preoccupations and he had no scruples in tempting them to bid for the valuable asset that lay in his power alone to give or to withhold. Only one question troubled him; which party would pay the higher price?

Parnell's choice is a matter of history. He held his hand till two days before the election and then on November 21, 1885, he issued a manifesto instructing the Irish in Great Britain to vote against all Liberal and Radical candidates. In appearance the verdict of the electorate realized Parnell's most sanguine hopes. The Nationalists, securing a bloc of 86 seats, held the balance in the new House. As a result, although the Liberals secured 335 seats to the Tories' 249, yet their dreams of a majority over Tories and Nationalists combined, as Morley sadly observed, 'had glided away through the "ivory gate"'. 'As he [Gladstone] reads in his Midlothian retreat', commented *United Ireland* in a superb flight of fancy, 'the tale of disaster wrought by the Irish vote, it were little wonder if the aged enigma spinner were to think of the anathema of the Hanoverian king on the causes which nerved the Irish arm at Fontenoy.'[3] It would in fact have been great wonder for Gladstone self-confessedly knew nothing of Irish history, but that apart *United Ireland*, and indeed Parnellite supporters generally, tended at first to overlook their liabilities in a generally favourable situation. Thus a week later *United Ireland* acclaimed the outcome in a

---

[1] Cf. R. C. K. Ensor, *England, 1870–1914* (Oxford, 1936), pp. 91–2.
[2] July 24, 1885.
[3] November 28, 1885.

leading article, entitled *Te Deum*, which declared that the Irish electors 'have made Mr Parnell as supreme between rival English parties as Irish constituencies have effaced Whig and nominal factions who dispute his supremacy'.[1] But they were mistaken. In fact, while Parnell could keep either English party out of office, he could put only the Liberals in. Before the end of the year the Nationalist Tory alliance was sundered and the Liberal Nationalist entente was an established fact.

The terms Parnell had obtained from the Tories, though for long somewhat obscure, are now tolerably clear.[2] The Viceroy, Lord Carnarvon, had acted at once as initiator and intermediary in private conversations, first with Justin McCarthy in July 1885 and then on August 1st in melodramatic circumstances in an empty house in Mayfair, with Parnell himself. It is quite wrong to think of Carnarvon, scholarly and now something of a valetudinarian, his incoming correspondence filled with enquiries about his health and his outgoing letters complaining of the damp of Dublin—'the Irish climate always actively develops rheumatic tendencies'[3]—as a 'man with no aggressive traits' who disliked 'political strife almost as much as war'.[4] Behind the mannerisms which earned for him his soubriquet of 'Twitters' from Disraeli, there lay the high-minded purpose of a man who believed in Empire, who had been Colonial Secretary when Canadian confederation was enacted and who sought first by diplomacy and then by more forceful means to bring about federation in South Africa ten years later. This was an essay, albeit one that failed, in imperial expansion and it indicated the settled purpose of Carnavon's principal political aim. It was the strengthening of Empire. The difference between Carnavon and the majority of his Conservative Cabinet colleagues was that he believed that this might be done in appropriate circumstances by self-government, consolidation and conciliation. In the case of Ireland Carnavon proceeded accordingly from the premise that union between the two countries must remain, but that union did not necessarily preclude a local parliament, which, in his own words, would 'give the shadow without giving the substance or at least the substance of that which would be perilous'.[5]

Lord Salisbury was committed to Carnavon's Irish initiative only

---

[1] December 5, 1885. See also later and more realistic thoughts on December 19, 1885.

[2] See L. P. Curtis, *Coercion and Conciliation in Ireland 1880–1892. A Study in Conservative Unionism* (Princeton, 1963), Chap. III and more especially pp. 49–54.

[3] Carnavon MS.: Public Record Office. The quotation is from a letter dated August 27, 1885.

[4] L. P. Curtis, *Coercion and Conciliation*, p. 38.

[5] O'Brien, p. 103. See also Ensor, p. 92.

by his acquiesence in the conversations with Parnell taking place and he kept himself free to disown Carnavon if or when considerations of public or party interest made that desirable. The Cabinet had no prior knowledge of them, nor was their substance reported by the Prime Minister to his colleagues. Carnavon was disappointed by this, for he had hoped his conversation with Parnell would have led to a full Cabinet discussion of Irish policy. '. . . I really staid on in London', he wrote to Lord Cranbrook on August 5, 1885,[1] 'thinking they might like to question me as to the present state of things here. But I did not desire to moot the subject and after the fashion of many cabinets we dawdled over some matters and galloped over others and finally broke up for the H. of C. before Ireland came up for consideration. I also *rather* regret that they did not hear what I had to say; for the position here is a *very peculiar* one—in some respects wonderfully favourable, in others threatening'. Salisbury's speeches in the autumn of 1885, however, left it to be supposed that substantial concessions in terms of Irish self-government were not excluded in the event of a Tory-Nationalist majority in the election. When that majority did not materialize Lord Salisbury in his brief, remaining period of office felt free to return to the more familiar Tory expedient of coercion.

'I have never looked much in Irish matters', Gladstone had written to Hartington on May 30, 1885,[2] 'at negotiation or the conciliation of leaders. I look at the question in itself.' This was at once admirable and substantially true, but it did not assist political or public understanding. In the Irish mind Gladstone was less a man with a mission, than the man who used the resources of civilization to enforce coercion. In England, and even among associates who knew how strongly he felt on Irish affairs, none could tell with assurance to what end his emotions, his thoughts and his calculations would lead him.

During the critical autumn of 1885 Gladstone's attitude to Irish problems continued to be one of cautious reserve and the Delphic ambiguity of his utterances gave the public no clue as to his intentions. Subsequently his friends asserted that this silence marked the caution of a statesman waiting till the hour should strike; his enemies that it cloaked the ambitions of a man anxious to return to office, even at the price of corrupt capitulation to Irish demands. Neither assertion was entirely true. Gladstone was a convert to Home Rule before the elections. But he was much concerned to conceal his conversion, not only

[1] Carnavon MS.: P.R.O.30.6.
[2] Morley, Vol. III, pp. 197–8.

from the electorate, but also from the majority of his colleagues and from Parnell. Why? Morley's general explanation does not take us far.

Mr Gladstone had pondered the matter deeply. His gift of political imagination, his wider experience . . . planted him on a height whence he commanded a view of possibilities and necessities, of hope and of risks, that were unseen by politicians of the beaten track. Like a pilot amid wandering icebergs, or in waters where familiar buoys had been taken up and immemorial beacons put out, he scanned the scene with keen eyes and a glass sweeping the horizon in every direction. No wonder that his words seemed vague, and vague they undoubtedly were. . . . This was no moment for ultimatums. There were too many unascertained elements.[1]

Less reverent critics, incapable of regarding Gladstone as a pilot amid wandering icebergs, remained sceptical. No doubt, Gladstone, as many lesser statesmen, was occupied in 'exploring every avenue', but what principle guided his footsteps? And where would it lead him?

More material evidence of Gladstone's changing attitude to Ireland in the autumn of 1885 is to be discovered in letters to certain colleagues and friends. In September Hugh Childers, the distinguished bearer of a name, destined later to be inscribed on the page of Irish history, 'a most capable administrator, a zealous colleague, wise in what the world regards as the secondary sort of wisdom, and the last man to whom one would have looked for a plunge',[2] wrote to Gladstone seeking his approval for a 'tolerably full-fleged scheme of home rule'. Gladstone replied,[3] 'I have a decided sympathy with the general scope and spirit of your proposed declaration about Ireland. If I offer any observations, they are meant to be simply in furtherance of your purpose.' The observations he offered, suggested that Childers, while stating his readiness to consider an Irish legislature for all matters not of imperial concern, should mention the details 'veiled in language not such as to commit you'. All the evidence available suggests that this response to Childers reflected with reasonable accuracy the state of Gladstone's opinion on Ireland at this time. He foresaw the necessity of a separate Parliament in Dublin, but he was determined not to shoulder prematurely the political liability of public commitment.

Why did Gladstone consider secrecy imperative for so long? Was it

[1] *Gladstone*, Vol. III, pp. 234–5. [2] Ibid.
[3] On September 28, 1885.

merely because he delighted to play the role of a prophet, whose inspired message pronounced at the appropriate hour would show his followers the road to the promised land? Certainly such a role afforded him pleasure, and the intricate sentences of his Midlothian address admirably fulfilled the design of mystifying his audience. When he spoke on the legislative union he was true to the portrait which Lytton Strachey[1] was one day to paint with epigrammatic malice; the portrait of a man the fibre of whose being was speech, and when he spoke 'the ambiguity of ambiguity was revealed. The long, winding, intricate sentences, with their vast burden of subtle and complicated qualifications, befogged the mind like clouds, and like clouds, too, dropped thunderbolts.' 'I believe history and posterity', said Gladstone, 'will consign to disgrace the name and memory of every man, be he who he may, and on whichever side of the channel he may dwell, that having power to aid in an equitable settlement between Ireland and Great Britain, shall use that power not to aid but to prevent or to retard.' And so the speech rolled on, profuse in language, ranging widely in thought, but indecisive on the one question it discussed, and so either admitting or excluding a policy of Home Rule as the hearer might care to think. The performance was the more remarkable inasmuch as Gladstone instead of minimizing, was at pains to emphasize the gravity of the Irish Question.

But Gladstone had more substantial reasons for his prolonged silence. He might favour Home Rule, but he was extremely averse to anything that might resemble 'bidding' between the two English parties for Irish votes. 'Apart from the term of whig and tory, there is one thing', he said in a well-remembered appeal, 'I will endeavour to impress upon you, and it is this. It will be a vital danger to the country and to the empire, if at a time when a demand from Ireland for larger powers of self-government is to be dealt with, there is not in parliament a party totally independent of the Irish vote.'[2] And he added a little later, 'for a government in a minority to deal with the Irish Question would not be safe'. If bidding was to be avoided, then Gladstone argued that proposals for Irish reform should come from the Government of the day. 'It is not', he wrote to Lord Rosebery, 'the province of the person leading the party in opposition to frame and produce before the public detailed schemes of such a class.'[3] From these premises he

---

[1] *Eminent Victorians* (London, 1918), pp. 272–3.
[2] November 9, 1885. Quoted in Morley, *Gladstone*, Vol. III, pp. 237–8.
[3] Ibid., p. 239. Letter dated November 13, 1885.

argued that his support of Home Rule would destroy all reasonable hope of its adoption. Such a plan proposed by the Liberal Party would have to face the opposition of the Tories *en bloc*, and this opposition and 'the appeals with which it will be accompanied', he added prophetically, 'will render the carrying of the measure, difficult even by a united Liberal Party, hopeless, should there be serious defection'. He concluded, 'The idea of constituting a legislature for Ireland . . . will cause a mighty heave in the body politic. It will be as difficult to carry the Liberal party and the two British nations in favour of a legislature for Ireland, as it was easy to carry them in the case of Irish disestablishment.'

The dislike of 'bidding' for the Irish vote, the danger of arousing uncompromising and unrelenting Tory opposition to all proposals for Irish self-government, the risk of Liberal division—these were the negative reasons for Gladstone's silence in 1885. That they were reinforced by something more positive was indicated by some casual references in letters published in Morley's biography, and was confirmed by the publication, in Sir Robert Ensor's *England, 1870–1914*, of some hitherto unpublished documents in the Gladstone papers.[1] From this evidence it becomes clear that Gladstone, reluctant in any case to embark on so doubtful a venture at the age of seventy-six, hoped that Lord Salisbury, despite the opposition of the old Tories, would carry Home Rule with Liberal and Nationalist support. Such a prospect did not appear altogether improbable. Parnell's negotiations with Carnarvon and Salisbury were known to Gladstone from information supplied by Parnell himself. Though the actual content was not revealed, the conversations could concern only one subject—the measure of self-government to be granted to Ireland. Parnell had attempted to secure better terms from Gladstone, but Gladstone's response was decided.

I am aware of . . . the altered attitude of the Tory Party, and I presume its heightened bidding. It is right I should say that into any counter-bidding of any sort against Lord R. Churchill I for one cannot enter.[2]

This firm and high-principled refusal to bid against the Conservative Government naturally induced Parnell to continue the Carnarvon-Salisbury conversations. But when invited by Parnell (through Mrs

---

[1] Op. cit. vide Appendix A, p. 558 et seq.
[2] Dated August 8th.

E

O'Shea) in late October to consider a paper on Home Rule policy, Gladstone drafted two replies; the first was never sent; the second, which Parnell received a few days before the election, was entirely non-committal. The first draft, after reminding Parnell that Gladstone could not enter into competition with the Conservatives 'upon the question of how much or how little can be done for Ireland in the way of self-government', continued:

Further I have seen it argued that Mr Parnell and his allies ought to seek a settlement of this Question from the party now in office, and I am not at all inclined to dissent from this opinion, for I bear in mind the history of the years 1829, 1846 and 1867 as illustrative of the respective capacity of the two parties to deal under certain circumstances with sharply controverted matters. In this view no question can arise from those connected with the Liberal Party until the Ministers have given their reply upon a subject which they are well entitled to have submitted to them.

It is easy to understand why this too revealing draft was never sent, for Gladstone's idea was quite simply that of a Tory initiative backed by the Liberal party for an Irish settlement enacted with some, but not undue regard for Irish wishes. Influenced by the precedents of Catholic Emancipation (1829), of the Repeal of the Corn Laws (1846), of the Second Reform Bill (1867), Gladstone considered that the repeal of the Union could most surely be carried by a Conservative Government, supported by Liberal votes to counterbalance the defection of the extremist Tories. And that belief underlay both his reluctance to take office and his long silence on the question of Home Rule. Lord Salisbury, too, had thought of a 'forward' policy. But whilst Gladstone might contemplate disruption in Tory ranks not without some satisfaction, Salisbury pondered the fate of Peel in '46 and remembered Lord Randolph, his brilliant and ambitious lieutenant so admirably equipped to play the part of Disraeli.[1] But in any event, the Conservative Party in 1885 was so different in character from that of half a century or even twenty years earlier, as to render illusory any prospect of executing such a manœuvre with success. Gladstone might well have remembered that while historians often repeat themselves, history rarely does.

[1] Vide Ensor's opinion, op. cit., Appendix A, pp. 558–62.

The result of the election put a very different complexion on Salisbury's pact and Gladstone's reticence alike. For the Nationalists, though returned in much increased numbers, were not strong enough to maintain the Conservatives in office. Pressure from within the party urged Salisbury to drop his allies, at all times uncongenial and now of slight Parliamentary value. At the same time Parnell approached Gladstone once more. The veteran leader, still anxious to retain the Conservatives in office, realized that only the most judicious reserve on his side could induce the Conservative Premier to sponsor a 'forward' Irish policy. A Conservative-Nationalist majority had not materialized, but Gladstone still nursed the hope that Salisbury might play the role of Peel. And so by early December 1885 he was moved, it would seem, by two considerations; first, that Home Rule was necessary, possibly even inevitable and second, that any such measure would be better enacted by the Tories. On the first point, he had before him a memorandum dated December 11, 1885, by James Bryce, recently returned from a visit to Ireland.[1] Bryce reported that 'the general feeling in Dublin, and among educated men in Ireland generally, outside of Ulster, is that things cannot longer go on in their present State. . . . The success at the election of the Parnellite candidates, coupled with the conduct of the present ministry, has given rise to a feeling of contempt for the authority of Parliament. One is told everywhere that many persons, especially young men of education, are going over to the Nationalist party.' All this accorded with and no doubt reinforced conclusions Gladstone had already reached. But how were they best to be implemented? There is among his papers a note, somewhat smudged, in his hand dated 'D.12.'85'. The more relevant points read:

1   Irish Question ought to be handled without delay.
2   And if possible by Tories with aid of Nationalists.
3   As they are half the House of Commons, this would *warrant* the adoption of a waiting policy by the Liberals.
4   The basis ought to be:
    a perfect political equality of Ireland with England and Scotland
    b Equitable, not illiberal, partition of Imperial Charges
    c Protection for the Irish minority

---

[1] *Gladstone Papers* British Museum Add Ms. 44770 ff. 5–14.
See also Fisher, op. cit., Vol. I, p. 211, for Bryce's later recollections of his visit.

d Management of Irish affairs, legislation and administration by
  Irish authority.
5 But *if* Tories and Nationalists part company, what then?[1]

What—indeed?

Gladstone did not content himself with writing notes on possible
developments. On the contrary three days later, on December 15,
1885, he took strange and precipitate action to further what he deemed
to be the appropriate policy. Without consulting any of his colleagues,
he drove over that day to see Arthur Balfour at Eaton Hall, where he
was staying as the guest of the Duke of Westminster, to tell him he
believed that, unless Home Rule were granted immediately, there
would be disorder and assassination in England as well as in Ireland.
Whatever the prospect, and it was clearly very slight, of his unsought
advice being carefully weighed by the Tory leaders, it was lost the
next day, December 16th, when Herbert Gladstone by one costly
indiscretion destroyed the harvest his father still hoped to reap. The
details of the son's unhappy disclosure are of no interest, in comparison
with the one plain fact, that Herbert Gladstone inadvertently communi-
cated to the press the news of his father's conversion to Home Rule.
Denial and subterfuge were no longer possible. The news published to
the world on December 17, 1885, heralded the most dramatic party
conflict of the century.

Lord Salisbury saw the Hawarden kite flying in the sky and he
hastened to drop his compromising allies; Lord Hartington saw it also,
and he warned Gladstone of the coming breach; Chamberlain observed
it with doubt and irritation; and Parnell watched it, another kingmaker
determined not to perish on a later Barnet field. Gladstone, secluded
at Hawarden, saw it too, saw the final frustration of his slowly maturing
plans and yet with a resolute determination, remarkable indeed in a
man entering on his seventy-seventh year, prepared to convert the
country and his party to the policy of Home Rule for Ireland. On the
evening of the fatal day, December 17, 1885, the son, in staccato sentences and an unusual metaphor recorded in his diary:

Fat all in the fire. *Standard* publishes 'Authentic plan' of Mr G. and the
evening papers and telegraph agencies go wild. . . . Hawarden flooded
with telegrams and all the world is agog. The NPA has sent [*sic*] the
whole cat out. . . . Father quite *compos*.[2]

[1] *Gladstone Papers*, ibid. Add. Ms. 44770, ff 15–16.
[2] Lord Gladstone, *After Thirty Years* (London, 1928), pp. 312–13.

But the father in his diary referred but casually to 'telegrams on the Irish rumours about me' and concluded 'worked much on MS. Huxley controversy'. Gladstone was seeking to defend the literal truth of the account of the Creation given in the Book of Genesis and the dialectical embers kindled by this dispute were not to be damped down even by the events of this unfortunate day. His article *Proem to Genesis* was posted on it to *The Nineteenth Century* and when it appeared in January 1886, it was a stock jest to ask 'Have you read Gladstone's Genesis' and to answer 'I'm waiting for his Exodus'.[1]

THE HOME RULE GOVERNMENT

Even now Gladstone did not abandon all hope of a Tory initiative. On December 20th he wrote to Arthur Balfour, repeating the warnings he had given on the December 15th and adding that, in his opinion, it would be a calamity, if the settlement of the Irish question should become a matter of party conflict and that it might best be dealt with by 'the *present* Government', who could be assured of his general goodwill and support. The invitation to public-spirited self-immolation— for such it was—left the Tory leaders incredulous, suspicious and, in the case of Lord Randolph Churchill, irreverent. On Christmas Day 1885 he wrote to Labouchère,[2] '*Very Private*. GOM has written what is described to me as a 'marvellous letter' to Arthur Balfour, to the effect that he thinks 'it will be a public calamity if this great question should fall into the lines of party conflict' and saying that he desires that the question should be settled by the present Government. He be damned!' There was nothing left in fact but for Gladstone to see, what had for some time been apparent to most observers, that responsibility for a final settlement of the Irish question was to be his and not anothers.'

Lord Salisbury resigned on January 28, 1886, after defeat by Liberal and Irish votes and on January 30th, Gladstone was invited by the Queen to form his third administration. The names of his Cabinet colleagues were made known on February 3rd. Though Gladstone's conversion to Home Rule was no longer a secret, the public and indeed his colleagues still remained unaware of the measure of Home Rule to be conceded. A heavy penalty was now to be exacted for the well-intentioned, but unfortunate, tactics of the previous year. Gladstone's

---

[1] Magnus, op. cit., pp. 348–9.
[2] R. R. James, *Lord Randolph Churchill* (London, 1959), p. 226.

apparently sudden conversion threw into opposition men who otherwise might have been conciliated. Of his leading colleagues, Chamberlain, Hartington, Bright, Harcourt, Selborne and James, only Harcourt
and Chamberlain joined the Cabinet, and within two months Chamberlain had resigned. Yet the Cabinet was not unimpressive. Harcourt
became Chancellor of the Exchequer, Hugh Childers Home Secretary,
Lord Rosebery went to the Foreign Office, and Lord Spencer, recognizing that firm government was now impractical, accepted the Lord
Presidency of the Council as token of his highly significant conversion.
John Morley, a most ardent Home Ruler, accepted the thankless post of
Chief Secretary. When Bright met him for the first time in the Lobby
after his appointment he said, 'Do you know what I say about you?'—
'What do you say?'—'I keep wondering whether it is courage or folly
in you.' Morley speculated on whether the question was prompted by
good nature or good manners. But Huxley expressed himself unam-
biguously. Having 'his own quarrels with Mr Gladstone about Gadarene swine and other critical affairs', as the agnostic Morley happily
records, Huxley's low opinion of the Prime Minister may perhaps be
discounted. 'Ah, he is sending you, my dear friend, to Ireland', Huxley
remarked, 'as he sent Gordon to Khartoum. I advise you to look out
for yourself; that's all.'[1]

With the notable exception of Chamberlain all the leading members
of the Cabinet were strong supporters of Home Rule and carried with
them the great bulk of the Liberal Party. Despite the secession of
Whigs and Radicals, despite the sundering of old and valued friendships as that between Morley and Chamberlain, the Liberals fought the
battle of Home Rule with a vigour and vitality that made the struggle
the most memorable in the annals of English parliamentary history.
Above all the veteran Prime Minister, with unflagging energy and
unswerving courage, set off on his last crusade. The Bill might be
defeated, but the Liberals, having inscribed it on their banner, were
determined that once for all the spirit of Anglo-Irish relations was to
be changed. Sir William Harcourt spoke no more than the sober truth
when he warned the Unionists:

You may reject this Bill, but its record will remain. The history of
England and Ireland can never be as if this offer had never been made. You
may kill it now, but its ghost will ever haunt your festivals of coercion.[2]

---

[1] Morley, *Recollections*, Vol. I, pp. 221–2.
[2] Hansard's *Parl. Deb.*, Vol. CCCIV, Col. 1458.

No better illustration of the strength of the case for Home Rule is to be found than the presence of men of such widely different outlook as Spencer, Morley and Rosebery in a Cabinet pledged to enact a measure, so profoundly distasteful to the vast majority of Englishmen. Moreover, the support that was given to Gladstone was ungrudging, even though the reason for it varied. Lord Spencer—whose departure from Ireland with the change of government in the summer of 1885 was signalized by an article in *United Ireland* despatching to his 'lugubrious limbo' a Viceroy who had shown that Liberal rule 'in the last quarter of the nineteenth century can be as savage and unbearable as in the days of the worst of monsters',[1] such as Carew and Cromwell—was a Home Ruler because party politics made a prolonged trial of resolute government impossible; Morley because it appeared the just solution of the Irish Question; Lord Rosebery because he thought it a rather unpleasant necessity. Few Liberals, indeed, were able to preserve the detachment essential for assessing the policy on its merits. The split in the party produced recriminations that inevitably influenced judgement. Nor did the advocacy of Home Rule come easily to those who had followed Gladstone in his denunciation of Home Rule only a few years earlier. Yet the majority backed him in his new course, because they sensed that he was right.

The choice of a young Liberal elected to Parliament for the first time in November 1885, open-minded, unshackled by the past, scrupulous, without marked ambition, who felt it was open to him without inconsistency to be either a Home Ruler or a Unionist, has a more than personal significance. His name was Edward Grey, better remembered as Lord Grey of Fallodon. 'That a man of Mr. Gladstone's importance should advocate Home Rule was a fact so arresting', he recalled later, 'as to make me feel the necessity for thought: the suddenness of the change puzzled and made me doubt. Then I came across the articles written by John Morley in the *Pall Mall Gazette*. . . . They seemed irresistible in their argument that coercion was not, under modern conditions, possible as a permanent system of governing Ireland. The only alternative was Home Rule. I was intellectually convinced.'[2]

Lord Rosebery, too, upon whom Gladstone, much to Chamberlain's chagrin, had showered high praises that marked him out for the Liberal succession, was intellectually but reluctantly converted to Home Rule.

---

[1] *United Ireland*, June 13, 1885.
[2] *Twenty-Five Years 1892–1916* (8th Edition, London, 1935), 3 Vols., Vol. I, pp. 39–40.

His reasoning, typical product of the mind of this gifted political amateur, was founded on illusions. 'I detest separation', he wrote to Reginald Brett, 'and feel that nothing could make me agree to it. Home Rule, however, is a necessity both for us and for the Irish. They will have it within two years, at the latest. Scotland will follow and then England. When that is accomplished Imperial Federation will cease to be a dream.'[1] In public speeches he struck a stirring note.

'Are you as weary as we are', he said to the electors of Glasgow, 'of that fatal and dreary policy of giving Ireland everything except that which she wants and that which according to every principle of Liberalism . . . she has a right to obtain.'

But more than thirty eventful years were to pass before the English people finally tired of that fatal policy.

THE SECESSION OF THE WHIGS

In retrospect past events are apt to slip into place as links in an unbreakable chain. One wonders, not why a thing happened, but merely why contemporaries failed to see that it was inevitable. And yet such an event as the defeat of the first Home Rule Bill does give rise to doubts. If Parnell had not thrown the Irish vote on the Conservative side, if Gladstone had not maintained his unprofitable silence in the autumn of '85, if his son had not been indiscreet, or even if later the father had been more conciliatory to his colleagues, above all to Chamberlain, would the Bill have been defeated by thirty votes? And if it had not been defeated might not the Irish Question have pursued a happier and a more peaceful way to the same goal as it has reached by more devious and violent paths today? Idle perhaps to speculate on what might have been, but not unprofitable to ponder the pardonable though not inevitable mistakes of English statesmen—and of an Irish leader—in one of the three most critical years in the history of Anglo-Irish relations.

Gladstone was prepared for the secession of the Whigs. In his second Cabinet an uneasy balance had been preserved between Hartington and the Radical Chamberlain. Opposition even to moderate constitutional reform in Ireland had made it plain that the former would never swallow Home Rule. Gladstone, however, having assembled

[1] Lord Crewe, *Lord Rosebery* (London, 1931), 2 Vols., Vol. I, pp. 279-80.

and studied some of Hartington's more important pronouncements on Irish policy[1] sought to persuade him at least to keep an open mind till the Home Rule proposals were formulated. But his success was only in respect of the timing of the breach. Hartington did not, as Gladstone had feared, feel it his duty at the opening of the new session in January 1886 to declare his determination to 'maintain the Legislative Union' and so 'proclaim a policy of absolute resistance without examination to the demand made by Ireland through five-sixths of her members'.[2] But his silence indicated no shift in his opinions. While he complained that he found Gladstone increasingly unintelligible, he was clear from what he did understand that he was opposed in principle to Gladstone's Irish policy. When the new Ministry was in course of formation in early February, James Bryce saw Gladstone sitting on the Front Opposition Bench 'in a long and earnest conversation with Hartington, who sat erect, stiff, and stolid, saying very little while Gladstone plied him with argument. One knew how much was going to turn upon that talk and felt the significance of Hartington's unyielding look'.[3] Yet the secession of Hartington and the Whigs, though expected, was profoundly regretted. All Gladstone Cabinets, with the exception of the last, had a strongly aristocratic tinge. He believed the presence of such men to be an asset and once he spoke 'of the old and invaluable habit of Liberal England which looked to a Liberal aristocracy and to a Liberal leisured class as the natural and therefore the best leaders of the Liberal movement'. The Home Rule Bill had among its consequences the final loss of such leadership and in consequence the enduring hostility of the Lords to the Liberal party. Before the election Hartington wrote to Gladstone explaining that, while he had done as much as he could in the past to minimize his differences with Chamberlain in respect both of domestic and foreign policy, he believed the hope of avoiding disruption in the party to be vain, quite regardless of any possible split on Irish policy. He urged Gladstone to take a strong and decided line against the Radicals—who in a few months were to be his allies. Towards the end of December Hartington indicated unmistakably that he could not join a Home Rule Government.[4] From that attitude he never wavered. He refused all

[1] *Gladstone Papers*, Add. Ms. 44770. f235.
[2] Agatha Ramm, *The Political Correspondence of Mr Gladstone and Lord Granville 1876–1886* (Oxford, 1962), 2 Vols., Vol. II, *1759*.
[3] Fisher, op. cit. Vol. I, p. 213.
[4] The correspondence is published in Bernard Holland, *The Life of Spencer Compton, Eighth Duke of Devonshire* (London, 1911), 2 Vols., Chapter XXI.

Gladstone's invitations to do so, on the ground that he disagreed fundamentally with the new Irish policy.

The secession of Hartington and his Whig followers was a more serious blow to the prestige than to the actual voting strength of the Liberal Government. Gladstone had taken considerable pains to conciliate Hartington, who received in the summer of 1884 one of the earliest indications that a separate legislature for Ireland would have to be considered when the Liberals returned to power.[1] A public statement by Gladstone before the election could only have hastened the day of disruption. Yet that the breach with Hartington should have come on Irish policy at a most critical moment, when it might have come, as indeed Hartington himself thought it should have come, on general policy one or two years earlier, had unfavourable reactions on the prospects for Home Rule. Even in the event many of the Whig leaders including Kimberley, Spencer and Harcourt, did not follow Hartington in his refusal to accept office in Gladstone's administration. Lord Granville, too, joined the Cabinet and, as his biographer tells us, 'like Peirithous in the Athenian legend, he plunged after his king into the gulf'.[2] This inspiring spectacle afforded no pleasure to Hartington, who supposed to the last that all the Whig leaders would support his refusal. This division in their ranks reinforces the conviction that Gladstone would have been wiser to effect the breach earlier. Had he been less conciliatory, Hartington would have resigned on general policy and so his immense personal influence would not have been thrown with such effect in the scales against Home Rule. For if Lord Hartington was slow, he was also greatly respected both in Parliament and in the country. The weight of his opposition may not lightly be discounted. Admirers of Lytton Strachey[3] will recall the portrait of a man beloved by the British people because 'they could always be absolutely certain that he would never, in any circumstances, be either brilliant, or subtle, or surprising, or impassioned, or profound. As they sat, listening to his speeches, in which considerations of stolid plainness succeeded one another with complete flatness, they felt, involved and supported by the colossal tedium, that their confidence was finally assured'. But that portrait would not lead us to suppose that Lord Hartington, one of the ablest debaters of the day, delivered perhaps the most effective denunciation of the Home Rule Bill in the House. The

---

[1] Lord Fitzmaurice, *The Life of the Second Earl Granville* (London, 1905), 2 Vols., Vol. II, p. 461.
[2] Fitzmaurice, op. cit., Vol. II, p. 489.   [3] *Eminent Victorians*, pp. 285-7.

speech was ponderous, but even in the dusty columns of *Hansard* the words of this Anglo-Irish landlord convey—it is a remarkable achievement—an impression of cool, judicial, detachment.[1] There is no attempt to minimize the consequences of rejection, merely a balanced but authoritative statement of the case against change. Goschen perhaps came close to the truth, when he remarked that the Duke of Devonshire (as Hartington had then become) 'is like myself a moderate man, *a violently* moderate man'. Lord Hartington also had something in common with Parnell, a reticence, a certain aristocratic disdain best described by Harcourt as 'Hartington's you-be-damned-ness'. 'Once', recalled Herbert Gladstone,[2] 'Tim Healy was flashing out a bitter attack. Hartington was on the front Opposition Bench with his hat over his eyes, apparently asleep. Healy turned on him suddenly: "There is the noble Marquis. Like a pike at the bottom of a pool." Hartington's hat never stirred, but I saw his whole body shake with laughter.' Herbert Gladstone records that Hartington's failure to form any progressive views on the Irish Question was to many who had to part from him, little less than a tragedy. But on a personal plane, it was understandable. It was his brother, Lord Frederick Cavendish, who had been assassinated, even if not of deliberate intent, by the surgical knives of the Invincibles[3] in Phoenix Park in May 1882 and the recollection of the event is unlikely, apart from all other considerations, to have predisposed him favourably to Irish claims for self-government.[4] The opposition acquired no mean recruit when this man of solid ability, the heir to a great Whig dukedom, crossed the floor of the House.

THE SECESSION OF THE RADICALS

Gladstone, who had a profound distaste for Radicals, probably never understood Joseph Chamberlain. He shared to the full Parnell's

[1] It was after these sentences had been written that I came across James Bryce's contemporary impression. 'The best speech made against the Bill was, to my thinking, Hartington's on the First Reading.' See Fisher, op. cit., Vol. I, p. 214.

[2] Op. cit., p. 175.

[3] P. J. P. Tynan in *The Irish National Invincibles and Their Times* (London, 1894), purports to give an inside account of their motives and methods. See also P. S. O'Hegarty, op. cit., p. 154.

[4] Lady Frederick Cavendish was Mrs Gladstone's niece. She was with Gladstone immediately after the assassination and hoped even in that hour that her husband's death might serve as a sacrifice for peace. (Magnus, op. cit., p. 202, and Holland, op. cit., Vol. I, pp. 353–4.) She had great nobility of character and in her widowhood devoted much time and thought to the advancement of higher education for women. She was invited to become Mistress of Girton College, Cambridge, but declined.

illusion that Chamberlain was a friend of Irish self-government. The mistake indeed was pardonable. Chamberlain had taken an active part in securing the release of Parnell from Kilmainham, he had protested against coercion, he absented himself from a banquet in honour of his colleague Lord Spencer, he had opened the electoral campaign of 1885 with the famous declaration:

The pacification of Ireland at this moment depends, I believe, on the concession to Ireland of the right to govern itself in the matter of its purely domestic business. Is it not discreditable to us that even now it is only by unconstitutional means that we are able to secure peace and order in one portion of her Majesty's dominions? It is a system as completely centralized and bureaucratic as that with which Russia governs Poland, or as that which prevailed in Venice under Austrian rule. An Irishman at this moment cannot move a step . . . without being confronted with, interfered with, controlled by an English official, appointed by a foreign government, and without a shade or shadow of representative authority. I say the time has come to reform altogether the absurd and irritating anachronism which is known as Dublin Castle.[1]

Is it surprising that even politicians so experienced as Gladstone and Parnell failed to understand that such incisive language concealed unrelenting opposition to Home Rule? Yet the failure was to prove costly indeed, and gibing references in debate to those eloquent sentences on Poland and Venice were to provide indifferent compensation for the loss of radical votes.

The rather fine distinction which Chamberlain drew between his own proposals for federal devolution and Gladstone's Home Rule policy was more important than it appeared[2] and Chamberlain's insistence upon its validity even to the point of resignation from the Cabinet on March 23rd was not a matter for cavil or surprise. It is undeniable, too, that he was treated with scant consideration by Gladstone. Had the latter been less secretive, had he consulted Chamberlain at the time of his conversion to Home Rule, had he been more conciliatory in respect of Chamberlain's reasonable representations on behalf of his political associates, persuasion might have yielded happier fruits.

But doubts intrude, Chamberlain was ambitious; he had resented the compliments showered on Rosebery; he was jealous of Morley's

---

[1] Speech of June 17, 1885. Quoted Morley, *Gladstone*, Vol. III, pp. 233-4.
[2] See below, p. 159-163.

promotion; and while it would be ungenerous to say that the motives which drove him into opposition were those of an ambitious self-seeking man, yet it is difficult to believe that his rigid insistence upon a distinction between Home Rule and Federal devolution was not powerfully reinforced by a growing personal antagonism to the Liberal leader. Not for nothing did Morley liken him to 'the envious Casca' and Gladstone, the most generous of opponents, said of Chamberlain in the House of Commons: 'He has trimmed his vessel, he has touched his rudder in such a masterly way that in whichever direction the winds of heaven may blow they must fill his sails.' The passage of time, the distinguished, if in one case controversial, national record of the Chamberlains have combined to soften, but not to reverse, that verdict.

The defection was final. Not only was Chamberlain's opposition to Home Rule bitter and unrelenting for the remainder of his life, not only were his speeches in Parliament decisive, but the loss of the Radical vote in industrial England was a blow from which the Liberal Party never recovered. As Sir Robert Ensor pointed out,[1] London and Lancashire as well as Birmingham voted heavily against Home Rule in subsequent elections and the radicalism dominant behind Gladstone after 1886 was that of districts hitherto in the background. The Liberal party came to depend visibly on the Celtic fringe and save in the landslide election of 1906 the party never again won an English majority. Parnell was right when he said Chamberlain had killed Home Rule and today it may be asked whether he had not signed the death warrant of the Liberal party as well.

The intervention of John Bright, less spectacular than that of Chamberlain, was but little less effective. A contemporary and personal friend of Gladstone, a champion of Ireland in earlier days when her English friends were few indeed, Bright was an elder statesman whose prestige was second only to that of the great Liberal leader. Curiously enough the influence he exercised on the fortunes of Home Rule was due to the entirely mistaken belief that he had an open mind on Irish policy. Nothing could have been further from the truth. When he first heard of Home Rule he condemned it out of hand, saying that to have two legislative assemblies in the United Kingdom would be 'an intolerable mischief'.[2] His unflattering opinion of Irishmen strengthened

[1] Op. cit., p. 207.
[2] Letter of January 20, 1872. This and following extracts are taken from letters printed in G. M. Trevelyan, *John Bright* (London, 1925), pp. 444–8.

his conviction. 'Tell the merchant', he said, 'he must not rely for one moment on Home Rule for any one thing that is wise or good, nor indeed on any combination of Irishmen.' Parnell he termed a rebel and early in '86 he counselled Chamberlain, 'If the *rebel* party were not *rebels* an arrangement would not be difficult, but with *rebels*, how can one negotiate with or trust them.' To his friend Gladstone he was entirely frank, stating in May 1886, 'I think your Bill is full of complexity and gives no hope.' Yet in spite of these opinions Bright was invited to the famous conference in Committee Room 15—invitations to which were issued not to unequivocal opponents of Home Rule as Lord Hartington but to 'Liberal members who being in favour of some sort of autonomy for Ireland' disapproved of the terms of Gladstone's Bill. Bright did not go, but sent a letter expressing his own intention of voting against the Bill on the second reading. Chamberlain read out the letter and afterwards admitted that its effect on the 'trimmers' was decisive. John Bright had hammered another nail in the coffin of Home Rule—and yet Gladstone felt no personal resentment. A chance meeting in a London street some two years after the defeat of Home Rule brought these two venerable survivors of early Victorian England face to face. John Bright recorded the conversation in his diary and recorded, too, that at parting Gladstone 'took his glove off to shake hands with me as indicating more cordiality of feeling'. But Joseph Chamberlain was not forgiven.

PARNELL'S MISCALCULATION

In the autumn of 1885 Parnell said that, if the English would not concede self-government, at any rate the Irish would determine which English party was to hold office. In the event such a prospect was not fulfilled, for while Parnell could turn either Conservatives or Liberals out after the election he could keep only the Liberals in. This simple fact imposed a serious limitation on his independence, a limitation that made an understanding with the Liberals a necessity. So it was only in a negative sense that the Nationalists controlled the parliamentary destinies of the British Isles in 1886.

Parnell had miscalculated in anticipating that the Nationalists would hold an unrestricted balance of power in the new Parliament. His political judgment would seem to have been more seriously in question in counselling that the Irish vote in British constituencies should be cast against Liberal and Radical candidates and in effect therefore on the

Conservative side. Contemporary politicians, including Salisbury and Morley, reckoned that the Irish vote was worth twenty-five to forty seats and, while this cannot be regarded as established fact, there seems little reason to doubt their estimate. Parnell's election manifesto in handing over these seats to the Conservatives had in fact ensured the defeat of Home Rule in the Commons. Even if only twenty-five seats had been decided by the Irish vote they would have been sufficient to reverse the verdict in the House some six months later. To all appearances the Irish leader had made the one disastrous political blunder of his career—and yet one hesitates to pronounce confident judgment, for Parnell had to weigh imponderables whose substance defies analysis to this day.

The Catholic clergy were profoundly concerned with the threat in the Radicals' 'unauthorized programme' to Church schools. What would have been the force of an edict from Parnell instructing the Irish in Britain to vote for candidates some of whom at least incurred the open hostility of the Catholic clergy because of their attitude on the Schools question? Might it not have meant a divided and therefore ineffective vote?[1] In so far as *United Ireland* may be regarded as the mouthpiece of radical, constitutional nationalism, opinion in Ireland inclined towards the Tories both for this particular reason and also on more general considerations. 'On religious and educational grounds', stated an editorial of June 20, 1885 'the Irish people approach much nearer to those of the English Church party than they do to the Radicals . . .' More generally it was noted that if the Tories ceased to be the landlords' party and 'cut off its Orange tail . . . the Irish question is settled'. These were big 'ifs'. But on the other hand there was no doubt that had Parnell thrown the Irish vote on the Liberal side, he had to anticipate the defeat of Home Rule in the Lords; and in addition a possible Liberal majority over Conservatives and Nationalists combined. Had the latter contingency materialized Gladstone doubtless would have been forced either to modify his plans in order to conciliate colleagues, or else to resign the leadership of the party. In either event the course of Irish self-government would have been retarded. Then again Parnell had reached some implicit understanding with Salisbury; Gladstone had maintained a mystifying silence. When Parnell made his choice the political prospect was unusually obscure. Dr

[1] On this point see especially C. H. D. Howard, *The Parnell Manifesto of November 21, 1885 and the Schools Question*. English Historical Review. Vol. LXII, No. 242. January 1947, pp. 42–51.

Cruise O'Brien lends the weight of his authority to the view that in these circumstances the policy of a tactical alliance with the Tories was in itself 'perfectly correct' even though undercurrents in the Irish party and 'the incalculable momentum that accompanies any grave political choice' carried it 'to the extreme of administering an insulting rebuff to a radical section, whose secession was to defeat the Home Rule Bill'.[1] But if such an alliance was tactically correct, does not that suggest, as indeed may well be the case, that even by 1885 Parnell had become the prisoner of his own tactical conceptions? Had he not, also, something to learn by looking at the question as it was? Was it really within the bounds of political possibility at any time that Lord Salisbury, who in May of the following year was speaking of Ireland as not one but two nations and suggesting, even if in an unguarded moment, that the Irish might be numbered with those races, like the Hottentots or even the Hindoos, who were incapable of self-government,[2] and his principal lieutenant, Lord Randolph Churchill, so well remembered for his most effective and inflammatory anti-Home Rule intervention in Ulster, would have sacrificed party and personal position—and no less would have been required of them—in order to give a form of government to Ireland, to which neither of them were committed by principle and to which both of them were by instinct opposed? That Parnell miscalculated in political terms seems the harder to dispute the more the evidence of the inner feelings of Conservative leaders is revealed; what remains doubtful is whether any decision taken by the Irish leader could have exercised a decisively favourable influence on the destiny of Home Rule.

The more closely the political scene of 1886 is examined, the stronger grows the conviction that even the most skilful use of the Irish votes could not ensure the repeal of the Union. For in the last analysis the decision lay, not with Parnell, but with the English parties. Parnell had built up a coherent, disciplined phalanx pledged to the cause of Home Rule. It was a remarkable achievement—but it did not alter the decisive fact that the Nationalists could never hope to return more than a small minority of members to the House of Commons. Eighty-six members followed the 'uncrowned king' to Westminster after the election, but that number represented the high tide of Nationalist success. The eighty-six of '86 was not destined to be surpassed. So it was by tactics alone that Parnell could hope to decide the issue of the day; and tactics were not enough with the Liberals, who were his

[1] Op. cit., p. 118. [2] *The Annual Register*, 1886, p. 181.

natural allies in the Commons and in the country unable to command a majority in the Lords.

THE LIBERAL-NATIONALIST ENTENTE

While the defeat of the Home Rule Bill in the House of Commons may not be attributed conclusively to Parnell's decision to throw the Irish vote on the Conservative side at the election, yet that decision had unhappy consequences. The Irish manifesto threw the Liberals, in constituencies where there was an Irish vote, into direct and angry antagonism to the Irish cause and its leaders. Passions were roused, things were said that were not easily forgotten, and in consequence, as Morley recalled, the task of conversion in 1886, difficult in any case, was made a thousand times more difficult still by the arguments and antipathies of the electoral battle of 1885.[1] The record of Gladstone's second administration, as it had been depicted in colourful electoral phrases by Nationalist speakers, was in itself sufficient to widen the gulf between the Liberal and the Irish Party. Yet such recriminations, the result in part of the Parnell Manifesto of November 21, 1885, heralded the birth of the Liberal-Nationalist entente. While it never attained the rigidity of a formal alliance, the understanding between the two parties was destined to endure. It was a most important political consequence of the events of 1886.

The strength of the Liberal-Nationalist entente was tested in the summer of 1886. For Gladstone, defeated by thirty votes on the second reading of the Home Rule Bill in the early morning of June 8, 1886, decided to appeal to the country. The new allies fared badly. Three hundred and ninety-four seats fell to the Unionists (a number which included 78 dissentient Liberals), while Home Rule mustered but 276 supporters, made up of 191 Liberals and 85 Nationalists. The verdict was decisive, for it showed that the country was more opposed to Home Rule than the House. Many reasons are advanced to explain the aversion of Englishmen to Home Rule. Racial and religious antipathies aroused by the Ulster Question, the English working man's dislike of Irish competitors in the labour market, the growing Imperialist reaction, a characteristic distrust of a final and radical solution of a political question all contributed to the result. But perhaps the decisive blow was struck by the territorial aristocracy. The English people, as Bagehot remarked, were a 'deferential people'. For the first time at this

[1] *Gladstone*, Vol. III, pp. 244–5.

election a virtually united peerage, fighting for the future of the landed interest in Ireland, threw its influence in the scale against the Liberal Party. The support of the great Whig magnates had passed under the lead of Hartington from Liberals to Conservatives. and this defection involved a loss of votes in rural constituencies that could be ill afforded.

Despite the double disaster of defeat in the Commons and defeat in the country, the Liberal Party did not waver in its allegiance to Home Rule. Yet its leaders lived under no illusions. 'You have no regrets at the course we took?' enquired Gladstone some four years later. 'None,' replied John Morley, 'none. It was inevitable. I have never doubted. That does not prevent bitter lamentation that inevitable it was.'

After 1886 a reaction set in and electoral omens improved. By the late autumn of 1890 the 'quicksilver stood delightfully high' in the Liberal barometer, but the hopes of Home Rulers were dashed in a moment by the news of Parnell's fall. 'History was ransacked for a parallel. Parnell was Mirabeau, in whom private fault destroyed a saviour of his country. He was Robespierre brought to the scaffold at the reaction of Thermidor. He was the Satan of *Paradise Lost* "hurled with hideous ruin and combustion down".'[1] But these unromantic comparisons of Victorian England could not banish uneasy foreboding from the minds of Liberals, trying to counteract the fissiparous character of the Nationalist party and understanding full well that the enactment of Home Rule was now indefinitely postponed. The situation was worsened by the letter Gladstone wrote, and which in haste and with encouragement from Harcourt he decided to publish, saying that the continuance of Mr Parnell at the present moment in the leadership of the Irish Party 'would render my retention of the leadership of the Liberal party, based as it has been mainly upon the prosecution of the Irish cause, almost a nullity'.[2] It was a letter, the publication of which did great and lasting damage to Gladstone's reputation in Ireland.

Gladstone formed a fourth Cabinet in August 1892, he introduced a second Home Rule Bill, it passed the Commons to be thrown out by the Lords. But in fact no progress had been made, for faith had been dimmed by disaster, the desire for resolute action had gone and the Liberal Cabinet declined the risk of an appeal to the people, as Gladstone wished, to challenge the veto of the Lords. Too well they

---

[1] Morley, *Recollections*, Vol. I., p. 251.
[2] Morley, *Gladstone*, Vol. III, pp. 436–7 and more generally pp. 430–40. For a recent, authoritative account of the episode see F. S. L. Lyons, *The Fall of Parnell 1890–91* (London, 1960), Chap. III generally and especially pp. 84–93.

remembered the summer of 1886. Morley in Dublin once again as Chief Secretary, in recalling a meeting with Asquith on October 25, 1893, reflects the pessimism of the time: 'A truly satisfactory man', he noted. 'Takes my view, and the view of everyone else, I should think, that there was never a political prospect so obscure, if only all political prospects were not obscure. We agreed that the chance of a Liberal majority at the general election is uncommonly slender. "Why did they give us one at the last election?" said Asquith. We agreed that a worse stroke of luck than such a majority had never befallen political leaders.'[1] When Morley, the man to whom Parnell paid so high a tribute in the last speech he ever made in England, voices such sentiments, then one understands the price exacted of the Liberal Party for its support of Home Rule.

The Liberal Party had been converted by Gladstone and while he remained leader, Home Rule was assured of unwavering support. His devotion to this solution of the Irish Question was well nigh fanatical in its intensity. M. Waddington, the French Ambassador to the Court of St James's, lamented Gladstone's absorption. In earlier days they could discuss other subjects—Gladstone would always rise to Homer or some other literary topic, but now even Homer failed and there was only Ireland, always Ireland. While he was brilliant as ever in point of language, his judgment, thought M. Waddington, was impaired, for one idea had full possession of his mind.[2] Even John Morley, hurriedly though he pushed aside the impious thought, felt that the GOM's undeviating fixity of purpose hindered the work of his last administration. It is probable indeed that a more flexible outlook on Ireland would have proved more popular in the House—but then Home Rule would not have been so ineffaceably inscribed on the creed of the Liberal party. For the last seven years of his political life Gladstone had lived wholly for the Irish Question, and though in 1892 he resigned ostensibly on another issue, it was really because his colleagues denied him the opportunity of a last electoral battle on Home Rule. He was then in his eighty-fifth year. 'Resigned!' he said in after years, 'I did not resign—I was put out.' Asquith has left a record of Gladstone's last Cabinet. Ministers were deeply moved and some of them on the verge of tears. Harcourt 'produced from his box and proceeded to read a well-thumbed MS. of highly elaborated eulogy'. Gladstone 'looked on with hooded eyes and tightened lips at this maladroit per-

---

[1] Morley, *Recollections*, Vol. I, pp. 373–4.
[2] Trevelyan, *Life of Bright*, p. 460.

formance', and was so little mollified that in after days he was accustomed to speak of this meeting as the 'blubbering Cabinet'.[1] On Home Rule Gladstone in truth had never wavered, and his successors, living under the shadow of a great name, could not be unmindful of an ideal, which had won the unstinted loyalty of the greatest of Liberal statesmen.

So the entente between Liberals and Nationalists, cordial at times but more often uneasy, continued to the last. Home Rule constituted the only bond of union between these strangely assorted allies and many of the planks in the Liberal programme at the landslide election of 1906 were as repellent to Nationalists as to Unionists. No Irish sympathies were stirred by the triumph song of Liberalism:

> The Churchman and the brewer we will drive them from the
>   land,
> For the Nonconformist children are marching hand in hand.

For in the Ireland of 1906, as in the Ireland of today, bishops were esteemed and brewers not only the most valued of citizens, but among the most substantial contributors to party funds. It must indeed have been with mixed feelings, that Irish Party veterans, seasoned campaigners of the Parnellite years, reassembled in a House in which their Liberal allies enjoyed the independence that an absolute majority affords and the invigoration of young and radical reinforcement. It was the least Anglican House of Commons since the Reformation, no less than 180 of its members being Protestant Dissenters.[2] Yet despite the wide gulf in outlook of which such things were symbolic, Campbell-Bannerman reaffirmed, in defiance of Rosebery, the Liberal allegiance to Home Rule. Lord Randolph Churchill was thinking of Gladstone when he challenged Chamberlain: 'That is the man you have deserted. How could you do it?' The Liberal Party could not—and when one reads again the moving eloquence of Gladstone's final appeal[3] for the passage of the first Home Rule Bill its loyalty seems justified indeed—

Ireland stands at your bar expectant, hopeful, almost suppliant. Her words are the words of truth and soberness. She asks a blessed oblivion

[1] Quoted in Spender and Asquith, *Life of Lord Oxford and Asquith* (London, 1932), 2 Vols., Vol. I, pp. 89–90.
[2] R. B. McCallum, *The Liberal Party from Earl Grey to Asquith* (London, 1963), p. 147.
[3] Hansard's *Parl. Deb.*, June 7, 1886, House of Commons, Vol. CCCVI, coll. 1239–40.

of the past, and in that oblivion our interest is deeper than even hers. My right Hon. Friend the Member for East Edinburgh (Mr Goschen) asks us tonight to abide by the traditions of which we are the heirs. What traditions? By the Irish traditions? Go into the length and breadth of the world, ransack the literature of all countries, find, if you can, a single voice, a single book, .. in which the conduct of England towards Ireland is anywhere treated except with profound and bitter condemnation. Are these the traditions by which we are exhorted to stand? No; they are a sad exception to the glory of our country. They are a broad and black blot upon the pages of its history; and what we want to do is stand by the traditions of which we are the heirs in all matters except our relations with Ireland. . . .

AFTERMATH

In the long, unhappy history of Anglo-Irish relations few events are more tragic than the rejection of Home Rule in 1886. The opportunity of settlement had come, perhaps the greatest of English statesmen was ready to grasp it, but the chance passed by through failures in perception, whose consequences not even time can wholly repair. Yet partly because the harvest never ripened, but still more because of the changed political outlook and preoccupations of later generations, the story of Home Rule is too often dismissed alternately with condescension or in Ireland with bitter contempt. Left-wing intellectuals in England, whose knowledge of the Irish Question could not be termed intimate by the friendliest of critics, maintain that the Gladstonian solution was superficial. For Gladstone, unaware of the economic basis of politics, suffered, in this view, from the illusion that the Anglo-Irish question was in fact, as in appearance, a political problem. Then on the other hand, Irish opinion, recalling all too well that the Nationalist party failed to achieve the one thing that could have justified its long sojourn at Westminster, has regarded Home Rule in retrospect as a carrot dangled by scheming English politicians before the nose of the Irish Donkey—a carrot always to be chased but never to be eaten. Neither criticism is entirely without foundation, yet both are unprofitable. Gladstone's policy can be judged only in relation to the Liberal principles which he professed. It is as idle to lament that the GOM viewed Irish problems with the eyes of a Liberal, not of a Marxist, nor of an Irish Nationalist, as it was for Wordsworth to deplore that

A primrose by the river's brim
A yellow primrose was to him
And it was nothing more.

To say that Liberal policy must be viewed in relation to Liberal principles is not to say that it offered the only possible or the best possible solution of the Irish Question. While it may reasonably be supposed that the enactment of Home Rule in 1886 (but not in 1914) would have allowed the peaceful re-emergence of an unpartitioned though possibly federal Irish state, it is clear that the renascence of Irish political and cultural nationalism that would almost certainly have followed, would not have afforded unmixed pleasure to Liberals. For in common with the vast majority of their fellow countrymen they did not comprehend the existence of an Irish mind and a distinctive Irish outlook. Liberals looked on the problem of Ireland as the great Whig historian once looked on those of India. As it was right, in Macaulay's eyes, that natives of the higher ranks should be educated for positions of responsibility in the English services, so it was right too that the Indians should be fitted for their future in a way which, intellectually, meant to detach them from their past and to graft them, if they could be grafted, on the stock of Western science and culture. 'The sceptre may pass from us. Victory may be inconstant to our arms. But there are triumphs which are followed by no reverse. There is an empire exempt from all natural cause of decay. Those triumphs are the pacific triumphs of reason over barbarism; that empire is the imperishable empire of our arts and our morals, our literature and our laws.'[1] Irish government was viewed with the same air of confident superiority, with the same lack of instinctive sympathy for another and an older civilization. The last lesson which intelligent, high-minded, Liberal Englishmen had to learn was that Irishmen had no more, and possibly even less, desire to have their affairs determined or their footsteps guided by intelligent, high-minded Liberal Englishmen than by that noxious, but part indigenous, ascendancy establishment which Gladstone had set out to destroy. If this proved for some of them too painful a lesson to absorb, that was partly because Liberal intentions towards Ireland while good indeed, were good with something of the terrible, devastating goodness of the unimaginative. The Gaelic League was a not unfitting reminder of the existence of a heritage other than theirs.

---

[1] This is quoted in G. M. Young's Introduction to his selection of *Speeches by Lord Macaulay* in the World's Classics.

While English Liberals and Irish Nationalists might see the distant scene in sharply contrasted colours, yet they were united in their immediate aim. Could that aim have been won, and could courageous statesmanship have achieved the obliteration of a sense of age-long injustice, future divisions could never have assumed the same bitter intensity. But it was not to be. The alliance forged by Gladstone and Parnell in 1886 in truth brought little fortune to either. For the history of Home Rule, the policy which alone could unite them, is a history of much endeavour, but no achievement. It is a story of violent controversy, in which statesmanlike vision and abysmal ignorance of Irish life, lofty purpose and sordid intrigue, generous action and mean betrayal, produce a picture of bewildering contrasts. It is a story that is told because one English party gave an allegiance, wavering and ineffective at the last, to the principle of self-government for Ireland; a story that might have had a climax, had that party pondered the detail, as well as the principle of its policy. 'Think, I beseech you', said Gladstone as in the early hours of June 8, 1886, the House of Commons listened in deathly silence to the ending of his speech on the first Home Rule Bill, 'think well, think wisely, think, not for the moment, but for the years that are to come, before you reject this Bill.'[1] Gladstone knew that the future of Ireland and of Anglo-Irish relations was at stake, but though some such suspicion would seem to have crossed his mind, he could not have known that the future of the Liberal Party was also weighed in the balance that night.

The influence of Irish policy upon the fortunes of the Liberal Party may not be determined with absolute precision. That it was destructive is clear, but whether it was fatal is open to doubt. It seems probable that the changing social conditions in England, so favourable to the growth of Labour, were in themselves sufficient to undermine its foundations; it is possible too that the system of power politics in Europe, with its recurrent threat of war, deprived Liberalism of its essential cosmopolitan background of free exchange of ideas and trade; it has been maintained that a party, whose creed was essentially political, was unfitted to solve the economic and social problems of later times, and it has been argued that the party perished simply because of internal dissension. It is certain that all these causes were contributory to the fall of the Liberal Party and to dissociate them in order to determine the exact effect of each is a task as difficult as it is unprofitable. Caesar's body bore the marks of many wounds; it is idle

[1] Hansard's *Parl. Deb.*, Vol. CCCVI, col. 1240.

to speculate how many of them were fatal. Suffice to say that the two parties which united in support of Home Rule in 1886 were to survive for but some thirty years, and then in 1916 in the midst of a world war the one was to be weakened by intrigues and personal rancour; the other to be the unnoticed and unlamented victim of an Easter Rising in the streets of that city, to which Parnell had aspired to restore the dignity of a National Parliament.

CHAPTER V

SOME ENGLISH STATESMEN AND THE IRISH QUESTION 1880–1914

When in office, the Liberals forget their principles and the Tories remember their friends.

TOM KETTLE

From the fall of Disraeli's last administration in 1880 till the outbreak of the Great War, there was general agreement amongst English states- men that the government of Ireland needed reform. But there existed a wide divergence of opinion as to the principle which should guide such reform. On the one hand Gladstone was convinced that an Act of Union, born in dishonour, cradled in corruption, was destined to perish of political penury; on the other, Arthur Balfour believed that better government was an alternative to national government. In the event Gladstone's analysis was shown to be susbtantially accurate; Balfour's policy, though by no means unfruitful in the field of social and administrative reform, to be in essence misconceived.

The outline of both the Liberal and Conservative policy for Ireland in these years is familiar. But it is well to remember—since the former was never put into practice and the latter was unsuccessful—both that their historical significance may well be over-estimated and that the political atmosphere, which made possible the adoption of such policies, may be of more lasting importance than the actual policies themselves. It is the purpose of this chapter to recapture something of the sense of that broader background, common both to Home Rule and to 'killing Home Rule by kindness', by studying the reactions of three English statesmen of the period 1880–1914, who were *only incidentally* con- cerned with the Irish problem. As a consequence the names most familiar in Ireland like those of Gladstone, Balfour and Lloyd George, are of set purpose excluded; and attention is for the moment confined to a brief analysis of the policies and constitutional proposals put forward by Joseph Chamberlain, by Lord Randolph Churchill and by Herbert Henry Asquith. Neither Chamberlain nor Lord Randolph were solid, representative party men, whilst Asquith, a Liberal by temperament and conviction, was a leader, whose capacity for analysing an intricate problem was not matched by an equal capacity for resolute action. Since none of them, with the arguable exception of Asquith, was principally preoccupied with Ireland, their attitudes afford some useful indication of the responses of political Englishmen to the peculiarities of the Irish problem. It goes far to explain both why Home Rule proved unacceptable to the majority of the English people, and why English political thought could offer no other solution whereby a disastrous climax to British rule in Ireland might be averted.

JOSEPH CHAMBERLAIN: A RADICAL ALIENATED AND AVENGED

There were wild cheers for Gladstone from the Irish members as he left the House after the defeat of the first Home Rule Bill and for Chamberlain angry cries of 'Traitor! Judas!' 'There goes the man who killed Home Rule', said Parnell in his quiet, vibrating tones as Chamberlain passed by in the Lobby of the House.[1] For the rest of his life Chamberlain had to face the envenomed hostility of the Irish members, not because he had voted against Home Rule—343 members had done that—but because the Nationalists had reckoned this most deadly of antagonists a sympathetic ally. To later generations, who remember Chamberlain as a great Colonial Secretary, as a tariff reformer, as a stirring leader of the new Imperialism, such a mistake appears incomprehensible. But in 1886 all this lay in the future; and Parnell could judge only from the past. And that was easily misinterpreted.

Chamberlain had entered national political life as an advanced Radical. The fall of the Second Empire in 1870 prompted him to say that for his part he did not feel 'any great horror at the possible establishment of a republic in this country. I am quite sure that sooner or later it will come.' And he scandalized the dominant Victorian middle class more by his utterances on social policy. In a famous Birmingham speech he spoke of the 'ransom', which the rich must pay to the poor for the enjoyment of their wealth. He declared himself an uncompro-

[1] J. L. Garvin, *The Life of Joseph Chamberlain* (London, 1932–34), 3 Vols. Vol. II, p. 250.

mising opponent of the orthodox *laissez-faire* economy and urged that
the State must intervene—'it must intervene on behalf of the weak
against the strong, in the interests of labour against capital, of want and
suffering against luxury and ease'.

Chamberlain was interested in social policy; he was not much interested in the Irish Question till after 1880. In that year he accepted office
under Gladstone and he represented the Left-wing Liberals in the
cabinet against Hartington on the Right. From the first session of the
1880 Parliament, Chamberlain found that Ireland blocked the way to
Liberal reforms in England. This was one, and perhaps the principal
reason, why he decided that the Irish incubus must be removed. But in
any case, faced with the agrarian depression and the discontent in
Ireland in the early eighteen-eighties Irish claims upon his attention were
in themselves virtually irresistible. Chamberlain sought to persuade his
Cabinet colleagues to give a thorough trial to conciliatory and remedial
measures, maintaining that a wise and liberal policy of reform would
do much to satisfy the Irish people and incidentally would have the
further and beneficial effect of lessening the influence of agitators,
exploiting what Chamberlain acknowledged to be 'their just discontent'.[1] Circumstances were, however, altogether unfavourable, the
measures insufficient and Irish outrages gave occasion for united Whig
and Tory hostility to their continuation. Moreover Chamberlain, while
still opposed to repression, felt increasingly that 'Parnell had got
beyond us. He was going for "No Rent" and Separation and these could
not be adopted by us as part of a Radical Programme.'[2] The climax came
with the arrest of Parnell and his lodgement in Kilmainham Jail on
October 13, 1881. Morley was troubled, but Chamberlain resolute.
'For heaven's sake' he wrote to Morley on October 18th, 'do not let
us "wobble".' And he proceeded to outline to Morley the reasons for a
step not seemingly easy for Radicals to support. The avowed objects of
the Irish Party, Chamberlain argued, had developed and changed since
the first formation of the Land League and the organization was no
longer being used to abolish practical evils, but to create sentimental
grievances and national hatred, in order to further the success of a
revolutionary programme which had separation as its goal. This was a
demand which could not be met—'national independence cannot be
given to Ireland'—and no other *modus vivendi* with Parnell was

[1] *Joseph Chamberlain. A Political Memoir 1880–92.* Edited by C. H. D. Howard
(London, 1953), p. 5.
[2] Ibid., p. 17.

possible. Therefore it was war to the knife 'between a despotism created to re-establish constitutional law, and a despotism not less complete elaborated to subvert law and produce anarchy as a precedent to revolutionary changes. Coercion was hateful but "coercion with a silk glove would be ridiculous".'[1]

The sharpness of Chamberlain's reaction to early Parnellite suggestions of a separatist goal was significant; so also was his readiness for strong measures to maintain order, should the occasion in his view demand it. Yet support for strong measures did not necessarily imply a lessening of reformist zeal. With characteristic energy Chamberlain himself tried to design in 1882 a scheme of planned public works to afford relief. Nothing was done. He protested. 'It may be the work of the Tories', he said, 'to crush out discontent. It is the better and higher work of the Liberals to find out the cause of disaffection and to remove it. It is not right to destroy liberty in order to preserve law.' In the same year (1882) the Prime Minister's treatment of Irish discontent led Chamberlain to write a letter on November 16th, threatening resignation from the Cabinet on this issue. He wrote: 'Redress of acknowledged grievances should precede, or at least accompany, the suspension of the safeguards of liberty. The widespread disaffection of the Irish people grows out of causes of just complaint, and it is empirical to try to crush the one without first enquiring into and dealing with the other. I think the necessity for destroying the Constitution in Ireland is not proved. . . .'[2]

Such expressions of opinion made plain once more Chamberlain's conviction that the constructive approach to the Irish Question lay along the lines of radical social reform. Parnell believed that a man who was so radical on social policy, must also be radical on constitutional questions. But Parnell was mistaken. For all the time Chamberlain was hardening in his attitude against the Nationalists and against any form of Irish independence. As early as 1880 he had declared: 'For my part I hate coercion. I hate the name. I hate the thing. . . . But I hate disorder more.' And he added significantly, 'We want to bind the Irish people to this country in bonds of unity and cordial union'. This emphasis on Union became more pronounced. In a letter of December 17, 1884, addressed to W. H. Duignan, Chamberlain remarked of the term 'Nationalist':

---

[1] Garvin, op. cit., Vol. I, p. 329, where Gladstone's reply is also reprinted.
[2] See esp. C.H.D. Howard, *Joseph Chamberlain, Parnell and the Irish "central board" scheme 1884–5*, I. H. S. 1952–3 pp. 237–63, 324–61.

'. . . I should like to know exactly what this word means and what the people really want. . . . I do not consider that wishes and rights are always identical, or that it is sufficient to find out what the majority of the Irish people desire in order at once to grant their demands. I can never consent to regard Ireland as a separate people with the inherent rights of an absolutely independent community.'[1]

Even if Parnell was not a professed separatist at this time, there was a deep difference in emphasis between his conception of a nation, marching to a boundary no man could fix and Chamberlain's notion of the underlying and integral unity of the British Isles. The implicit conflict of opinion and purpose boded ill, in the happiest of circumstances, for co-operation between the two men.

Circumstances, in fact, were not happy. There were also personal and particular reasons behind the alienation of Chamberlain from Parnell, while the Irish nationalist newspapers, *The Freeman's Journal* and *United Ireland* vied with each other in criticism of Chamberlain and his Radical friends. 'Mr Chamberlain', declared *United Ireland*[2] early in 1885 'is a sort of shopkeeping Danton, probably the very best imitation a nation of shopkeepers could produce. . . . He is strong, daring, not too scrupulous, knows the currents . . . has in a sense a soul for storms. . . . But if he expects by any amount of high sounding demagogy to cajole the Irish people into his camp, or to constitute themselves a wing of English radicalism one hour sooner or for one hour longer than the supreme interests of Ireland make it desirable, we warn him frankly he is nourishing a wild delusion.' The phrase 'a sort of shopkeeping Danton' may well have rankled even though it was not particularly original. Chamberlain had long since been described as 'this pinch-beck Robespierre', by Lord Randolph Churchill[3] and likened to Jack Cade by Salisbury. Danton might well have been deemed preferable to either, were it not for the deliberately offensive epithet which prefaced it.

In the summer of 1885, after the fall of the Liberal Government, Chamberlain and Dilke proposed to visit Ireland, chiefly in order to discover what the Catholic Hierarchy desired. Dilke asked Cardinal Manning for introductions; Manning fearful of 'your Midlothian in Ireland' declined.[4] The Nationalist newspapers were discouraging to

[1] Quoted ibid. p. 241. See also pp. 330–1 on Duignan.
[2] *United Ireland*, January 24, 1885, p. 5, coll. 4–5.
[3] James, op. cit., p. 115.   [4] Garvin, op. cit., Vol. II, p. 14.

the point of rudeness, Chamberlain and Dilke being depicted as petty intriguers, seeking to further their English Radical ambitions, by making use of Irish grievances and deserving 'to be ducked in a horse-pond or a bog-hole'.[1] 'We tell Mr Chamberlain . . .' declared *United Ireland* 'that if he imagines he can dupe the National party with his bastard, out-of-date sympathy, he has a much higher opinion of his powers than is entertained on this side of the Channel.' And the paper concluded that 'Messrs Chamberlain and Dilke . . . if they are wise . . . will keep out of our country altogether. We do not want them here. . . . They can learn all they want to know (and a great deal more) about Irish affairs from Irish representatives in the House of Commons, and they ought to be able to realize for themselves the offensiveness of that all-wise John Bullism, which proposes to prepare a course of dogmatic lectures on Ireland on the strength of a £5 return ticket.'[2] A later and direct approach to Archbishop Walsh by the Radical leaders produced no more encouraging result, the Archbishop explaining that he was prepared to give no introductions lest his doing so might 'be interpreted as hostile to the excellent tenor and promise of Lord Carnarvon's Conservative régime'. The 'generous and manly hand' which, in the words of his biographer, Chamberlain had held out was accordingly not clasped but 'bitten to the bone'.[3]

In personality and in political philosophy the Radicals were anti-pathetic to the essential conservatism of the Home Rule leadership, but the rudeness of the rebuff, even if provoked in part by a certain brash-ness in the radical approach to Irish affairs, was at the least, as Davitt well understood, ill-advised. It derived once again from the over-riding Parnellite preoccupation with tactics. Relations with the Tories were encouraging, there was a prospect of an understanding with them and therefore it was idle even to repress a dislike—in part no doubt instinctive—for the rising radicalism of the Birmingham school. But if, once more like Gladstone, the Irish leadership had looked at the Irish Question itself, instead of the tactical problems connected with it, they would surely have allowed broader considerations of possible long-term Irish interest to curb their language and to determine their response to radical overtures.

However it is also true that over and above such personal antipathy,

---

[1] Garvin, op. cit., Vol. II, p. 16.
[2] *United Ireland*, June 27, 1885. For discussion of this question generally see O'Brien, op. cit., pp. 99–102.
[3] Garvin, op. cit., Vol. II, p. 12.

there were matters of much substance dividing Nationalist from Radical. Chamberlain believed, as he reminded O'Shea in a letter of July 11, 1885 intended for communication to Parnell, that the Irish people were entitled to the largest measure of self-government consistent with the continued integrity of the Empire. He was opposed to the idea of a national Parliament in Dublin, but entertained the hope that a complete and effectual system of local government might be found sufficient to satisfy Irish sentiment. Parnell, through O'Shea, replied that he doubted whether it would be worth while to encumber the Irish Question with a larger extension of local government to Ireland than to England.[1] The statement, or restatement, of respective views was thus explicit—and should have removed the possibility of further and future misunderstanding. Was there not a clear difference in principle and ultimate purpose between a Home Rule measure and increased powers in local government? Yet in practice it was not altogether easy to maintain a sufficiently sharp distinction between Home Rule as Parnell conceived it and Chamberlain's proposals for a large extension of local government powers to Ireland. This was probably by no means unwelcome to Chamberlain.

Again, the Irish Party, in respect of leadership at least, was a protectionist party. When James Bryce visited Ireland in 1885, he noted that the question of customs either generally or at any rate against English manufacturers was much debated among Nationalists, with many holding that the people did not really care about the issue, but with the certainty that Parnell would demand the right to impose them.[2] The last at least was true and in the light of past British destruction of, or discrimination against, Irish industries, inevitable. 'I claim this for Ireland,' said Parnell in September 1885,[3] 'that if the Irish Parliament of the future considers that certain industries can be benefitted by Protection, nursed by Protection, until they can be placed by Protection in a position to compete with similar industries in other countries . . . then Ireland's Parliament ought to have the power to carry out such a policy.' To this Chamberlain reacted, and continued to react, sharply. The imposition of Irish protective duties against all British manufactures was a threat he was later to deploy with effect against Home Rule. It is true that Gladstone under pressure later amended his Home Rule proposals so as to keep control of customs

---

[1] The letters are reprinted in Chamberlain, op. cit., pp. 151–6.
[2] *Gladstone Papers*, Add. Ms. 44770, Vol. DCLXXXV, ff. 5–14.
[3] Quoted in O'Brien, op. cit., p. 110.

in the hands of the Imperial Parliament but that, and rightly, did not dispose of the question. Chamberlain was at one with Parnell, at least in this; neither believed that Home Rule would mark the end, but rather the beginning, of a phase in Anglo-Irish relations. And both, again surely rightly, believed that implicit in that phase was the progressive if gradual enlargement of the jurisdiction of the Irish parliament. The argument could not, therefore, be settled by what was decided in 1886; it was too much of a question of future probabilities for that.[1]

The election of 1885 was a landmark in English history, not only because it brought into rivalry the three great political personalities of the age—Gladstone, Parnell and Chamberlain—or because it marked the opening of a new era in Anglo-Irish relations, but also and perhaps chiefly because it afforded the first opportunity for expression to new forces in English politics. It was Chamberlain fighting on the left wing of the Liberal Party, who brought into prominence the demand for a progressive social policy, and his proposals were embodied in the Radicals' 'unauthorized programme'. His own words best explain its aims. He said:

'We will fight alone; we will appeal unto Caesar; we will go to the people from whom we come and whose cause we plead; . . . We have been looking to the extension of the franchise in order to bring into prominence questions which have been too long neglected. The great problem of our civilization is still unsolved. We have to account for and to grapple with the mass of misery and destitution in our midst, co-existent as it is with the evidence of abundant wealth and teeming prosperity. It is a problem which some men put aside by references to the eternal laws of supply and demand, to the necessity of freedom of contract, and to the sanctity of every private right of property.

---

[1] E. Strauss, op. cit., p. 176, and O'Brien, op. cit., pp. 109–14, are at issue on the importance of the fiscal issue in determining Chamberlain's hostility to Home Rule. The weight of evidence would seem to support the principal contention submitted by Dr Cruise O'Brien. He buttresses his argument, however, with one questionable speculation, by suggesting that Chamberlain may have feared that Ireland, once she had Home Rule would demand, and get, Protection and 'that her example would be imitated by Canada and other portions of the empire'. (p. 114). But Canada had asserted through Alexander Galt her right to impose protective tariffs against Britain as an integral part of responsible self-government in 1859 and the principle had then been conceded in effect in respect of all self-governing colonies. The exact reverse of what Dr. O'Brien says is more likely to be true, namely that Chamberlain feared that Canadian precedents would stimulate and reinforce Irish demands for the right to impose protective duties. On the Canadian precedent and how it was established see Professor Gerald Graham *The Listener*, November 5, 1959, *A Canadian Declaration of Independence*.

But, gentlemen, these phrases are the convenient cant of selfish wealth.'[1]

Such was the temper and tone of the radical appeal and in the 'unauthorized programme' it was accompanied by proposals for the settlement of Ireland, which, as might be expected after the July exchanges between Chamberlain and Parnell, fell far short of Home Rule.

The Radicals suggested that Ireland might be pacified by a Federal Scheme of Government to be known as Home-Rule-All-Round. Their proposals contemplated the devolution of powers upon local legislatures to be known as National Councils, not merely in Ireland, but also in England, Scotland and Wales. Such powers as the local legislatures exercised would be of a purely domestic character and the integrity of the United Kingdom would be preserved by continued representation at Westminster. Chamberlain explained what was in mind in a letter to Labouchère. He wrote:

'There is only one way of giving *bona fide* Home Rule, which is the adoption of the American Constitution.

1   Separate Legislatures for England, Scotland, Wales and possibly Ulster. The three other Irish provinces might combine.

2   Imperial Legislature at Westminster for Foreign and Colonial affairs, Army, Navy, Post Office and Customs.

3   A Supreme Court to arbitrate on respective limits of authority.

There is a scheme for you. It is the only one which is compatible with any sort of Imperial unity, and once established it might work without friction. . . . I am not going to swallow separation with my eyes shut.'[2]

And in an election speech Chamberlain outlined the purposes the radical proposals were designed to serve. He said:

'We have also to recognize and to satisfy national sentiment which is in itself a praiseworthy feeling and which both in Scotland and Ireland has led to a demand for a local control in purely domestic affairs. And these objects I believe can only be secured by some great measure of devolution, by which the Imperial Parliament shall maintain its supremacy and shall nevertheless relegate to subordinate authorities the control and administration of their local business. I believe . . . that in

[1] Quoted in J. L. Garvin, op. cit., Vol. II, p. 63.   [2] Ibid., p. 145.

F

the successful accomplishment' of this constitutional experiment 'lies the only hope of the pacification of Ireland and of the maintenance of the strength and integrity of the Empire. . . .'

From the letter and the speeches there emerges a clear picture of Chamberlain's main objectives. He aimed at the pacification of Ireland, but in order to achieve it there was a limit beyond which he was not prepared to go. The continued supremacy of the Imperial Parliament was to him the supreme necessity. This explains his anxiety to secure a federal solution, which would preserve the integrity of the United Kingdom, his desire for uniformity, as between the governments of Ireland, Scotland and Wales, and his frequent (if misleading) analogies with the Constitution of the United States. It is possible that in practice such a scheme of devolution would have developed in Ireland into a system of self-government. But it is not probable and Parnell was almost certainly right in thinking that such proposals were intended and, if adopted, would prove a means by which Home Rule would be effectively shelved. The issue indeed was clear. It was the essence of Parnell's claim that the Irish Question was a distinctive national issue; it was the aim of Chamberlain to show that it was part of a general demand for better local or regional government *within* the United Kingdom.

The Liberal failure to win a decisive victory in the country at the 1885 election left Chamberlain in an advantageous strategic position. This was recognized somewhat wryly in the columns of *United Ireland*, where the hope was expressed in late December that Chamberlain with 'the best grace he can' would dry his eyes, not sulk and support Gladstone and Home Rule.[1] Chamberlain, however, had seen no cause to modify his views. On the contrary the evidence of the election had suggested to him that Home Rule, apart from all other considerations, was not an electoral asset. 'If there were a dissolution on this question,' he wrote to Gladstone on December 19th, 'and the Liberal Party or its leader were thought to be pledged to a separate Parliament in Dublin, it is my belief that we should sustain a tremendous defeat. The English working classes, for various reasons, are distinctly hostile to Home Rule carried to this extent, and I do not think it would be possible to convert them before a General Election.'[2]

When the Salisbury administration fell, Chamberlain accepted Gladstone's invitation to join the Cabinet with reluctance, but with the

[1] December 26, 1885.   [2] Chamberlain op. cit., p. 171.

assurance that he would give 'an unprejudiced examination' to Gladstone's draft proposals for the reform of Irish government. From the first he was uncomfortable and his antagonism to his own Prime Minister was such as to allow him, seemingly with an easy conscience, to keep the Tories, through Lord Randolph Churchill, fully informed about Cabinet discussions on Irish policy.[1] Chamberlain disagreed with Gladstone on two specific points. In the first place he disliked the Land Purchase Bill, which the Prime Minister regarded as an integral part of his policy for the settlement of Ireland. His objections were not so much objections in principle, as objections on the particular ground that the compensation proposed was unduly favourable to the Irish landlord. At the election the Radicals had gained many votes in rural constituencies with the slogan of 'three acres and a cow'; and they felt that English agriculture was being sacrificed to Irish landlord interests. Later in opposition they were to draw vivid pictures of a train of railway trucks two miles long, loaded with millions of bright sovereigns, all travelling from the pocket of the British son of toil to the idle Irish landlord. Secondly, Chamberlain disagreed with the Prime Minister on the vital issue of Home Rule. Gladstone aimed at the establishment of a separate Parliament in Dublin and no Irish representation at Westminster. The moment of confrontation came on March 26, 1886. Chamberlain then asked the Prime Minister in a Cabinet memorandum four questions:

(i) Whether Irish Representation at Westminster was to cease.
(ii) Whether the power of taxation was to be vested in the Home Rule Parliament.
(iii) Whether the Judges were to be appointed by an Irish authority.
(iv) Whether the Irish Parliament was to have authority in every matter not specifically excluded from its jurisdiction. . . .

Here were the acid tests of Chamberlain's distinction between Home Rule consistent with Federal Union and Home Rule weakening the visible links of unity. It was, Chamberlain's biographer wrote,[2] a great and plain issue. To all the questions Gladstone replied in the affirmative and so in the negative to Chamberlain's ideas. Chamberlain said 'Then, I resign'. With these words the destiny of Home Rule was decided.

---

[1] See James, op. cit., pp. 235–6. On March 24, 1886, Lord Randolph reported to Lord Salisbury *inter alia*, 'Joe is becoming very ferocious in his hostility to his chief. The moment the scheme is out he means to resign'.

[2] Garvin, op. cit.

For the rest of his life Chamberlain adhered to a Federal solution of the Irish Question. For he knew that he had killed Home Rule, and he was probably well satisfied that Home Rule had killed his scheme of devolution. From Chamberlain's point of view the important thing was that Gladstone's Home Rule and Land Bills should be killed and as has been shrewdly surmised, it was all the better to kill them 'from a position fairly close to Gladstone and simultaneously consolidate Birmingham radicalism behind some sort of Unionism distinct from the pure negation of Lords Hartington and Salisbury'.[1] Yet it is ironic to reflect that, in this way, the two constructive proposals for the solution of the Irish Question, even if rightly regarded by Chamberlain as antagonistic, were destined to prove mutually destructive. Chamberlain opposed the second Home Rule Bill for the same reason that he had opposed the first. But his interests were soon to be drawn to other fields, to South Africa and then to Europe. When the Count von Bülow visited Windsor in 1899 with the Kaiser, he recorded an unusually favourable impression of Chamberlain, who was then working for an Anglo-German Alliance, which may help to explain a side of his character, which Irishmen did not easily understand. 'Chamberlain', wrote von Bülow, 'the modern merchant, very decided, very shy, very scrupulous, very much aware of his own advantage, and yet sincere, for he knows that without sincerity there can be no big business.'[2]

Like the Gods of Olympus Chamberlain heard the demands of Nationalist members:

Streaming up a lamentation and an ancient tale of wrong,
Like a tale of little meaning though the words are strong.

Certainly the words were strong: and it was not infrequently that the Irish members continued to see a striking resemblance between the character of Joseph Chamberlain and that of Judas Iscariot. But despite the unhappy exchanges in the summer of 1885, and despite Chamberlain's well-known sensitivity to criticism, it would be a mistake to believe that the basis of this hostility was no more than petty personal antipathies, even though these assuredly played their unhelpful part. It was rather a division of opinion on a vital matter of principle.

[1] M. C. Hurst in *Joseph Chamberlain and West Midland Politics 1886–1895*. Dugdale Society Occasional Papers No. 15 (Oxford, 1962), p. 19. Mr Hurst's study is essential to an understanding of the development of Chamberlain's Irish policies in relation to the views of his Birmingham supporters.

[2] E. T. S. Dugdale, *German Diplomatic Documents 1871–1914* (London, 1930), 4 Vols., Vol. III, p. 114.

Parnell after all was a separatist; Chamberlain was one of Nature's imperialists.

LORD RANDOLPH CHURCHILL: A TORY BEGUILER

While Joseph Chamberlain remains in Irish minds as the man who killed Home Rule, Lord Randolph Churchill is less well, but more kindly remembered as the author of the jingling refrain, 'Ulster will fight; Ulster will be right'. In both instances the association is as inevitable as it is incomplete. What is now apt to be overlooked in both cases is the element of pained surprise, in the one instance that Chamberlain should kill Home Rule; in the other that Lord Randolph Churchill should arouse Orange opposition to fever pitch against it.

It might be supposed from Lord Randolph's intervention in Belfast that he was a stern, unbending Tory. But nothing could be more misleading. This vivid and vital personality, whose brief career was over at the age of forty-six, still lends a certain charm to those grim political contests, which marked the close of the Gladstonian era. His sympathies with the injustices of Ireland and his realization of the inadequacies of her system of government, might be superficial but were seemingly sincere. One of his early political speeches in 1877 indicated the distance that separated the attitude of a progressive Tory from that of the vast majority of his party. In that year Lord Randolph declared that he could not vote for Home Rule, because that would mean the exclusion of the Irish members from Westminster. Without them more than one-third of the life and the soul of the House of Commons would be lost. Banish them, he said, and a House composed only of Englishmen and Scotsmen would sink to the condition of a vestry.[1] And more seriously, he added, 'I have no hesitation in saying that it is inattention to Irish legislation that has produced obstruction. There are great and crying Irish questions which the Government have not attended to, do not seem to be inclined to attend to and perhaps do not intend to attend to—the question of intermediate and higher education, and the question of the assimilation of the municipal and parliamentary electoral privileges to English privileges—and as long as these matters are neglected, so long will the Government have to deal with obstruction from Ireland.' This speech attracted a lot of attention. Parnell, speaking at Paisley three days later, declared that if the Government would pass the measures alluded to by Lord Randolph, they would not be troubled

[1] W. S. Churchill, *Lord Randolph Churchill* (London, 1906), 2 Vols., Vol. I, pp. 90–1

by Irish obstruction in the next session. In the Tory Party this speech was regarded with unqualified disapproval. *The Morning Post* was vigorous in denunciation and Sir Michael Hicks-Beach wrote at once in protest to Lord Randolph's father—the Duke of Marlborough. The latter replied, 'My dear Beach,—The only excuse I can find for Randolph is that he must either be mad or have been singularly affected with local champagne or claret. I can only say that the sentiments he has indulged in are purely his own! . . .'[1] But Lord Randolph's logic was plain enough. It was because he hoped that these issues of social policy would be settled by the Government and not by the Liberal or Home Rule Party, that he brought them into prominence.

The motive force behind Lord Randolph's Irish policy was consistent with the ideas which led him to enunciate his creed of Tory democracy. The Act of Union, as he said, was passed; but in the passing of it all the arsenal of political corruption and chicanery was exhausted in order to inaugurate a series of remedial and healing measures. If the Act was not productive of such measures then it would be entitled, he said, to be unequivocally condemned by history. It was for these reasons that he opposed the coercive measures advocated by the other members of the Tory Party and objected to the sanction by the House of extreme penalties against the Irish members, believing as he did that the cure for discontent and for obstruction lay in the enactment of conciliatory legislation. For this cause he was throughout his life a consistent and able advocate of educational reform in Ireland.

Lord Randolph's attitude to Ireland is so closely related to the doctrine, if indeed it merits such a description, of Tory democracy that it is worth recalling something of what he meant by this phrase. In 1884, he said, 'The Whigs are a class with the prejudices and vices of a class, the Radicals are a sect with the tyranny and fanaticism of a sect . . . but the Tories are of the people.' Therefore Tory democracy is a democracy which supports the Tory Party . . . 'because it has been taught by experience to believe in the soundness of true Tory principles But Tory democracy involves, also, another idea of equal importance. It involves the idea of a government who, in all branches of their policy and in all features of their administration, are animated by lofty and by *liberal ideas*'.[2] So much at least was not inconsistent with Lord Randolph's general attitude to Irish affairs.

---

[1] Ibid., p. 92.
[2] A sympathetic account is given in W. S. Churchill, *Lord Randolph Churchill*, Vol. I, Chap. VI, and in Lord Rosebery's *Lord Randolph Churchill*, (London, 1906), p. 160 et seq.

Churchill had an indifferent opinion of the Ulster wing of the party, which he expressed with his usual candour. In November 1885 he was complaining to Salisbury about these 'abominable Ulster Tories', foreseeing great difficulties in future relations with Parnell, because of the 'monstrous alliance' with them and concluding that 'these foul Ulster Tories have always ruined our party'.[1] On the other hand from the summer of 1885 he was most forward among Tory leaders in seeking to cement the Tory-Nationalist entente. In many respects he was well fitted in this adventure to lead and to mislead. His eloquence delighted, his social charm beguiled and his aristocratic background appealed most strongly to many Irish party members. Why should they heed the rasping voice of Birmingham radicalism, with its disturbing overtones of secularism and social revolution, whilst they were being wooed by this gifted scion of an historic dukedom? His appeal was to the people over against the wealthy bourgeoisie of the great cities and when he championed the claims of the Irish peasant against the superiority, indifference and incomprehension 'of the lords of suburban villas, of the owners of vineries and pineries',[2] his appeal for many of the Irish party members, as Michael Davitt noted with misgiving, was immediate and potent.[3] Indeed the only apprehensions *United Ireland* seemingly entertained were that 'some time must elapse before the views of Lord Randolph Churchill, influential as they will now be, can "permeate" his colleagues on the Irish Question' and that 'of course, the landlord party will work heaven and earth against him'.[4] But if Lord Randolph knew there was a time to speak, he knew also there was a time to keep silent. And it was not by speech but by silence that he misled. He was at all times opposed to Home Rule; yet no man, with the possible and honourable exception of the Viceroy, Lord Carnarvon, did more to persuade the Irish leaders that co-operation with the Tories might bring them to their cherished goal. What part did Lord Randolph play in Parnell's historic decision to advise the Irish in Britain to vote Tory in the election of November 1885? There was no direct or personal connection, but may it not have been that Lord Randolph more than any other man created the atmosphere, in which such a decision appeared to Parnell a not unreasonable one to take? If indeed this were so, Lord Randolph has a second, less familiar, but more important,

[1] Quoted in James, *Churchill*, p. 223.
[2] Churchill, *Lord Randolph Churchill*, Vol. I, p. 345.
[3] Cf. C. C. O'Brien, op. cit., p. 117.
[4] *United Ireland*, June 20, 1885.

claim to a place in Irish history, than the one traditionally accorded to him.

Lord Randolph, his hopes of having Gladstone 'pinned to Home Rule' once realized, was seized, as was no other Tory leader, with an awareness of the possibilities of ingrained Ulster suspicions of Irish Catholic, Nationalist intentions. In Belfast he had heard, like Kubla Khan of old, 'ancestral voices prophesying war'. It was a feat of no great difficulty—they remained quite audible. But Lord Randolph resolved that the menace they conveyed should be used to break Home Rule. On February 16, 1886, while the first Home Rule Bill was still in process of gestation he wrote: 'I decided some time ago that if the G O M went for Home Rule, the Orange Card would be the one to play. Please God it may turn out the ace of trumps and not the two . . .'[1] On February 22nd he travelled to Ulster. On landing at Larne he first used the phrase by which he is best remembered in Ireland: 'Ulster will fight, and Ulster will be right'. The enthusiasm was great; Lord Randolph voiced sentiments that were deeply entertained; he found a mood of belligerence and, of deliberate purpose, he intensified it. He concluded his speech at Belfast with words 'which are best expressed by one of our greatest English poets:

> The combat deepens; on ye brave,
> Who rush to glory or the grave.
> Wave, Ulster—all thy banners wave,
> And charge with all thy chivalry,[2]

It was not surprising that when Lord Randolph appeared in the House of Commons the next evening, he was greeted by a loud demonstration of hostility from the Nationalist members, taking the form of prolonged and dismal groaning.[3]

Had there been more conviction, and a less cynical search for party advantage, in Lord Randolph Churchill's intervention in Ulster much, even in Nationalist Ireland, might have been forgiven him. But the evidence, however much allowance is made for the characteristic ebullience of his language, is against him. He played 'the Orange Card' with reckless abandon and during the next half-century the Unionist Party, following his example, were to play it with frequency and, be it added, with great effect.[4]

It was this conscious endeavour, to play off the North against the

---

[1] Churchill, *Lord Randolph Churchill*, Vol. II, p. 59.   [2] Ibid., p. 63.
[3] Ibid., p. 64.   [4] See below pp. 195–200.

South, that did more than anything else to undermine the prestige and the good name of English parties amongst the Irish people. Lord Randolph felt no uneasiness. In 1886, when Leader of the House of Commons and Chancellor of the Exchequer, he was charged by Sir William Harcourt and others with a very real responsibility for the riots against Home Rule, which had occurred in Belfast. Lord Randolph replied with characteristic boldness: 'There was not', he said, 'a shred of a shadow of a shade, or a shade of a shadow of a shred of foundation for the indictment.' But history records another verdict.

At all times Lord Randolph had been in fundamental accord with his party on the necessity of preserving the Union. He was prepared for reforms and progressive social policies in Ireland: he was utterly opposed to constitutional change. In a speech at Edinburgh in 1884 he had said, 'We owe the Irish a great deal for our bad government of them in the past' but 'by giving continuous support to the Tory Party let the Irish know', though they cry day and night, though they vex you with much wickedness and harass you with much disorder . . . though they cause you all manner of trial and trouble, there is one thing you will detect at once, in whatever form or guise it may be presented to you, there is one thing you will never listen to, there is one thing you will never yield—and that is their demand for an Irish Parliament . . .'.[1] And in his memorably outrageous electoral address of June 20, 1886 to the electors of Paddington, treated by Winston Churchill in his biography of his father with a mixture of defensive admiration and evident embarrassment,[2] Lord Randolph declared that Gladstone in his Home Rule Bill had 'reserved for his closing days a conspiracy against the honour of Britain and the welfare of Ireland more startlingly base and nefarious than any of those other numerous designs and plots which, during the last quarter of a century, have occupied his imagination. . . .' This 'design for the separation of Ireland from Britain, this insane recurrence to heptarchical arrangements, this trafficking with treason, this condonation of crime, this exaltation of the disloyal, this abasement of the legal, this desertion of our Protestant co-religionists, this monstrous mixture of imbecility, extravagance and hysterics . . . this farrago of superlative nonsense' were such as 'the united genius of Bedlam and Colney Hatch would strive in vain to produce . . .' And why? 'For this reason and no other: to gratify the ambition of an old man in a hurry!'

[1] Quoted in W. S. Churchill, *Lord Randolph Churchill*, Vol. II, p. 145.
[2] Ibid., Vol. I, p. 281,

Lord Randolph Churchill's policy towards Ireland, it might be argued, was clear-sighted and generous within its self-imposed limits. If it *was* possible to maintain the Union, then the application of the principles of Tory democracy was one practical means by which it might be achieved. For whatever may be thought of the substantial content, or the lack of it, in this new Tory programme, it represented an approach psychologically sympathetic to many Irish nationalists. It marked a break from established ideas of rule by coercion with interludes in its application during which older Tories, resentful at signs of continuing Irish agitation, rarely failed to express surprise at such evidence of Irish ingratitude. Again while many old-fashioned Tories professed the comfortable belief that Providence would settle the Irish Question and thus absolve them from the necessity of doing anything very much about it, Lord Randolph outlined a programme which was at once constructive and conservative in social purpose. Balfour was to give practical effect to some parts of it; and retrospectively it seemed more attractive in embryonic Churchillian outline than in ruthless Balfourian application. This was as it had to be. In the longer run, irrespective of Ulster, even Lord Randolph's charm could not have reconciled Irish nationalists to his fundamental purpose —which was by new means to maintain and strengthen the union.

HERBERT HENRY ASQUITH: LIBERAL EPILOGUE

In one of his novels (*Endymion*) Disraeli wrote that 'an insular people subject to fogs, and possessing a powerful middle-class requires grave statesmen'. Mr Asquith was grave. He was a man of the highest intellectual attainments. To an unimpeachable integrity of mind he added the sagacious scepticism of an Oxford humanist. Yet he made no personal contribution to the solution of the Irish Question. To a degree surprising in one 'who was a master of so many of the arts of government, he was without initiative in ideas and policy. . . . We may speak of an Asquithian phrase or an Asquithian attitude, but not of an Asquithian doctrine or idea. It was not his mission to find the raw materials of policy, but rather to shape and direct them, when the course of events brought them within his reach'.[1] So one of his biographers has written, and in Irish affairs this lack of intellectual initiative was reinforced by the history of Home Rule. When Asquith succeeded Campbell-Bannerman in 1908, Gladstone's Irish policy was

[1] R. B. McCallum, *Asquith* (London, 1936), p. 12.

invested with all the sanctity of a traditional Liberal cause. The shadow of a great name, the memory of an heroic conflict, hung over the deliberations of the Liberal party. No alternative seemed possible. Gladstone's policy of 1886 must be adopted as Asquith's policy in 1910.

Asquith's analysis of the Irish Question was at no time lacking in distinction. In his maiden speech in the Commons delivered as early as 1887, he attacked Balfour's administration of Ireland. What value, he asked, lay in representative institutions when the voices of the representatives were systematically ignored 'What conceivable advantage', he went on, 'can there be either to Ireland or to Great Britain from the continuance of this gross caricature of the British Constitution? There is much virtue in government of the people, by the people, for the people. There is much also to be said for a powerful and well-equipped autocracy, but between the two, there is no logical or statesmanlike halting-place.

For the hybrid system which the Government is about to set up, a system which pretends to be that which it is not . . . a system which cannot be either resolutely repressive or frankly popular—for this half-hearted compromise there is inevitably reserved the inexorable sentence, which history shows must fall on every form of political imposture'.[1] By 1912 further point was added to Asquith's criticism, for by then the vast majority of the representatives of the Irish people had demanded Home Rule for close on forty years. Could a demand constitutionally pressed and consistently supported be indefinitely ignored under a democratic system of government? That was the question Asquith felt bound to meet.

The question, though allowing of simple statement and seemingly inviting a straightforward answer, was none the less heavily loaded with perplexing political problems and highly charged with more than political emotions. These were things of which Asquith was, if anything, too well aware. They inhibited his judgment and restrained his actions. He had lived with the Irish question all through his political life and had sat in Cabinet, when Gladstone had made his last effort in 1893. He knew, as his biographers so justly remarked,[2] the Irish controversy by heart. That may well have been his greatest liability. All his thoughts were second thoughts.

The burden of the past rested upon his followers as well. They

[1] Quoted in Spender and Asquith, op. cit., Vol. I, pp. 53–5.
[2] Op. cit., Vol. II, p. 14.

accepted the need for Home Rule; they did not generally welcome it. Behind them lay a depressing record of frustration and failure. Too well they remembered the electoral defeat of 1886 and the disaster of 1895. Even if the latter might reasonably be attributed only in part to Home Rule, reflections upon the fate of the Second Bill and its immediate sequel were hardly calculated to inspire enthusiasm. Introduced by Gladstone in February 1893, it had passed through the Commons to meet with resounding defeat, by 419 votes to 41, in the Lords on September 8th. The GOM was almost alone in his desire to fight on and his successor, Lord Rosebery, who had enjoyed Asquith's support against Harcourt's rival claims, in his first speech as Prime Minister inadvertently betrayed lack of faith, and what seemed worse to his angry Irish listeners, lack of serious intent in the Home Rule cause. Rosebery, so he said, found himself on this occasion in entire accord with an observation of Lord Salisbury's to the effect that before Irish Home Rule was conceded by the Imperial Parliament, 'England as the predominant member of the Three Kingdoms will have to be convinced of its justice and equity'.[1] Was Home Rule now to be made conditional upon the support of a majority in England over and above the majority of elected members for the United Kingdom which it had, in fact, secured in 1893? 'I blurted it out', Rosebery remarked by way of explanation to John Morley. 'For Heaven's sake', replied Morley, 'blurt out what you please about any country in the whole world, civilized or barbarous, except Ireland. Irish affairs are the very last field for that practice.'[2] Rosebery, however, remained unmindful, or more probably indifferent, to the need for discretion in the handling of Irish issues and, not unfittingly, his Government, dependent upon the Irish vote, lurched to final and deserved disaster on a proposal to erect a statue of Oliver Cromwell in Parliament Square.

As if the record of his Government on Home Rule were not enough Rosebery, no longer party leader but still ambivalent in his attitude to the leadership, campaigned early in the new century for a 'clean slate'. By a 'clean slate' he meant a Liberal Party programme from which Home Rule, among other lesser things, had been erased. He spoke contemptuously of party colleagues who sat still 'with the fly-blown phylacteries of obsolete policies bound round their foreheads', who did not remember that while they had been mumbling their incantations to themselves the world had been marching on. What was

---

[1] R. R. James, *Rosebery* (London, 1963), pp. 337-8, and Ensor, op. cit., p. 216.
[2] Morley, *Recollections*, Vol. II, p. 21. See also James, ibid.

needed, he concluded, was a policy adapted to the new century and not one adapted to 1892 or 1885.[1]

Rosebery professed to be ploughing a lonely furrow but his enigmatic and in part incomprehensible[2] utterances provoked a challenge from the solid, substantial figure of Sir Henry Campbell-Bannerman. He repudiated the idea of a 'clean slate', renewed his adherence to Home Rule and enquired of Rosebery on February 19, 1902, whether he spoke from 'the interior of our political tabernacle or from some vantage ground outside'. Rosebery replied next day: 'I remain outside, but not I think in solitude.' In this, and in so far as Home Rule was the principal question at issue, he was certainly correct. Was Asquith with him? In general terms, yes. Within a week the Liberal League was formed with Rosebery as President and Asquith as one of the three Vice-Presidents. It was not Irish but South African issues that had brought them together under the elusive banner of Liberal Imperialism. Asquith did not repudiate the doctrine of the 'clean slate'; he reinterpreted it. He spoke of it as the putting on one side of the unattainable and the relatively unimportant and combining the energies of the party upon a few things which were 'weighty, urgent and within reach'. Home Rule was not among them. 'Is it', he wrote, in March 1902, 'to be part of the policy and programme of our party that, if returned to power, it will introduce into the House of Commons a Bill for Irish Home Rule? The answer, in my judgement, is No. And why? ... Not because we think that the Irish problem has been either settled or shelved. But because the history of these years, and not least that part which is most recent, has made it plain that the ends which we have always had, and still have, in view ... can only be attained by methods which will carry with them, step by step, the sanction and sympathy of British opinion. To recognize facts like these is not apostasy; it is common sense.'[3] Reason was Asquith's guide and his conclusions were eminently reasonable. The lessons of experience were learned; there was to be no repetition of the events of 1886 or 1893. He was without illusions; what remained to be tested was the strength of his Home Rule convictions.

Step by step was an approach psychologically attuned to party

---

[1] James, *Rosebery*, pp. 430–1.

[2] Campbell-Bannerman, after subjecting the phrase 'fly-blown phylacteries' to patient analysis, concluded that it was without meaning in this context. More generally there is much evidence on this controversy in the *Campbell-Bannerman Papers* in the British Museum.

[3] Spender and Asquith, op. cit., Vol. I, p. 144. See generally pp. 141–5.

opinion. Thoughts in this one field inclined towards the cautious advance and judicious limitation of immediate purpose. The electorate must have no reason to be affrighted; moderation, even if it meant some retrogression from the comprehensive aims of 1886, seemed to be demanded by political realities. On the 27 November, 1905, Sir George Newnes, the veteran proprietor of *The Westminster Gazette*, a paper which 'thro' all the dark days has been very loyal', besought Campbell-Bannerman for a letter of reassurance which he might publish—a letter which would say that while 'Ireland should be governed according to Irish ideas, and full control of their own affairs should be left to the people of Ireland',[1] a Liberal Government 'would not consent to separation between the two countries'. Gladstone, recalled Newnes, had told him he would not assent to it, but in the country there remained a need for renewed reassurance. 'It is', he concluded, 'this horrible word "separatists" which has killed us in the past and now that we have come to life again' still had 'its power to wound'.

Electorally, no doubt, this was sound advice. But as the Irish policy of the Liberals became hedged about with caution, the Gladstonian sense of mission was succeeded by a circumspect appreciation of the supposed political temper of the electorate. 'A Home Ruler *in despair*, adopting it as the least of a choice of evils and being far from hopeful as to the results.'[2] This was the impression earlier formed by a friend of James Bryce, who in December 1905 became Chief Secretary for Ireland in Campbell-Bannerman's administration. The Gladstonian goal remained, but there are no Gladstonian echoes here.

Asquith, however, was not a Home Ruler 'in despair'. He was a man of too sanguine a temperament for that. He was intellectually convinced that Home Rule was the right policy and, in the manner of intellectuals, he believed that the logic that had determined his conclusion would influence others to the same end. His were the politics of reason; not those of virtuous passion. He lacked the Gladstonian sense of moral purpose and something of Gladstonian political artifice as well. Nor did he possess the warmth of personality which endeared Campbell-Bannerman—whom he succeeded as Prime Minister in April 1908—to Afrikaners and Irishmen alike. What Asquith brought to the last phase of Home Rule was easy, almost effortless, intellectual mastery of a highly complex subject. In power of analysis he stood alone

---

[1] *Campbell-Bannerman Papers*, British Museum. Add. MS. 42138, f. 283.
[2] Fisher, op. cit., Vol. 1, p. 221.

and the papers[1] he submitted to his colleagues and to an anxious and questioning Monarch on the Irish problem as it neared its climax in 1913–14 are supreme examples of his gifts. But, alas, it did not suffice to analyse the Irish question; the time had come when it had to be resolved. This Asquith failed to do. How far responsibility rests with him, and how far other men and circumstances made the problem so intractable as to be insoluble by peaceful means, is a question history has yet to determine.

Asquith had advantages such as Gladstone had never enjoyed and liabilities with which he had not been burdened. Chief among Asquith's advantages must be numbered the conversion of England to Home Rule and the limitation of the power of the Lords by the Parliament Act of 1911. In 1894 Salisbury had argued—and Rosebery, as we have seen, agreed—that before Home Rule could be enacted England as the predominant partner in the United Kingdom must assent. The elections of 1906 and of January and December 1910 suggested that a majority of members for English constituencies now supported Home Rule. This was certainly a source of strength to the Liberal Government—even if the Tories no longer regarded the existence of such a majority as being relevant to the argument. The Parliament Act, successfully carried through all its stages, despite intemperate and provocative opposition, by Asquith's calm and resolute leadership, brought a more evident and immediate gain. The Lords could delay, but no longer defeat, Home Rule. Yet the advantage was not so clear as might at first sight be supposed. There remained a period of some two and a half years in which the Lords could, and in the case of the Third Home Rule Bill did, hold up legislation; and two and a half years afforded ample time to those who were resolved to organize armed resistance to it in Ulster.

Against these advantages—and however qualified they were very considerable—must be set out the peculiar liabilities of Asquith's position. First, and by no means least important, were the now tepid convictions of many of his followers. Home Rule was a historic cause; it was not a new one nor any longer first in importance to younger members of the party. Secondly there was the perceptibly declining force of the Irish Party. Its leader, John Redmond, had a commanding position but was not a commanding personality. After 1910, with Liberals and Unionists evenly balanced, Redmond held the scales. All that Parnell had sought, and sought in vain, was his. But he took little

[1] The *Asquith Papers* are in the Bodleian Library, Oxford.

advantage of it. He did not threaten to turn the Liberals out, because he could not afford to put the Unionists in. Paradoxical as it may seem, this was perhaps Asquith's greatest liability. He needed a formidable and independent ally; he had a conscientious and increasingly anxious associate. Confronted with the Tory challenge in Ulster, Asquith's natural inclination was to concede, and to concede not upon the merits of a well-established case at the outset, but under pressure. Step by step he gave ground, with Redmond forever protesting, but never acting. Nationalist action, or even a realistic threat of action on their part, was not a factor in the scales. Asquith was almost certainly the loser by such default. His opponents were minatory and bombastic; his friends could always be relied upon to behave with constitutional rectitude. *Irish Freedom*, the journal of the Irish Republican Brotherhood, described Sir Edward Carson as 'the only Irish member of Parliament who has any back-bone'. The Irish Republican Brotherhood believed in physical force, they had more regard for an Orange leader prepared to use it than for an Irish Nationalist, to whom departure from constitutional methods was unthinkable.

And that brings one to the last and greatest of Asquith's liabilities—there were no lengths, in the words of Andrew Bonar Law, Balfour's successor as leader of the Unionist Party, to which that party was not prepared to go to defeat Home Rule. Asquith said that the use of such language was a declaration of war against constitutional government. His description was just. But as provocative words were succeeded by provocative acts, Asquith always found solid and substantial reasons for not taking decisive measures. A Provisional Government was formed in Ulster, with Sir Edward Carson at its head and with the declared purpose of organizing armed resistance to measures that would be embodied in an Act of Parliament. An Ulster Volunteer force was organized with an Anglo-Indian general in command. Arms were imported from Germany. Asquith, in this acting in conformity with the advice he received from his Irish allies, decided against intervention, against the institution of criminal proceedings and against any step that might be regarded as the coercion of Ulster. In each instance the arguments[1] against action were substantial and persuasive; collectively they led almost certainly to a wrong conclusion. The climax came with the Curragh Mutiny in March 1914. Liberal and radical opinion was outraged at the evidence of association between

[1] They are set out in Spender and Asquith, op. cit., Vol. II, pp. 22–4.

high ranking officers of the Crown and those who were plotting resistance to its laws. Asquith acted. He himself assumed responsibility for
the War Office. Sir Robert Ensor described it as a 'heroic gesture' and
he proceeds to say all that need be said in one epigrammatic sentence,
'His [Asquith's] followers supposed that this betokened a drastic
policy, such as only a prime minister could put through; in fact, it
heralded a policy of surrender, such as only a prime minister could
put over'.[1]

Yet if Asquith conceded, he never in fact surrendered. He continued
to advance in accord with his own declared principle, step by step,
towards the goal. He never abandoned the principle of an all-Ireland
parliament, even if he never understood the extent to which his own
gradualist approach had undermined it. Yet such misapprehension,
contrary to what is so often alleged, was not at the heart of the matter.
Asquith had been prompted to expound his step by step advance by
Rosebery's enunciation of the 'clean slate' doctrine. The circumstances
that had elicited his exposition made clear the motives behind it. In
respect of Home Rule, Asquith within his own party was pre-eminently
a man of the centre. Rosebery was to the right, Campbell-Bannerman
to the left. And a man of the centre Asquith remained. There was a
point beyond which he was not prepared to force the Irish issue. Gladstone had split the party on Home Rule; Asquith was neither prepared
to do so once more, nor was he ready to imperil the law and the constitution for an Irish cause. Gladstone recked little of the price in a
cause he deemed supremely just; Asquith at all times weighed it in the
scales before judging if payment were warranted. In some measure this
presupposed an attitude of wait and see: at a deeper level it indicated a
reluctance to take the initiative. In April 1912 Lloyd George said of
Asquith 'He is like a great counsel in whom solicitors and clients
have faith . . . . He has splendid judgement.' And a year later he remarked: 'He is a big man. He never initiates anything, but he is a great
judge.'[2] Certainly in Irish affairs judgement was important: but lack
of initiative, of the element of political surprise, in Asquith's tactical
approach left the running to those who weighed grave matters less
judiciously than he did.

Asquith's Irish policy was never brought to a conclusion. When in
the summer of 1914 the Buckingham Palace Conference attempted a
settlement of the Irish deadlock, the future of Great Britain depended,

[1] Op. cit., p. 479.
[2] Lord Riddell, *More Pages from My Diary* (London, 1934), p. 56.

as Churchill later noted with undisguised revulsion, upon the disposition of clusters of humble parishes in Ulster.[1] But the deliberations of the Conference were in vain. No agreement was reached. A few weeks later the European War broke out. Asquith's reputation depends accordingly upon questions to which the answers are unknown—would his Irish policies have ended in civil war in Ireland had not a greater European conflict intervened? Or was the Conference the first indication of a *détente* in party feeling, which would have allowed of an Irish settlement in substantial accord with Liberal policy? Or would the approaching election have vindicated the Unionist opposition? Since one cannot answer, the verdict must remain in suspense. Yet the evidence available suggests at the least that, had war not intervened, Asquith's policy would not have been vindicated. It is improbable that the Liberals would have secured a majority at the next election. Quite apart from growing Unionist strength, the Labour Party were preparing to contest many of the hitherto safe radical seats. Leith and Midlothian had already been lost to the Government in by-elections. The Liberal tide was ebbing and Asquith's Irish policy was deemed largely responsible for it.

The third Home Rule Bill had all the qualities of an epilogue, and in fairness to Asquith it has always to be remembered that, in addition to the normal difficulties of the Irish Question, he was faced with the problem of dealing with a reckless and unconstitutional opposition in Ulster. In these circumstances his sagacity and foresight were wasted. He was the first English statesman to recommend Dominion Status for Ireland in 1919; and perhaps even while advocating Home Rule, he realized it would provide no lasting solution. It was later said in criticism of George Lansbury that he allowed his bleeding heart to run away with his bloody head. It is a curious commentary on this phase of Anglo-Irish relations to say that the spontaneous enthusiasms of Mr Lansbury might well have contributed more to an agreement in the critical months of 1914, than the sceptical benevolence of Mr Asquith.

SOME CONCLUDING REFLECTIONS

This brief survey of the record and policies of three of the more notable of English statesmen of the period between the introduction of the

[1] W. S. Churchill, *The World Crisis, 1911–1918*, Revised Edition (London, 1931), p. 109.

first Home Rule Bill and the signature of the Anglo-Irish Treaty thirty-five years later reflects some at least of the psychological reactions of English leaders to Irish problems. All three exercised a notable, if mainly negative, influence upon the course of Irish history. In no case, Asquith possibly excepted, does their reputation depend to a decisive extent upon their attitude to the Irish Question. Lord Randolph Churchill's place in history stands or falls by his conception of Tory Democracy; Joseph Chamberlain must be judged as a radical imperialist and as a tariff reformer; and historians, despite their criticism of his conduct of the war, honour Asquith as the leader of the last of those Whig-Liberal administrations, which adorned the golden age of English parliamentary government. It is for this reason that an analysis of the attitudes of these statesmen to Ireland throws some light upon Anglo-Irish relations. Their Irish policies were not the product of major interest nor, in the case of Chamberlain or Churchill, of specialized study, but rather were implicit in their political outlook, and for that reason contribute to an understanding of attitudes widely adopted and opinions as widely and instinctively entertained.

The basis of policy in each instance was provided by the relative or absolute failure of the Act of Union. It was the purpose of Chamberlain to strengthen Union by a general scheme of devolution; Lord Randolph, wishing also to preserve and to strengthen it, believed that something at least to this end might be achieved by measures of conservative social reform; while Asquith, in this the heir of Gladstone, saw no hope save in Repeal and the enactment of a measure of Home Rule. The three statesmen agreed, therefore, that the existing government of Ireland was unsatisfactory, but the conflict between them as to the principle of reform was fundamental. It went deeper and extended further than the field of Anglo-Irish relations. No more suggestive remark on this phase of English statesmanship towards Ireland was made than that of Lord Salisbury. He said that Gladstone, in championing Home Rule, had 'awakened the slumbering genius of Imperialism'. Chamberlain and Churchill were among its spokesmen and in the case of Chamberlain there was a direct connection between his opposition to Home Rule and his emergence as the most formidable of the new imperialists.

It would be presumptuous to draw general conclusions from so slight a study of particular men or particular events. But a few observations may be allowed. In the first place it is curious that there is no development in the views on the Irish Question entertained by these English statesmen. Lord Randolph advocated certain reforms in social policy, notably in education, in his earliest political speeches. He was advocating the same reforms in 1895, the year of his death. Chamberlain proposed a federal solution in his unauthorized programme in 1885. No later speeches indicate that he was prepared to advance any other solution, even though devolution was obviously impracticable by the close of the century. Asquith was a member of Gladstone's ministry when the second Home Rule Bill was introduced in 1893. When he put forward his own Bill in 1912, the only significant alteration was the reduction of the authority of the proposed Home Rule Parliament. When one remembers the changes in other fields, this inelasticity in outlook is remarkable. It indicates either a problem insoluble in accordance with their preconceived assumptions or unreceptive minds. It may be significant that it was Gladstone who said, 'I have been a learner all my life and a learner I shall continue unto the end'.

The failure of English statesmen to resolve the Irish Question at a date earlier than 1921, and then only after violence, was due to continuing inability to understand the Irish political outlook, to some confusion of mind as to the distinction between good government and national government, and by the refusal of the electorate to decide finally in favour of one particular policy. These are the things which help to explain why so many Englishmen were so slow, or alternatively so reluctant, to recognize that, after a certain point in time, a new order in Ireland was *inevitable*. English statesmen did nothing to facilitate its emergence. The indictment against them indeed is not so much that they hoped the Irish Question would, like Swinburne's river, 'wind somewhere safe to sea', but that in its last stage they resolutely tried to check its flow. In so doing, to vary the metaphor they prolonged the travail and the birthpangs of a new state.

But when so much is said a question remains. Lord Randolph Churchill once exclaimed to John Morley, 'Ah, but then Balfour and you are men who believe in the solution of political questions'.[1] The remark was well founded. Morley was the most devoted champion of Gladstonian Home Rule, and Balfour was the only Conservative statesman, who aspired to achieve a final and constructive settlement of the Irish Question. But none-the-less it may well prompt a doubt as to whether any peaceful settlement was possible. For while John Morley

[1] Morley, *Recollections*, Vol. I, p. 191.

firmly repudiated the implication that the statesman is a man who does not believe in the solution of political questions, yet even he did not fail to remind us that in history there is such a thing as an insoluble problem. May it not be that the settlement of Ireland by English statesmen in fact presented one?

CHAPTER VI

THE ULSTER QUESTION, 1886–1921.
THREE CRITICAL YEARS

The sound of fight is silent long
That began the ancient wrong;
Long the voice of tears is still
That wept of old the endless ill.
In my heart it has not died. . . .

A. E. HOUSMAN

If the Ulster Question were not one of the tragedies of history it might well be regarded as one of the more remarkable of its curiosities. The intensity of political and religious divisions in that province has been equalled and indeed surpassed in other countries at other times; the vivid and enduring mistrust of a minority for government by the majority of their fellow-countrymen is the consequence of a historical process familiar to many continental peoples; but where else have the divisions of other days been used with such final effect to determine the issues of contemporary politics—issues to which to all outward seeming they bear no relation whatever? Casual observers frankly bewildered at the significance attached by politicians in Ulster down to the present-day to the victory of a Dutch Prince over an English King nearly three centuries ago, are tempted, like Marx, to dismiss as fantasies these

> Party cries of long ago,
> Still *bombinans* in vacuo.

But from long experience Irishmen know better. They have learnt to pierce that camouflage of tradition which serves so well to obscure the realities of Northern politics. Had Parnell and Gladstone better comprehended the Ulster mind some eighty years ago, Ireland might not be partitioned today; had Asquith learned from the experience of 1886 he would hardly have brought Ireland to the brink of civil war in 1914, had Irish Republicans understood it, their tactics in the critical years 1919–22 would surely have been different. In the end the misapprehensions of English statesmen and of Irish Nationalists, fostered as they were by the Ulstermen's fervent concentration on the politically irrelevant, combined to produce a Home Rule government in Northern Ireland, accepted and worked by the very party which protested so loudly against Home Rule under any guise or in any form. This result, less paradoxical in fact than in appearance, is the outcome of events which illuminate in an especial degree the more curious qualities of the Ulster Question. Gibbon, in the light of all his experience in the handling of a vast and complicated mass of material, warned historians 'never to pursue the curious'. Perhaps only intrinsic significance could justify a disregard of this all too frequently disregarded advice, and heretical though the doubt may seem in Ireland, it is sometimes tempting to wonder whether the Ulster Question could furnish such a justification.

The study of political forces in Ulster has been seriously hampered by the observations of writers and politicians who are determined at all costs to interpret developments in such a way as to accord with their own strongly entertained but frequently somewhat limited views. 'Beaucoup de gens', observed Balzac, '*aiment mieux nier les dénouements que de mesurer la force des liens.*' Reluctance to recognize the logic that has governed the recent phases of the Ulster Question is as common in Irish political thought as in those more personal affairs which inspired Balzac's aphorism. This chapter seeks to redress the balance by recalling the process and by analysing the forces which have guided the destinies of Ulster in the thirty-five years between the first Home Rule Bill and the 'Partition Act' of 1920. Since it is not possible to describe in so brief a compass all the changes and chances of this eventful period it is perhaps most instructive to recall the demands of Ulster and the response that they elicited in London and in Dublin at the most critical moments in the shaping of Anglo-Irish relations. This approach to the Ulster Question may have the advantage of bringing out developments that have in fact taken place in the often supposedly static creed of Ulster Unionism.

1886. ULSTER WILL FIGHT

The Ulster Question did not originate with the Unionist opposition to Home Rule, but its present-day character was moulded by the events of 1886. In that year it became for the first time apparent that the forces in

Ulster working for the division of Ireland might prove stronger than the forces working for unity. Since the relative strength of these conflicting pulls constituted a question in Irish politics less important only than that of the true nature of Irish nationalism in the early part of the nineteenth century, the predominance of the one revealed in 1886 marks out that year as a turning point in Irish history.

The plantation of Ulster with settlers of English and Scottish birth was more successful, chiefly because closer, than that of any other part of Ireland, yet these new inhabitants soon displayed an independence of character that brought them into conflict alternately with their British kinsmen and their Irish fellow-countrymen. From the time when they stood by the Scots in their quarrel with the Long Parliament and were in consequence denounced by John Milton as 'a generation of Highland thieves and red-shanks who, being neighbourly admitted . . . by the courtesy of England, to hold possessions in our province, a country better than their own, have with worse faith than those heathen, proved ungrateful and treacherous guests to their best friends and entertainers',[1] to the day some century and a half later, when a Chief Secretary, seeing in the democratic opinions so popular in Belfast 'the source of all the mischief', denounced 'the levellers of the North', political opinions in Ulster were apt to be independent with a distinctive flavour of settler radicalism. Differences in history and in creed marked off the descendants of the Ulster settlers from the majority of Irishmen, but these differences in themselves did not necessarily cause the political division of the Irish nation. Too often is it forgotten today that little more than a hundred and sixty years ago the Ulster dissenters provided some of the most notable champions of Irish parliamentary independence. In that generous national enthusiasm which illuminated the Irish political scene for two brief decades at the close of the eighteenth century, the Northern Protestants associated themselves with the demands of the Irish people and in notable measure supported the movement for Catholic Emancipation. 'The Irish Protestant could never be free', said the conservative Henry Grattan, 'till the Irish Catholic ceased to be a slave.' But Wolfe Tone, who aspired to overthrow the privileged order in Ireland through a union of Catholics and Dissenters, stirred an Ulster already permeated with the doctrines of the French Revolution more profoundly. The 'Society of United Irishmen' formed by Tone in October 1791 had its first headquarters

[1] Quoted in J. W. Good, *Ulster and Ireland* (Dublin, 1919), pp. 11–12, from John Milton's *Observations*.

in Belfast. Its objects were to abolish all unnatural religious distinctions, to unite all Irishmen against the unjust influence of Great Britain and to secure their true representation in a national Parliament. The real danger to the established order, Professor Curtis[1] justly observed, came at this time from the democratic Presbyterians of the North.

As now in retrospect there is a disposition to think that the whole Protestant population of Ulster has been solidly anti-nationalist in sentiment since 1886, so too there is a tendency to minimize the force of continuing religious animosities during the last two decades of the eighteenth century. In fact despite the influence of the United Irishmen, agrarian-religious feuds persisted in the Northern counties. Yet when every allowance has been made it cannot too frequently be recalled that there was a period, not so very long distant, when the aspirations of Ulster coincided with those of the rest of Ireland. Wolfe Tone had seemingly convinced Catholics and Dissenters alike that they 'had but one common interest and one common enemy; that the depression and slavery of Ireland was produced and perpetuated by the divisions existing between them, and that consequently, to assert the independence of their country and their own individual liberties, it was necessary to forget all former feuds, to consolidate the entire strength of the nation and to form for the future but one people'. After 1798 these seemed but the empty words of an unpractical visionary, for when the crisis came mistrust was revived and that spirit of magnanimity which had momentarily stirred the Irish people was replaced once again by older antipathies and cruel, dividing hatreds. Yet the student of Ulster politics may be wise to remember that such popular aspirations, transient though they appear, do not vanish as though they had never been.

It was the evidence of division, not fast fading recollections of unity, that impressed visitors to Ireland in the early years of the Union. Gustave de Beaumont recorded in graphic phrases what he saw and learnt on his Irish travels. Ulster was the Protestant stronghold and, as Connaught was the prototype of old Ireland, so might Ulster be regarded as symbolic of the newer Protestant settlements. '*L'Ulster*', he wrote, '*résume l'Irlande protestante.*' Yet, as de Beaumont recognized, there was here an element of over-simplification. Ulster was not merely protestant; it was above all puritan; '*l'Ulster est l'Écosse de l'Irlande*'.

---

[1] E. Curtis, *A History of Ireland* (London, 1937), 3rd Ed., p. 331. See generally Chap. XVII.

It had retained '*dans toute son amertume les vieilles passions antipapistes que lui apportèrent les colons de Jacques Ier, et que ravivèrent les soldats de Cromwell et de Guillaume III. L'habitant de l'Ulster n'est séparé que par un fleuve de celui du Connaught; mais la religion établit entre eux une plus puissante barrière; et bien de temps encore s'écoulera avant que le puritain écossais du nord de l'Irlande regarde et traite comme ses frères les catholiques du Connaught?*'[1]

Nassau Senior, at his most didactic, analysed the situation at once with less regard than de Beaumont for traditional explanations and with a formidable air of precision. 'It may be necessary', he wrote, 'to inform a portion of our readers, that under the general term "Ireland" are included two countries very different in their social conditions—namely the province of Ulster, or, as it is usually called, the "North of Ireland"; and the provinces of Leinster, Munster and Connaught, which together, constitute what is usually called the "South of Ireland".'[2] In this one sentence, it will be noted, is implicit the presumption that underlay the Government of Ireland Act, 1920—the 'two countries'—and it employs also the terminology—North of Ireland, South of Ireland—which was to find its way on to the Statute Book in that Act. As befitted a professional economist, Nassau Senior laid much stress upon differences in social conditions and, indeed, he would seem to have been most influenced in his analysis by his observation of the fact that, with some exceptions, 'the state of the population in the North and in the South is not merely dissimilar but opposed'.[3] These differences, statistically documented in respect of land in the Report of the Devon Commission, did not diminish but, on the contrary, increased with the passage of time.

Throughout the nineteenth century Leinster, Munster and Connaught remained, despite very considerable differences in their living standards, predominantly agricultural, but Ulster found a new prosperity in rapid industrial expansion. Much of it was concentrated in Belfast, the growth of which from a small market town with some 65,000 inhabitants, to the great industrial city of today provides one of the most notable tales of expansion afforded even by the age of the Industrial Revolution. By 1926 the population of Belfast[4] was six times what it had been a century earlier and was double what it had been in 1886. This remarkable and rapid growth had political consequences which Irishmen rarely ponder. Badly housed workers, with a low standard of

[1] Op. cit., Vol. I, pp. 193–4.
[3] Ibid.
[2] Op. cit., Vol. I, p. 22.
[4] In 1926 census, 415,151.

wages and long hours, business men and manufacturers[1] absorbed in the task of amassing new and hardly acquired wealth composed the most important classes in this expanding city. Its inhabitants were brought up in an atmosphere of sectarian strife; the educational system which might have counteracted it was here, as in the rest of Ireland, notoriously inadequate. Enlightened political guidance from the ruling classes was not forthcoming largely because the leaders of political opinion were, till the close of the century, drawn from the landowning classes who understood little and sympathized less with the triumphs of industrialism. As a result this city, where inflammable memories still smouldered, was the prey to unreasoning passions easily played upon by demagogue and politician. Self-assertive of its wealth and achievement, Belfast none-the-less was both mindful of its past and somewhat apprehensive of its future. 'Strange to say', wrote Lord Morley,[2] 'this great and flourishing community where energy, intelligence, and enterprise have achieved results so striking, has proved to harbour a spirit of bigotry and violence for which a parallel can hardly be found in any town in Western Europe.' The observation is just, but the surprise is unwarranted. It was because Belfast was flourishing, expanding and, above all, a highly competitive community that the spirit of bigotry survived in all its intensity.

Throughout the modern phase of the Irish Question religious divisions played a dominant role in Ulster. This was so, not necessarily because they constituted the fundamental issues, but because party leaders on either side knew that religious prejudices, especially where there existed, as in Belfast, a substratum of economic competition, were most easily exploited. In consequence, after 1886, religious antagonisms hardened in accordance with the alignment of political parties. The Dissenters who attacked the privileged order at the close of the eighteenth century, the Presbyterian farmers and business men, with their traditional hostility to the Episcopalian landlords, buried their differences when confronted with Home Rule. The fusion was not spontaneous and was not rendered final till the destinies of Ulster had been placed in Sir Edward Carson's hands. Yet broadly speaking, after 1886, the terms Unionist and Protestant, Nationalist and Catholic became synonymous. Since then religious and political divisions have

---

[1] W. J. Pirrie, Managing Director and Chairman of Harland and Wolff and Lord Mayor of Belfast 1896 and 1897, was the most widely known among them. For a portrait see R. D. C. Black, 'William James Pirrie' in *The Shaping of Modern Ireland*. Ed. by Conor Cruise O'Brien (London, 1960), pp. 174–84.

[2] *Recollections*, Vol. I, p. 222.

coincided, and by what economic and social historians are apt to regard as this unreal and artificial alignment of forces the history of Ulster has been moulded. One may despise the survival of medieval intolerance; one may condemn or scorn the attitude of mind which makes it possible, but one cannot ignore its existence. This was the legacy of the fierce fanaticism of the religious wars, fostered and nourished through the centuries by a chain of calamitous circumstances till at last it became embedded as a well-nigh ineradicable habit in the mind of an enterprising and otherwise progressive community.

It was the prospect of change, culminating in the introduction of the first Home Rule Bill, that made 1886 a critical year in the development of the Ulster question. Home Rule was in no sense the cause of sectarian division, but the possibility of its receiving legislative sanction brought to the surface all the suspicions and the fears latent in the settler mind. They were further increased by lack of psychological preparedness. At Eastertide 1885, James Bryce warned Ulster liberals in Belfast that Home Rule in some form was imminent and urged them to prepare some plan for safeguarding the interests of the Protestant part of Ulster. 'They were startled and at first discomposed', he recorded,[1] 'but presently told me that I was mistaken.' Incredulity gave way some nine months later to consternation and then a hardening resolve to resist. In the memorandum which he submitted to Gladstone in December 1885, and to which reference has already been made, Bryce noted that his informants, who were apparently mostly of Liberal sympathies, believed that an Irish legislature 'would act in a spirit hostile to the Protestants of the North, and even attempt to injure their trade. The Orange populace there assumes that the Protestants would be attacked.'[2] Here again, party manœuvres and Gladstonian silences exacted a price. But even more important was the interplay of Irish Nationalist and Ulster Unionist politics.

There is an element of political determinism in the working out of majority-minority relations in dependent societies as the time for a transfer, or possible transfer, of power approaches and the pattern in Ireland had so much in common with events as they later unfolded in India, in Cyprus and in parts of Africa, as to suggest that the freedom of choice before majority and minority community leadership was more limited than may retrospectively be supposed. In theory the Nationalist party in the eighties had a choice between the conciliation of the Ulster

[1] H. A. L. Fisher, *James Bryce*, Vol. I, pp. 199–200.
[2] *Gladstone Papers*, Add. Ms. 44770, ff. 5–14. See also above p. 131.

minority or its coercion constitutionally or, if need be, otherwise. A
policy of conciliation carried with it one grave liability. It conceded, of
necessity, the existence of two communities, Nassau Senior's 'two
countries', and by recognizing the separate identity of the minority
community, almost inevitably encouraged a heightening of its claims.
Could it be certain that conciliation implying, again of necessity,
concession would win Ulster minority acceptance of Home Rule even,
for example, in a federal form safeguarding minority rights? In retrospect it seems unlikely. That being so, was not the wiser course to
pursue a policy, not of conciliation, but of undermining the Ulster
minority's will to resist and, as a corollary, its means of support?

The question might have been—there is no evidence that it was—
and may still be, debated in these terms. Historically, if choice there
were before the Nationalist leadership, there is no doubt what choice
was made. From Parnell to Redmond, to Pearse and de Valera no Irish
leader consistently pursued a policy of conciliation. For this there
were many, and by no means insubstantial, reasons. Nationalists
accepted as an article of faith that Ireland, like Mazzini's Italy, had 'her
own irrefutable boundary marks'; that the sea had made of her for
ever one nation. They believed, given this premise, that within that
nation the will of the majority would, and should, prevail. The Ulster
question was not a question between two countries, still less between
two nations, but a domestic question for settlement by Irishmen and
by Irishmen alone.

Theoretic preconceptions were reinforced by tactical considerations.
Ulster was not a solidly Unionist and Protestant province but a province so divided that in parliamentary terms a small majority of
Unionist members was at best likely to be returned. Was not the right
course once again, and especially for a highly organized, constitutional
party, to seek, not to conciliate, but, in electoral terms, to capture the
province? Here, the Protestant Parnell, that master of tactics, set the
pattern by embarking on a policy of electoral 'invasion', intended to
consolidate support for Home Rule in the North and to convey the
impression of its inevitability[1]. The policy was crowned with significant success. Of the 89 contested Irish seats in the election of November
1885 the Nationalists won 85 and Ulster returned 18 Nationalists

---

[1] Parnell, a landowner, almost certainly thought of the minority in land-owning terms.
In a memorandum for Gladstone dated January 6, 1886, he commented with reference to
'the concession of a full measure of autonomy to Ireland' that 'the Protestants, other than
the owners of land, are not really opposed to such concession'. Quoted Ensor, op.
cit., p. 451, fn. 2.

as against 17 Unionists. Here, if indeed required, was convincing and conclusive evidence that there was no question of a united northern province resolutely resisting Home Rule, but of a minority concentrated in the north-eastern counties of that province whose co-religionists were strongly entrenched, but not numerically preponderant, in other parts of it. Yet electoral 'invasion' exacted its price. By giving the appearance of an external threat, it contributed significantly to the closing of the anti-Home Rule ranks. More important, perhaps, it encouraged illusions in Nationalist thinking about the minority problem in Ulster.

Electoral inroads in Ulster in fact reflected no weakening in Unionist resistance to Home Rule but were more simply the fruits of improved party organization and of the response to Parnell's dynamic leadership among the Nationalist Party's natural supporters. In so far as they suggested otherwise, they were misleading. And the evidence suggests that, if not Parnell himself, then at least Parnell's successors were in fact misled. From his tactical approach to the Ulster question they never departed and superficially at least they had little reason to, for it continued to achieve notable successes on the road to ultimate failure. It involved, almost of necessity, the discounting of minority misgivings, reasonable and unreasonable alike, the neglect of realistic reappraisal, in socio-economic as well as religious terms, of the true character of Ulster opposition and, in the period of the struggle over the third Home Rule Bill, of the dismissal of threats of organized Orange resistance as 'mere bombast'. In all these things the impress of the personality of Parnell and of the events of 1886 is clear. They determined, even predetermined, the pattern of the future. And if the outcome was, as it certainly was, a failure to achieve unity, that is not to say other policies and other tactics would necessarily have succeeded.

Parnell's Ulster policy carried with it another important corollary. If it was unsuccessful, it could serve only to underline the existence of a third party in Anglo-Irish relations, a party, moreover, which the Nationalists were not seeking to reconcile by negotiation and possible concession. Just as there was not a united Ulster resisting Home Rule so, too, there was not a united Ireland demanding it. This was very evident to the opponents of Home Rule and, moved by conviction and by considerations of party advantage alike, they sought to exploit this weakness in the joints of the Home Rule armour. Their awareness of it preceded the 1885–6 climax of the Home Rule struggle. In an unsigned article in the *Quarterly Review*, 1883, reviewing a volume of W. E. Forster's speeches, and entitled 'Disintegration', Lord Salisbury expressed the belief that:

'The highest interests of the Empire, as well as the most sacred obligations of honour, forbid us to solve this [Irish] question by conceding any species of independence to Ireland; or in other words, any licence to the majority in that country to govern the rest of Irishmen as they please. To the minority, to those who have trusted us . . . it would be a sentence of exile or of ruin. All that is Protestant—nay, all that is loyal—all who have land or money to lose . . . would be at the mercy of the adventurers who have led the Land League, if not of the darker counsellors by whom the Invincibles have been inspired.'[1]

Unionist statesmen became most acutely conscious of feeling in Ulster and its implications after Gladstone's public conversion to Home Rule in December 1885. Their concern, though confessedly prompted by solicitude for the welfare of Ulster, was not diminished by the prospect of undeniable party advantage. When Lord Randolph Churchill decided early in 1886, 'that if the GOM went for Home Rule the Orange card would be the one to play' and prayed that it might turn out 'the ace of trumps, and not a two', he meant an ace to trump Home Rule as a policy altogether. When he crossed to Belfast and cried 'Now may be the time to show whether all those ceremonies and forms which are practised in the Orange Lodges are really living symbols or only idle meaningless ceremonies' he was not thinking of stirring his hearers to resistance which would ensure safeguards for the Ulster minority. Far from it. He was seeking to rouse Ulster to defeat Gladstone's grand design. And what was it? Home Rule? No, but rather something greater, of which Home Rule was only symbolic. 'Like Macbeth before the murder of Duncan,' explained Lord Randolph with an eloquent flourish, 'Mr Gladstone asks for time. Before he plunges the knife into the heart of the British Empire he reflects, he hesitates. . . .' Loyalists in Ulster therefore, should wait and watch, organize and prepare so that the blow if it came, should not come upon them 'as a thief in the night'.[2]

---

[1] *Quarterly Review*, 1883, No. 312, p. 584. For an account of the circumstances in which it was written and Lord Salisbury's indignation at public recognition of the identity of the author, see Cecil, *Salisbury*, Vol. III, pp. 69–70.

[2] Churchill, *Lord Randolph Churchill*, Vol. II, pp. 59–62. See also above pp. 168–9.

The appeal for readiness and, if need be, resistance, was directed to Ulster but it was not for Ulster. It was for the integrity of the Empire that Ulster was to fight. This was the larger cause in which an English statesman, lately Secretary of State for India, and soon to be Chancellor of the Exchequer, incited Ulster to physical resistance to Home Rule. However much older Tories may have been scandalized and shocked that a leader of the 'party of law and order' should use such language, words had been spoken that were not forgotten either in Ulster or in the Unionist Party. Twenty-seven years later, 'Ulster will fight, Ulster will be right' was to be the accepted slogan of the Unionist Party. And it was still accepted that the cause was greater than Ulster or than Ireland. It was the cause of Empire. And it was that which gave to the Ulster and to the Irish Question its critical significance in the history of British Imperialism.

At this point two questions, one hypothetical and having, therefore, no historical answer and the other historical, may be posed. Firstly had Parnell negotiated with, rather than campaigned against, the Ulster minority, would not the more alarmist of the fears professedly entertained by English Unionist friends of Ulster have had at least some sobering answers, and accordingly less influence in swinging opinion in England against Home Rule? And then, it may be asked, why did not Gladstone with this in mind take the initiative and include safeguards for Ulster in the draft of his Bill? He gave his reasons to the House of Commons as follows:[1]

'I cannot conceal the conviction that the voice of Ireland, as a whole, is at this moment clearly and Constitutionally spoken. I cannot say it is otherwise when five-sixths of its lawfully-chosen Representatives are of one mind in this matter. . . . Certainly, Sir, I cannot allow it to be said that a Protestant minority in Ulster, or elsewhere, is to rule the question at large for Ireland. I am aware of no Constitutional doctrine tolerable on which such a conclusion could be adopted or justified.'

But, he proceeded, the wishes of the minority should be considered to the utmost extent and he expressed himself ready to examine any practicable scheme proposing 'that Ulster itself, or, perhaps with more appearance of reason, a portion of Ulster, should be excluded from the operation of the Bill' or alternatively that some special safeguards be included to protect minority interests. But nothing practicable, in his

[1] Hansard's *Parl. Deb.* Vol. CCCIV, col. 1053.

view, had been proposed and so in the Bill itself existence of an Ulster problem was ignored. The oversight is understandable—as it was Home Rule was coupled with a complicated measure of land reform—but it was disastrous. Had some form of federalism been proposed for a limited or even indefinite period, had the Ulster Unionists been safeguarded by some express provision of the Bill, a reasonable basis for negotiation and amendment would have been provided and thereby Lord Randolph's militant exuberance would have been deprived of its only possible justification and fears, so passionately voiced by Charles Spurgeon, for the future of Irish Protestantism would presumably have been substantially allayed. For there is no doubt that this Bill in its actual form aroused uneasiness among men whose opinion could not lightly be disregarded. John Bright wrote to Gladstone in May 1886 saying, 'I cannot consent to a measure which is so offensive . . . to the whole sentiment of the province of Ulster so far as its loyal and protestant people are concerned. I cannot agree to exclude them from the protection of the imperial parliament'.[1] John Bright had his faults but insincerity was not among them. The emphasis that he placed on possible discrimination against Protestants by a Home Rule government profoundly influenced the opinion of Liberal Nonconformists throughout the British Isles. It would not have been difficult for Gladstone to insert safeguards which would have eased, if not removed, these fears.

Gladstone's speech introducing the First Home Rule Bill was followed immediately by no less than three speeches from Ulster members,[2] all expressing the opposition of what the first among them, Col. Waring, the member for North Down, called 'for want of a better name, the West Britons of Ireland'[3] to the measure. The Hon R. T. O'Neill, the member for Mid-Antrim, and the last of the three to speak, affirmed that the result of the enactment of Home Rule would be constant pressure from Ireland, with every restriction a grievance and 'grievance after grievance . . . agitated, until total separation resulted, and the result would be the establishment of an Irish Republic . . .'[4] He was magnificently mistaken. Home Rule was *not* enacted and an Irish Republic was established. But what mattered in May 1886 was not the distant prospect, but the immediate challenge. In the first exchanges on the Second Reading of the Home Rule Bill the gage was thrown down in the House and to friend and foe alike Ulster stood

---

[1] Quoted in Morley's *Gladstone*, Vol. III, p. 327.
[2] Hansard's *Parl. Deb.*, Vol. CCCIV, col. 1085–95.
[3] Ibid., col. 1089.
[4] Ibid., col. 1095.

G

revealed as the vulnerable joint in the armour of Home Rule. Joseph Chamberlain, a man rarely slow to press home a political advantage, exploited the opening to the full: 'Sir', he said, 'it is the difficulty, one of the great difficulties of this problem that Ireland is not a homogeneous community—that it consists of two nations—["No, no!"]—that it is a nation which comprises two races and two religions ["No, no!"] . . .'[1]

In some measure the notion of 'two countries' or 'two nations', and the violence of the controversy over it, helped towards bringing them into existence. In Ulster itself the antipathy to Home Rule was exploited to bring the Liberal-Unionists within the Tory fold though not all Liberals at first were content to become 'mere circus riders in the Tory Hippodrome'. A Presbyterian Minister, Mr J. B. Armour, noting that after the 1886 election Presbyterians in all Ulster had only two representatives, believed that Unionism in its new militant form was but a device to secure the ascendancy in the enjoyment of their privileges. Presbyterians in his opinion did not get fair play and in Dublin Castle nobody appeared qualified if he happened to be a Presbyterian. 'The sacred cause of Unionism', Armour complained, 'is made at the present day a stalking horse to cover a multitude of political hypocrisies. We have been true to the Union. But those who under cover of patriotic sentiment take advantage of the political crises will be responsible if any breach in the [Liberal-Tory electoral] truce takes place.'[2] But later the reaction to Home Rule submerged Liberalism in Ulster. Till the Wyndham Act of 1903, the Land Question gave it a *raison d'être*. After that date the process of absorption continued unchecked. It was perhaps the most significant legacy of 1886 to Ulster. Henceforward liberalism in politics as in sentiment had no admirers in the North. One possible bridge between Unionism and Nationalism had been carried away.

Parnell declared in the House of Commons that no single dissentient voice had been raised against the Home Rule Bill by any Irishman holding Nationalist opinions. This consensus of opinion, he argued, made impossible any half-way house between the concession of legislative autonomy to Ireland and her government as a Crown colony. He was mistaken. There was a third possibility—*divide et impera*. So long as Irish divisions endured they could be used by the opponents of Home Rule as a justification for inaction. Ulster blocked Home Rule.

[1] Hansard's *Parl. Deb.*, Vol. CCCIV, col. 1200.
[2] W. S. Armour, *Armour of Ballymoney* (London, 1934), p. 78.

Yet for Unionist leaders, it should be repeated, the Ulster Question was the *occasion*, it was not the *cause* of their opposition. It was, as Lord Randolph so confidently hoped, 'the ace of trumps'. Sincerely opposed to a measure which was reckoned likely to promote the disintegration of the Empire, some Unionist statesmen played their winning card in a spirit of light-hearted cynicism, which transgressed the spirit of the English constitutional government and which boded ill for the future reconciliation of Irishmen of different outlook and different creed.

SEPTEMBER 1913–JULY 1914. DEADLOCK.

On November 8, 1911, Arthur Balfour yielding to the mounting pressure of the B.M.G. (Balfour Must Go) movement in the ranks behind him, resigned the leadership of the Unionist Party. The succession was disputed. The two strongest candidates, Austen Chamberlain and Walter Long, both stood aside when it was understood that the choice of either would divide the party. Andrew Bonar Law was then selected.[1] He was reputed to be a 'first-class fighting-man' and in his first speech delivered at the Albert Hall he lived up to this reputation. He described the Liberal Government as 'humbugs', as 'artful dodgers' dealing in 'trickery' and 'cant', and going down the steep place like the Gadarene swine.[2]

The choice of Bonar Law as leader of the Conservative Party was an event of no small moment in the history of the Ulster Question. For Bonar Law was a Scots-Canadian and a Presbyterian; his father had once occupied an Ulster manse. His sympathy with Ulster Unionism was whole-hearted, his language indiscreet. He was, wrote Sir Walter Raleigh, a man *without unction*. Sir Walter added that he liked men without unction. None-the-less it was unfortunate that the leader of the Conservative Party at this juncture should be a man who was reluctant to impose any restraint on the activities of the Ulster Unionists and who at the last was prepared to pledge an English party to the unconditional support of an Irish faction. No stranger episode is to be found in the history of conservatism than its abandonment of all pretension in the three years before the First World War to be the party of 'law and order'. For this Bonar Law carried his full share of responsibility, not least because of his indifference to the existence of that nice distinc-

[1] For an account of the circumstances, see Robert Blake, *The Unknown Prime Minister* (London, 1955), Chapter IV.
[2] Vide Spender, *Great Britain, Empire and Commonwealth* (London, 1937), p. 416.

tion which divides conservatism from reaction, a distinction which his predecessors in the Conservative leadership had, for the most part, wisely sensed and scrupulously observed.

When Asquith moved for leave to introduce the Third Home Rule Bill on April 11, 1912, he quoted in protest a passage from one of Bonar Law's more recent utterances. 'The present Government turned the House of Commons into a market place where everything is bought and sold. In order to remain for a few months longer in office, His Majesty's Government have sold the Constitution. . . .' This dialogue followed:

THE PRIME MINISTER: 'Am I to understand that the right hon. Gentleman repeats here, or is prepared to repeat on the floor of the House of Commons—?'

MR BONAR LAW: 'Yes'.

THE PRIME MINISTER: 'Let us see exactly what it is: It is that I and my colleagues are selling our convictions'.

MR BONAR LAW: 'You have not got any'.

THE PRIME MINISTER: 'We are getting on with the new style'.[1]

A new style it was indeed—far removed from those elegant rapier thrusts with which Balfour had delighted the House. A new style which denoted a new rancour in English politics; a style which played on every Irish fear, which could only inflame every Irish passion.

The casual observer might suppose that the greatly intensified resistance to Asquith's Bill was the response to a measure more extreme in character than that sponsored by Gladstone. He would be utterly mistaken. The Third Home Rule Bill conferred only a very moderate measure of self-government on Ireland, and the main question about it as an administrative measure was whether, after the numerous concessions made to Unionist sentiment, it would prove workable. The financial authority of the Dublin Parliament in particular was restricted to an extent that would deprive the new institutions of many of the rights customarily conferred in any grant of responsible self-government to British colonies overseas. But to Unionists, opposed to Home Rule on principle, the extent of the powers to be surrendered was immaterial. Their resistance was stiffened by two quite different considerations. On the one hand the Bill, like its predecessors in 1886 and 1893, made no provision for possible safeguards for Ulster; on the

[1] House of Commons Debates, 1912, Vol. XXXVI. col. 1425.

other the passage of the Parliament Act in 1911 deprived the Lords of their absolute veto. Since the Unionists could no longer rely on the Upper House to block the way, the probability was that the Bill would become law within two and a half years. Such an outcome was well calculated to sharpen the edge of controversy.

The Prime Minister was fully aware that the opposition would concentrate on Ulster in the belief that without Ulster a Home Rule Parliament could not work. He had also carefully considered in the Cabinet whether Ulster or those counties in which the Protestants were in a clear majority should be given an option to contract out, in the Bill as introduced, or whether this should be reserved as a possible concession to be made at a later stage. Eventually the Cabinet decided that the Bill should be applied to all Ireland. This was a decision in complete accord with Asquith's own views. He had a strong personal preference that the Government policy should be a policy for the whole of Ireland. He had also a characteristic and lively sense of the possible objection to any more positive course of action. It was entirely true, as Asquith argued, that there were Nationalist minorities in considerable parts of Ulster, that in the province as a whole representation was evenly divided, that exclusion would be deeply resented by the Nationalists and that it would never propitiate extreme Unionists like Carson.[1] But while the existence of such facts complicated the problem, they did not warrant its oversight for the second time. Ignoring an issue which could not be ignored, played into the hands of the opposition. If, with the lessons of 1886 before him, the Prime Minister had made provision in the Bill for some scheme of local autonomy for the Northern counties under the aegis of the central Parliament in Dublin, he would thereby have given a clear lead to his party and a challenge to the Unionists to define precisely the cause of their opposition.

As it was, no one, least of all Asquith himself, believed that the Bill could go through without amendment. Before the measure was introduced in the House, the Cabinet warned the Nationalist party that 'the Government held themselves free to make changes, if it became clear that special treatment must be provided for the Ulster counties, and that in this case the Government will be ready to recognize the necessity either by amendment or by not pressing it [the Bill] on under the provision of the Parliament Act'.[2] Within the Cabinet, so Churchill

[1] See Memorandum printed in Spender and Asquith, *Life of Lord Oxford and Asquith*, Vol. II, pp. 31–4.
[2] Cabinet Letter to the King, February 6, 1912, quoted in Spender and Asquith, op. cit., Vol. II, pp. 15 seq.

recalled, both he and Lloyd George had consistently advocated the exclusion of Ulster on the basis of county option. But 'we had been met by the baffling argument that such a concession might well be made as the final means of securing a settlement, but would be fruitless till then'.[1]

The Home Rule Bill was introduced on April 11, 1912. In the following year it was rejected by the Lords by a majority of 257. None-the-less, under the provisions of the Parliament Act, the Bill would automatically become law if passed in two successive sessions by the House of Commons. This was the prospect that provoked the Unionist opposition to such a storm of indignation as might be thought likely to leave the Government in no doubt as to its reality. At Blenheim on July 27th, Bonar Law described the Liberal Government as 'a Revolutionary Committee which seized by fraud upon despotic power'. He continued:

'In our opposition to them we shall not be guided by the considerations, we shall not be restrained by the bonds, which would influence our action in any ordinary political struggle. We shall use whatever means seem most likely to be effective. . . .'

This Blenheim speech was justly characterized by the Prime Minister as 'a declaration of war against constitutional government' but did he really believe it? All the evidence suggests that the Liberals, reluctant in any event to use force, deluded themselves into the belief that Bonar Law and Carson were 'bluffing'. Certainly not till late in 1912 did it occur to Asquith and his colleagues that the language of Bonar Law, the drilling of Volunteers and the creation of a provisional government in Ulster might be the sober indication of actual intentions, and even then the Liberal Government were not fully convinced. After all, when Asquith had devoted his brilliant gifts of exposition to an analysis of the Ulster Question, Liberal policy did appear unassailable. The Prime Minister acknowledged that 'minorities have their rights; they also have not only their rights but susceptibilities which ought to be considered and provided for'. This the Liberal Government was prepared to do by some measure of 'open' or 'veiled' exclusion, even though such a concession would be greatly resented by their Nationalist allies. But this was not what the Unionists demanded. They went

---

[1] W. S. Churchill, *The World Crisis* (London, 1931), 4 Vols. revised edition, Vol. I, p. 104.

much further. They claimed, said the Prime Minister, a totally inadmissible right 'to thwart and defeat the constitutional demands of the great majority of their fellow-countrymen'.[1] At every election for twenty-six years four-fifths of the Irish people had voted for representatives pledged to Home Rule. Was it reasonable to suppose that the Irish people would view with equanimity the destruction of hopes constitutionally expressed? Was it just that a Parliamentary majority at Westminster should submit 'to the naked veto of an irreconcilable minority'?

Had Sir Edward Carson confined himself to the declaration, 'Ulster asks to remain in the Imperial Parliament and she means to do so', his cause would have been assured of a sympathetic hearing from both the English parties. It was his avowed intention to wreck Home Rule by any means that lay in his power that caused so sharp a division of English opinion on an Irish problem. 'If Ulster succeeds,' said Sir Edward Carson in a moment of candour in Dublin, 'Home Rule is dead.'[2] The aim of Ulster resistance was not therefore and on this view, to secure guarantees or even exclusion for the minority; it was quite simply to make Home Rule impossible. Even when war threatened in 1914, Bonar Law contemptuously rejected any compromise that would place Ulster outside the jurisdiction of a Home Rule Parliament. In the House of Commons he said:

'The position of the Unionist Party on that question [exclusion] has never been in doubt. We have always said that we are utterly opposed to Home Rule, with or without exclusion, and that we will not in any shape or form and to no degree accept any kind of responsibility for any kind of Home Rule.'

The belief that a Home Rule Parliament could not function without Ulster was the foundation of Unionist policy. Subsequent events showed that the economic resources of the North were not, as was supposed, indispensable to self-government in the rest of Ireland, yet this illusion was responsible for the extreme character of Unionist resistance. For if Home Rule was impracticable without Ulster, then its final defeat depended upon unflinching resistance by the Orangemen. It was the resolve, melodramatically proclaimed by Carson, to use the Ulster Question to wreck Home Rule that prompted the Prime

[1] Speech in Dublin, July 14, 1912.
[2] October 10, 1911. Quoted in E. Marjoribanks and Ian Colvin, *The Life of Lord Carson* (London 1932–6), 3 Vols., Vol. II, (Colvin), p. 104'.

Minister to say that between the opponents and supporters of Home
Rule there lay 'a deep and hitherto unbridgeable chasm of *principle*'.
The issue was no longer political; it was constitutional. Ulster could
claim for herself what she wished, but Ulster, as Lord Randolph's son
declared, 'cannot stand in the way of the whole of the rest of Ireland'.[1]

Sir Edward Carson was a Southern Irishman. In his youth he visited
his uncle at Ardmayle, a small village in the Tipperary plains by the
upper reaches of the River Suir, and often he must have seen the Rock
of Cashel crowned with the mingled ruins of the Cathedral and the
Palace of the Munster Kings silhouetted against the skyline. But the
memorials of the past, no more than the discontents of the present,
sufficed to kindle no nationalist feeling in the young Protestant lawyer.
Sir Edward was fifty-six years old, a famous advocate, a member for
Dublin University, when on February 27, 1910, he was chosen to succeed Walter Long as chairman of the Ulster Unionist Council. He led
the Ulster Unionists in the most decisive decade of their history.
Sombre, melancholy, a man of notable courage and great forensic
ability, he brought to the Orange cause a considerable capacity for
organization, a moral fervour almost fanatical in its intensity and an
instinctive feel for high, political drama.[2] It is told how on the final day
of the House of Lords debate on the third Home Rule Bill, he was met
by a young Peer in the lobby who asked him 'What's the betting?'
'Betting', was the cold answer, 'is that all you think about when the
constitution is in the melting-pot'? But seemingly it never occurred to
Sir Edward to enquire how far responsibility for its being there was his
own.

Ruthless, defiant, with a thinly veiled contempt for the conventions
of democratic government, Sir Edward organized resistance in Ulster.
The Provisional Government in Belfast was formed in 1912. In
September of the same year amid enthusiastic demonstrations the
Covenant was signed. The responsible leaders of Church and State:
'Being convinced in our consciences that Home Rule would be disastrous to the material well-being of Ulster as well as of the whole of
Ireland, subversive of our civil and religious freedom ... perilous to the
unity of the empire' pledged themselves 'throughout this our time of
threatened calamity to stand by one another . . . in using all means
which may be found necessary to defeat the present conspiracy to set

---

[1] W. S. Churchill, *House of Commons Debates*, Vol. XXXVII, col. 1720.
[2] For an appreciation of his political outlook see R. B. McDowell, 'Edward Carson',
in C. C. O'Brien, *The Shaping of Modern Ireland*, pp. 85–97.

up a Home Rule parliament in Ireland'.[1] And the use of 'all means' was
not only threatened but contemplated. Carson, before he started for
Ireland in 1912, said, 'he intended to break every law that is possible'
and his 'galloper', F. E. Smith, whose utterances at that time, it is true,
were not regarded with grave solemnity, assured the world that he
'would not shrink from the consequences of his convictions, not
though the whole fabric of the commonwealth be convulsed'. On the
recommendation of Field-Marshal Lord Roberts, Lieutenant-General
Sir George Richardson, 'who had learnt to know men and war fighting
the Afghans and the Pathans on the North-West Frontier', was placed
in command of the Ulster volunteer force.[2] The Rev. J. B. Armour,
almost a lone voice surviving from Ulster's more liberal past, continued to maintain that 'Carsonism is not really popular outside the
Orange Lodges' and that his Provisional Government was 'the most
outlandish proposal ever made by a sane man', but he added, not
surprisingly in view of the military preparations being made, that in
Ulster 'the terror is so great that sane men prefer to sit silent and say
nothing'.[3] For in retrospect the wonder is not that 'Carson's bluff' was
never called, but rather that its immediate consequences were not
more violent.

The policy of the Orangemen had permeated the Conservative Party
by introducing even to its inner counsels a spirit of intolerance, curiously out of place in the leisurely atmosphere of English politics. In
the autumn of 1913 Lord Esher, for many years a confidential adviser
both to the Crown and to its Ministers, one of the most influential men
in England, joined the ranks of elder statesmen and distinguished
academics who had advised that the King should intervene, either by
the exercise of the royal prerogative of dissolution or by royal veto of
the Home Rule Bill[4], with the further suggestion that he should use the
power of remonstrance. How exactly this obsolete power should be
used was a matter requiring 'grave consideration', but, argued Lord
Esher, 'it may be urged that the constitution is for the moment abro-
gated and that the House of Commons is, in point of fact, a "Con-
stituent Assembly" of a revolutionary character, and not a Parliament'.[5]

---

[1] Curtis and McDowell, *Irish Historial Documents*, p. 304.
[2] *The Life of Lord Carson*, Vol. II, p. 187.
[3] Comment of the Rev. J. B. Armour. Quoted W. S. Armour, op. cit. p. 282.
[4] For an account of the pressure upon the King see H. Nicolson, *King George the Fifth*
(London, 1952), p. 200.
[5] *Journals and Letters of Reginald Viscount Esher* (London, 1934–38), 4 Vols., Vol. III,
p. 129.

The adjective 'revolutionary' was used on the ground that the Liberals had disturbed the traditional balance of the constitution by enactment of the Parliament Act, followed by the introduction of the Home Rule Bill.

So questionable a foundation for so grave a charge, advanced by a man so shrewd in judgement, reveals most clearly how disputes over Ireland had deprived Unionist statesmen of their sense of proportion. Two days later Lord Esher expressed a somewhat modified opinion to Arthur Balfour. 'Carson's methods to my thinking', he wrote, 'are the right and above board ones. Those who hate Home Rule sufficiently should be ready to risk their skins, not skulk behind the throne.' And later in conversation Lord Curzon, the noble representative of an antique order, urged that the contest must finally be allowed 'to solve itself in battle on the soil of Ireland'. Lord Esher assented, adding that Carson should 'be encouraged to provoke a contest at an early date'.[1] And in the meantime Lord Milner was active and astonishingly successful in raising funds from some of the most distinguished names in the country to combat, if need be, by force of arms the application of an Act of Parliament for the better government of Ireland.[2]

The party system is essentially Whig alike in origin as in character. The Tory tendency to designate opposition to their party as 'faction' expresses an outlook, impressive in office, but liable to mislead in opposition. Never has this been more clearly seen than in the years before 1914. A policy introduced by the Government of the day, supported by a clear majority in the House of Commons, approved by the most influential political leaders in the Dominions[3] was termed a 'conspiracy' against the Crown and Empire and 'all means' were regarded as defensible in opposing it. Bonar Law, wrote Lord Esher to Balfour, 'made a great mistake, I think, in admitting for a moment that the Ulster question could be settled by a General Election. It has always been obvious that the Ulster people would not and ought not to yield even if a General Election were to go in favour of the Government.'[4] In such circumstances the prospect of settlement by constitutional means inevitably became more and more remote.

[1] *Journals and Letters of Viscount Esher*, Vol. III, pp. 134 and 135.
[2] A. M. Gollin, *Proconsul in Politics* (London, 1964), pp. 187–8. See Chap. VIII generally.
[3] Vide Spender, op. cit., p. 420.
[4] Op. cit., Vol. III, pp. 163–4.

While the signs and portents were of war, the weight of a now long-established English tradition in favour of the peaceful settlement of the gravest issues by party compromise and concession, none-the-less remained. Was there no possibility at least of a narrowing of issues by discussion? In a letter to *The Times* on September 11, 1913, Lord Loreburn, who had been Lord Chancellor in successive Liberal governments from December 1905 till his resignation in June 1912, proposed a settlement by a Conference between the party leaders. In one sense the letter was well-timed. It was published at a moment when there was mounting concern at what the end of the unloosing of sectional and party passions might be. Five days earlier, on September 8th, Lord Crewe, the Lord Privy Seal, reported to Asquith the substance of a conversation at Balmoral with King George V. The King, while not at all attracted by 'the impudent demand' of some Unionist leaders that he should either veto the Home Rule Bill or dissolve Parliament before the beginning of the next Session, was 'not less convinced that the passage of the Bill will mean what he calls civil war in Ulster than that its failure will make the government of the rest of Ireland impossible'.[1] On that same day, September 8, 1913, Augustine Birrell, the Chief Secretary, reported, with a familiar excess of underlining, to Asquith: '. . . the *appearance* of the Measure on *the Statute Book* is *all in all*—to our sturdy friends and allies'. And he proceeded: 'I still adhere to the opinion that *Civil War*, as Balfour is willing to call it, is at least as *unthinkable* as anything he finds unthinkable, but that the *Riots* and *Disturbances* will be on a *great scale* and beyond the powers of the *Police* to cope with.'[2] Here, even on Birrell's somewhat more sanguine view, was a situation no government, and least of all a pacifically minded Liberal administration, could contemplate with equanimity. But did Loreburn's proposal for a Conference settlement offer a way out? Asquith thought not. He wrote to his former colleague asking what precisely he meant by his letter to *The Times*. There was, wrote the Prime Minister,[3] 'an irreconcilable difference of opinion between the supporters and opponents of Home Rule; . . . the one affirmed and the other denied the necessity for a subordinate legislature with a local Executive responsible to it; and that neither party was likely to enter into a conference, if the abandonment of the position which it had hitherto held was to be a preliminary condition'. Asquith put the point even more forcibly in a long memorandum submitted to the King and

[1] *Asquith Papers*, Dep. 38.
[2] Ibid.   [3] Ibid.

circulated to the Cabinet:[1] 'It is', he commented 'no good blinding one's eye to obvious and undeniable facts, and one of those facts, relevant to the present case, [settlement by conference] undoubtedly is, that there is a deep and hitherto unbridgeable chasm of *principle* between the supporters and the opponents of Home Rule. It is a question not of phraseology but of substance. Four-fifths of Ireland, with the support of a substantial British majority in the present and late House of Commons, will be content with nothing less than a subordinate legislature with a local executive responsible to it.' Until that was accepted, there was no fruitful basis from which conference deliberations could proceed.

Lord Loreburn's initiative, which provoked the greatest anxiety in the Irish party, lapsed,—Morley delivering a last, unkind thrust on September 30, 1913, in a letter to Asquith—'Loreburn is pure moonshine for any practical purpose whatever;... I have seen a good many mushroom schemes in my time but never a more fungoid growth than this.'[2] The Prime Minister then summed up the problem for the King once more, and in reply to anxious royal enquiry[3] on October 1st:[4] 'Either alternative [coercion of Ulster or of Ireland] is in the highest degree repellent; but unless we are to abandon once and for all the reign of law, every Act of Parliament must be carried into execution; and if its execution is resisted, it is the duty of the State to see that that resistance is overcome by whatever modes of enforcement are appropriate and adequate in the particular case.' The argument was logical but the conclusion was not reassuring. Both the King and his Prime Minister were already aware of the existence of misgivings and the risk of uncertain loyalties were the Army to be used to impose Home Rule upon Ulster. And the King's misgivings were the greater for he never doubted that Ulster would resist.

While Loreburn's proposal for an immediate conference came to nothing, his letter stimulated ideas for a negotiated settlement. They all, as Redmond so greatly feared, followed one line—the exclusion of Ulster, or some part of Ulster, from the jurisdiction of a Home Rule Bill. What form of exclusion and for what period of time? The Government, willing to acquiesce in *de facto* exclusion as a basis of settlement by early 1914, remained none-the-less resolved to retain the

[1] *Asquith Papers*. Dep. 38. Also reprinted in Spender and Asquith, op. cit., Vol. II, pp. 31–4.
[2] *Asquith Papers*. Dep. 38.
[3] Reprinted in Nicolson, op. cit., pp. 225–9, and also in *Asquith Papers*.
[4] *Asquith Papers*. Dep. 38.

principle of unity. But was this acceptable even to moderate Unionists? The King was quite clear it was not. 'I have always given you my opinion', he wrote to Asquith on January 26, 1914, 'that Ulster will never agree to send representatives to an Irish Parliament in Dublin, no matter what safeguards or guarantees you may provide.'[1] In the early months of 1914 negotiations proceeded privately on the issues of 'naked' or 'veiled' exclusion of Ulster, or some part of Ulster, either for a period of years or indefinitely. But behind and parallel with these negotiations there continued the simpler conflict Home Rule or no Home Rule with developments in Ulster watched, anxiously or hopefully according to the party viewpoint, for any opportunity they might offer for the final wrecking of the Bill. In July 1914 Lord Loreburn's proposal for a party conference yielded belated fruit. But the Conference summoned by the King at Buckingham Palace bore out Asquith's initial objections. It met; its members agreed to debate exclusion in terms of the area to be excluded and the time for which it was to be excluded. They failed to reach agreement on the former; and so the latter was never discussed. Yet one suggestion was made at the Conference, which though later retracted, foreshadowed the future. On July 22nd Sir Edward Carson substituted 'for his demand for the exclusion of the whole of Ulster, the exclusion of a *block* consisting of the Six Counties: Antrim, Down, Armagh, Derry, Tyrone, and Fermanagh, *including* Derry City and Belfast: *all to vote as One Unit*'.[2]

The predicament of the Unionist Party by 1914 was clear enough. It did not consist in the lack of an Irish policy, but in the fact that its policy having been put into practice under exceptionally favourable conditions, had failed. Balfour's social reforms conferred benefits on Ireland, but killing Home Rule by kindness was destined to failure in a country in which good government was not accepted by the majority as a substitute for national government. The Unionists, therefore, could only hope to maintain the Union by uncompromising opposition to the wishes of the majority of the Irish people. In 1912–14 Unionist policy sought therefore not to secure special treatment for the minority in Ulster, but to use the Ulster Question to block Home Rule. 'Ulster', cried Carson, 'will be the field on which the privileges of the whole nation will be lost or won.' So it was that Unionist Ulster in a cause

---

[1] *Asquith Papers.* Dep. 39.
[2] *Redmond Papers.* John Redmond kept a day to day record of the Proceedings of the Conference.

she considered just and loyal, was encouraged to take every step which
she had for centuries condemned in her southern neighbours. But
Unionist Ulster in her own eyes was justified. For Ulster was in the
right; the Nationalists in the wrong. And in that view she had the support of the English Unionist Party and its leader, Andrew Bonar Law.

By 1914 the faith of Irishmen in English parties and English pro-
mises was dead. The Home Rule Bill which John Redmond had welcomed with a warmth that cloaked anxiety as a 'great measure', was, it
is true, placed on the Statute Book in October 1914, but accompanied
by an Act suspending its operation till after the ending of the War and
by an assurance of its amendment in respect of Ulster; that division of
the nation which Redmond had denounced at Limerick in 1912 as 'an
abomination and a blasphemy', had been the subject of negotiation in
which Redmond, under pressure from his Liberal allies, agreed to the
exclusion of Ulster for six years as the 'extremest limit of concession'
without eliciting any favourable response from his Unionist opponents. It was a concession which the more advanced Nationalists were
not prepared to make. 'So long as England is strong and Ireland is
weak', was the comment of Sinn Féin, 'she may continue to oppress
this country, but she shall not dismember it.' In the south there were
men who had observed the Ulster rebellion, who had learnt from
the organization of the Ulster Volunteers, who had watched the *Fanny*
unload her cargo of arms at Larne. Like Sir Edward Carson—'the
only Irish member of Parliament who has any backbone' observed
Irish Freedom, the newspaper of the Irish Republican Brotherhood—
they did not share John Redmond's belief in the wisdom and good faith
of majorities at Westminster; like Bildad the Shuhite they answered and
said, 'how long will it be till ye make an end of words?'

1920. THE UNIONIST STATE

As Chancellor of the Exchequer in Asquith's pre-War administration,
Lloyd George had been fertile in expedients to resolve the Ulster
deadlock. But when he came to power in late 1916, he deemed himself
free from particular past commitments in respect of an Irish settlement.
Tom Jones, his trusted adviser, believed that the key to Lloyd George's
Irish policy in succeeding years was to be found in views expressed on
March 7, 1917[1] and again on December 22, 1919, when Lloyd George
made clear his unwillingness to coerce the people of Ulster into accep-

[1] Thomas Jones, *Lloyd George* (London 1951), p. 187.

tance of an all-Ireland Parliament. They were, he thought, 'as alien in blood, in religious faith, in traditions, in outlook—as alien from the rest of Ireland in this respect as the inhabitants of Fife or Aberdeen. . . . To place them under national rule against their will would be as glaring an outrage on the principles of liberty and self-government as the denial of self-government would be for the rest of Ireland'.[1] If Tom Jones is right, conviction alone might, therefore, have prompted the Prime Minister to isolate and dispose of the problem of Ulster as a first step towards an Irish settlement. But even if conviction were absent, political circumstances strongly suggested such a course. Lloyd George was a Home Ruler; but he was also the Prime Minister of a Coalition Government which, after the 1918 election, was heavily dependent on Unionist support. He was, in respect of Irish policy, where past passion was by no means spent, in a peculiar sense the prisoner of the Coalition, with far less freedom for manoeuvre than critics of his Irish policies are wont to allow. Lloyd George, 'the great little man' who had 'won the war', still stood in 1920, it is true, at the very pinnacle of popular esteem. But he presided over a Cabinet in which Bonar Law, that formidable supporter of Ulster Unionism, was Lord Privy Seal and Arthur Balfour, whose Irish reputation had been determined once for all by reaction to events in Mitchelstown as long ago as 1887, Lord President of the Council. Lord Curzon was at the Foreign Office, Lord Milner at the Colonial Office, Austen Chamberlain at the Exchequer, Lord Birkenhead with memories of more active, jauntier days as Galloper Smith not so very far away, was Lord Chancellor and Churchill, a Liberal Home Ruler, it is true, but from the Irish point of view not a particularly reassuring one, was at the War Office. And, what was of equal importance, the weight of Unionist influence in the Cabinet, reflected Unionist strength in the House of Commons. Of the 484 supporters of the Coalition returned in the 'coupon' election of December 1918, 383 were Conservatives. Nor was their conservatism of the compromising kind. These were the victors in an electoral campaign that has gone down to history for its platform clamour for the hanging of the Kaiser and the squeezing of the lemon till the pips squeaked. And if it has been shown to be unjust to think of the House of Commons returned at the election as having been, in Keynesian

[1] *House of Commons Debates*, December 22, 1919, Vol. 123, col. 1171. This extract is reprinted in Thomas Jones ibid. but incorrectly attributed to House of Commons Debates for March 7, 1917 (Vol. XCI, col. 459) when the Prime Minister made the same points in somewhat different terms.

parlance, composed of 'a lot of hard-faced men who look as if they had done very well out of the war',[1] assuredly they were not men who would concede gracefully any substantial measure of self-government to Ireland. If the Cabinet was strongly Unionist, the House of Commons had the strongest 'diehard' representation of modern times.

To the Unionist phalanx there was no sufficient counterpoise either within or outside Coalition ranks. The 383 Coalition Conservatives were reinforced by 48 Conservatives returned without the Coalition Coupon. The Liberals, painfully divided since the Maurice debate of May 9, 1918[2] between supporters of Lloyd George and Asquith, returned 136 supporters of the Coalition and a mere 26 Asquithians, or 'Squiffies' as this much abused remnant of halcyon pre-war days were contemptuously called. There was, it is true, the foreshadowing of ascending Labour fortunes but the actual number of Labour members was only 59. There was no organized Irish Nationalist vote. 'The two supreme services', commented Churchill,[3] 'which Ireland has rendered Britain are her accession to the Allied cause on the outbreak of the Great War, and her withdrawal from the House of Commons at its close.' His observation was at once facile and, in one minor but important respect, inaccurate. It was not Ireland that withdrew from the House of Commons; it was Sinn Féin, which represented some four-fifths of Irish constituencies, that boycotted Parliament at Westminster. Ulster Unionists attended. Unionist presence and nationalist absence were not without importance. In conjunction they added one further element to a situation which, in parliamentary terms, was more favourable to Ulster claims than any that had existed since 1886. It was in this situation that Ulster Unionists obtained a settlement in 1920 which in substance, though not in form, gave them all they had asked for, for themselves. It would have been astonishing if it had been otherwise.

The preamble to the Act of 1920[4] was confined to the sanguine description of it as 'an Act to provide for the better Government of Ireland'. Section 76 (2) explained one of its principal purposes. It read: 'The Government of Ireland Act, 1914, is hereby repealed as from the

---

[1] J. M. Keynes, *The Economic Consequences of the Peace* (London, 1920), p. 133. The remark was quoted by Keynes with approval but not in fact first made by him. For some critical reflections upon its justice see R. B. McCallum, *Public Opionin and the Last Peace* (Oxford, 1944), Chap. I.

[2] There are many accounts of the debate which was provoked by Major-General Sir Frederick Maurice's letter to *The Times* of May 7, 1918. For one of the more recent see Blake op. cit. pp. 368–75.

[3] *The Aftermath*, p. 283.

[4] 10 and 11 Geo V, ch. 67.

passing of this Act.' So much for the crowning achievement of the unfortunate Redmond—an Act repealed without ever having been in force. With the Act of 1914 went the principle of unity on which it rested. The essence of the 1920 Act, which was division, was to be found appropriately in the first section of it. This called into existence, not an Irish Parliament, but two Parliaments, one for the North of Ireland and one for the South of Ireland. 'For the purposes of this Act, Northern Ireland shall consist of the parliamentary counties of Antrim, Armagh, Down, Fermanagh, Londonderry and Tyrone, and the parliamentary boroughs of Belfast and Londonderry, and Southern Ireland shall consist of so much of Ireland as is not comprised within the said parliamentary counties and boroughs', the most northerly county, Donegal, therefore, being part of it.

Section 2 provided for the constitution of a Council of Ireland, composed equally of members of Parliament from the North and South of Ireland with minimal powers relating to railway administration, fisheries and contagious diseases in animals. The hope was expressed that the existence of this Council might open the way in time to unity by agreement and an all-Ireland parliament.

Lloyd George told the House of Commons late in 1919 that there were four ways in which the Ulster problem might be resolved.[1] Ulster as a whole might be excluded from the jurisdiction of a Home Rule Parliament; counties in Ulster might be excluded on a basis of county option, leaving substantial Unionist minorities outside the excluded area, the six counties might be excluded as a bloc or finally the six counties might be excluded with some adjustment of their boundaries. The Act of 1920 came down in favour of the third of these possibilities, namely the exclusion of the six Plantation counties but Lloyd George, as subsequent exchanges during the Anglo-Irish Treaty negotiations showed, was himself reluctant to abandon the tactical advantages implicit in the fourth. But the Act itself was explicit, and once it was on the Statute book, the Northern Ireland Government could rely upon the solid sanction of a statutory definition of area.

How was that area determined? The answer is that it was proposed by the Government, debated and agreed by the Ulster Unionist Council on March 10, 1920 and then finally approved by Parliament. In the debate in the Ulster Unionist Council[2] it was accepted that a Parlia-

[1] *House of Commons Debates*, December 22, 1919, Vol. 123, col. 1175.
[2] For an account see Colvin, op. cit. Vol. III, pp. 382–6 and Ronald McNeill, *Ulster's Stand for Union* (London, 1922), pp. 277–80.

ment for the nine counties of Ulster, consisting of 64 members, would be likely to give a Unionist majority of 3 or 4. 'No sane man', Captain Craig told the House of Commons later,[1] 'would undertake to carry on a Parliament with it.' On the other hand in a six-county area, returning 52 members, there would be a Unionist majority of 10 or more. 'We quite frankly admit' Captain Craig told the House of Commons, 'that we cannot hold the nine counties. . . . Therefore, we have decided that in the interests of the greater part of Ulster, it is better that we should give up those three counties (Donegal, Monaghan and Cavan) rather than take on a bigger task than we are able to carry out.'[2] Parliamentary endorsement of that decision resolved the question of area, on which the Buckingham Palace Conference had foundered, in accord with the views of the Ulster Unionists. This was a signal triumph for their cause.

In an area, such as the province of Ulster, where the voting strength of two communities was nearly equal, a plebiscite offered no satisfactory solution and in fact a plebiscite was not popular with the party leaders on either side just because it would have settled none of the real problems involved. The issue in 1920 thus turned once again, as it had in 1914, on the precise area to be excluded. On a basis of county option the four north-eastern counties would certainly have voted for exclusion, but no such certainty existed about the wishes of Fermanagh or Tyrone. Indeed, voting as a single constituency, they would presumably have produced a small nationalist majority. Yet the Unionists, who could not hope to maintain a majority in Ulster as a whole, insisted that the six-county area was a cardinal point in any possible settlement. Since 1914, observed Winston Churchill[3] with imperial revulsion, 'every institution, almost, in the world was strained. Great Empires have been overturned. The whole map of Europe has been changed. . . . The mode and thought of men, the whole outlook on affairs, the grouping of parties, all have encountered violent and tremendous changes in the deluge of the world, but as the deluge subsides and the waters fall we see the dreary steeples of Fermanagh and Tyrone emerging once again. The integrity of their quarrel is one of the few institutions that have been unaltered in the cataclysm which has swept the world'. But the quarrel was settled in 1920 by the

---

[1] *House of Commons Debates*, Vol. 127, Coll. 990–1. Captain Craig was a brother of Sir James Craig and spoke for the Ulster Unionists.
[2] Ibid., col. 991.
[3] *The Aftermath*, p. 319.

imperial government and Parliament in favour of one party, without consulting the inhabitants of the two counties whose destiny was in dispute.

The Ulster Unionist Council approved the six counties as the area of jurisdiction for the Northern Government, in order that their party might govern as large an area as was consistent with assured Unionist supremacy. Since the area so determined was not changed, as the Irish Free State had substantial reason to hope, by the Boundary Commission of 1924, the Unionists have remained in office in Northern Ireland for more than forty years. No government in Europe, is the boast, has been so stable. In this respect, therefore, the calculations of 1920 have proved well founded. In a province where political parties are founded on differences in creed, where a Protestant who is not a Unionist, where a Catholic who is not a Nationalist is as rare as a swallow in March, a floating vote does not exist. A party that has a majority retains it, for at the least threat of disaffection, the old party cry is raised and every issue of political or social reform is subordinated to the chill hand of sectarian prejudice. As a result the Unionist majorities at successive elections have remained virtually unchanged. Predominance is secure, but at the price among other things of political vitality. The forms of democracy remain, but its spirit can scarcely flourish in a political atmosphere so frozen that up to 70 per cent of the seats have been uncontested at a general election.

Unionist determination of area was matched by Unionist success in respect of time-limit. There was no time limit set to Northern Ireland's exclusion from an all Ireland Parliament and so the other major issue before the Buckingham Palace Conference in 1914 was also decided in favour of the minority. This meant the abandonment of the principle of unity. Austen Chamberlain, for the Coalition Government, disclaimed British responsibility for this. 'It is', he said,[1] 'a paradox of ours that the only hope of union in Ireland is to recognize her present division . . . It is not we who are dividing Ireland . . . not we who made party coincide with the religious differences. . . .' Before 1914 it had also been proposed to recognize it, but on the Liberal-Nationalist side always for a limited period of time with the presumption of unity when it had elapsed. It was for that reason that Asquith declared that calling the Act of 1920 a Home Rule Bill was 'a manifest and almost aggressive abuse of language'.[2] Home

[1] *House of Commons Debates*, 1920, Vol. 127, col. 981.
[2] Ibid., col. 1111.

Rule had always meant a single legislature with a single executive responsible to it. There had been a pledge to the dissentient minority that they should not be coerced but there was another pledge— equally solemn—to the vast majority of the Irish people that they would have what they had demanded for thirty years and what after two elections the people of Great Britain had conceded. The Home Rule Act should not have been repealed with that pledge left un- redeemed. Yet this was what was proposed with the consequence that the foundation would be no longer unity but dualism.[1] And Asquith, in this at least surely justified, dismissed in language that they deserved the 'fleshless and bloodless skeleton' of the Irish Council with the 'spectral' figure of an Irish Parliament behind it. What was of sub- stance was the fact that the Act of 1920 left it open to 'an Ulster minority for all time to veto, if it pleases, the coming into existence of an Irish Parliament'.[2]

There was no doubt that Northern Ireland was vested with the power to veto unity under the provisions of the 1920 Act and little doubt that a Unionist Government in Belfast would exercise its power for that purpose, if not for all, at least for a long time to come. The Act of 1920 not only divided Ireland but in so doing it equated majority and minority. There was thus *equal* representation from North and South on the Council of Ireland and achievement by the minority of parity with the majority in effect gave to the minority its power of veto on any step towards unity. Complacent Coalition commentaries on the theme of a broad conciliar road to unity, were given as short shrift by Captain Craig as they were by Asquith. 'I would not be fair to the House', he said[3], 'if I lent the slightest hope of that union arising within the lifetime of any man in this House. I do not believe it for a moment.' There was good reason for this confident and correct asser- tion. Captain Craig explained it. It was the creation of separate par- liamentary and administrative institutions for Northern Ireland. Had Northern Ireland remained, as would have been theoretically more acceptable to staunch Unionists, under the direct control of Westminster and Whitehall, her position as a separate political entity in Ireland would sooner or later be reviewed, and possibly reconsidered by Liberal or Labour politicians of whom Ulster Unionists were equally and profoundly mistrustful. The existence of a separate Parliament was regarded, and rightly regarded, as a safeguard against

[1] *House of Commons Debates*, 1920, Vol. 127, col. 1109.
[2] Ibid., coll. 1112–3.   [3] Ibid., coll. 984–5.

such an eventuality. 'We see our safety . . .', said Captain Craig, 'in having a Parliament of our own, for we believe that once a Parliament is set up and working well . . . we should fear no one, and . . . be in a position of absolute security.'[1]

Paradoxical as in many respects it must appear, the creation of a Unionist State in North-Eastern Ireland was not welcomed by the Orangemen in 1920. Ulster Unionist members refrained from voting for the Bill in the Commons, though the prospect of its defeat in the Lords caused them anxious concern, on the ground that it destroyed the Union. Extreme reluctance was displayed in accepting self-governing institutions. The British government was reminded in 1921 that Ulster had made the 'supreme sacrifice' in accepting the Act. The Prime Minister of Northern Ireland, Sir James Craig (later Lord Craigavon), wrote to Lloyd George, on July 29th that year, not long after the signing of the Truce and while the British Government and Sinn Féin were exchanging views about the basis of a possible Anglo-Irish settlement, to 'call to your mind the sacrifices we have so recently made in agreeing to self-government and consenting to the establishment of a Parliament for Northern Ireland. Much against our wish, but in the interests of peace, we accepted this as a *final settlement* of the long outstanding difficulty with which Great Britain has been confronted'.[2]

The note of self-sacrificing patriotism was maintained; but expressions of opinion as to the value of self-governing institutions later underwent a remarkable transformation. With the passage of time the Unionist leaders tended to place less emphasis upon the 'supreme sacrifice' and more and more upon the 'final settlement' that had been achieved in 1920, till the preservation of these self-governing institutions became a cardinal point in the Unionist creed. The change in opinion was brought about to some extent by the administrative benefits conferred by the existence of a local Parliament, but more notably by a growing conviction that, as Captain Craig had correctly foreseen, local self-government gave the most explicit guarantee possible, amid the play of changing political forces, of permanent

---

[1] *House of Commons Debates*, 1920, Vol. 127, col. 990. Captain Craig spoke with customary candour in remarking: 'We profoundly distrust the Labour Party and we profoundly distrust the right hon. Gentleman the Member for Paisley [Mr Asquith]'. Ibid., 989.

[2] Northern Ireland. *Parl. Deb.* House of Commons Vol. I, Coll. 48–9. See also *Correspondence between H.M.G. and the Prime Minister of Northern Ireland*, 1921, cmd. 1561, in which Sir James Craig returned to the same point.

supremacy to the Unionist Party. A restoration of the Union so far as
the six counties were concerned came to be denounced as a heresy.
'The cry "back to Westminster"', warned the Report of the Ulster
Unionist Council for 1936, 'is a subtle move fraught with great
danger. Had we refused to accept a Parliament for Northern Ireland
and remained at Westminster, there can be but little doubt that now
we would either be inside the Free State or fighting desperately against
incorporation. Northern Ireland without a Parliament of her own would
be a standing temptation to certain British politicians to make another
bid for a final settlement with Irish Republicans.' The North was, and
is, determined to maintain its Parliament.

The air of finality, which so completely reconciled Ulster Unionism
to its destiny, proved the most repellent feature of the settlement to the
majority of Irishmen. The partition of Ireland was regarded as a crime.
It might be explained; it could not be justified. Emotional though the
detestation of the Boundary might be it has not proved transient. It is
true that before the First World War the Nationalists under Redmond's leadership ultimately assented under Liberal pressure to the
exclusion of the North Eastern counties from the jurisdiction of the
Dublin Parliament. For this reluctant acquiescence Redmond was not
forgiven, even though it was his hope that the concession of local
autonomy to this area, or of Home Rule within Home Rule as it was
popularly called, would suffice to pacify the Unionists and so secure
the *inclusion* of these counties in principle in an all-Ireland Parliament.
Far different was the effect of the Act of 1920, for by setting up a
Parliament in Belfast it gave strength and permanence to Partition.
This settlement, which appealed to Lloyd George because of its tactical advantages, was viewed quite differently on the other side of the
Irish Sea where a people suspicious by temperament, and rendered still
more suspicious by experience, interpreted it as a deliberate blow at
Irish unity. Such was almost certainly not the Prime Minister's inten-
tion, yet had it been so, he could have devised no more effective means
of furthering his aims.

As early as May 30, 1920, C. P. Scott of the *Manchester Guardian*
analysed in a letter to John Dillon, in temperate terms, objections to the
Bill which gave contemporary expression to this view.

'As you say', he wrote, 'the present Bill has no relation to the needs
of the situation. Its real objects so far as I can make out are, first to get
rid of the Home Rule Act, and secondly to entrench the six counties
against Nationalist Ireland. Its effect, one fears, will be not to make a

solution easier but to make it harder, by creating a fresh and powerful obstacle.'[1] These were prophetic words.

Beautifully situated, on a hillside some miles from the centre of Belfast, stand the Northern Ireland Parliament Buildings at Stormont. Looking from the foot of the hill at the long façade, it is easy to understand why so much money was lavished in building so imposing a home for the Northern Legislature. For Stormont was the offspring of no wanton extravagance, but rather was conceived as the symbol of the permanence and stability of the Northern State. It remains the visible indication of the Unionist intention to perpetuate the seemingly makeshift solution of the Ulster Question enacted in 1920.

A life-size statue of Lord Carson dominates the approach to the Parliament Buildings. No more fitting tribute could seemingly be paid to the leader whose policy resulted in the establishment of a Belfast Parliament. The Government of Ireland Bill, declared Captain Redmond, by 1920 a lone survivor in the House of Commons of the party his uncle, John Redmond, had led, 'is the price that has been paid to the right Hon. Member for Duncairn (Sir Edward Carson) by the Government which is beholden him'. Yet for Carson there was defeat as well as victory. Craig might say 'the Bill gives us practically everything we fought for'; he might, and again with substantial justice, repudiate the charge that Ulster was attempting to prevent Home Rule for the rest of Ireland as 'utterly false'. But Carson could not. The Bill did not give him everything he was fighting for, just because in his case, though not in Craig's, he was fighting for the maintenance of the Union and against Home Rule in any form. He was not an Ulster Unionist but a Unionist without qualification.

It is true that until 1920 Unionist policy had been directed to the maintenance of the Union. To that all else was secondary and subordinate. Unionist leaders since 1886 had confessedly used the Ulster Question to wreck Home Rule, since without Ulster, Home Rule was deemed to be impracticable. Carson had said many times that the Ulstermen, whom he led, but of whom he was not one, were not fighting for themselves alone. He had assured the Southern Unionists specifically that no circumstances could justify a settlement which left them at the mercy of 'Rome Rule', that the Ulster Volunteers would march from Belfast to Kinsale to avert such a calamity. But when the hour of decision came the fate of the Southern Unionists, who had never been

---

[1] Quoted in J. L. Hammond, *C. P. Scott of the Manchester Guardian* (London, 1934), p. 273.

216 THE IRISH QUESTION

uncritically receptive either of Carson's leadership or of their Orange champions, received scant consideration in Belfast. This indeed had been foreshadowed by the growing divergence between Northern and Southern Unionists, deriving at root from differences in numbers, social structure and interests, but provoked more immediately by the intransigence of the North. Uneasy at the intention of Ulster to block Home Rule, critical of the uncompromising character of Ulster's resistance before 1914, the Southern Unionists ultimately came into direct conflict with the Ulster Unionists at the Irish Convention, an unrepresentative body boycotted by Sinn Féin, but nonetheless called together in 1917 by Lloyd George and given the thankless task of making a final bid for a peaceful settlement.[1] The 'inexorable opposition' of Ulster to any form of Home Rule made negotiation impossible, and though her representatives went into the Convention with stated willingness to consider reasonable terms of settlement, they did not contribute a single concrete proposal in eight months and ended it by voting against what the leader of the Southern Unionists, Lord Midleton considered 'the most advantageous and best-guarded scheme which has yet been devised to keep Ireland united'.[2] Without subscribing to this all too sanguine judgement, the fact remains that the partition of Ireland was in prospect, neither to the liking, nor in the interest of the Southern Unionists and many of them deeply resented in 1920 what they deemed to be their desertion. As a minority they had been encouraged to resist Home Rule by the Ulster leaders, but when the crisis came the North made terms for itself alone. This was not what Carson desired but in the years of his leadership he had pursued his aims in such a way as to accentuate, not only the inherited divisions between Unionist and Nationalist in every corner of Ireland, but also so as to divide the Irish Unionists. When he died, in 1935, the leading Southern Unionist paper wrote in its editorial 'Edward Carson's career was one of the tragedies of Irish history. . . . He has died at the age of eighty-one after a life crammed with great achievements and yet strangely barren of great results.'[3] He was at once a principal beneficiary and the outstanding victim of Lloyd George's Irish policy, which in one legislative enactment safeguarded Unionist Ulster and destroyed the Union.

Irish nationalist opinion credits neither Carson nor Craig with final

[1] *The Report of the Proceedings of the Irish Convention* was published in Cd. 9019.
[2] The Earl of Midleton, *Ireland. Dupe or Heroine* (London, 1932), p. 109.
[3] *The Irish Times*, October 23, 1935.

responsibility for Partition. That is attributed personally to Lloyd George and collectively to the British Government. 'They have created for the first time in history' protested Joe Devlin, leader of the Ulster Nationalists, 'two Irelands. Providence arranged the geography of Ireland and the right hon Gentleman (Mr Lloyd George) has changed it.'[1] But in respect of individuals there are in fact other British claimants to such responsibility. Chief among them stands the Canadian, Andrew Bonar Law. He declared that until War came in 1914 he had cared for only two things in politics, Ulster and Tariff Reform. 'Over Ulster', writes his biographer Mr Robert Blake, 'his success was indisputable, and her survival as an autonomous province wholly independent of the Irish Republic is in no small measure the achievement of Bonar Law.' Mr Blake recognises the greater popular appeal of Carson's theatrical leadership, and Craig's contribution in building up a solid backbone of indigenous resistance but he nonetheless concludes that 'without the uncompromising support of Bonar Law, without his much criti cized decision to pledge the whole of the English Conservative Party to the Ulster cause, it is very unlikely that Ulster would stand where she stands today'.[2] It is a judgement well grounded in evidence but hardly to be accepted as conclusive, unless and until the Lloyd George papers are made available for historical study. But of two things, there can be little doubt. In respect of Irish policy Bonar Law had stronger backing in Cabinet and Parliament than Lloyd George and he was moved by a single-mindedness of aim to which Lloyd George laid no claim. And a third provokes ironic reflection. Irish assertions of ultimate British responsibility for partition receive unlikely, but nonetheless substantial vindication from the biographer of the Canadian leader of the Conservative Party, who goes down to history as the 'Unknown Prime Minister'.

[1] *House of Commons Debates*, Vol. 127, col. 1149.
[2] Blake, op. cit., p. 531.

PART III
REVOLUTION:
DOMESTIC AND EXTERNAL FORCES

CHAPTER VII

THE POLITICAL, ECONOMIC
AND SOCIAL BACKGROUND
TO THE SINN FÉIN REVOLUTION

In the last three chapters successive developments in Anglo-Irish relations have been analysed in the context of political pressures and forces at Westminster, for the reason that there was only one authority, which could reform the government of Ireland and that was the Parlia ment of the United Kingdom. In the nineteenth century agitation in Ireland was a commonplace, rebellion smouldered beneath the surface, but the failure of Smith O'Brien in '48 and of the Fenians in '67 made it all too clear that no rising was likely to endanger English rule. The goal of Irish endeavour was accordingly restricted to reform by stages. The disestablishment of the Church of Ireland was achieved first, and it was followed by a succession of Land Acts, culminating in the Wynd-ham Act of 1903, and placed on the Statute book as a result of parliamentary pressure, powerfully reinforced by well-organized and, at times, violent land agitation. Repeal of the Union by means which were constitutional, even if behind them there remained, as a strong incentive to action, the threat of an unconstitutional alternative, would have provided the logical climax to an age of Irish reform. But logic has little or no place in the history of Anglo-Irish relations. The fall of Parnell convinced many and especially younger Irishmen, Arthur Griffith not least among them, that the campaign for constitutional reform had failed at least for many years to come and possibly for ever. The result was a shift of interest from Westminster to Ireland, from the source of constitutional reform, to the breeding-ground of rebellion. Indeed Parnell himself would seem to have sensed that this would necessarily be so, for in his last desperate electoral campaign in Kilkenny in November 1890 the threat of unconstitutional action was implicit in his appeals to the 'hill-side' men.[1]

[1] F. S. L. Lyons, *The Fall of Parnell*, Chap. VI.

THE NATIONALIST PARTY IN DECLINE

Parnell was a Protestant landlord, whose capacity for leadership was so commanding, whose championship of the cause of Irish nationalism so unusually combined the intensity of angry conviction with a cool and sure sense of tactics, that for over a decade he was, and deservedly, in fact as well as in name an 'uncrowned king'. The obedience he exacted from his supporters, his unwavering concentration on the end to be achieved, gave to the Irish people a new confidence and a new hope. Parnell's intellect was not profound, but it was incisive and since the problem with which he was confronted was in essentials simple, the directness of his approach was his greatest asset. So long as he remained to give forceful leadership and a clear sense of direction to the Nationalist Party, Irishmen had reasonable hope that Home Rule would sooner rather than later pass from the region of debate to that of reality. For this cause the Irish members at Westminster were written of as men who were fighting in the vanguard of the national movement. Martial metaphors were used to describe their participation in parliamentary battles. There were 'hot eager man-to-man conflicts' with the foe and moments of 'exultation comparable to a Benburb or a Fontenoy'[1]. The authority of the Nationalist Party was fatally undermined only when Home Rule appeared unattainable to younger or more extreme nationalists, by verbal engagement, however bellicose the language used, while still continuing to embody all the hopes of the Parliamentary party.

Gladstone once observed that men ought not to suffer from disenchantment, since they ought to know that ideals in politics are never realized. The Irish were not willing, nor perhaps even able at this time, to survey their disappointments with such philosophic detachment. The fall of Parnell marked the beginning of a period of profound disillusion in Ireland, a period in which is to be noted little of obvious interest or activity in the political field and which was yet a period of significant development in national consciousness.

For ten years after the Parnellite split the ever-powerful fissiparous tendencies of Irish politics reasserted themselves. National life was devitalized by faction, the Nationalist Party divided.[2] Parnell's opponents were led by John Dillon, Tim Healy and William O'Brien; the remnant who remained faithful to him after a tribute to him by his

[1] See C. C. O'Brien, op. cit., p. 81. The quotations are from *United Ireland*.
[2] For an account of the politics of the period see F. S. L. Lyons, *The Irish Parliamentary Party, 1890–1910.*

supporters had been condemned by a Papal Rescript, and in the face of the denunciation of his leadership by the Catholic Hierarchy, was led by John and William Redmond. Slowly this remnant acquired prestige, but it was not till 1900 that the party was reunited under the leadership of John Redmond.

John Redmond, born of a County Wexford family with strong parliamentary associations, was a devoted follower of Parnell in the years of his ascendancy and his allegiance to his chief never wavered in the stormy sunset of his days. This was in a sense the more remarkable, because there was a gulf between the two men in age, social background and political temper. Parnell, the descendant of generations of Anglo-Irish settlers, the undergraduate sent down from Magdalene College, Cambridge, the Protestant landlord, owner of a great and beautiful estate at Avondale among the Wicklow Hills, the country gentleman, by circumstance if not by choice leading a peasant revolution, had both a knowledge of the English social structure and the splendid contempt of an aristocrat in revolt for the English establishment of his day. But Redmond, while coming also of country stock was a scion of the Roman Catholic squirearchy, imprisoned in his early days for denunciation of an evicting County Wexford landlord, educated, till parliamentary responsibilities called him to Westminster, at Trinity College, Dublin and in revolt neither against his background nor his class, but seeking rather to restore it to what he conceived to be its rightful place in Irish life and politics. From Parnell Redmond inherited uncritical faith in a Home Rule settlement of the Irish Question, and a firm belief in the efficacy of political tactics and from his father and family, respect for Parliament as an institution. When occasion demanded Redmond's criticism of the Union could be as sharp as Parnell's. 'For us,' he said, in 1905,

the Act of Union has no binding moral or legal force. We regard it as our fathers regarded it before us, as a great criminal act of usurpation carried by violence and fraud, and we say that no lapse of time and no mitigation of its details can ever make it binding upon our honour or our conscience.

And as late as 1907 Redmond declared in Dublin, 'the methods of resistance' to be adopted remained merely a 'question of expediency', and that an appeal to arms would be 'absolutely justifiable' if it were likely to succeed.[1] But nonetheless behind the strong words was no

[1] D. R. Gwynn, *The Life of John Redmond* (London, 1932), p. 77.

longer a ruthless, single-minded personality but rather a man temperamentally pre-disposed to the compromises of the parliamentary system.
Redmond, whatever he might say with an eye on his more extreme
supporters, would never act unconstitutionally.

When Asquith formed his government and still more when the
Liberal-Nationalist victories at the 1910 elections made Home Rule
once more a question of practical politics, Redmond's tone became
markedly conciliatory. Ireland, he said, wanted Home Rule, which he
defined as self-government in purely Irish affairs, subject to the
supreme authority of the Imperial Parliament. This moderate demand
did not, as Redmond was well aware, secure the support of all Irish
nationalists, but he believed the dissenting separatists to be of slight
significance, both in number and ability. In respect of the first he was
right; in respect of the second he was mistaken.

Home Rule in the twentieth century was in essentials a sound and
prudent policy. The report[1] published in 1896, of the Commissioners
appointed under the Chairmanship of the Right Hon. C. E. Childers
to enquire into the financial relations between Great Britain and Ireland, while exploratory rather than conclusive in character, strongly
suggested that Ireland, far from gaining financially from the Union,
had in fact been consistently over-taxed, and thus provided solid
material argument for the control of Irish administration and taxation
by an Irish Government. Sir Horace Plunkett's endeavours to revive
agriculture in Ireland, through the co-operative system, emphasized
by implication and example the material benefits that would be derived
from the intelligent encouragement, which could be given to Irish
industry and agriculture by a local legislature and administration,
which alone would possess the time and the knowledge they required.
But prudence and material advantage were not the qualities that
appealed to the younger generation. Encouraged in their romanticism
by the poetry of Yeats and his circle, dreaming of the regeneration
of Gaelic Ireland with Douglas Hyde, the young men marked out as
their goal, not the pedestrian Home Rule haven of the Nationalist
party, but the independent Ireland of the Fenians. Parliamentary
tactics seemed to them, not as they seemed to Redmond, a common-
sense means of attaining that goal by Fabian methods, but rather a dis-
honourable indulgence in dangerous compromise.

The failure of the Fenian Rising in 1867 had not finally discouraged
those who believed that an independent republic was the true aim of

[1] C. 8262. 1896. XXXIII.

Irish nationalism and who were convinced, not without reason, that this aim was so revolutionary in character that it could be achieved only by violence. In 1873 the Irish Republican Brotherhood was reorganized in the United States.[1] Its strength even at the end of the century was small and a member of its Supreme Council reckoned that at that time 'its whole membership could have been comprised in a concert hall'.[2] The oath of membership was:

In the presence of God I . . . do solemnly swear that I will do my utmost to establish the National Independence of Ireland, that I will bear true allegiance to the Supreme Council of the Irish Republican Brotherhood and the Government of the Irish Republic; that I will implicitly obey the constitution of the Irish Republican Brotherhood and all my superior officers, and preserve inviolable the secrets of the organization. So help me God![3]

The Brotherhood had its selected group ready to act as 'The Provisional Government of the Irish Republic' when the moment for revolution should come. As a secret society it was condemned by the Church, but its activity behind the scenes was continuous. Thomas Clarke, who was associated as a young man with the Fenian Rising, devoted himself to the revival of the Republican Brotherhood after his release from fifteen years' imprisonment in 1898, took part in the 1916 Rising and was executed with the other leaders. He afforded a personal link between two generations of Irish republicans, whose outlook was different but whose aims were identical.[4]

The work of the Irish Republican Brotherhood was abetted and financed from the United States by the Clan na Gael.[5] Sinn Féin, which was founded by Arthur Griffith, was more dependent on support at home. Griffith first published his paper *The United Irishman* in 1897, though Sinn Féin was not founded as a party till 1906. His policy was as uncompromising as that of the Republican Brotherhood, but he did not share its belief in the efficacy of physical force. Redmond's Parliamentary policy he dismissed with contempt as 'useless, degrad-

---

[1] Cf. Miss D. Macardle, *The Irish Republic* (New Edition, London, 1951), Chapters II and IV.

[2] P. S. O'Hegarty in *The Victory of Sinn Féin* (Dublin, 1924).

[3] Constitution of 1894. Reprinted in Macardle, op. cit., p. 64.

[4] There is a biographical study by Louis N. Le Roux entitled in translation from the French, *Tom Clarke and the Irish Freedom Movement* (Dublin, 1936).

[5] Macardle, op. cit., p. 64.

H

ing and demoralizing'. In 1910 Griffith prophesied in the columns of *The United Irishman:*

Ireland has maintained a representation of 103 men in the English Parliament for 108 years. The 103 Irishmen are faced with 567 foreigners. . . .

Ten years from now the majority of Irishmen will marvel they once believed that the proper battleground for Ireland was once chosen and filled by Ireland's enemies.

The Sinn Féin policy, unlike that of the Nationalist Party, was separatist, and unlike that of the Republican Brotherhood it was monarchical. Griffith believed that the Austro-Hungarian Dual Monarchy as established in the *Ausgleich* of 1867 provided the prototype most appropriate for the solution of Anglo-Irish relations.[1]

Griffith's programme at first received the sympathetic support of the IRB, but the Nationalist Party and Sinn Féin never co-operated. The reason was to be found in the nature of Griffith's diagnosis. 'Only on the soil of a nation can a nation's salvation be worked out.'[2] So Kossuth had said and, in his saying, Griffith saw the sovereign remedy for Ireland's ills. The Hungarians had refused to recognize the abrogation of their constitution. The Irish should do the same. The Union was a usurpation and a fraud 'and no lapse of time, no ignorant acquiesence, can render legal an illegal act'. The existence of a Union Parliament accordingly should never, and should certainly no longer, be recognized by Irishmen. 'From the inception of *The United Irishman*,' wrote Griffith, 'we have opposed the sending of Irishmen to sit in the British Parliament on two grounds (1) That it is a recognition of the usurped authority of a foreign assembly to make laws to bind the people of Ireland and (2) That the policy of Parliamentarianism has been materially and morally disastrous to the country.' O'Connell, he thought, had had one statesmanlike idea in his latter life when 'it flashed across his mind to summon the Irish Parliament to meet in Dublin, and, ignoring the illegal "Act" of Union, proceed to legislate for the country'.[3] Griffith urged that this should be done and it was a course of action which might, and did, commend itself to republican

---

[1] His views were set out first in a series of articles in *The United Irishman* and in 1904 reproduced in a booklet entitled *The Resurrection of Hungary: A Parallel for Ireland*. The third edition, from which later references are taken was published in 1918.
[2] Ibid., p. XIII.   [3] Ibid., pp. 89–91.

separatists, even if they did not approve Griffith's monarchical goal. But it could never win the acceptance of the parliamentary party, because it undermined the foundation of their existence and all their action at Westminster. They were, in Griffith's view, trying to achieve what was neither desirable nor indeed possible—for how could there be a legal repeal of an illegality?

The differences which divided the Nationalist Party and the separatists, whether Sinn Féin dual monarchists or republicans, has been attributed to differences in class and even in racial origins. It is true that the Nationalist Party, even if it had not always been, had become an essentially bourgeois party,[1] but it is also true, that both Griffith and the majority of the republican leaders, who were executed in 1916, sprang from the same class. No doubt Redmond and his party became infected during their long sojourn at Westminster with something of the English spirit of compromise, but that was due to the influence of environment. There was little racial or ethnic reason for distinguishing between the Nationalist 'West Britons' and the separatist Gaelic Irish. On the contrary it is remarkable how many of the more uncompromising of the separatist leaders were not Gaelic but Anglo-Irish in origin. The father of Patrick and Willie Pearse was English, Sir Roger Casement was the son of Ulster Protestants, the Countess Markievicz was the daughter of an Anglo-Irish landlord, Maud Gonne's mother was English, Erskine Childers was the son of an English father and an Irish mother, whilst de Valera was the son of a Spanish father and an Irish mother. In truth the difference between the rival parties was temperamental. It was in this respect the difference between the Feuillants and the Jacobins in the French Revolution, the difference between those who believed in the expediency of Burke and those who gave uncompromising allegiance to the ideology of a theoretic conception. In Ireland this division, which finally resulted in civil war, was obscured during the first decade of the century. Miss Macardle writes, with reference to Irish affairs, 'the reign of Edward VII covered a decade very deceptive to the superficial observer'.[2] This observation is just and it makes it the more necessary to supplement our political knowledge of the period by a consideration of the economic forces at work, in order to bring the character of this critical interregnum in Irish history into clearer relief.

[1] For an analysis of the social and occupational background of Parnellite members in 1880, see C. C. O'Brien, op. cit., pp. 32–4.
[2] Op. cit., p. 61.

THE CONFLICT OF ECONOMIC INTERESTS

In the early years of the century the economics of the Irish Question were manifested in two distinct fields: on the one hand in the struggles for ownership of the land, on the other in the capitalist-labour conflicts in the large cities, which culminated in strikes and lock-outs in Belfast and Dublin in the years just before the First World War. As in each case the object was different, so, too, the method and even the principles which dominated the struggle were different. The peasantry, devoutly Catholic, had nothing but hostility for the Socialist programme of universal application, which proved so effective a rallying force in the large cities. James Connolly, the Labour Leader, a man of passionate sincerity, who was executed in 1916, directed his appeal to the urban poor, to the 'men of no property'. He echoed the words of Wolfe Tone: 'Our freedom must be won at all hazards. If the men of property will not help us they must fall; we will free ourselves by the aid of that large and respectable class of the community—the men of no property.' Connolly claimed that 'the Irish Socialist alone is in line with the thought of this revolutionary apostle of the United Irishmen'[1] and the nature of his appeal to the urban unskilled workers and workless was inspired at least as much by French revolutionary ideas, as interpreted by Tone, as it was by Marx. But Connolly also thought that Marx's recognition of the class war 'as *the* factor in the evolution of society towards freedom' was 'his chief and crowning glory'.[2] Such appeals and reflections aroused more misgivings than sympathy in rural Ireland. The small peasant proprietor was not a man of 'no property'—after the Wyndham Act, he was, or else was well on the way to becoming, a freehold farmer—a man of property. And like the peasants of France who guarded so tenaciously the lands they had won from the privileged class, from the nobles and from the clergy in the Revolution, so too the Irish farmer viewed with extreme suspicion appeals of a Socialist or even a vaguely Utopian character, which might ultimately deprive him of the ownership of his land. Thus the interests of the workers in the towns were not then, as they are not today, the same as those of the agricultural classes.

The union in 1916 of the working-class leaders with their internationalist background and of the rural classes, who were intensely nationalist in outlook, was accordingly one of the more remarkable and decisive of the turning-points in modern Irish history. As yet it is

[1] James Connolly, *Labour in Ireland* (Dublin and London, 1917), p. 90.
[2] Ibid., p. 118.

too early to say whether this fusion, brought about by the pressure of contemporary events, possesses a lasting quality. On the whole the evidence suggests that it has not. The ideals of Labour, however moderately presented, have made little headway in rural Ireland since 1916. Labour candidates outside the large cities have had little success, though proportional representation enabled the party to capture one seat in seven in some of the large county constituencies, like Tipperary, before their size was reduced. Yet so long as the rural constituencies divide their representation almost wholly between two parties, whose programmes emphasize political rather than economic ideals, so long, too, will Labour remain a small minority party, for these constituencies decide the government of Ireland. The Labour Party after 1921, partly because of electoral considerations and also under the necessity of conformity to the dominant Church, was careful to dissociate itself from the more advanced working-class movements, whether Socialist or Communist, in other parts of the world.[1] But in the country nonetheless, mistrust of its internationalist, socialist background survived.

THE INFLUENCE OF THE LAND QUESTION

During the nineteenth century the violence of land agitation bore little direct relation to the degree of distress in rural Ireland. On the contrary, as the material condition of the tenant farmers improved, so the agitation against the land system became more intense. The Famine was not followed by general revolt. It was followed by emigration and passive despair as Smith O'Brien soon learned in '48. The insufficient but nonetheless beneficial reforms incorporated in the Land Acts of 1880 and 1881, though counteracted in some measure by the slump in agricultural prices experienced in the following decade, were in any event the natural precursors to more aggressive action by the Land League. Increased security of tenure rendered all the more irksome injustices and restrictions that survived. De Tocqueville noted that on the eve of the Revolution the peasantry in the country around Paris, where the land system was the most enlightened and the feudal dues the least onerous in the whole of France, were the most active revolutionaries, whilst the peasants in the country of the Loire and in Brittany where the *ancien régime* survived almost intact, fought a civil war against the revolution. Such apparent inconsistency is to be

---

[1] The deletion of a 'Workers' Republic' in 1940 from the declared aims of the Labour Party was due largely to the representations of the Church.

encountered not once but many times in history. The most dangerous moment for a bad government, said de Tocqueville, is normally that at which it begins to reform and he concluded from this that only a great statesman could save a government which decided to lighten the burden on its people, after they had endured long years of oppression.[1] These observations might well have been prompted by the last phase of English rule in Ireland, alike of its political and its economic aspects. In relation to the land, it is sufficient to recall that the Land League was founded after, and not before, the first reforming land legislation had been enacted, and that the appeal of Davitt was directed essentially, not to a prostrate, but to a resurgent class. If that had not been so, the 'fall of Feudalism' in Ireland might well have been long delayed.

The land question was supremely important in nineteenth-century Irish history because it was, in Marx's words, 'the exclusive form of the social question in Ireland'. When the cry in England was for shorter working hours, for improved conditions of work in factories and mines, for schemes of state insurance and for the rights of trade unions, Irish agitation was concentrated almost entirely on the alleviation of the lot, not of the industrial, but of the agricultural classes. The difference fixed a wide gulf between the interests of the English and Irish working classes and so ultimately the predominance of the land in Ireland served to accentuate national division.

Lord Dufferin in a letter to *The Times*, which acquired a spurious immortality from the sarcasm which it evoked in the pages of *Das Kapital*, sought to explain by picturesque simile why the land question had acquired such desperate intensity in nineteenth-century Ireland. 'Debarred from every other trade and industry,' he wrote, 'the entire nation flung itself back upon the land, with as fatal an impulse as when a river whose current is suddenly checked rolls back and drowns the valley which it once fertilized.' A backward glance at the trends in Irish population indicates the dimensions of this invasion of the land. In 1800 the population of Ireland was about 5,000,000, by 1841 it had risen to 8,175,000, by 1851 it had decreased to 6,623,985, by 1866 it had shrunk to some 5¼ millions. The evidence and experience of more recent times suggests that a non-industrial Ireland could not support a population of eight millions in tolerable comfort, even with vastly improved methods of agricultural production and distribution and a wholly reformed system of land tenure.

The decline in population after the Famine might lead one to antici-

[1] Alexis de Tocqueville, *L'Ancien Régime et la Révolution* (Paris, 1859), Livre 14.C.IV.

pate an alleviation of the lot of those remaining on the land. To some extent this was certainly the case. Between 1851 and 1861 the number of holdings between 15 and 30 acres in size increased by 61,000, the number of holdings over 30 acres increased by 109,000, while the total number of farms *decreased* by 120,000. The number of holdings under 15 acres had therefore materially diminished. There is also evidence of capital accumulation by tenant farmers. But many of the benefits that might have accrued to the survivors were sensibly lessened by two things: on the one hand the depopulation of the country threw much of the land out of cultivation so that agricultural output declined, whilst on the other hand the consolidation of holdings made possible by the disappearance of the smaller farms, encouraged the extension of cattle-rearing, thereby facilitating the decline of agriculture and lessening the demand for labour. The consequence was that the major advantages were secured by the larger farmers and landowners, who benefited from the sale of the 'surplus product' until the slump in livestock prices, and were not distributed evenly throughout the population.

The revolutionary changes in Irish agriculture, which were themselves the product of a changing economic pattern meant that the reproduction of relative over-population more than kept pace with absolute depopulation. The process, which was described by Marx[1] as one which might serve the orthodox economists supremely well for the illustration of their dogma, that poverty is the outcome of absolute over-population and that equilibrium can be re-established by de-population, in this case provided no solution on economic quite apart from humanitarian grounds. So much was admitted by implication in Lord Dufferin's correspondence to *The Times* [2] in which he maintained that Ireland was still overpopulated and that increased emigration would afford the proper outlet for her surplus population. Such an outlet, though it had less to recommend it, at least on social grounds, than industrial development at home, had been used by nearly all European nations, either in the form of colonial expansion in the Graeco-Roman sense of the term, i.e. in the settlement of colonists overseas, or of emigration to the New World, and if used in the *Irish* interest in a humane and orderly way the process might well have proved beneficial. But there was no guarantee at the time that further depopulation would not result once more in less intensive cultivation, followed in turn by relative over-population.

'What condescension in so great a lord!' commented Marx derisively

[1] See *Das Kapital*, Chapter XXIV, part VII.   [2] In 1866–67.

on Lord Dufferin's interest in the Irish problems; but the day was soon coming, when the attention of the English governing classes was riveted on Ireland. For the land question there were two possible solutions, dual-ownership or a peasant ownership and both had serious implications for them. The former was adopted in principle in the Land Act of 1881, the latter was the solution finally embodied in the Wyndham Act of 1903. It is ironic that the Act of 1881 was sponsored by a Liberal Government, for had it been enacted some years earlier it might well have afforded a foundation for a hierarchical system of land tenure, essentially Conservative in character and complexion, and one in which the rights of the tenants would have been safeguarded, the obligations of the landlords rendered inescapable. So at least Sir Horace Plunkett believed, and he observed, not without regret, that the Magna Carta of the Irish peasant, famous as the three F's—fixity of tenure, free sale, fair rent—was a concession that was made too late. Had it been granted in time, even if the Act had been launched at the eleventh hour on a rising market, the principle of dual ownership might have proved acceptable and finally led, in Plunkett's view, 'to a strengthening of the economic position and character of the Irish tenantry which would have enabled them to . . . meet any condition which might arise'.[1] In the event, however, the dual-ownership established in 1881, proved no more than a stepping-stone to the principle of single ownership—peasant proprietorship—which was accepted in 1903. Gladstone, having found the land system intolerable for one party, made it intolerable for the other as well and so paved the way for a land system, quite out of accord with that which he had planned.[2] The transition was undoubtedly hastened by the consistent pressure of the Land League—a pressure that was not always pleasing to Parnell. 'He spoke of anarchy', complained Davitt the founder of the Land League in 1882, 'as if he were a British Minister bringing in a coercion Bill.' At the same time Parnell wanted the Ladies' Land League suppressed. 'They have kept the ball rolling', said Davitt. 'I don't want them to keep the ball rolling any longer', snapped Parnell. 'The League must be suppressed or I will leave public life.' The difference of opinion was representative of the wider difference in outlook between the conservative Nationalists, who followed Parnell and Social Democrats, who looked for as revolutionary a change in the social, as in the political system.

[1] Sir Horace Plunkett, *Ireland in the New Century* (London, 1904), pp. 22–4.
[2] Ibid., p. 25.

The land question found its lasting solution in the Wyndham Act of 1903. The Conservatives who sponsored the Bill regarded it as part of the wider policy of appeasement known under the name of killing Home Rule by kindness. The Act had the support of all parties on the ground of expediency. Ministers calculated that a nation of peasant proprietors would become progressively conservative in outlook, and historical justification for this belief was afforded by weighty arguments derived from Sir Henry Maine's study of Ancient Law, the influence of which was then very great. In one respect their predictions proved not ill-founded. Ireland, like France, a nation of peasant proprietors, has remained fundamentally conservative in social policy, and like France, too, it has remained strongly nationalist in sentiment. That was where Balfour miscalculated. He believed that a solution of Ireland's great economic problem would undo the nationalist movement; he believed, that is to say, like Marx, that the economic problem alone was fundamental. It was not. The political claims of Ireland possessed a vitality quite independent of any economic issue, and in fact the solution of the land served to concentrate attention on the national question. The removal of the social grievance assisted the union of remarkably divergent forces on the national claim to independence.

The relative significance of economic and political issues may be weighed by considering the position of the Conservative Government, intent on its policy of killing Home Rule by kindness. Gladstone had justified Home Rule by claiming that Irish nationalism was not a passing mood, but an inextinguishable passion. The Conservatives believed that a judicious combination of coercion and concession would sap its vitality. In pursuit of their policy they introduced material reforms whose effect was undoubtedly beneficial.[1] The reforms were enacted under conditions most favourable to their practical application. Twenty years of absolute government was Salisbury's panacea in 1886. The condition was granted. During the next twenty years his party was in office for seventeen, and the brief Liberal interlude, thanks to the House of Lords, left its Irish policy intact. Salisbury himself was Prime Minister for thirteen years, he was succeeded by his nephew for the remaining four. For almost the whole time during which Salisbury was Prime Minister, one or other of his nephews was Chief Secretary. The policy, therefore, was applied continuously and consistently by

[1] Professor L. P. Curtis in *Coercion and Conciliation in Ireland 1880–92* (Princeton N.J., 1963), has added new and substantial evidence in support of this conclusion.

the men who had advocated it. Parliamentary criticism was powerless
to move the solid Unionist majority, and in any event since Chamberlain and Hartington had crossed the floor, the balance of debating
ability lay heavily on the Unionist side.[1] The Nationalist ranks were
divided by internecine strife. To complete the good fortune which
attended this experiment, there was the co-operative movement in Ireland founded by Sir Horace Plunkett with the purpose of reviving Irish
agriculture and effecting material regeneration from within. All the
omens were favourable, yet the experiment was a miserable failure. In
1905, the year in which the Unionist Government fell, the Sinn Fein
movement was founded. Truly did de Tocqueville say that the most
dangerous moment for an oppressive government is that at which it
begins to reform.

The facts make it clear that the land question, though associated with
national sentiment, was not its motive force. It had, however, a great
significance of its own. 'I agree', said Sir Horace Plunkett, 'with most
Englishmen in thinking, though for a different reason, that the passing
of the Land Act marked a new era in Ireland. They regard it as productive of . . . the dawn of the practical in Ireland. I antedate that event
. . . and regard the Land Act rather as marking a new era, because it
removes the great obstacle which obscured the dawn of the practical
for so many, and hindered it for all.'[2] Sir Horace was right as to its
material, but he misjudged its political consequences. 'The patient and
constructive wisdom of that mild and noble Triptolemus of modern
Ireland', wrote John Eglinton of Sir Horace, 'was not combined with
the daemonic attributes of a leader[3]. . . .' This was an understatement.
Plunkett was not interested, nor did he understand the politics of
nationalism. As John Eglinton also remarked of him with wit and truth;
'his indifference to politics bewrayed him for a Unionist, his indifference
to religion bewrayed him for a Protestant'. The indifference to politics
was certainly responsible for Plunkett's miscalculation of the consequences of this climax to land agitation. It acted as a stimulus, not as a
check, to national aspirations. Davitt had understood the tremendous
potentialities of organized pressure against an unpopular system and
the example of the Land League was not to be neglected in the political
field. The Land League found the farmers weak and divided; it made
them an effective force for political ends. Consequently the chief

---

[1] Vide, Hammond, op. cit., pp. 730–1.
[2] Op. cit., pp. 11–12.
[3] *Irish Literary Portraits* (London, 1935), p. 53.

legacy of the land question was not a peasantry reconciled to 'good' government, but a peasantry who, conscious of their new economic status as owners of land, had been brought once for all into the national struggle. It was a decisive development in the political as in the social history of Ireland. The solution of the Land Question heralded the emergence of a rural middle class, whose control over the Nationalist movement has been challenged frequently, but never successfully, a class whose social and political philosophy is embodied in the constitution of 1938.

In the early years of Queen Victoria's reign the French traveller, de Beaumont had spoken of the 'vindictive cruelty', of the 'savage violence' of the Irish peasant in his acts of revenge. For some seventy years from the time when he first visited Ireland, outrage and reprisal disturbed the peace of the countryside. A tradition was established, men became accustomed to brutal scenes, and, as those who have read the opening scene of the *Playboy of the Western World* will recall, revenge even on helpless animals might in certain circumstances be referred to with pride. The passions of rural Ireland lingered on after the wounds which had excited them had been healed, and they permeated the more humane outlook of the towns,[1] so that a tradition of cruelty and violence was a significant legacy of the land struggle to the political conflict that was to be.

LABOUR AND SINN FÉIN

A chance phrase at times makes one fully aware of that change in outlook towards social questions which, in the last century, has been even more remarkable than the change in material conditions. That 'we are all socialists nowadays' is perhaps true, but it is not very enlightening and it conveys little idea of the underlying change in temper and opinion. But to read Bagehot's *English Constitution*, published first in 1867, is to gaze at the picture of another world. That so penetrating a critic should describe the English people as essentially 'a deferential people', that he should regard this characteristic as an outstanding political virtue in itself, gives his study that antiquarian flavour, which has long made the book so attractive to the older Universities. 'A nation of respectful poor is', he wrote, 'far happier than a nation in which there are no poor to be respectful.' It is delightful, it might conceivably be true, but it is so alien to the twentieth-century mind that it is hard to

---

[1] This was inevitable for in a predominantly agricultural country the majority of townsmen were only at one remove from the land.

credit that the circumstances which provoked it, were ever representative of the English social pattern. Certainly that outlook had disappeared more completely from the Irish than from the English scene by the end of the first decade of the twentieth century, owing to the social disintegration resulting from the land war. In Ireland the change in social relations was more marked in the country than in the towns. In Dublin the Vice-regal court and the administration at Dublin Castle preserved up to the eve of the war the appearance and the forms of an established social order. But in the country, peasant proprietorship by freeing the tenants from all obligation to the landlord, clearly constituted the death warrant of an *ancien régime*. For this reason the trend of social development in Ireland is in marked contrast to that in contemporary England, where the aristocracy preserved its authority in the country for decades after its collapse in the towns.

The settlement of the land question with the liquidation of the Anglo-Irish ascendancy as landlords—many remained as landowners farming their own demesnes—had one unforeseen sequel. It proved the preludee to a class struggle which threatened at one moment to divide and indeed to bring into direct hostility the working class and the rapidly expanding middle class; the Labour movement and Sinn Fein, the men who were primarily socialists, like Connolly and James Larkin, and those who were nationalists like Redmond and Griffith. This was not wholly fortuitous. So long as the land question remained the predominant social question, all else was subordinated to the struggle for its resolution, on the only terms ultimately acceptable to the tenant-farmers. But once that aim was achieved a nationally unifying social issue no longer existed.

Labour discontent in the Irish cities before the First World War was not the expression of an abstract revolutionary feeling, but the outcome of very real grievances. Wages were low, especially for unskilled labour, which was unorganized almost up to the outbreak of the war. Housing conditions in Belfast, and even more in Dublin, were amongst the worst in Europe. Sir Charles Cameron, Superintendent Medical Officer for Health in Dublin, in evidence[1] before a Committee of Enquiry in 1900 stated: 'We exceed all other towns [in the United Kingdom] in the number of families in one house.' He also recalled that the Census returns had shown that out of 54,000 families who inhabited the 24,000 houses in the city, 32,000 families resided in only 7,000 houses, the average number of rooms being one and a half per family. It is

[1] Cd. 244. 1900. XXXIX, pp. 18–19.

true that by 1911 it was, in the terms employed in the General Report[1] on the Census of that year, 'manifest' that 'a material improvement has taken place in the housing conditions of the people' (of Dublin) since 1901. But it is also important to understand its limitations. It was the case in 1911 that 75·8 per cent of all the tenements in the city, and they numbered 62,365, had less than five rooms, that 21,000 consisted of only one room and nearly one-third of these were occupied by more than four people. Conditions in other respects than housing were little or no better.[2] . . . 'I do not think', said Sir Charles Cameron in 1900, 'there is a more underfed population than the poor of Dublin.'[3] According to the Medical Press[4] the death-rate in Dublin in 1911 at 27·6 per 1,000 was higher than that of any other city in Europe, the next highest being Moscow with a rate of 26·3. In 1905, Sir Charles Cameron reckoned child mortality among the professional classes at 0·9 per thousand, for the children of labourers 27·7. It was a remarkable contrast, since the unskilled workers, whose children alone came into the second category, comprised almost a quarter of the total adult male population of the city. In brief, the condition of the working classes cried aloud for improvement. The issue between Labour and Sinn Féin leaders was in effect one of priorities. Should attention be concentrated, and at once, on social reforms or should they be regarded as properly dependent on the achievement of national freedom and therefore subordinate to it? Larkin and Connolly maintained that the former was first in importance, Griffith and Sinn Féin leaders that material conditions were secondary to national aims.

The division between Labour on the one hand and both the Sinn Féin and the Parliamentary Nationalist Party on the other tended to become more acute according as Labour policy became more active in the years before the war. The 1905 programme for Sinn Féin, drafted under the inspiration of Griffith, advocated a moderate social policy akin in many respects to the Radical-Liberal programme enacted in England between 1909–14 and to the contemporary Radical-Socialist reforms in France. Even though the nationalization of certain services was contemplated, its essential character was not socialist. On the contrary the social reforms outlined by Griffith reflected the thinking of a man moved by a political conception of nationalism and deter-

[1] Cd. 6663. 1913. CXVIII, p. XXII.
[2] For a summary of the statistics of wages earned by tenement dwellers see R. M. Fox, Green Banners, The Story of the Irish Struggle (London, 1938), p. 119.
[3] Cd. 244.
[4] Quoted by Fox, op. cit., p. 83.

mined to make his economic and social programme subservient to his political aims. He advocated the economic nationalism of Friedrich List,[1] not because he was impressed by its abstract validity, but because it suggested the economic system best equipped to further his national programme. Griffith's ambition, a critic maintained, was to make Ireland a 'Gaelic Manchester'. The phrase was only a half-truth. If Griffith desired to make Ireland a Gaelic Manchester that was only because he felt the 'Manchester' element necessary to the full realization of Irish potentialities as a nation. Not surprisingly his programme elicited the strongest sympathy from the middle classes, though it is always well to remember the limits to it and the fact that Sinn Féin, founded in 1905, reached its pre-war high-water mark in 1908, after that declining to such an extent that its historian has said, 'From 1910 to 1913 the Sinn Féin movement was practically moribund'.[2]

James Connolly was to the Labour movement what Arthur Griffith was to Sinn Féin. His most notable achievement was that in 1916 he succeeded in effecting a junction between revolutionary Labour and revolutionary National forces as represented respectively by the Citizen Army and the Irish Volunteers. Before the war the possibility of such fusion appeared extremely remote. Connolly had always emphasized strongly the national side to the Labour programme, more strongly indeed than could command the sympathy of many trade unionists, and yet, despite this, the division between him and the various nationalist organizations was very great. 'Only the Irish working class', said Connolly, 'remain as the incorruptible inheritors of the fight for freedom in Ireland.' The implications of such a statement could never be accepted by the nationalist organizations, largely dependent, as they were, for support on the smaller shop-keepers and the agricultural community. And in 1898, in the first issue of *The Workers' Republic*, Cononlly had declared, 'We are Republicans because we are Socialists'. While Connolly was never a rigid doctrinaire, yet the dependence of national on socialist aims was repugnant to the majority of Irishmen, whose outlook accorded ill with the conception of a fundamental economic struggle, essentially international in character.

In 1913 the issue became clearer. The strike of the dock labourers in Belfast in June 1907 was the herald of a militant-revolutionary movement in Irish Labour, which was not an isolated event, but had its

[1] Cf. *The Ressurection of Hungary*, pp. 124–6 and p. 142. Griffith said he would like to see List's work on the National System of Political Economy 'in the hands of every Irishman'.

[2] R. M. Henry, *The Evolution of Sinn Féin* (Dublin, 1920), p. 88.

counterpart in most European countries and in the USA in the years before the war. The Belfast strike was organized by James Larkin, a man of crude but fiery eloquence and picturesque appearance, whose ability to sow the wind was as undoubted as his inability to control the whirlwind. The strike was remarkable in that it effected a momentary union between the workers of different creeds in Belfast, despite the interests of employers in fomenting sectarian strife. On July 12, 1907, Belfast witnessed the unusual sight of a great demonstration waving both Orange and Green banners march down to the Customs House to listen to Larkin's crusade for Labour unity, 'Not as Catholics or as Protestants, as Nationalists or as Unionists, but as Belfast men and workers stand together and don't be misled by the employers' game of dividing Catholics and Protestants'.

Such was the theme of Larkin's campaign; but after a transient success sectarian passions reasserted their traditional sway. For this reason the strike did not foreshadow a transformation of political life in the North, but it did portend a period of intense strike activity all over Ireland. The technique of the sympathetic strike was exploited probably to excess, even if the interest of the unskilled workers alone be considered, while the skilled workers showed marked resentment at Larkin's harsh advocacy of industrial strife.[1]

The return of Connolly to Ireland in 1910 brought a man of less eloquence, but of far superior organizing ability, to assist in guiding the Irish Labour Movement. Connolly's ideal for Ireland was a Workers' Republic.[2] In England in the early years of the century he had associated himself with the revolutionary as distinct from the Fabian wing of the Socialist movement, and in the USA he was closely associated with international socialism, notably with the IWW (Industrial Workers of the World) which was founded at a convention in Chicago in 1905. He had gained a significant victory for Ireland in the Labour world in 1900, when delegates of his party were given credentials as representing a separate nation at the Paris Internationalist Socialist Congress.[3] Yet this international activity was not reassuring to non-Socialist Nationalists. Griffith from the outset denounced the strike

[1] R. M. Fox, op. cit., p. 84.

[2] The pattern of his thinking is best studied in *Labour in Irish History* and *The Re-Conquest of Ireland* published in one volume with a Foreword by Robert Lynd in Dublin in 1917 under the title *Labour in Ireland*. See also Nora Connolly O'Brien, *Portrait of a Rebel Father* (Dublin, 1935), and R. M. Fox, *James Connolly: The Forerunner* (The Kerryman, Tralee, 1946).

[3] Fox, op. cit., p. 96.

policy of Larkin and Connolly. In 1908 he wrote a series of articles in *Sinn Féin* attacking Connolly as the 'strike organizer'. He denounced the activity of the Irish Transport and General Workers' Union, founded in 1909, as 'English trade unionism', and he was outspoken in his disapproval of strikes unauthorized by the executives of the unions to which the men were affiliated, even though this involved the sanction of an English executive for an Irish strike.[1]

The climax to industrial strife came in 1913. The rival leaders were James Larkin standing on the one side, and William Martin Murphy, leader of the Employers' Federation, who possessed a controlling interest in the Press and in the Tramway Company, on the other. Larkin was a man who provoked passionate controversy. He wore a dark wide-brimmed hat and it was rumoured among the more credulous that he never removed it—because he was Anti-Christ and obliged to hid the third eye that was in the centre of his forehead.[2] In the Belfast strikes he was denounced as a Papist; when he came to Dublin it was said that he was at once an Orangeman and an Atheist. Larkin delighted in dramatic challenges and melodramatic action—preferring, for example, to bring food to the strike-hungry workers of the city in ships steaming up the Liffey, as though to a beleagured city, with banners waving and torch-light processions along the quays, to the prosaic alternative of using subscriptions to buy food in the city itself.[3] But, whatever his extravagances—and a price was exacted for them— he knew well, possibly better than any other man of his time, how to sustain the morale and to stir the emotions of the hungry workless of 1913.

The conflict was protracted and it was waged with much bitterness. It was chiefly remarkable for the relentless tenacity shown by both sides. A E, who was a normally independent observer, penned an open letter, passionate in its anger against the employers, addressed 'To the Masters of Dublin' and published in *The Irish Times* on October 7, 1913,[4] and he commented on another occasion:

We no longer know people by the old signs and the old names. People are to us either human or sub-human, they are either on the side of those who are fighting for human conditions in labour or they are

---

[1] Fox, op. cit., p. 71.
[2] Cf. James Plunkett's fiftieth anniversary article published in *The Irish Times*, August 26, 1963, under the title 'Larkin and the Great Lock-Out'.
[3] Ibid.
[4] It is reprinted in full in James Connolly, *Labour in Ireland*, pp. 341–6.

with those who are trying to degrade it and thrust it into the abyss. . . .

In the event the victory lay with the employers after a conflict of eight months, but it was not final, for the Irish Transport Union was not crushed. What were the consequences? A new belief in the efficacy of violence and even more important a *rapprochement* between revolutionary Labour, radical-social-reformist sentiment and revolutionary Nationalism, with Arthur Griffith, however, remaining critically apart.

Lenin surveyed the struggle from Geneva. 'At the present moment', he wrote in August 1913, 'the Irish Nationalists (i.e. the Irish *bourgeoisie*) are the victors: they are buying up the land from the British landlords; they are getting national *Home Rule* (the famous Home Rule for which such a long and stubborn struggle between Ireland and Britain has gone on), they will freely govern "their" land in conjunction with "their" Irish priests.

'Well, this Irish nationalist *bourgeoisie* is celebrating its "national victory", its maturity in "affairs of state" by declaring a war to the death against the Irish labour movement.' But the unions had begun to develop 'splendidly' and so 'on the heels of the Irish bourgeois scoundrels engaged in celebrating their "national" victory' there was following 'the Irish proletariat' which had found a leader of 'remarkable oratorical talent, a man of seething Irish energy' in the person of 'Comrade Larkin'. 'A new spirit' had awakened in the country, for the unskilled workers had introduced 'unparalleled animation into the Trade Unions'. The outcome was hailed with rejoicing. 'The Dublin events', wrote Lenin, 'mark a turning-point in the history of the labour movement and of socialism in Ireland. Murphy has threatened to destroy the Irish Labour Unions. He has succeeded only in destroying the last remnants of the influence of the Irish Nationalist *bourgeoisie* over the Irish proletariat. He has helped to steel the independent, revolutionary working class movement in Ireland, which is free of Nationalist prejudices.'[1]

Lenin was quite mistaken. After 1913 Irish Labour tended to become not less, but more nationalist in outlook. This was due in part to the growing absorption of Connolly in the National movement, an absorption which provoked the witticism that, while Irish Nationalism had gained an advocate, Irish Labour had lost a leader. But it was due still more to the greater significance attached to the political, as distinct

[1] *Collected Works*, Vol. XIX, pp. 332–6.

from the economic struggle, by the working classes themselves. The outbreak of the world war undoubtedly hastened this shift in opinion and the traditional feeling that England's difficulty was Ireland's opportunity distracted attention from social to political issues.

The sequel is well-known. In Easter Week, 1916, the Citizen Army, conceived at first purely as a strikers' defence force, came out to fight in the national struggle. Connolly declared his policy in an article in the *Workers' Republic* on April 8th of that eventful year.

The cause of Labour is the cause of Ireland, the cause of Ireland is the cause of Labour. They cannot be dissevered. Labour seeks that an Ireland free should be the sole mistress of her destinies, supreme owner of all things within and upon her soil. Labour seeks to make the free Irish Nation the guardian of the interests of the people of Ireland and to secure that end would vest in that Free Irish Nation property rights as against the claims of the individual. . . . Is it not well that we of the Working Class should fight for the freedom of the Irish nation from foreign rule as the first requisite for the free development of the national power needed for our class?

Under Connolly's leadership the Irish working class brought a distinct and clearly-defined force into the national struggle. In prison Connolly, thinking of the association between Labour and Nationalist movements remarked, 'The Socialists will not understand why I am here. They forget that I am an Irishman.' It was quite true. Though the execution of Connolly, a wounded man unable to walk, produced an immense revulsion of opinion in his favour, yet in August 1916 the Trades Union Congress at Sligo declined to identify itself with Connolly's participation in the Easter Rising. Thomas Johnson, a moderate socialist and later a much respected leader of the Labour Party in the Dáil, then declared as Chairman of the National Executive that 'as a Trade Union Movement we are of varied minds on matters of history and political development and consequently this is not a place to enter into a discussion of the right or the wrong, the folly and the wisdom of the revolt'. That attitude still represents the attitude of Irish Labour whatever personal opinions individual Trade Unionists hold. After the Treaty, unlike Fianna Fáil, the Labour deputies took their seats in the Dáil and for many years gave support to President Cosgrave's constitutional programme.

EPILOGUE

The course of Labour's policy in Ireland should not be viewed in isolation, for its programme, its reaction to the pressure of outside events may be paralleled in the history of the Labour movement in other countries. The technique of the sympathetic strike was adopted from experience of its effectiveness in the New World, whilst the climax of the capitalist-labour conflict in Dublin in 1913 found a counterpart in the great Chicago strike and in the French railway and industrial strikes of 1909 and 1911.[1] If the conflict assumed a less responsible form in Ireland than in France or in the United States, that was largely because Ireland was not a self-governing country. Where the Socialist, Briand, ended the French strikes by mobilizing the strikers, in Ireland the State did not intervene to impose its own solution—such action, apart from all other considerations, being politically impossible for an alien authority. But despite such differences, the motive force in both cases was similar and it is interesting to observe that the response to external pressure was similar too. The German menace tended progressively to diminish the international and to strengthen the distinctively national character of socialism in France. Consequently the extension of the period of military service just before the war was generally accepted, despite the violent opposition which the proposal encountered from Socialists and Pacifists under Jaurès' leadership. The reaction of the working classes in Ireland to external pressure, different in character but the same in principle, followed similar lines. After the great strikes, Labour under Connolly's leadership became more national in outlook and, though never completely identified with the national movement, nonetheless contributed to its ultimate success.

After the war the history of Labour in Ireland and in other countries is contrasted, in as much as in Ireland it could not hope to secure a majority in a predominantly agricultural country. Indeed, the steady decline in Labour representation in the successive Dálà for many years after 1922 was to be attributed largely to the tepid response to its programme amongst the rural community. In part this was due to indifferent leadership and to a failure to appeal directly to the smaller farmers, as the Socialist and even the Communist parties appealed in France to the farmers of the North-West and to the vine growers of

---

[1] Cf. the account of the strike during M. Briand's ministry in Émile Bourgeois, *History of Modern France 1815–1913* (Cambridge, 1919), 2 vols., vol. II, p. 366 et seq.

Burgundy and of Provence, but more fundamentally was it due to the Irishman's distaste for the rigidity of a Socialist system and to the mistrust of a people, at that time self-consciously nationalist in outlook, for the international character of the Socialist creed. Lenin was quite mistaken in thinking the strikes of 1913 heralded the overthrow of the *bourgeoisie* and the triumph of the proletariat in Ireland. On the contrary, they foreshadowed the partial absorption of Labour into the national movement, thereby confirming what the history of the land question had clearly suggested, namely, that in Ireland the economic motive force was subordinate to the political throughout the last phase of the Union.

CHAPTER VIII

THE INFLUENCE OF THE ROMANTIC IDEAL IN IRISH POLITICS

Was it for this the wild geese spread
The grey wing upon every tide;
For this that all that blood was shed,
For this Edward Fitzgerald died,
And Robert Emmet and Wolfe Tone,
All that delirium of the brave?
Romantic Ireland's dead and gone,
It's with O'Leary in the grave.
                    W. B. YEATS, *September 1913*[1]

The ode which Yeats wrote in moving tribute to his erstwhile **mentor** and friend, the Fenian, John O'Leary, was also a contemptuous protest against the complacent inertia, as it seemed to poets and revolutionaries alike, of the Ireland of the early years of the new century. John Eglinton in his critical, if all too brief, study of Yeats and his circle advanced the opinion that 'Yeats, and the literary movement in which he was the commanding figure, may be said to have conjured up the armed bands of 1916'[2] and questioned more particularly whether the scornful refrain:

> Romantic Ireland's dead and gone,
> It's with O'Leary in the grave

had not been the spark which had fallen upon the inflammable minds of the young Gaelic enthusiasts and kindled their vague aspirations into a realistic purpose.[3] The casual judgement, as it must seem to historians, and the speculation reflected the high political significance attributed by members of a literary circle to the utterances of one another and need not be taken too seriously. But it is true both that

---

[1] *The Collected Poems of W. B. Yeats* (London, 1934), pp. 120–1.
[2] John Eglinton (W. K. Magee), *Irish Literary Portaits*, p. 26.
[3] Ibid., p. 33.

Ireland began to be romantic once again in Yeats's sense just before the war, and that the stimulus of an intellectual revival proved a direct precursor to revolution.

National sentiment in Ireland had long found a romantic refuge. The unhappiness of the present was counterbalanced by legends of a golden age long ago or by dreams of the happiness that would be realized once national independence were regained. Such romantic illusions afforded a natural escape, and an antidote to despair. It is quite wrong to suppose that it was a new influence that came into Irish life in the early years of this century; on the contrary the romanticism was very old, only its forms of expression were new. They were two-fold: one Gaelic and indigenous, the other Anglo-Irish, and indigenous only in its inspiration. Both were revolutionary, or, to be more precise, revolutionary in their popular impact even if, and when, they were not revolutionary by deliberate and self-conscious intent.

The Gaelic League was founded in 1893. Its first President was Douglas Hyde, later to be the first President of Eire. The declared purpose of the League was the revival of the Irish language, a revival which had much the same political significance as the revival of Magyar, Czech, Serb and Croat earlier in the century. Hyde, though following a well-worn nationalist path, was none the less resolute in his determination that the League's activities should be confined to its purely linguistic purpose. It was to remain 'non-political and non-sectarian'. In fact, however, the revival of Gaelic inevitably constituted a powerful incentive to separatist feeling. '. . . I believe it is our Gaelic past', said Hyde in his address[1] to the Irish National Literary Society in November 1892, 'which, though the Irish race does not recognize it just at present, is really at the bottom of the Irish heart, and prevents us becoming citizens of the empire.' Sir Horace Plunkett, though a Unionist, shared Hyde's rather curious underestimate of the influence of the language revival. In his book, *Ireland in the New Century*' Plunkett wrote: 'Of this language movement I am myself but an outside observer, having been forced to devote nearly all my time and energies to a variety of attempts which aim at doing in the industrial sphere much of the same work as that which the Gaelic Movement attempts in the intellectual sphere—the rehabilitation of Ireland from within.' But nothing, he went on to complain, would induce his Unionist friends to believe that the language movement was not, in the political sense, separatist. The

[1] Text reprinted in Curtis & McDowell, *Irish Historical Documents 1172–1922*, pp. 310–13.

sequel has shown that their conviction on this score was in fact well founded. From the Unionist point of view there was solid political objection to the revival of Irish, for it threatened to stimulate a consciousness of nationality in precisely the same way as the revival of Magyar earlier, and of the Czech, Polish and Croat later in the century, stimulated the ambitions of the nationalities within the Habsburg Empire. Yet the issue was, perhaps deliberately, confused, Dr Mahaffy, later Provost of Trinity College, for example, informing the University Commission of 1900 that it was impossible to find a text in Irish that was not 'either religious, silly or indecent'. Such eccentric expression of opinion did the Unionist cause the doubtful service of disguising the gravity of the implicit political challenge.

In retrospect Plunkett, and in less certain measure, Hyde himself, were clearly mistaken in their view of the non-political character of the Gaelic League. It is not necessary to have a definite political programme in order to influence political thought and political action. Moreover, the conception of a national language had a strong appeal to a generation wearied of the sordid political quarrels that followed the fall of Parnell. Patrick Pearse, leader of the Easter Rising of 1916, expressed opinions far removed from those of Plunkett. 'We never meant', he said in November 1913,[1] 'to be Gaelic Leaguers and nothing more than Gaelic Leaguers. We meant to do something for Ireland, each in his own way. Our Gaelic League time was to be our tutelage . . .' but 'we do not propose to remain schoolboys for ever. . . . I say now that our Gaelic League education ought to have been a preparation for our complete living as Irish Nationalists. . . . For if there is one thing that has become plainer than another it is that when the seven men met in O'Connell Street to found the Gaelic League, they were commencing, had there been a Liancourt there to make the epigram, not a revolt, but a revolution. The work of the Gaelic League, its appointed work, was that: and the work is done. To every generation its deed. The deed of the generation that has now reached middle life was the Gaelic League: the beginning of the Irish Revolution. Let our generation not shirk *its* deed, which is to accomplish the revolution.' It was in the light of this reasoning that Pearse pronounced early in 1914 a judgement on the Gaelic League often quoted misleadingly in isolation. 'The Gaelic League', he wrote in February that year, 'will be recognized in history as the most revolutionary influence that has ever come into

[1] Quoted in *The Irish Volunteers 1913–1915. Recollections and Documents* edited by Professor F. X. Martin (Dublin, 1963), pp. 62–3.

Ireland.'[1] An overstatement? Perhaps. It is still too early to assess the significance of the language movement. But the verdict is in all probability not far from the truth, especially when the League is seen, as Pearse saw it, as an influence that released revolutionary forces.

The spirit of the Irish Literary Revival, as it is known to a wider world, was at once more romantic and less Irish than that of the Gaelic League. Later, indeed, the more exclusive shades of national thought denied the title even of Anglo-Irish to the more notable figures of the Literary Revival. Thus Professor Daniel Corkery, drawing rather fine distinctions on the meaning of 'Anglo-Irish', maintained that Anglo-Irish literature was mostly the product of men who neither lived in Ireland nor wrote for the Irish people. This literature may have been a homogeneous thing but Irishmen could not think of it as indigenous. Professor Corkery allowed, it is true, that the work of Yeats and his colleagues at the Abbey Theatre was *in intention* genuine Anglo-Irish literature, but he sounds several warning notes. 'We must not', he admonishes us, 'be waylaid into thinking because it shed for the nonce its Colonial character it became genuine Anglo-Irish literature, or that because the world accepts it as Irish literature, it may really turn out to be Anglo-Irish literature, or that because it is neither quite English nor quite Irish it must be Anglo-Irish.' For his own part Professor Corkery was disposed to regard it as 'no more than an exotic branch of English literature'. And his argument, which is important and illuminating, might be presented, necessarily in brief compass, as follows.[2] There cannot be a distinctive literature which is not a national literature; Anglo-Irish literature is not a national literature, therefore, it cannot be a distinctive literature; and not being a distinctive literature it does not merit a distinctive (and misleading) description. The critical stage in the argument, in an historical context, is the second. Professor Corkery sets out his reasons fully and fairly. The most important of them, again in an historical context, was that, positively, Anglo-Irish literature—'if it be correct so to describe it'— was all written by spiritual exiles for their motherland, England. Negatively these writers springing from the Ascendancy, insensitive to and unmoved by the three great forces which 'working for long in the Irish national being, have made it so different from the English national being, namely '(i) The Religious Consciousness of the People; (ii) Irish Nationalism; and (iii) The

---

[1] Quoted in Macardle, op. cit., pp. 62–3.
[2] See D. Corkery, *Synge and Anglo-Irish Literature* (Cork, 1955), Fourth Impression, pp. 1–27.

Land',[1] had no share in the Irish national memory, and were accordingly as 'un-Irish as it is possible for them to be'.[2] Yet Professor Corkery in his enunciation of exclusivist Irish literary doctrine, which in its emphasis upon social, cultural and political difference would win unqualified acceptance from the Orange protagonists of a two-nation theory, concedes that in time of national revival, 'when the land is under the stress of a national movement', Irish 'Colonial' literature 'makes an effort to seat itself on the Truly Anglo-Irish stool—the writers make an effort to express their own land'. All the work done for the Abbey theatre from its beginning to 1922, for this reason, 'may be reckoned as Anglo-Irish literature, for whether good or bad in itself, it made an effort to express Ireland to itself' and by so doing, with some exceptions, freed itself from 'the Colonial strain'.[3]

Professor Corkery's analysis, manifestly correct in respect of much nineteenth-century Anglo-Irish literature, which was written about Ireland from outside and self-consciously catered for English predilections or prejudices, may seem too doctrinaire to be wholly convincing in respect of a later period. But even if so much be allowed, his analysis in itself goes far to explain why the influence of the Literary Renaissance on Irish politics remains so difficult to assess. Yeats, Synge, Moore and Joyce, though influenced in a greater or lesser degree by the early Ireland of history and of legend did not, and if one follows Professor Corkery in the case of the first three, were not by inheritance fitted to appeal to 'political' Ireland. 'All the great literatures', wrote John Eglinton, 'have seemed in retrospect to have risen like emanations from the life of a whole people, which has shared in a general exaltation: and this was not the case with Ireland. How could a literary movement be in any sense national when the interest of the whole nation lay in extirpating the conditions which produced it?'[4] In logic such criticism is irrefutable; in fact this late flowering of Anglo-Irish letters was, in historical terms, national both in inspiration and in effect. It was also revolutionary in its impact.

The de-Davisization of Irish history and letters, as the inelegant phrasing went, was a task to which young writers, William Butler Yeats most notable among them, devoted their public energies in the late nineteenth and early twentieth centuries. Romantic, perverted tales of the Sack of Baltimore, or of Spanish expeditions to the coast

---

[1] See D. Corkery, *Synge and Anglo-Irish Literature* (Cork, 1955), Fourth Impression p. 19.
[2] Ibid., p. 15.   [3] Ibid., p. 11.   [4] Op. cit., p. 5.

of Kerry were little to the taste of this more realist generation. Thomas
Davis was chiefly blamed, but not altogether justly. Romanticism in
letters, as in politics, was the product, it must be repeated, of an 'esca-
pist' philosophy. A low standard of life, the horrors of famine, the
failure of revolt, all that depressed Irish life, that inflamed a seemingly
hopeless discontent against the existing social system and the English
rule which buttressed it, found some compensation for the ills of the
present in romantic interpretations of the past and an eschatological
view of the future. Thomas Davis, Clarence Mangan, Standish
O'Grady, Sir Samuel Ferguson and others in greater or lesser degree
satisfied a people's need, but they did not create it. Nor are Thomas
Davis and the writers in the Young Ireland tradition to be dismissed as
impracticable visionaries, lost in the labyrinths of imaginative re-
creations of a heroic past. Indeed, one need only recall the influence of
Davis on Arthur Griffith, that most practical of patriots, to realize that
though romanticism coloured Davis's writings, it remained an influence, but not a guide, to his political thinking. Independence, said
Davis, was the goal of the national movement; but the achievement of
this ideal was not an end in itself, but the all-important means for the
building up of a new, united and happier country. For this reason
Davis, like Tone before him, cared little for the political abstractions
which divide. By no means all of his critics were as clear-sighted as he
was in this very important respect.

The cause of Yeats's reaction against Thomas Davis, the Young
Ireland Movement generally and the influence of their writings was
precisely stated and indeed many times restated. Young Ireland had
deliberately subordinated art and letters to political ends. Yeats thought
this was wrong. 'Young Ireland', he wrote,[1] 'had sought a nation
unified by political doctrine alone, a subservient art and letters aiding
and abetting. . . . To recommend this method of writing as literature
without much reservation and discrimination, I contended, was to be
deceived or to practise deception.' And elsewhere, in the course of an
essay on *Ireland and the Arts*, written in 1901, Yeats remarked:

I will not . . . have all my readers with me when I say that no writer,
no artist, even though he choose Brian Boroihme or St Patrick for his
subject, should try to make his work popular. Once he has chosen his
subject he must think of nothing but giving it such expression as will

[1] Donald Davie, *The Young Yeats* in C. C. O'Brien, *The Shaping of Modern Ireland*,
p. 141 and pp. 140–151 generally.

please himself. . . . He must make his work a part of his own journey towards beauty and truth. He must paint saint or hero, or hillside, as he sees them, not as he is expected to see them, and he must comfort himself, when others cry out against what he has seen, by remembering no two men are alike, and that there is no 'excellent beauty without strangeness'.[1]

Others indeed did cry out. In seeking to create a more imaginative tradition in Irish literature by a criticism at once remorseless and enthusiastic, Yeats was launching an attack on the national literary establishment of the day. 'Every young Catholic man', he recalled later, 'who had intellectual ambition fed his ambition with the poetry of Young Ireland; and the verses of even the least known of its poets were expounded with a devout ardour at Young Ireland Societies and the like . . .' And the attack was fundamental in the sense that Yeats was criticizing not only the poems but the conscious national purposes that had inspired them. 'Young Ireland's prose', Yeats complained,[1] 'had been as much occupied with Irish virtue, and more with the in-vaders' vices, than its poetry, and we [in the National Literary Society] were soon mired and sunk into such problems as to whether Cromwell was altogether black, the heads of the old Irish clans altogether white, the Danes mere robbers and church burners . . . and as to whether we were or were not the greatest orators in the world. . . . All the past had been turned into a melodrama with Ireland for blameless hero and poet, novelist and historian had but one object, that we should hiss the villain, and only a minority doubted that the greater the talent the greater the hiss.'[2] With critical overstatement went a certain emotional detachment, even coldness, that was the more resented. Thus when Yeats learned from a newspaper that Sir Charles Gavan Duffy recited upon his deathbed his favourite poem, he was moved only to comment that it was one of the worst of the patriotic poems of Young Ireland.

In later years Yeats wrote and spoke with greater balance and moderation but it was clear that his standpoint remained unchanged down the years. In November 1914 at the invitation of the newly-formed Gaelic Society of Trinity College, Dublin, Yeats delivered a Thomas Davis centenary memorial lecture—not, as might be expected, in Trinity College, but in the Antient Concert Rooms, Dublin, because of the objection of the Vice-Provost, Dr J. P. Mahaffy, to the name of

[1] W. B. Yeats, *Essays* (London, 1924), pp. 254-5.
[2] W. B. Yeats, *The Trembling of the Veil* (London, 1922), p. 89.

'a man called Pearse', then actively engaged in discouraging recruitment to the British forces, among the speakers. In reflective retrospect[1] Yeats allowed that 'the new generation is but little merciful to the old' and that when his criticisms of Thomas Davis were first advanced he might have remembered, had he not been so anxious to show what was lacking in the gift of Davis, 'that reaction is a good ploughman, who never waits long before he readies the field for the new crop, and that he would not have failed to bring out his old tackle while I slept'. But at the time it had seemed 'as if our new generation could not do its work unless we overcome the habit of making every Irish book, or poem, shoulder some political idea; it seemed to us that we had to escape by some great effort from the obsession of public life and I had come to feel that our first work must be to close, not knowing how great the need of it still was, the rhymed lesson book of Davis'. How great the need of it still was? Yeats did not make explicit what he had in mind. But if one thing emerges from his centenary lecture, it is his new understanding of the magnanimity of Thomas Davis. Had young men of his own time copied Davis's magnanimity, he felt, the history of a generation might have been changed. Not uncharacteristically, however, Yeats's fuller and, it may be thought fairer, appreciation of Davis came by way of what may equally well be thought unfair disparagement of O'Connell, in whose very genius 'there was demoralization, the appeal—as of a tumbler at a fair—to the commonest ear, a grin through a horse collar' and whose personal influence 'had been almost entirely evil'. It was partly because Yeats was more mindful that Davis began his work 'in the meridian hours' of O'Connell that he made more generous appraisal of Davis's contribution and most of all of 'his magnanimities'.

What was at issue between Yeats and Young Ireland was, like so many things on the small stage of Irish history, of great and universal import. Was a writer's first, or only, loyalty to his country and its cause or to his art? To this question Thomas Davis gave one and Yeats another answer. '... I have never been quite certain', Yeats wrote again in 1901,[2] 'that one should be more than an artist, that even patriotism is more than an impure desire in an artist.' And whatever his uncertainties on that particular score, there was no doubt in his mind that poetry

---

[1] The lecture was reprinted in 1947 with a Foreword by Denis Gwynn and a hitherto unpublished letter of protest from A. E. at the Vice-Provost's exclusion of Pearse from speaking in Trinity College in honour of Thomas Davis under the title *Tribute to Thomas Davis* by W. B. Yeats (Cork, 1947).

[2] *Essays. What is Popular Poetry?* p. 4.

should not be subordinated and shackled, as Young Ireland had subordinated and, by precept and example, shackled it to the national
cause, or as Yeats more critically phrased it, to the abstractions of
nationality and politics. And Yeats liked to think that in this, his
principal contention, he had at the least understanding from an improbable but unimpeachable national source—John O'Leary the
Fenian friend and mentor of his youthful Dublin days, richly commem-
orated in the refrain in the poem *September 1913*, one verse of which
is reprinted at the beginning of this chapter.

When O'Leary died Yeats could not bring himself to go to the
funeral because he shrank 'from seeing about his grave so many whose
Nationalism was different from anything he had taught or that I
could share'.[1] If Yeats in later years was much troubled by his sensitive
fastidiousness on that occasion, it testified at the least to the careful
regard of the young Anglo-Irish poet for the thought and opinions of
the dead Fenian. In one sense this was paradoxical. John O'Leary, the
son of a shop-keeper in Tipperary town, had been converted to
nationalism by Thomas Davis[2] and in long years of imprisonment he
found in Davis's writings a source of strength and consolation. But
later in exile in Paris, in the company of writers and artists, Whistler
among them, he came, it would seem, to sense the limitations as well as
the virtues of the literature of Young Ireland and to accept the need for
a new literary movement, analogous to the old, but discarding its
faults. Psychologically, therefore, he was prepared for Yeats's critical
assault and, in principle at least, he would seem to have considered
it a proper and timely contribution to the intellectual life of the
nation.

In rejecting the romanticism of Young Ireland, Yeats sought not
realism but a new romanticism. In literary terms he was his own
master; but in that borderland between literature and politics where
Yeats so often strayed, O'Leary's influence was surely greater than
that of any other man. This was historically important. O'Leary was a
revolutionary and the authentic sense of revolution conveyed in so
many of Yeat's earlier poems would seem to have owed much to
O'Leary, while that poem, whose scornful and provocative refrain was
thought by John Eglinton to have been the spark, that had kindled the
minds of Young Gaelic enthusiasts to realistic purpose, was, as has

---

[1] *Essays. Poetry and Tradition*, p. 304.
[2] John O'Leary, *Recollections of Fenians and Fenianism*, 2 Vols. (London, 1896),
Vol. I, pp. 2–3.

been noted, directly inspired by the memory of him. 'In this country', O'Leary told Yeats, 'a man must have upon his side the Church or the Fenians, and you will never have the Church.' After the Abbey Theatre's first production of *The Playboy of the Western World* it seemed equally certain he would not have the support of the Fenians. But he continued to have the support, and what was more important, the understanding of one Fenian. And that Fenian was 'one of Plutarch's people'.

Yeats later felt he should have asked O'Leary whether he had had some teacher who had expounded Roman virtue but 'I doubt if I would have learnt anything, for I think the wax had long forgotten the seal if seal there were'.[1] Perhaps, it seems not unlikely though there is no evidence that it was so, he had learned of it in his very early years at the Abbey School[2] in his native town of Tipperary. What is certain is that it served him well in the nine years he served of a twenty-year sentence of imprisonment given in 1865 for subversion as an editor of *The Irish People*. When the Governor of the prison asked him why he did not report some unnecessary discomfort O'Leary replied: 'I did not come here to complain.' He would speak only of the humours, never of the hardships of his prison life. 'I was in the hands of my enemy, why should I complain?'[3] With his noble appearance and his Roman courage went an independence of mind and judgement which at times disconcerted his associates of earlier days. He was, as the Irish saying goes, a cross-grained man. He scorned the emotion that swept the country when Gladstone's conversion to Home Rule was known. 'Nations', he said, 'may respect one another; they cannot love.' Yeats was once told how O'Leary had said to a great gathering of Tipperary farmers assembled to welcome him on his return from prison and exile: 'The landlords gave us some few leaders, and I like them for that, and the artisans have given us great numbers of good patriots, and so I like them best: but you I do not like at all, for you have never given us any one.'[4] The anecdote if authentic—and it may be for O'Leary would no doubt have had his recollections of Smith O'Brien and the

---

[1] *The Trembling of the Veil*, p. 95.
[2] It was one of four Erasmus Smith Grammar Schools and it offered an education, rigorous in every sense, down to its closure in 1922. O'Leary went from there to school at Carlow and thence to read law at Trinity College, Dublin, a course which he abandoned when he learned he would have to give an oath of allegiance to Queen Victoria before he practised and he went instead to Cork and Galway to study medicine.
[3] Ibid.
[4] *Essays*, p. 321.

events of 1848 much in mind[1]—may serve to illustrate one thing
O'Leary and Yeats shared—dislike or mistrust of the middle-class,
whether in the country or the town.

> Sing the peasantry, and then
> Hard-riding country gentlemen,
> The holiness of monks, and after
> Porter drinkers' randy laughter;

wrote Yeats in one of his *Last Poems*. But the bourgeoisie of town and
country were to be left unnoticed and unsung. Yeats and O'Leary were
also at one in their individualistic dislike of organization. 'No gentleman can be a socialist', he [O'Leary] said, and then, with a thoughtful
look, 'He might be an anarchist'.[2] But their understanding rested on
deeper and more lasting things. 'I think', reflected Yeats, 'it was because he [O'Leary] no more wished to strengthen Irish Nationalism
by second-rate literature than by second rate morality, and was content that we agreed in that.'

O'Leary, in this like Mazzini, entertained a strong sense of the moral
foundation of nationality. As in the eighties he would not lend his
countenance to sporadic acts of violence or outrage, so later by precept
and in public utterances—O'Leary's oratory, Yeats recalled, 'was
noble, strange, even beautiful'—he had his own clear perception of
what might, and what might not, be done even in the great cause of
national freedom. 'A man', he said, 'was not to lie, or even to give up
his dignity on any patriotic plea. . . .' 'A man must not cry in public to
save a nation.' Justice must not be forgotten in the passion of controversy, and most memorably, and how well Yeats remembered it,
'There are things a man must not do to save a nation'. Yeats applied
this to his own circumstances and concluded that even to save the
nation he must not write poetry inspired, not by artistic, but by political considerations. If his critics alleged, and rightly, that his verse
lacked rhetoric, enunciated no doctrine and disregarded the necessities
of a cause, such neglect was not casual, but to Yeats a matter of principle. His poetry, or much of it, was revolutionary but it contained, it
could contain, no principle, still less a programme of revolution. To
Yeats, and, as he liked to think, to O'Leary also, life was greater than
any cause, even the cause of country.

[1] They are set out in *Fenians and Fenianism*.
[2] *The Trembling of the Veil*, p. 94.

Yeats was not concerned with political influence or leadership. Nor
on grounds of temperament was he equipped to exercise them. His
romanticism, different but certainly no less pronounced than that of
the Young Ireland leaders whom he criticized, predicated that any
political influence he exercised would be at once fortuitous and im-
pulsive and that a literary movement, in which he was the principal
figure, would not possess a serious political character. He wrote—and
few more extreme expressions of the Romantic ideal have found utterance—

> God save me from those thoughts men think
>   In the mind alone,
> He that sings a lasting song,
>   Thinks in a marrow bone.
>
> I pray—for fashion's word is out
>   And prayer comes round again—
> That I may seem, though I die old,
>   A foolish, passionate man.

The reaction against intellectual analysis goes far when it comes to
thinking with the marrow;[1] and while one may sympathize with Yeats
in his contention that it is worse to have too little passion, as some
modern intellectual poets, than too much, yet it must also be allowed
that self-conscious reversion to instinctive thinking renders coherent
guidance in a political movement out of the question. Even if it be
unreasonable to ask of a poet any but the aesthetic standard, which in
this case he deliberately set himself, yet the historian may none the less
observe that the edifying, the moral, function of literature was so
completely neglected by Yeats and his circle as to deprive the Irish
Literary revival of the more serious character, which from time to time
some of its more notable figures liked to claim for it and which otherwise it might conceivably have acquired.

The absence of an undertone of moral seriousness in Yeats's work in
some respects consorted ill with his political outlook, for he believed
as ardently as any Whig of the Glorious Revolution in the leadership
of an aristocracy. Like so many of his associates in the Literary Revival
his admiration was for the 'tall unpopular men', the women who were

---

[1] This expression of opinion runs counter to George Moore's comment: 'Yeats can
no longer think with his body, it is only his mind that thinks. He is all intellect, if that
isn't too cardinal a word.' *Hail and Farewell*, Vol. I: *Ave*, p. 216.

beautiful in the proud old way,[1] and surely in giving it, he was thinking of the Anglo-Irish aristocracy of the late eighteenth century and most of all of Charles Stewart Parnell who symbolized the qualities Yeats so greatly admired:

> Every man that sings a song
> Keeps Parnell in his mind.
> For Parnell was a proud man,
> No prouder trod the ground,
> And a proud man's a lovely man,
> So pass the bottle round.[2]

'I am proud', Yeats told the Senate during the Cosgrave regime, 'to consider myself a typical man of that minority. We are the people of Burke; we are the people of Grattan; we are the people of Swift, the people of Emmet, the people of Parnell. We have created the most of the modern literature of this country. We have created the best of its political intelligence.'[3] It was a contribution to debate—on divorce of all topics—that was *not* listened to with satisfaction by most of Yeats's Senatorial colleagues.[4]

Among the Ministers of the Free State, Kevin O'Higgins commanded Yeats's admiration—

> A great man in his pride
> Confronting murderous men.

because, as J. M. Hone justly observed,[5] O'Higgins seemed to come nearest to the realistic and authoritarian tradition of Irish leadership. Yet despite this admiration for the qualities of leadership, such leadership was the one thing that the Irish Literary Movement did not give to Ireland.

[1] Dr Gogarty's lines:
> Tall unpopular men,
> Slim proud women who move
> As women walked in the islands when
> Temples were built to Love,
> I sing to you.

[2] *Last Poems.* 'Come Gather Round Me, Parnellites.'
[3] The speech is reprinted in D. R. Pearce, *The Senate Speeches of W. B. Yeats* (London, 1961), and the extract quoted is on p. 99.
[4] Nor by the then Clerk of the Senate. See Donal O'Sullivan, *The Irish Free State and its Senate* (London, 1940), pp. 167–8.
[5] In the *London Mercury*, March 1939.

I

The comparative lack of moral seriousness in the work of Yeats and his contemporaries was in considerable measure responsible for a later disposition in Ireland to underrate the 'national' character of the Literary Revival. It is true, of course, that the leaders of the Irish Literary Movement were for the most part Anglo-Irish in origin, but their failure to appeal more directly to the 'Irish' Ireland was less because of difference in origin, to which it may be thought an unhistorical significance came later to be attached, than to their imaginative conceptions of Irish nationality. Yeats in his search for some national ideal, which he could associate with his romantic belief in Ireland, thought not with the politicians though he might at times employ some of their phrases, but essentially with the mystics. His detachment may have been a political liability but far more important it was, in his view, a condition of his integrity as a poet. He could claim for himself at the end—and it was not mean or unworthy pretension:

> He never sang a poorer song
> That he might have a heavier purse,
> Nor gave loud service to a cause
> That he might have a host of friends.

In the end Yeats's romantic conception of Irish nationality left him in mind and in sympathy divorced from the makers of the new Ireland. His ideal of an aristocratic, intellectual, liberal state was indeed repellent to, and repelled by, the new conception of a Gaelic-Catholic country with its Puritan outlook and its Censorship Act. But that later conflict should not obscure Yeats's own contribution to the making of the New Ireland. If it was indirect because (as has been suggested) the Irish Literary Movement neglected the edifying function of literature, it was none the less, and in its own way, decisive. The Ireland of the 'Celtic Twilight' which in following the *Wanderings of Oisin* thought again of the Fenian

> heroes lying slain
> On Gabhra's raven-covered plain;

and learned of how Cuchulain met his death, which was brought

> to the cairn heaped grassy hill
> Where passionate Maeve is stony still,

could not but grow restive under rule which though becoming in-creasingly benevolent was yet branded as alien. The last question and answer in *Cathleen Ni Houlihan* first spoken on the Abbey stage by Maud Gonne, 'a woman Homer sang', in the title role of the old woman who is Ireland, gave expression to the Irish Nationalist ideal in a form whose emotional appeal to Irishmen was intense. 'Did you see an old woman going down the path?' 'I did not, but I saw a young girl and she had the walk of a queen.'

Yeats's vision of Ireland was imprecise, but in one sense it was that very imprecision that made it so stirring an inspiration, for it meant different things to different men and in so doing filled the minds of his countrymen with dreams and clothed in glamour his country's past. Douglas Hyde, the founder of the Gaelic League, was honoured in his old age as first President of an Irish state that was republican in all but name, but his achievement was more dependent for success, than many Irishmen now care to admit, on the poetic inspiration of Yeats and on his foundation of the Abbey Theatre. Had Yeats's poetry been more didactic this truth would have been acknowledged. But it was not for nothing that he had been so critical of the Young Ireland poets and for his part:

> when all is said
> It was the dream itself enchanted me:
> Character isolated by a deed
> To engross the present and dominate memory.
> Players and painted stage took all my love,
> And not those things that they were emblems of.[1]

And who of all who have enjoyed his poetry could wish that it had been otherwise?

Yeats's influence on Irish history tends, perhaps most of all, to be discounted because so many of his famous associates in the Literary Revival became highly critical of the course of the National Movement. Those among them who survived into the post-Union age had little sympathy with the new Ireland which (in some cases unconsciously) they had helped to bring into being and many of them, unlike Yeats, preferred to live out their days in exile. But it were idle to pretend that Moore and Joyce, to take two notable examples, could have found in Ireland a congenial home, whatever the prevailing intellectual outlook.

[1] *Last Poems.* 'The Circus Animals' Desertion.'

Indeed, even in pre-war years there had been some degree either in aloofness or of artificiality in these writers' conception of Ireland as it was and Ireland as it should be. Lady Gregory's self-conscious endeavours to bring herself 'nearer to Ireland' were largely self-defeating, whilst in the association of George Moore and Yeats there are occasions when the intended artifice verges on the ridiculous. If George Moore is to be believed,[1] Yeats and Moore contemplating the composition in collaboration of an heroic drama—*Diarmuid and Grania*—considered the wisdom of writing the play in French, translating it into English and then into Irish in order to suit the dialogue to the theme. Anecdotalism, not accuracy, was Moore's *forte* and this may well be one more product of his often malicious invention. But George Moore's own association with the Literary Movement, temporary, though at one time assuredly genuine, in itself bears most striking testimony to the detachment of some at least of these Anglo-Irish writers from the Irish national background.

George Moore, while strongly attracted by the country of his birth, never idealized it, as those who have read his Triology on Irish life will remember:

The Irish 'do not know themselves, but go on vainly sacrificing all personal achievement, humiliating themselves before Ireland as if the country were a god. . . . And these sacrifices continue generation after generation. Something in the land itself inspires them. And I began to tremble lest the terrible Cathleen ni Houlihan might overtake me. She had come out of that arid plain, out of the mist, to tempt me, to soothe me into forgetfulness that it is the plain duty of every Irishman to dissociate himself from all memories of Ireland— Ireland being a fatal disease, fatal to Englishmen and doubly fatal to Irishmen.'[2]

Such an approach to Ireland was, it need hardly be said, altogether remote from that of the single-minded patriots who were determined that at whatever cost Ireland should regain her freedom, but what remains remarkable is that a man with such an outlook should be so drawn to the Ireland of the Literary Movement. Scornfully in the *Confessions of a Young Man*, Moore condemned the ignominy of a modern world which was enfeebled by its weak acceptance of humani-

---

[1] *Hail and Farewell*, 3 vols. (Ebury edition, London, 1937), Vol. I: *Ave*, p. 268 seq.
[2] Ibid., Vol. I: *Ave*, pp. 220–1.

tarian scruples. 'That some wretched farmers and miners', he wrote, 'should refuse to suffer that I may not be deprived of my *demi-tasse* at Tortoni's, that I may be forced to leave this beautiful retreat, my cat and my python—monstrous! And these wretched creatures will find moral support in England—they will find pity. Pity, that most vile of all virtues, has never been known to me.'

Even in jest such language could not but appear in bad taste to the self-conscious political Ireland of his day. Moore, in his early aesthetic Parisian phase, was not the same man who came to Ireland many years later, but he was still a dilettante in all things save the art of letters. The political significance of his association with the Literary Movement is negligible, but it is suggestive. Moore's one dominating interest was writing. He came to Ireland because he was impressed by the vitality of the Literary Movement. He did not regard its political influence seriously because he saw no reason to do so. Yeats, who maintained that the softness, the weakness, the effeminacy of modern literature should be attributed to ideas, was assuredly not one to impress on his disciples the need to consider the probable influence of letters on practical affairs. Moore, though he possessed the Irishman's characteristic interest in personalities, had no serious concern with politics and he illustrated in extreme form, and indeed deliberately caricatured, the political irresponsibility of this literary renaissance.

At Coole, says John Eglinton,[1] 'Yeats's defects as a leader became evident. He lived completely in an Ireland of his own imagination, and without the least perception of the real trend of events.' This verdict may be too pronounced. But it is true that the romantic idealist conception of Ireland, which has found enduring expression in the imagery of some of Yeats's plays and poems, involved a marked degree of remoteness from political realities. Even AE, the secretary of the Agricultural Co-operative Society, the indefatigable cyclist who journeyed all over Ireland in the service of Plunkett's prosaic ideals, the member of the Literary Movement whose contact with practical affairs, whose interest in the material regeneration of Ireland was close and continuous, none the less at times made only too clear his detachment from the painful and pressing political anxieties of his contemporaries. One example will suffice. In 1921, at the height of the Anglo-Irish war, AE was writing about ideal politics in a futurist symposium. His theme was 'What relation have the politics of time to the politics of eternity?' or alternatively, 'Why does the Earth Spirit inspire its

[1] Op. cit., pp. 8-9.

children in such contrary directions?' And on the conclusion of the
Treaty he published the pamphlet, whose intention was to give some
kind of lead to Irish opinion, but in fact only revealed 'the remoteness
of his idealism from the actualities of politics'.[1] In it the arguments on
both sides were set out, but a verdict on their respective merits was left
to the transcendental wisdom of the National Being.

One consequence of such detachment, admirable in so many respects, was seen in AE's belief that Ulster would form a part of the new
Ireland. An Ulsterman himself, he claimed to know Ulster well, and
yet he never appears to have contemplated the secession of the Northern counties. If such unawareness of political forces was possible in
AE, whose pronouncements on Irish affairs were often penetrating,
then one may conceive the remoteness of other members of the Literary Movement, who had few or no practical interests.

Arthur Griffith, who was reputed to have had little use for poets,
whom he was inclined to consider a trifle mad, reflected thereby the
reaction of the mundane Irishman to the national idealism of the Celtic
Renaissance. Possibly Michael Collins came to share his opinion. When
he was on the run with a price upon his head, Collins came at considerable risk one evening to meet AE in Dr Gogarty's house. AE
poured forth in his rich, golden voice a mystic monologue, 'which was
all music and half poetry'. 'Your point, Mr Russell?' enquired Collins
sharply. This interruption was symbolic of the two worlds which had
met but did not understand each other.[2] The Sinn Féin leaders, the
members of the IRA, looked on politics with different eyes to
the writers, who in no small degree had instilled in the minds of a
generation a national feeling that was at once militant, idealist, and
ruthless.

The nationalism of the Celtic Renaissance was militant. The later
reactions of the poets to the horrors of the revolution, to the tragedy of
civil war at times led outside observers to believe that their outlook was
tinged with pacifism. This was not so. Lionel Johnson, in dismissing
the belief in a last heroic insurrection as but a dream,[3] gave most

---

[1] John Eglinton, *Memoir of AE* (London, 1937), pp. 140–2.
[2] O. St. J. Gogarty, *As I was walking down Sackville Street* (London, 1937), p. 175.
Dr Gogarty's son, Dr O. D. Gogarty, at the Yeats Summer School in Sligo in August
1964 recalled how President Cosgrave had sent an offer of a seat in the Senate to George
Russell, who told the President's emissary, 'I must consult my God'. 'Codding apart,
what shall I tell him?' was the emissary's down to earth rejoinder. *Irish Times*, August 19,
1964.
[3] On this point see Yeats *Essays*, p. 319.

telling, if paradoxical, expression to the ideal of a final sacrifice for the nation which inspired the men of 1916.

> A dream! a dream! an ancient dream!
>   Yet ere peace come to Inisfail
> Some weapons on some field must gleam
>   Some burning glory fire the Gael.

Yeats in one of the poems of his closing years wrote:

> You that Mitchel's prayer have heard,
>   'Send war in our time, O Lord!'
> Know that when all words are said
>   And a man is fighting mad,
> Something drops from eyes long blind . . .[1]

The Easter Rising did not take the form, and was not inspired by the motives, which stirred the hearts of these Anglo-Irish poets, yet each in his own way paid tribute to the men who died. AE wrote:[2]

> Their dream had left me numb and cold,
>   But yet my spirit rose in pride,
> Refashioning in burnished gold
>   The images of those who died
> Or were shut in the penal cell.
> Here's to you, Pearse, your dream not mine,
>   But yet the thought for this you fell
> Has turned life's waters into wine.

And Yeats in lines long famous:[3]

> I write it out in a verse—
> MacDonagh and MacBride
> And Connolly and Pearse
> Now and in time to be,
> Wherever green is worn,
> Are changed, changed utterly:
> A terrible beauty is born.

[1] *Last Poems*, 'Under Ben Bulben'.
[2] Quoted John Eglinton, *A Memoir of AE*, p. 119.
[3] *Collected Poems*, pp. 202–5, 'Easter, 1916'.

There was no protest because appeal had been made to the final arbitrament of force and Yeats thought, as always, in aesthetic terms. It was beauty that had been born.[1]

Looking back over the past, Yeats had the misgivings of a sensitive man about the impact of his poetry upon the men and events of the revolutionary years.

> All that I have said and done,
> Now that I am old and ill,
> Turns into a question till
> I lie awake night after night
> And never get the answers right.
> Did that play of mine send out
> Certain men the English shot?
> Did words of mine put too great strain
> On that woman's reeling brain?
> Could any spoken words have checked
> That whereby a house lay wrecked?
> And all seems evil until I
> Sleepless would lie down and die.

Men noted that Lamartine's hair had turned grey in the Revolution of 1848; and Yeats's influence in Ireland, though less measurable, probably went deeper than that of Lamartine in France.

Yeats looked back on Irish history:

> Cast your mind on other days
> That we in coming days may be
> Still the indomitable Irishry.[2]

And he had little but the inspiration to be drawn from the past to offer for the future. AE, by contrast, looked resolutely to the Ireland that was to come:

> We hold the Ireland in the heart
> More than the land our eyes have seen
> And love the goal for which we start
> More than the tale of what has been. . . .
> We would no Irish sign efface,
>   But yet our lips would gladlier hail

---

[1] This point is made by D. Davie, op. cit., p. 143. See generally pp. 143–7.
[2] *Last Poems*, 'Under Ben Bulben'.

The firstborn of the Coming Race
Than the last splendour of the Gael.
No blazoned banner we unfold—
One charge alone we give to youth,
Against the sceptred myth to hold
The golden heresy of truth.[1]

It was a not ignoble ideal, but it was not the ideal of independent Ireland. It unfurled its 'blazoned banner' and the inscription on it was 'A
Gaelic Catholic State'.

In 1921 the romance of Irish independence was over, its history had
begun. Save only in the secession of the Northern counties the whole
series of politico-romantic ideals which had inspired so many generations of Irishmen had been fulfilled. Ireland at last possessed liberty and
independence, if not unity, but the fulfilment of such long-cherished
hopes left behind it a feeling of hollowness and disillusion among the
people. The seemingly hopeless character of the struggle made even
the wisest regard the achievement of independence as an end and not
as a beginning. What was to follow the achievement had always been
contemplated through rosy mists of optimism. The 'Golden Age' of
Irish history would somehow miraculously return in the free light of
independence, the bitter wrangles of politicians would be replaced by a
generous renunciation of individual ideals in order to unite for a
common purpose. Culture and learning would be reverenced in the
new Ireland as they had been honoured in the Ireland of long ago. But
in fact the 'harvesting of the dream' shattered many illusions, and
Irishmen felt as Italians had felt after 1870, that an heroic age was over,
'that prose had succeeded to poetry'.[2]

The disillusion in Ireland was probably more intense than in Italy.
The struggle for independence had been won, but the war of 1919–21
had loosed bitter and revengeful passions; the very character of the
struggle, ambushes and reprisals, terrorism and destruction hardened
men's minds to violence and to lawlessness. The traditions which
bound society were loosened, the principles of ordered government
challenged. That independence could have been won by non-violent
means, as some few isolated voices, mostly pacifist, suggested is alto-

---

[1] *Collected Poems* (London, 1928), 'On behalf of some Irishmen not followers of
Tradition'.
[2] Cf. B. Croce, *A History of Italy, 1871–1915*, trans. C. M. Ady (Oxford, 1929),
p. 2.

gether improbable, but there is no denying the reactions to the methods employed; reactions which found a tragic outlet in the civil war, whose memories long embittered public life in Ireland. Less happy than the Swiss who had won their freedom in medieval times, who have never shed the blood of the oppressors save in the field of battle, who had crowned an heroic struggle with a decisive victory over the last of the Burgundian Dukes; less fortunate than the Italians who had built a united nation in the heroic age of the nationalist movement, the Irish were confronted with the less enviable and less romantic task of carrying on by any means in their power an unequal conflict against modern weapons of war. The necessity was there, but the consequences were plain for all to see. A tradition of violence received a partial sanction if cloaked under the name of patriotism, and such a tradition, firmly implanted by earlier rebellions and more especially by the land war, takes long to eradicate. Many years after independence was won the curious might see inscribed in white on the grey walls of Kilmainham Jail the words, 'We shall rise again'. Irishmen did not regard such utterances lightly, for they knew that it might be possible by an appeal to the past to divide public opinion on the question of physical force or constitutional progress. The news-boys in the nineteen-thirties who cried *An Phoblacht*[1] in Grafton Street in the same strident and aggressive tones as those in which the newsvendors of Paris called *L'Action Française* or *L'Emancipation Nationale* in the shadow of the Madeleine, were for long a reminder to the sober citizens of a bourgeois state that dangerous currents still flowed beneath the surface of national life.

But it were wrong to ascribe the disillusion of Ireland wholly, or even in greater part, to the character of the Anglo-Irish war or to the consequences of civil war. In truth, whatever the antecedents, some such disillusion was bound to pervade public opinion in the new state. That background of romantic idealism which inspired the Celtic Renaissance and clothed with heroic glamour a wellnigh forgotten past, fostered an outlook on the future far removed from the realities of political and social life in the modern world. Those, for example, of whom Yeats liked best to sing, the peasantry and the hard riding country-gentlemen, the lords and ladies gay and the porter drinkers with their randy laughter, were collectively unlikely to contribute much to the stability of a new state or to the discharge of its political or economic responsibilities. The middle classes, like the middle aged, have no comparable poetic appeal, but it is they who support a modern

---

[1] *The Republic*. It was a news-sheet whose publication was periodically banned.

state and modern society. The art of government in the twentieth century is a sober, complicated, even a dull business concerned of necessity with problems of social and economic life, with the improvement of living standards. The simplicity of a single idea, national independence, fired the imagination of poets: the complexity of modern government aroused only their protest. And to the people as a whole, large political issues are more comprehensible, because they appear to present problems that are soluble, whereas economic and social problems frequently seem insoluble by statesmen, who can exercise control only over the economy of the state they govern and not over world conditions as a whole, on which that economy in the last analysis is dependent. In such circumstances it was not surprising that while the main current of Irish literary thought soon broke away from the romanticism of the Literary Movement and adopted a more realistic approach to contemporary life, the people generally were not easily to be persuaded that this was either necessary or desirable, intellectually or politically.

When Flaubert had written in *Madame Bovary* his sordid realist picture of the provincial France he knew so well, he felt the need to turn his back on the modern world *'qui le fatigue autant à réproduire qu'il le dégoute à voir'*, and to dream of the vanished splendour of the ancient world, to write of *'de grandes choses somptueuses'*, of battles, of sieges, of the decadence, the cruelty and the wealth of a Carthage confronted by the challenge of barbarian hordes. As Flaubert found an outlet in *Salammbô*, so Irishmen found an escape in imaginative pictures of their Gaelic past. The causes which drove them to seek such an escape had mostly vanished with independence in 1921, but the outlook remained and a romantic conception of Irish politics long appealed to popular sentiment. The call was not for a Fabian policy with its dullness and its solid achievement; it was for charismatic leadership, for personality rather than principle, with faith in oratory rather than in argument, in the picturesque rather than in the precise, in the spectacular triumph rather than in the steady advance. And so even today those who listen may still hear the voice of that ghost of romantic Ireland, which through the centuries has sat robed and crowned on the grave thereof. Its final deposition is something that may be devoutly desired by the rulers of an independent nation but nonetheless, be long delayed.

CHAPTER IX

THE IRISH QUESTION IN WORLD POLITICS

There has not been a Foreign Minister in this country during the last fifty years who has not felt, and indeed often stated, that the strength of England was diminished, and her moral influence jeopardised, by the unsolved position of the Irish question. This was felt . . . most of all in the United States of America, where the understanding which we so warmly desire has not only been rendered difficult, but almost impossible, by the existence of the Irish question.

THE MARQUESS CURZON OF KEDLESTON,
Secretary of State for Foreign Affairs, in a speech on the Anglo-Irish Treaty in the House of Lords, December 14, 1921.

'You cloud your speech with some eloquent expression of your desire to satisfy the natural aspirations of Irishmen. Rightly or wrongly, I have not the slightest wish to satisfy the natural aspirations of Ireland.' Many English Conservatives, and not a few Liberals, envied Lord Salisbury the caustic candour of his references to Irishmen and their politics, but calculated, since not everyone could count on the electoral immunity enjoyed by the head of the House of Cecil, that indulgence in such language, however agreeable, was likely to exact too heavy a political price. Nonetheless it would be wrong to suppose, as was often imagined in Ireland, that calculation of personal or party interest determined the expression and still less the nature of English interest in Ireland in the last decades of the Union. Certainly such considerations were rarely, if ever, absent from Parliamentary debates, but had they in fact been dominant, other courses would surely have been pursued. If, for example, the two English parties had resolutely determined to ignore the Irish demands; if they had been able to reach agreement on the measure of redress to be afforded to Irish grievances; if, as Gladstone once wished, they had declined to compete for the Irish vote; then it is very likely that the whole question of Anglo-Irish relations and of the Repeal of the Union could have been kept in the background perhaps right up to 1914. Sitting on the safety valve in this way might well have led to an explosion, but whether the explosion would have been as violent, as was in fact the case, is doubtful. In other words the probability is that the English parties by imposing a firm yet benevolent despotism on Ireland, by carefully relegating the Irish Question to the background could have both postponed and shortened the day of reckoning. Why did not the danger of party-competition for the Irish vote, of focussing the attention of the world on Irish grievances, produce such a concerted policy? The answer is partly that the conditions of party warfare made such agreement difficult if not impossible, but chiefly that the conscience of many Englishmen was too profoundly disturbed to allow the issue to be shelved in this way. Like Lord Salisbury they may have cared little about 'the natural aspirations of Irishmen', but they cared a good deal about the reputation of English government.

Home Rule failed in 1886, but Gladstone's campaign for Irish self-government stirred the English conscience, much as it had been stirred nine years earlier by the Midlothian campaign; and while in neither instance was the immediate end accomplished, in both, Englishmen were made to question the wisdom of, and still more the existence of, any moral justification for a traditional policy. The campaign for clearing the Turk 'bag and baggage from the province[1] he has deso-lated and profaned' was directed not primarily to the self-interest, but to the conscience of Englishmen. And the campaign for Home Rule followed the same pattern. It, also, was an essay in 'the politics of virtuous passion' and if indeed it be accepted that the Midlothian Campaign left Gladstone subject to heightened spiritual and emotional tensions which lasted till nearly the end of his life, the one was a necessary prologue to the other.[2] And though the majority of the electorate were in neither case converted to the Gladstonian view, yet the two campaigns created a sharper awareness of England's moral responsibilities. In turn this made a 'deal' between the two parties for the settlement of Ireland more difficult and in so doing placed in the forefront an issue which became the concern not merely of the two peoples most directly concerned, but also of enlightened opinion throughout the world.

In appearance the problem of Anglo-Irish relations was a local issue.

[1] Bulgaria.
[2] See R. T. Shannon, *Gladstone and the Bulgarian Agitation 1876* (London, 1963), pp. XI–XII and generally.

In reality, because its repercussions might become of international consequence, it possessed a direct interest both to the peoples of Europe and of the New World. Ireland was a pawn in the game of international politics; not one of first importance, it is true, but still not one to be overlooked. Bismarck, the Kaiser, Lenin all at different times and with different motives considered how Irish discontent might be turned to advantage. To the enemies of England the unsolved Irish Question was an opportunity; to her friends, to the United States and to the France of the post-Entente years, it was an unwelcome embarrassment.

EUROPEAN REACTIONS TO THE IRISH QUESTION

Count Cavour in the middle years of the nineteenth century observed, not without regret, how the press of every nation in Europe, and writers of every political shade were united only in the venom of their attacks on Britain. For such attacks the state of Ireland afforded an opening too favourable to be neglected. In *The Argus*, a propaganda journal written in English, which Napoleon had caused to be published after the Peace of Amiens, the attempt to ridicule British statesmen and to represent the state of England as one of near-revolutionary chaos acquired most substance in jeers at the contrast between 'the much vaunted freedom', 'the didactic attitude' of English utterances on European policy and the state of impending revolution in Ireland. The propagandist criticism of the French Emperor in respect of Ireland was echoed down the years almost as much by those who were well, as by those who were ill, disposed to England. Vincenzo Gioberti, in the *Primato* in which he championed the claims of the Papacy to lead the Italian nationalist movement, whilst acknowledging the English to be undoubtedly the first people in the world, for the energy of their public life and their sense of national personality, went on to speak of England's two 'internal ulcers', pauperism and Ireland. Ireland was to England, he remarked in unflattering comparison, as Poland is to Russia.[1]

European criticisms of English rule in Ireland were paralleled by general European sympathy for the Irish. Mazzimo D'Azeglio, a Piedmontese aristocrat, whose qualities of mind and character enabled him to render memorable service both to Italian nationalism and to the House of Savoy as Prime Minister of Piedmont during three critical

[1] Quoted G. F. H. Berkeley, *Italy in the Making* (Cambridge, 1932), 3 Vols., Vol. I (1815–46), p. 171.

years, once deplored the fact that the misfortunes of Italy under alien rule did not excite the pity of the world 'as it is aroused in the case of Poland and of Ireland our sisters. I mean the indignation which generous minds feel against those who oppress others, and the ancient honourable compassion that is a comfort and a hope, not an insult to the oppressed'. 'Ireland and Poland!', he said later. . . . 'The opinion, the sympathy and the wishes of the whole of civilization is with them, and nowadays these feelings are powerful allies.'[1] The first was true but the second was, and is, questionable. For the oppressed to rely on the sympathy of other nations may mean indulgence in dangerous daydreams. Good wishes count for nothing in international affairs, unless backed by force and statesmanship. Worse still, the easy sympathies of distant peoples may lure on to disaster those who place reliance on them. The Irish learned not, as we have seen, without disillusioning experience, to count upon 'ourselves alone'.

Arthur Griffith was asked in the years before the World War what was the foreign policy of Sinn Féin. 'In any issue', he replied, 'I find out where England stands. Ireland will be found on the other side.' Whether so negative a policy was ever in the best interests of Ireland may be doubted. What is certain, however, is that this was the presumption of England's enemies. From the Spain of the Armada, to the France of the Revolution, to the Germany of the Kaiser, Ireland in resentful subjection, seemed to present to England's foes a weak, and at times, the weakest link in the English armour. But neither their policies nor their actions were determined by interests other than their own.

No one who has studied the circumstances that existed and the calculations of the Central Powers at the outbreak of War in August 1914 will be inclined to dismiss lightly the European significance of the Irish Question. As the statesmen of the Western democracies observed how the 'Greater Serbia' and the 'Greater Roumania' agitation, both within and without the frontiers of the Dual monarchy, threatened with dissolution the Empire of the Habsburgs, so too the rulers of the autocracies of Central Europe saw in the discontent that simmered in India and in Ireland, first signs of the approaching disintegration of the British Empire. As early as 1910, the Kaiser returned from the funeral of King Edward VII apparently convinced that England was on the verge of civil war over the future of Ulster. Violence or the threat of violence in Ireland continued to offer an incentive to the Central Powers to strike while England was preoccupied in trying to maintain

[1] Quoted Berkeley, op. cit., p 232.

or restore peace and order there. The issues at stake in Ireland and more especially in Ulster may seem, as they seemed to Winston Churchill, 'inconceivably petty', yet, as he has recorded with an imaginative insight that survives even his unconcealed disgust, 'the political future of Great Britain turned' in the summer of 1914 'upon the disposition of clusters of humble parishes' in Fermanagh and Tyrone. It was true; and though there was not civil war as the Kaiser hopefully anticipated, yet in one sense the impression that was given to this impressionable ruler counted for more in deciding the destiny of Europe than the actual event itself.

The potential significance of Ireland to the prophets of ideologies was not less, but rather greater, than it was to the protagonists of power politics. As before 1914 the rulers of Germany surveyed with watchful eyes the course of Irish politics, to see what advantage there might be for exploitation in the coming conflict, so too Lenin, an exile in Geneva, working and waiting for the dawn of the proletarian revolution, reflected, as Marx and Engels had done before him, on the decisive part that Ireland might play, unconsciously perhaps, but nonetheless effectively, in hastening the overthrow of the existing social system. The Dublin strikes of 1913, though they failed to achieve their ostensible objectives, were, as we have seen,[1] interpreted by Lenin as marking the end of 'the influence of the nationalist *bourgeoisie* over the proletariat of Ireland'. All that happened in Ireland in the year that elapsed between the end of the strikes and the outbreak of the World War strengthened him in his belief, both that the Irish nationalist movement could be used to overthrow the capitalist régime in the British Isles and that, having served this purpose, it could be discarded without difficulty by a succeeding international-socialist government. Like the Kaiser, though for a different reason, he attached much significance to the Ulster Question. '. . . the British Conservatives', he wrote in March 1914,[2] 'led by Carson, the British version of our Black-Hundred Landlord, Purishkevich, have raised a frightful howl against Irish Home Rule . . . Lord Carson has threatened rebellion, and organized gangs of reactionary armed thugs for this purpose.' Carson's object 'is to scare the Liberals'. Had the latter appealed to the proletariat all would have been well. But 'the Liberals in England, the lackeys of the money-bags are capable only of cringing before the Carsons'. Lenin, however, consoled himself with the thought that Liberal inaction

---

[1] See above p. 241.
[2] *The British Liberals and Ireland, Collected Works*, Vol. 20, p. 150.

would widen the gulf between this *bourgeois* party and the proletariat. The Curragh mutiny[1] further nourished his hopes. By reopening the question of Parliamentary control over the army, the mutiny threatened the sovereignty of Parliament and in so doing, evidently weakened the strongest bulwark against violence. If parliamentary government broke down, then the working class, throwing off their reliance on constitutional reform, would be easily persuaded, so Lenin thought, to seek amelioration of their conditions by violence. He was, at the least, precipitate in his judgement.

'This revolt of the landowners against the British Parliament', Lenin wrote, 'the "all-powerful" Parliament (as the Liberal dullards . . . have thought and said millions of times) is of tremendous significance. March 21, 1914, will be an epoch-making turning-point, when the noble landlords of Britain tore the British constitution and British law to shreds and gave an excellent lesson in class struggle.

'The lesson stemmed from the impossibility of blunting the sharp antagonisms between the proletariat and the *bourgeoisie* of Britain by means of the half-hearted, hypocritical, sham-reformist policy of the Liberals. This lesson will not be lost upon the British labour movement; the working class will now quickly proceed to shake off its philistine faith in the scrap of paper called . . . the British law and constitution . . .'[2]

If Lenin was right in sensing the disturbing quality of the threat to English constitutional government implicit in the 'revolt of the revolutionaries from the Right', he underestimated—because he continued to discount the intensity, even the ruthlessness, of national sentiment—the consequences of the Curragh incident and what it portended in Ireland. In England the affront to constitutional tradition had less marked reactions than might reasonably have been anticipated. In Ireland it had greater. The interest of Lenin's observations and conclusions, however, lie less in the correctness of his analysis than in the purpose which inspired it. His aim was the destruction of the existing social order and the accomplishment of a world revolution. Because Britain was so formidable a buttress of that order, an Irish challenge to its political or social stability might be of world significance.

---

[1] For studies of it see A. P. Ryan, *Mutiny at the Curragh*, (London, 1956) and Sir J. Fergusson, *The Curragh Incident* (London, 1963), the second of which gives an authoritative account of the motives and actions of the officers principally involved.
[2] *Constitutional Crisis in Britain, Collected Works*, Vol. 20, pp. 226–9.

Lenin's forecast of the future patterns of Anglo-Irish development proved as ill-founded as the Kaiser's anticipation of civil war. In both instances their conclusions were coloured by their hopes. But that is not to say that they have no lasting importance. Far from it, for they emphasized, that whatever the wishes of her people, Ireland could not live detached from continental politics and political movements. Her geographical position, neighbouring a Great Power, made that well-nigh impossible.

AMERICAN REACTIONS TO THE IRISH QUESTION, 1914–21

'Ireland', said Metternich in the middle years of the nineteenth century, 'is passing forth. It is wending its way to the North American States ... to ask for an empty space of ground.'[1] The great exodus that succeeded the Famine years aroused the sympathy of all Europe. Conservative nationalists like Cavour and Gioberti, revolutionary nationalists like Mazzini and Kossuth, statesmen as sober as Guizot, reactionaries as implacable as Metternich—all were stirred to pity or to reproach at the sight of the thousands of exiles crossing the Atlantic. They understood, too, what Englishmen as a whole did not, that sooner or later the descendants of these exiles would demand retribution. But there were also some few Englishmen who saw the consequences with painful clarity. John Bright was one among them. On August 25, 1848, he warned[2] the House of Commons that Irishmen, driven out from their own land by poverty and famine, had emigrated in great numbers and 'in whatever quarter of the world an Irishman sets his foot, there stands a bitter, an implacable enemy of England. . . . There are hundreds of thousands—I suppose there are millions—of the population of the United States of America who are Irish by birth, or by immediate descent; and be it remembered, Irishmen settled in the United States have a large influence in public affairs. They sometimes sway the election of Members of the Legislature, and may even affect the election of the President of the Republic. There may come a time when questions of a critical nature will be agitated between the Governments of Great Britain and the United States; and it is certain that at such a time the Irish in that country will throw their whole weight into the scale against this country . . .'

[1] Quoted in G. F. H. Berkeley, op. cit. Vol. II, p. 164.
[2] The extract is reprinted in Thorold Rogers, *Speeches by the Rt. Hon. John Bright M.P.* (London, 1869), p. 159.

Twenty years later, on March 12, 1868, John Stuart Mill, in his brief period as a Member of Parliament, also warned the House of the danger from the Irish from across the ocean. The Fenian rising of '67 amounted to nothing because no one of consequence would commit himself to an insurrection foredoomed to failure but nonetheless, argued Mill,[1] the state of Ireland was more dangerous than at any former period. Why? Partly, he said, because of the growth of the feeling of nationality in Ireland and partly because of 'a circumstance which has never existed before'. 'For the first time', he proceeded,[2] 'the discontent in Ireland rests on a background of several millions of Irish across the Atlantic. This is a fact which is not likely to diminish. The number of Irish in America is constantly increasing. Their power to influence the political conduct of the United States is increasing, and will daily increase; and is there any probability that the American-Irish will come to hate this country less than they do at the present moment?'

What Bright and Mill foreshadowed largely came to pass. The Fenians found their followers, the Land League its resources, the Republic its champions among the Irish colonists in the New World. And more precisely, the contingency which Bright forecast, the time when questions of a critical nature were agitated between the governments of the United Kingdom and the United States, was substantially realized in the War of 1914–18.

In the United Kingdom the public and, even those in authority, for long remained unaware of the extent to which American policy during the First World War was influenced by unfavourable American reactions to developments, or rather the continuing lack of development, in British policy in Ireland. Sir Cecil Spring Rice, the Anglo-Irishman[3] who was English Ambassador in Washington, time and again warned his Government as to the extreme sensitiveness of American opinion on the Irish Question. On May 20, 1915, when the Allies, despairing of an early peace, were beginning to look more anxiously across the Atlantic in the hope that their reserves of material and man-power might be replenished by American collaboration on the democratic side, Sir Cecil emphasized in a letter from Washington, 'It is evidently of very great importance that no action should be taken in England

[1] The speech is reprinted in J. S. Mill, *The Irish Land Question*, pp. 108–25.
[2] Ibid., pp. 111–12.
[3] He was by reason of his origin sensitive to Irish feelings in the United States. He had also family reasons for knowing about the growth of national sentiment in Ireland since his niece, Mary Spring Rice, had helped Erskine Childers in gun running for the Irish Volunteers at Howth in July 1914.

which would arouse a strong anti-British sentiment among the Irish here'.[1]

In fact anti-British sentiment in the United States was stirred to fever-heat a year later when the leaders of the Easter Rising were shot. 'It is most unfortunate', wrote Sir Cecil, 'that it has been found necessary to execute the rebels.'[2] So unfavourably was he impressed by the consequent change in American opinion towards England that he concluded that the executions had made it hopeless to count on American help or even on American sympathy. It was possible that a settlement of the Home Rule Question might have a beneficial effect on the American public generally, but the Ambassador despaired of ever conciliating the Irish-Americans. 'Our cause for the present among the Irish here', he wrote, 'is a lost one. They have blood in their eyes when they look our way.'[3]

Lloyd George was made aware of the dangerous consequences that might follow from the alienation of American opinion at such a moment. As a politician he appreciated the influence of the Irish-American vote on the result of the 1916 Presidential election, and as a statesman determined to win the war at all costs, he realized the imperative need to counteract the growth of anti-British feeling in the States. His task, rendered far easier by German 'frightfulness' in the submarine campaign in the Atlantic, was to be furthered by the despatch of a mission under A. J. Balfour to Washington as tangible proof of a new British resolve to conciliate American opinion. 'It's sad to me', said Balfour to the American Ambassador just before leaving on it, 'that we are so unpopular, so much more unpopular than the French, in your country. Why is it? The old school books?' Mr Page doubted the influence of the school books. 'Certainly', he said, 'their influence is not the main cause. It is the organized Irish. Then it's the effect of the very fact that the Irish question is not settled. You've had that problem at your very door for 300 years. What is the matter that you don't solve it?'

'Yes, yes', replied Mr Balfour in plaintive tones,[4] but he had no positive suggestion, for indeed his own policy had been tried and failed more than a dozen years before. The wheel had come in full

---

[1] *The Letters and Friendships of Sir Cecil Spring Rice, A Record*, Edited by Stephen Gwynn (London, 1929), 2 Vols., Vol. II, p. 273.
[2] Letter of May 30, 1916.
[3] Letter of June 16, 1916.
[4] J. Hendrick, *The Life and Letters of Walter H. Page* (London, 1922–25), 3 Vols., Vol. II, p. 215 et seq.

circle. At the most critical moment of a war to prevent the German domination of Europe, the armed support of the United States was delayed, until the President could reassure the American people as to the direction of English policy in Ireland.

One of the notable products of the Balfour Mission was the communication of a request from President Wilson that Great Britain should take some decisive step to settle the Irish Question. 'The President', declared this message to the Ambassador, 'wishes that, when you next meet the Prime Minister, you would explain to him that only one circumstance now appears to stand in the way of perfect co-operation with Great Britain. All Americans, who are not immediately connected with Germany by blood ties, find their one difficulty in the failure of Great Britain so far to establish a satisfactory form of self-government in Ireland. In the recent debates in Congress on the War Resolution, this sentiment was especially manifest. . . . If the American people were once convinced that there was a likelihood that the Irish question would soon be settled, great enthusiasm and satisfaction would result and it would also strengthen the co-operation which we are now about to organize between the United States and Great Britain.'[1] Lloyd George, however, when confronted by the Ambassador with this statement of American views, broke out, 'God knows I'm trying. Tell your President that'. And then looking across the room he saw in Sir Edward Carson, his First Lord of the Admiralty, a convenient target. 'Madmen—madmen—' he cried. 'I never saw any such task. Madmen! But the President's right. We've got to settle it and we've got to settle it now.' It was a subject on which Sir Edward's idea of a settlement differed considerably from that of Lloyd George and still more from that of President Wilson.[2]

President Wilson was the son of a Presbyterian Minister of Scottish descent. He was born in Virginia and brought up in Georgia. His political thought was founded upon an uneasy union of the missionary zeal inherited from the Covenanters and of the devotion of the Southern Democrats to popular sovereignty or self-determination.[3] His insistence on the principle of self-determination might have predisposed him to sympathy even with the extreme national claims of Irishmen, had not an inherited mistrust of the Southern Irish caused

[1] J. Hendrick, *The Life and Letters of Walter H. Page* (London, 1922–25), 3 Vols., Vol. II, p. 255.
[2] Cf. the opinion of Sir Cecil Spring Rice. Gwynn, op. cit., Vol. II, p. 393.
[3] Sir A. Zimmern, *The League of Nations and the Rule of Law, 1918–35* (London, 1936), pp. 216–17.

him to look askance at their pretensions. The President impressed on the Prime Minister the need for an Irish settlement agreeable to American opinion, if the United States were to enter the war on the allied side. He did not, however, himself regard Ireland as one of the nations 'struggling to be free', and in the various proposals which he sponsored, the Irish were not numbered with the Poles or the Czechs or the Serbs as one of the peoples whose independence was a necessary condition of peace.

The President in fact preferred to regard the solution of the Irish Question more as a factor in home politics, than as an integral part of the new European settlement. His professed task at the Peace Conference was the re-arrangement of national frontiers according to the principle of self-determination. Before the President sailed for Europe in December 1918, more than a thousand Roman Catholic priests of the Diocese of New York sent him an appeal to make the principle of self-determination applicable to Ireland. A similar appeal was sent to him by wireless, after he had sailed, from a large Madison Square meeting of the Friends of Irish Freedom. To such appeals Wilson returned noncommittal replies, for he was well aware that his difficulties in Europe would be greatly increased, if he incurred British hostility in advance by a pronouncement in favour of Irish self-determination. At the same time his position as leader of the Democratic Party, which commanded the allegiance of the vast majority of Irish-Americans, rendered definite opposition to Irish claims out of the question. So he was compelled to pursue a middle course, uncongenial to his autocratic temper.

The sympathy of the people of the United States for Ireland was clearly shown when on March 4, 1919, the House of Representatives passed by 261 votes to 41 the Resolution of Thomas Gallagher of Illinois which read:

That it is the earnest hope of the Congress of the United States of America that the Peace Conference now sitting at Paris and passing upon the rights of the various people will favourably consider the claims of Ireland to self-determination.

Miss Macardle in her history of the Irish Republic draws the conclusion that by this vote 'the American people had instructed their President to support Ireland's claim'.[1] Such was not entirely the case. The resolu-

---

[1] Op. cit., p. 292. It should be observed that though the majority is large the vote is small. More than a quarter of the House abstained from voting.

tion was so worded—'the Peace Conference shall favourably consider' —as to attract the support of all sympathizers in the House of Representatives without committing them to any explicit course of action in the future. In the circumstances only a man of definite conviction would vote against the motion, since it would automatically entail the loss of Irish support at the next election, whereas the waverer would either abstain or vote for the motion. The issue is one of some significance, since the acceptance of Miss Macardle's interpretation in Ireland has prompted the inevitable enquiry, that if sympathy in the United States was so overwhelming as this vote suggests, why did not public opinion there insist on a hearing for the Irish case at the Peace Conference?

In 1919–20 support for Ireland in the States was sensibly weakened by divisions within the Irish-American ranks. John Devoy, leader of the Irish-American organization, the Clan na Gael, and Judge Cohalan, his intimate friend and adviser, were not prepared to give unqualified support to the extreme Republican claims in Ireland. Though Devoy had taken part in the planning of the German expedition to Ireland in 1916, which is associated with Sir Roger Casement's name, he rather unexpectedly refrained from according recognition in his paper, *The Gaelic American* [1] to the Irish Republic as established by the Declaration of Dáil Éireann in 1919. More serious even than these internal dissensions was Judge Cohalan's denunciation of the League of Nations. President Wilson, who displayed the arrogance of a citizen of the New World in his concern for the plight of the Old, could not forgive criticism of his most cherished project for the regeneration of Europe. This conflict of opinion on the League heralded the loss of the Irish vote to the Democratic Party in the 1920 elections. Yet despite internal dissensions political pressure from America was persistent. On June 6, 1919, the Senate resolved with only one dissentient voice that a hearing should be given to the representatives of Ireland at the Peace Conference. In addition the Senate expressed 'its sympathy with the aspirations of the Irish people for a government of their own choice'.[2]

The danger of an Irish appeal to the Peace Conference over the head of the British Government had occupied the attention of the Foreign Office, as soon as they came to consider the general principles of the Peace Settlement. President Wilson's enunciation of the right of self-determination implied that the Irish claim might henceforward be

[1] Macardle, op. cit., pp. 290–2.   [2] Quoted, ibid., p. 310.

placed on a new basis. Would the Peace Conference be entitled to discuss whether or no the Irish claim to self-determination was valid?
Could it refuse to consider the claim and yet remain true to the spirit of
the Fourteen Points? A Foreign Office paper entitled, *A Memorandum
prepared for the consideration of the British Government in connection
with the forthcoming Peace Settlement* was drafted in the Autumn of
1918. In it the difficulty likely to confront the British Government was
considered. 'Efforts will doubtless be made', read the fifth section, 'to
embody provisions in the Treaty safeguarding the rights of . . .
minorities and, further, to interpret the doctrine of "national self-
determination" as entitling such minorities, if they can claim to be
nations, to present their case to the Peace Conference.' On both these
points the memorandum recommended that as much discretion as
possible should be left in the hands of the Allied Powers. 'It would
clearly be inadvisable', the document continues, 'to go even the smallest
distance in the direction of admitting the claim of the American
negroes, or the Southern Irish, or the Flemings or Catalans, to appeal
to an Inter-State Conference over the head of their own Government.'[1]
Therefore the British Government should beware of encouraging a
right of appeal to the Conference from Macedonians or German
Bohemians, lest such a course should encourage more inconvenient
claims nearer home. The Conference and later the League of Nations
should trust member states 'to be true to their professions' rather than
encourage appeals to this international tribunal from some part of their
subjects. At the same time member states, which allowed propaganda
subversive of the governments of their neighbours, should be placed
outside the pale of the League's membership, a suggestion directed
against Communists, but also applicable to the activities of Irish-
American Republican organizations.

This Foreign Office document revealed the predicament of the
British Government. There was a strong case against the enunciation
and the application of the principle of national self-determination. It
was stated by Robert Lansing, who was for some time the adviser of
President Wilson on Foreign policy and who recorded the impressions
of an able, if somewhat opinionated, American observer at the end of
1918.

'The more I think about the President's declaration as to the right of
"self-determination", the more convinced I am of the danger of

[1] The Memorandum is quoted in full in Zimmern, op. cit., pp. 197–209.

putting such ideas into the minds of certain races. It is bound to be the basis of impossible demands. What effect will it have on the Irish, the Indians, the Egyptians, and the nationalists among the Boers? Will it not breed . . . rebellion? The phrase is simply loaded with dynamite. It will raise hopes which can never be realized. It will, I fear, cost thousands of lives. In the end it is bound to be discredited, to be called the dream of an idealist. . . . What a calamity that the phrase was ever uttered!'[1]

Outspoken criticism of this character did not come from the British Government. Why? It was largely because the principle of self-determination was generally accepted as the most hopeful basis for settlement in South Eastern and Central Europe, but also in part because of more ephemeral considerations. The American President could not be rebuffed. He might be cajoled. The only statesmanlike course was, therefore, the acceptance of the principle, reserving for later discussion the necessarily arbitrary distinction to be drawn between those who might claim a right to self-determination and those who might not.

By its tactics the British Government successfully averted a disastrous rupture in Anglo-American relations. On President Wilson fell the onus of refusing a hearing to the Irish delegates to the Peace Conference. He received the Irish deputation in Paris on June 11, 1919, and explained that the Committee of Four had decided that no small nation should appear before it without the unanimous consent of the whole Committee. An attempt to secure French co-operation had failed earlier in the year, when Sean T. O'Kelly wrote to M. Clemenceau, defining the Irish claims to self-determination and urging that these claims should be heard by the Conference. The letter received no reply. Moreover, French opinion, though traditionally friendly to Ireland, could not bestow upon the rising of 1916 its unqualified favour. M. Rivoallan expressed the French point of view when he wrote: '*Notre dilemme est aujourd'hui le même qu'en 1916: nous ne pouvions applaudir à une insurrection qui favorisait, non inconsciemment, l'ennemi que nous combattions devant Verdun, nous ne pouvions non plus refuser à l'héroisme des insurgés notre tribut d'admiration.*'[2] France might hope for the complete independence of Ireland, but only if her English ally was not thereby weakened.

[1] Robert Lansing, *The Peace Negotiations* (London, 1921), p. 87.
[2] *L'Irlande* (Paris, 1934), pp. 197–8.

The Irish claim was not considered at Versailles. But American sympathy for the Irish cause did not lessen, and when in March 1920 the American Senate had the ratification of the Treaty of Versailles under consideration, it resolved that when self-government was attained by Ireland, 'a consummation it is hoped is at hand', then Ireland 'should promptly be admitted as a member of the League of Nations'.[1] This new evidence of American sympathy was certainly not without effect in England, where it was understood that a discontented Ireland might seriously affect future co-operation between the United Kingdom and the United States. Continued repression could only alienate American opinion, and the ultimately successful endeavours to end the war in Ireland in 1921 acquired a sense of urgency, from the sharpness of the American reactions to Lloyd George's attempt to break up 'a small body of assassins'.

Diplomatic pressure by the United States on Britain alone would not, it seems clear, have advanced greatly the Irish cause. It became important when the Irish rose in insurrection. That insurrection was indigenous in origin. But once it had broken out, with evidence of careful organization and the prospect of sustained resistance, funds, which the British by early 1921 believed to be a condition of continued IRA operations, were supplied from the United States.[2] It was this twofold support, diplomatic and financial, that rendered American backing for Ireland in 1919–21 of great, though probably, despite British views to the contrary, not of decisive importance. It was, therefore, by no means unfitting that the first American Independence Day, July 4, 1921, after the signing of the Truce was celebrated in Dublin, so the American Consul reported to the State Department, in a manner that 'would scarcely have been exceeded in a city of similar size in the United States'.[3] President de Valera had specially requested that the Stars and Stripes should be generally flown in honour of America and in response to his request the Consul noted that 'not only a great many large flags were flown, but thousands of the populace had adorned themselves with small American flags'; the wearing of which 'was limited only by the exhaustion of the stocks for sale. There was, indeed, only one small doubt to mar the Consul's otherwise unmixed

[1] Macardle, op. cit., pp. 380–1.

[2] Some particulars of the extent of American assistance to Sinn Fein is given in a Report from the American Consul in Dublin, to the State Department, Washington. No. 195, March 22, 1921.

[3] Despatch from American Consulate, Belfast, to Department of State, Washington, July 6, 1921.

gratification. 'It is not altogether clear', he reported to Washington, 'to what degree De Valera's request to fly the American flag in Dublin was prompted by appreciation of America, or how far he may have been moved to the request by the desire to give offence to the English.'

CONCLUSION

CHAPTER X

SOME GENERAL REFLECTIONS ON THE DEVELOPMENT OF ANGLO-IRISH RELATIONS 1840–1921

All general judgements are weak and imperfect
MONTAIGNE
On the Art of Conversation

The Irish Question is customarily spoken of in the past tense and it is true that the Anglo-Irish Treaty of 1921 marked the ending of an age. But the legacies and the burdens of the past remained to influence and shape the future. In history there are no endings and no beginnings. In 1921 Ireland stood on the threshold of a new era, Anglo-Irish relations entered a new phase, but the past remained to encourage, to influence, and, most of all, to warn.

The absence of finality prevents the historian from saying with any assurance that one interpretation of history is true and that another is false. All he can do is to suggest that one interpretation explains the course of events more satisfactorily, that it throws more light upon the actions of men and peoples than another. Further, he will find it hard to go. Some historians, wrote H. A. L. Fisher,[1] have been fortunate enough to discern 'in history, a plot, a rhythm, a predetermined pattern' but his own study of the growth of European civilization only confirmed in him a spirit of historical agnosticism and a conviction that there was only one safe rule for the historian, that he should 'recognize in the development of human destinies the play of the contingent and the unforeseen'. An analysis of Anglo-Irish relations, such as is attempted in this book, fosters a similar scepticism. There would seem to be no ultimate, final or predestined solution of Anglo-Irish relations; there is only a continuous conflict of forces, whose

[1] In the Preface to *A History of Europe* (London, 1935), 3 Vols., Vol. I, p. vii.

direction and strength are always changing. What appears final to-day, may well be modified or even refuted, by the events of tomorrow. All one can discern are certain tendencies, which appear predominant at a certain time and the analysis of which, by deepening our knowledge of the past, assists our understanding of the future.

Two large interpretations of nineteenth-century Irish history have constantly recurred in this book, the one economic and the other predominantly political. The economic, in its extreme Marxist application, assumed that the class struggle alone was fundamental, and given the lack of a substantial urban middle class, saw in the land question, the only form of the social question in nineteenth-century Ireland. The land question was therefore decisive; but so long as the ascendancy landlords remained in control, the issue was clouded by considerations of a political, religious, or national character. Increasing urbanization, coupled with the 1903 solution of the land question, converting the tenant farmers into peasant proprietors, on this view, brought the fundamental conflict between the proletariat and the *bourgeoisie*, in country and in town, into the foreground. By 1913 Lenin, observing the rapid growth of an Irish middle class, singles it out for especial condemnation. But if this economic interpretation is correct, the emergence of a *bourgeoisie* should have heralded the beginning of a decisive class-struggle for power in Ireland. No such struggle was in fact joined. On the contrary the 1916 rising afforded conclusive evidence, at any rate at that time, of co-operation between the prospective protagonists. This fact alone would make one hesitant to accept this interpretation of Irish history.

The crudities of economic interpretation are not altogether confined to Marxist or pseudo-Marxist historians. They are apt to permeate the teaching and thinking of many who would repudiate, possibly with some indignation, any such description. The Professor of Modern History at Cambridge recalled in 1964 how he was told at another university ten years earlier, 'when an undergraduate was asked to write about the French Revolution he would write of Marie Antoinette, the *Philosophes*, Robespierre, Danton and so on. Now all this is changed. Apparently the standard essay revolves round the price of bread, the declining wage-rates of shoemenders and the falling profits of Paris wig-makers in 1789.'[1] Yet, if an historical fashion seems to go too far, that is ground only for testing its pretensions, and rejecting

[1] C. H. Wilson, *History in Special and in General. An Inaugural Lecture* (Cambridge, 1964), p. 8.

those that are unreasonable. And in the context of nineteenth–early twentieth-century Anglo-Irish relations, social and economic factors, until recently much neglected by Irish historians[1] still require analysis and further critical reappraisal. Irish history would be the richer, it may be thought, for some more general diffusion of knowledge about the growth of industry in the North-East, the wage-rates of farm labourers or even of the stone-breakers with their hammers and protective glasses once so familiar a sight on Irish country roads, the price of corn and cattle, fluctuations in the price of bread, and perhaps most of all, in so far as evidence is available, about the productivity of the soil. Even in respect of the dominant socio-economic factor of the early nineteenth century, the staple food of the great majority of the people, the potato, little more than generalities are interwoven in the interstices of political narrative. Is there not some lack of balance and perspective here? The great calamity of nineteenth-century Irish history derived from dependence upon this single crop; and if the fundamental questions are how and why did this dependence come about, the answers to which are to be sought well back in time, it is still, in the narrower context of nineteenth-century history, important to realize that because of dependence on that single crop calamity was at once foreseeable and foreseen.

On July 9, 1822, in a time of near famine, Maria Edgeworth wrote from Edgeworth's Town[2] in County Longford to David Ricardo inviting him to discuss 'the question *for* and *against* the potatoe which has for some hundred years past been alternately cried up as the blessing and cried down as the bane of Ireland. In Berkeley's Querist . . . there is this query

Whether it is possible Ireland should be well improved while our beef is exported and our labourers live upon potatoes.'

Miss Edgeworth proceeded to press home her enquiry by listing familiar

---

[1] Professor E. Curtis's *History of Ireland*, for example, widely accepted as a standard work is a political history of a nineteenth-century type and while admirable in other respects gives little or no consideration to the influence of social and economic factors upon the course of events.

[2] She spelt it in this way. It is now written Edgeworthstown. Miss Edgeworth was familiar in the literary and philosophical circles in London and also in Paris, though she had to exercise some care on her visit during the Peace of Amiens because her uncle, L'Abbé Edgeworth de Firmont, was confessor to Louis XVI and had attended him on the scaffold.

U

objections—that the potato crop was uncertain, that it was not easily stored, that it facilitated subdivision, that it encouraged over-population, then countering them in part and concluding with the enquiry whether people in England who did not live upon potatoes and who had 'gone through all the prosperity and adversity of manufactures are you better off—are you happier—I don't ask whether you are richer than we are in Ireland'.[1]

David Ricardo replied on December 13th with the expression of some doubt as to whether he had given 'the question *for* and *against* the potato that degree of attentive consideration to entitle me to speak with confidence upon it'. But in the otherwise even balance of argument one factor alone and in isolation sufficed to bring this most distinguished of the classical economists down against the potato. 'My objection', he said, 'rests almost wholly on the fact which we have so often witnessed of the crop being uncertain and liable to peculiar accidents.' And he developed his objection in moving and prophetic terms. 'The argument, that the failure of the potatoe crop is only occasional, and that at all other times there will be in the world a much greater number of happy and contented beings, appears to me defective. Judging by my own feelings, if, for five, six or seven years of easy competency, with respect to food, I had to endure one year of famine, and to witness the sufferings of my family and friends for that one dreadful year, I would rather that I had never been born;—no happiness . . . can compensate perpetual hunger, and all the evils in its train, for one year, much less can it compensate for the dreadful suffering of starvation, if that should be the consequence.'[2] Does not so precise a prediction, of what was to be the experience of so many in that terrible year almost a quarter of a century later, remind us at the least of the importance of seeking for causes, not merely in the immediate political context of the times, but also and equally in the broader social and economic pattern imposed upon a country by the circumstances of an earlier period?

Consideration of economic and social factors also suggests the need for some reconsideration of the familiar historical perspectives of the years between the famine and the Treaty. Historically this is a time dominated by personalities. Attention is given, and rightly, to parties and above all to their leaders. But the question is rarely asked, what was the relation of these parties and personalities to the social and economic

---

[1] *The Works and Correspondence of David Ricardo*, Vol. IX, pp. 230–2.
[2] Ibid., pp. 237–8.

circumstances of their time? Yet it may be as important, even with the
most outstanding of leaders, to understand not only the relation of
society to the individual but also the relation of that particular individual to the political and social context of his time. Is it not deserving of
consideration whether Parnell—to take the classic example—was in
part at least the product of a particular environment and, if so, why?
Could he have emerged as a leader twenty or thirty years earlier, in the
fifties or the sixties? The answer might well be the familiar one that the
physical and psychological depression of the post-famine years was
too great to allow of forceful and highly organized party leadership of
a Parnellite kind. But other questions might also be asked. Had the
tenant farmers accumulated enough capital, and in consequence did
they possess the necessary minimal independence, in those earlier
years, to make the politico-social struggle of the eighties under
Parnell's and Davitt's leadership possible? Did Parnell attain his
position because of or in spite of emigration? Could he have maintained the struggle without American funds? Would those funds have
been forthcoming twenty years earlier, before the Irish emigrants were
established in the United States? Even the asking of such questions
suggests the lacunae in historical knowledge which overmuch dependence on political narrative may leave.

In the concluding phase of the period under review there is another
question, arising from the interrelation of socio-economic and
political factors, which is of perennial interest in the conflict between
imperial powers and national movements. It is this. How far does the
force of national sentiment derive its strength from social injustices or
economic depression, and how far therefore may that force be blunted
by social and economic reforms? Communists and conservatives, apt
to be at one in discounting the authenticity of political nationalism,
incline, usually strongly, to the view that socio-economic factors are
fundamental, and they are accordingly predisposed to believe that
reforms and redress of grievances in these fields will sap the strength of
political nationalism. King George V put the point concisely to his
Prime Minister on September 22, 1913, '. . . is the demand for Home
Rule in Ireland', he enquired of Asquith,[1] 'as earnest and as National
today as it was, for instance, in the days of Parnell?'

'Has not the Land Purchase policy settled the agrarian trouble which
was the chief motive of the Home Rule agitation?'

Lest the answer to the King's enquiry should be thought altogether

[1] *Asquith Papers.* Dep. 38.

self-evident, it may be noted that the biographer of Michael Collins, Piaras Beaslai, after alluding to the wave of pro-British enthusiasm that followed the outbreak of war, went on to write, 'Never was there a period when the conquest of Ireland by England seemed more complete'.[1] Yet the events of 1916–21 were to expose the deceptiveness of popular appearances, and, far more important, to confound expectations by no means unreasonable in themselves. Ireland at this time gave to the world a classic example of the predominance of political over socio-economic factors, since the resolution of the land problem and the economic betterment of the country in the first two decades of the century combined, not to weaken, but to give final, concentrated explosive force to political nationalism. It was an object-lesson which British statesmen, in their dealings with national movements in South Asia and in Africa in succeeding decades, remembered not without profit, both to themselves and to their erstwhile subject-peoples.

In Ireland the lessons of revolutionary nationalism in one respect may have been learned too well. After 1921 there was a marked predisposition to re-interpret the aims and struggles of the pre-revolutionary and essentially reformist era in the light of subsequent revolutionary aspirations and achievement. This was to impose upon nineteenth-century Irish history a political concept as restrictive in its own way as those of the economic theoreticians. For in its more extreme form the concept predicated, not that nationalism became, but that it was in a single, indentifiable form and for far back in time, the dominant and all sufficient directing force in Irish historical development. This was at once, and it might be thought self-evidently, unhistorical and also by inference a depreciation of the achievements of the revolutionary movement, one of the most remarkable of which was the harnessing of many and diverse forces in a common, overriding purpose.

In nineteenth-century Ireland the idea of nationality passed through many phases and reflected many strands of thought and aspiration. Daniel O'Connell's notions of the Anglo-Irish settlement that might follow Repeal, rested upon an idea of nationality less absolute, if also less comprehensive, than that expounded by Thomas Davis, as he sought in romantic re-creation of the past, to reaffirm 'the pedigree' of Irish nationhood and was in undisguised conflict with the revolutionary, republican nationalism of John Mitchel. Later, in the early sixties, there were not lacking some indications that Irish nationality might find fulfilment in Liberal Unionism, while Charles Stewart Parnell, in

[1] Piaras Beaslai, *Michael Collins, Soldier and Statesman* (Dublin, 1937), p. 19.

his struggle for Home Rule, not only looked forward to the separatist state of later times, but also looked back to the Irish Parliament of the late eighteenth century—as indeed was movingly and dramatically shown in one last gesture of greatness when the Chief, his hair and beard ruffled, a bandage over an eye injured in an electoral demonstration against him, returned in December 1890 to Dublin from disastrous defeat in a by-election at Kilkenny and, passing the buildings in College Green where Grattan's parliament had sat, flung out his arm and without speaking pointed to it, the watching crowd responding with a deep roar of applause.[1] In sum there was a richness and variety in the Irish nationalist tradition in the nineteenth century which defies narrowing classification and was the stuff of history. It was the complexity, not the simplicity of the Irish national question that commanded the attention and held the interst of visitors from other lands, from de Tocqueville to Cavour, from Nassau Senior to Friedrich Engels. De Beaumont, indeed, in one brief sentence said all that was needed at the outset of his work—'*L'Irlande est une petite contrée sur laquelle se debattent les plus grandes questions de la politique, de la morale and de l'humanité.*'[2]

Reconsideration of the complex of problems and forces that collectively made up the Irish Question in these years suggests that past concentration upon politics (in the narrower sense) and personalities, sometimes to the exclusion of other factors, may have created an impression that governments, parties, classes and, most of all, individual leaders enjoyed a freedom of manœuvre and action greater than that which historically they possessed. Yet, to reflect upon the largest of issues, the Union itself, may it not be, quite apart from methods employed to secure its enactment, that it was predestined to failure because it lacked a necessary foundation in political and social realities? Was Henry Grattan endowed with eloquent and prophetic foresight in that speech of May 15, 1797, in which he warned Unionist supporters of the consequences of a successful imposition of union—'. . . a union! but what may be the ultimate consequences of such a victory? A separation!' Or was he rather stating the most likely outcome?

John Stuart Mill identified[3] one corroding canker in the Union settlement, when he spoke of the political and social lack of compatibility and of mutual comprehension between the two peoples thereby

[1] F. S. L. Lyons, *The Fall of Parnell*, pp. 174–6.
[2] Op. cit., Vol. I, p. ii.
[3] *England and Ireland* (London, 1868), p. 9.

united in one state. Anyone, he observed on one occasion, who reflected on the state of society in England and in Ireland, with any
sufficient knowledge of the states of society that existed elsewhere,
would be driven, however unwillingly, to the conclusion that 'there is
probably no other nation of the civilized world, which, if the task of
governing Ireland had happened to devolve on it, would not have
shown itself more capable of that work than England has hitherto
done' and the principal reason he advanced for this conclusion was
that 'there is no other civilized nation which is so far apart from Ireland
in the character of its history or so unlike it in the whole constitution
of its political economy' as England . . . 'and none therefore, which if
it applies to Ireland the modes of thinking and maxims of government
which have grown up within itself, is so certain to go wrong'. And
on May 17, 1866, in the House of Commons debate on Chichester
Fortescue's Land Bill, Mill observed 'Ireland is not an exceptional
country but England is. Irish circumstances and Irish ideas as to social
and agricultural economy are the general ideas of the human race; it is
English circumstances and English ideas that are peculiar. Ireland is in
the main stream of human existence and human feeling and experience;
it is England that is in one of the lateral channels. If we are to be guided
by experience in legislating for Ireland, it is continental rather than
English experience we ought to consider, for it is on the Continent,
and not in England, that we find anything like similarity of circumstances.'[1]

No doubt Mill was guilty of some overstatement, but the substance of
his argument is surely correct. And it may be added, if de Tocqueville's
passing impressions possess any general validity, that similarity of
circumstance between Irish and continental conditions was paralleled
by affinity of minds. 'The conversation', de Tocqueville recorded of a
dinner party on July 26, 1835, with the Catholic Bishop of Kilkenny[2]
'followed its course . . . for two hours. It was impassioned, superficial,
light, often interrupted by jokes and witty remarks. I might have been
in France. Nothing resembled England.' And of the journey to Cork a
few days later—'In our open diligence there were two young men both
very uproariously drunk. They talked to and made jokes at almost
every passer-by. All, men and women, answered with laughter and
other pleasantries. I thought I was in France.'[3]

[1] *The Irish Land Question*, pp. 98–9.
[2] *Journeys*, p. 153.
[3] Ibid., p. 159.

The causal relationship between difference in circumstances and difference in outlook may be a matter best left to speculation; but the consequences of the association of two nations so dissimilar in their economic and social conditions and so widely separated in their outlook, may be thought of as a deep-seated reason of the failure of the Union. Irish causes did not naturally commend themselves to the English people; Irish reforms, especially radical reforms, were not, as Joseph Chamberlain understood, an electoral asset but an electoral liability to the party which sponsored them. This was not a matter of class, though Marx was certainly correct in emphasizing the antipathy of the English working classes for their generally lower paid Irish competitors. It went, though by no means evenly, through the nation. And it had, it was bound to have, far-reaching consequences. 'We can never be qualified', wrote Thomas Munro, one of the most enlightened of early English administrators in India,[1] 'to govern men against whom we are prejudiced. If we entertain a prejudice at all, it ought rather to be in their favour than against them. We ought to know their character, but especially the favourable side of it; for if we know only the unfavourable, it will beget contempt and harshness on the one part, and discontent on the other.' What was true of India, was at the least equally true of Ireland. That there was 'a prejudice against' was common to both parties to the Union and the greater, on whom the major share of responsibility rested, made no sustained effort to transform it into 'a prejudice in favour'.

Lack of mutual comprehension, tension and antipathies between the English and Irish peoples were of historical moment, and indeed in large measure only existed and continued, because the two nations were rigidly confined after 1800 within a political and social system that in the last resort was unitary, however great the continuing diversity in ordinary practice. Nor was it only the Irish who found the Union irksome. 'Your restless nation', wrote Ricardo to Miss Edgeworth on May 26, 1823,[2] 'gives us a great deal of trouble in Parliament. The best amongst us do not know how to manage you, nor what course to take to give you the blessings of peace, order, and good government. . . . Coercion and severity have proved of little use, and I hope the system of indulgence, kindness, and conciliation will now be tried. If that system will not succeed I hope we shall get rid of you altogether;—we

[1] G. R. Gleig, *The Life of Major-General Sir Thomas Munro* (London, 1830), 3 Vols. Vol. II, p. 15.
[2] *Works of David Ricardo*, Vol. IX, pp. 295-6.

could do very well without you,—you are a great expence to us, and prevent us from making any great improvement in our own government, as all our time is taken up attending to yours.' But to abandon the attempt to govern Ireland was the one thing Englishmen were not prepared to do. And in stiffening their resolve to maintain the Union, the very nature of the Act of 1800 played an important part. To create a United Kingdom of Great Britain and Ireland had been a task of some magnitude; to unmake it was widely deemed to involve the undermining of the constitution.

The first article of the Act of Union declared that Great Britain and Ireland should 'upon the first day of January, which shall be in the year of our Lord 1801, and for ever, be united into one kingdom, by the name of "The United Kingdom of Great Britain and Ireland".' The air of finality, that 'forever', was not intended to, and did not, encourage flexibility. Fundamental law is a concept unknown to English jurisprudence, but if the Act of Union may not, therefore, be so described nonetheless it was invested with the authority of an enactment, respect for the provisions of which, was deemed a condition of the maintenance of the established order in Church and State. This did not predispose governments to contemplate reform or change to meet Irish circumstances, however great, or even overwhelming, the case for such reform or change might be, if it was in conflict with the settlement of Anglo-Irish relations embodied in the Act of Union. Sir Robert Peel, reluctantly persuaded to concede Catholic Emancipation, well expressed an attitude of mind, which the nature of the Union induced and to which the predispositions of English statesmen generally inclined. 'I do not think', he said in the House of Commons on February 27, 1829[1] of his long, and now unsuccessful, attempt to maintain the exclusion of Roman Catholics from Parliament and high offices of State, 'it was an unnatural or unreasonable struggle. I resign it, in consequence of the conviction that it can be no longer advantageously maintained; from believing that there are not adequate materials or sufficient instruments for its effectual and permanent continuance. I yield, therefore, to a moral necessity which I cannot control, unwilling to push resistance to a point which might endanger the Establishments that I wish to defend.'

These words have general application to British policies towards

---

[1] Quoted in Norman Gash, *Mr Secretary Peel. The Life of Sir Robert Peel to 1830* (London, 1961), p. 570.

Ireland from the Union to the Treaty. British statesmen delayed concessions as long as was practicable, and when procrastination was no longer possible they yielded less from conviction than from unwillingness to push resistance to the point at which it might endanger the Union they sought to preserve and defend. Gladstone, it may be argued, was the great exception. But in some measure, that also is debatable. Gladstone, and Asquith after him, believed that Home Rule, by timely concessions to the sentiment of Irish nationality, would not weaken, but rather strengthen Union. And what persuaded them each in turn to propose such concessions? Was it conviction independently formed? Or was it conviction inspired in the first instance by Irish agitation and outrage and strengthened both in 1886 and again in 1910 by the weighty pressure of some eighty Irish votes in the House of Commons? To pose such questions is not necessarily tantamount to casting doubt upon the authenticity of Liberal convictions, which on the evidence would be altogether unjust in the case of Gladstone, and indeed also of Asquith, but they are nonetheless important in so far as they suggest that throughout the nineteenth century the onus for securing redress or change whether in Church or State rested, and heavily, on Irish shoulders. The Irish had not merely to make their case; they had additionally to overcome the weighty English bias against any change that might impair the Union settlement.

In the light of such predetermining factors there were three possible British approaches to the Irish question in its post-famine phase. The first was the maintenance of the Union in all its essentials, with redress and reform only within its framework. The second was the creation, or rather the re-creation, of a separate but subordinate Irish parliament on the model of the parliament that had existed in Dublin, 1782–1800, but within the framework of Union. And the third was acceptance of the reality of separate nationhood in Ireland and an advance by deliberate stages towards its recognition. These alternative approaches commended themselves to British statesmen and the British, or at any rate the English, electorate in sharply descending order of preference; —or more realistically in sharply ascending order of objection.

Irrespective of party or creed there were few Englishmen indeed who were prepared to contemplate the break-up of the Union. They were prepared to acknowledge deficiencies in the established order in Church and State and to consider remedies for them; they were for the most part ready to condemn the evils of the Irish land system and to reform them, subject to the conditions that the true principles of

political economy, as they were then conceived, were not disregarded
and that the foundations of property in the rest of the United Kingdom
were not thereby undermined; and they were, again for the most part,
ready to consider greater decentralization in Irish government so that
in purely domestic affairs the Irish might enjoy a more direct control,
and develop a greater sense of political responsibility. But action in all
these matters, even when taken, as it was so often, under pressure, was
dependent upon a conviction or at least an argument—neither of which
was necessarily in every case well founded—that such action contributed to the strengthening of the Union. The English debate about
reform was accordingly a debate about reform within a limited context.
This was not sufficiently understood by the Irish at the time or indeed
universally by historians since. John Bright, for example, advocated
substantial reform in Church and land questions; the Irish presumed
that in consequence he must favour Home Rule and bitterly resented his
defection, as they deemed it, from the Home Rule cause. But it was no
defection. John Bright had consistently declared himself a Unionist in
the sense that he believed that Irish reform should be within the framework of the Union and designed not to weaken but to strengthen it.
He did not consider that Gladstone's Home Rule proposals fulfilled
this condition.

On the Irish side attitudes to the Union settlement and to the Act of
Union itself were very different and the area in debate was accordingly
widened. Behind Irish demands for the redress of particular grievances
and the reform of particular anachronisms or evils, lay a general and a
fundamental theoretic conception. The Act of Union by reason of its
origins, far from possessing some special sanction, was deemed not to be
binding on Irishmen, because it was constitutionally defective in its
origin. The Irish Parliament, it is true, voted itself out of existence in
1800, but the Irish people had neither part nor lot in the transaction.
It was idle to speak to them of a solemn compact; if there were any
such compact, they were not a party to it. They were not a party to it,
firstly because the majority of them were unrepresented, being dis-
franchised, in the Irish Parliament, and secondly, in the opinion of
Arthur Griffith, the founder of Sinn Féin and the large section of
opinion, moderate and extremist alike, which in this respect anticipated
or followed him, the Irish Parliament of 1800, in voting away its
separate and independent existence was acting *ultra vires*. President de
Valera indeed sought to turn the argument against Arthur Griffith
himself in the debate on the Treaty in Dáil Éireann in December 1921.

'We were elected here', he said,[1] 'to be the guardians of an independent
Irish State—a State that had declared its independence—and this
House could no more than the ignominious House that voted away the
Colonial Parliament that was in Ireland in 1800 unless we wished to
follow the example of that House and vote away the independence of
our people.'

The influence of constitutional conceptions upon practical politics
should not be exaggerated. Like economic theories they serve their
purpose best when they coincide with the views politicians and statesman already entertain. Nonetheless in this particular instance the dispute about the ultimate validity of the Act of Union, and consequently
the extent to which it was morally as well as legally binding, underlined the wide gulf that existed between English and majority-Irish
psychological attitudes to the 1800 settlement and in so doing at once
helped to explain why it was so difficult even for moderates on either
side to work harmoniously towards a common end and why the outcome of attempts to do so was generally disillusioning. 'A grain of
effectual boycotting', argued United Ireland, 'is worth a bushel of
Radical philandering.'[2] The paper had a particular target in mind but its
conclusion had its general application in respect of Anglo-Irish political
co-operation, much less for personal reasons than because of the deeper,
predetermining factors in the situation.

The lack, or given the circumstances, it might be nearer the truth to
write, the impossibility of understanding and agreement about ultimate
ends accounted for a concentration of attention upon immediate steps
that could, or might, be taken in association, without calling in question
the constitutional foundations of the State or even implying that they
were in question at all. English liberal and radical opinion was at one
with majority Irish opinion in its desire first to curb and then to destroy
the landlord system and to disestablish the Church of Ireland. But to
Radicals and to Liberals, even to Gladstone in 1868, all this appeared
as an end itself. They cherished the 'upas tree' theory of Irish ills. The
country and its people were shadowed by a great and noxious ascendancy growth. Its branches, as Gladstone thought, needed to be
lopped; the tree indeed, though at this point some paused, had best be
felled; and then the Irish people, the landlords dispossessed, their
Church disestablished, could move forward with an advancing Liberal
Party in an increasingly prosperous Liberal Union.

[1] Dáil Éireann Treaty Debate, December 1921–January 1922, p. 25.
[2] United Ireland, May 30, 1885.

De Tocqueville was told in 1835 by a young and able Protestant lawyer[1], among others, that a struggle for power in Ireland had now begun. It was a conflict between the hitherto ruling Protestant minority and the newly enfranchised Catholic electorate. It was also in such narrow terms that Liberals and Radicals conceived the struggle. They thought with Ricardo[2] that it was not England that was oppressing Ireland but an aristocracy which ruled the country with 'a rod of iron within it', and they inferred from this that once that class was dispossessed the Union would be correspondingly strengthened. They were to be sharply disillusioned. In the Irish view there was not one upas tree but two—and the more noxious was the Union itself.

In the national struggle for power which ensued, Liberals and Nationalists once more might travel some distance together along a Home Rule road but there was a predestined parting of the ways, for while most Liberals were concerned to strengthen the Union by broadening its basis in self-government, most Nationalists aspired to a separatist goal. There was, however, also a third party to complicate and confuse the issue.

Over most of Ireland the ascendancy was expendable and politically it had been, or was being, expended. But in the closely settled areas of the North-East there was more than a class, there was a community. It was resolved not to be, and it did not prove to be, expendable. In this time was on its side. The transfer of power, foreshadowed in 1886, was long protracted and, as so often elsewhere, the passage of time served at once to stiffen the demands and to strengthen the hand of the third party. In the period 1886–1920 it advanced its position from that of an indentifiable minority group within a recognized political entity to one of control of a semi-autonomous state equated by Act of Parliament with the remainder of the island of which it formed a part. Minority determination to resist incorporation in a unitary Irish state, the reality of which was recognized most clearly by republican opponents, could not have achieved so great a transformation without the backing of formidable English allies. At a favourable moment politically the minority were in consequence enabled to obtain not only a separate state but also the area for which they asked, on the ground that it was the largest in which stable Unionist government could be maintained. Twenty-seven years later, in not altogether dissimilar circumstances, Mohammed Ali Jinnah sought from Lord Mountbatten, the

---

[1] *Journeys*, pp. 149–52 See also p. 143.
[2] See above, p. 42.

last British Viceroy of India, the whole of six provinces of North-West and North-East India, which collectively contained a Muslim majority in favour of a separate Muslim state of Pakistan. But Lord Mountbatten in his broadcast of June 3rd stated: 'When the Muslim league demanded the partition of India Congress used the same arguments for demanding in that event the partition of certain provinces. To my mind that argument is unassailable'. The Punjab and Bengal were themselves accordingly partitioned and Jinnah was left, as he indeed had feared, with a 'moth-eaten,' 'truncated' Pakistan.[1] In Ireland the principle of partition applied; but there was no corresponding county or district division to determine its extent. Irish revolutionary nationalists would not have compromised in any event in respect of the principle of partition; they felt doubly aggrieved at the manner of its imposition.

Lord Acton, who if not the wisest, had at least some claim to be regarded as the most learned Englishman of his generation, maintained that the combination of different nations in a single state was as necessary a condition of civilized life as the combination of men in society, and it is the case that in many parts of Europe and Asia, the state must be, in Acton's words, a 'cauldron in which the fusion of different races takes place', if it is to survive as a unit. But in Ireland the existence of political and cultural diversity was for long discounted and, in so far as it was subsequently recognized, it was with reluctance. That was partly at least because bi-culturalism was conceived of as a source only of national weakness and division. But here again Acton thought otherwise. 'Where political and national boundaries coincide', he wrote, 'society ceases to advance, and a nation relapses to a condition corresponding to that of men who renounce intercourse with their fellowmen.'[2] The judgement may well be questioned, but at least it affords a corrective to uncritical acceptance of the view that a society in which the frontiers of nationality and state exactly coincide is alone ideal.

In Ireland the unitary concept of the State was taken as the model, and no doubt partly in consequence the ways in which federation in one of its many forms might contribute to the reconciliation of diversity with unity was at no time systematically explored. There is, of necessity, always some conflict between the political decentralization and the racial and cultural diversity, the existence of which federalism

[1] Alan Campbell-Johnson, *Mission with Mountbatten* (London, 1951), pp. 59–115, for a personal account of the circumstances leading to the statement.
[2] *Essays on Nationality*, London, 1862.

at once acknowledges and accepts and a strong self-conscious national
sentiment drawing inspiration from an historic past. But then, the
ideal of unity, like the ideal of national independence, demands its
own, if very different, forms of sacrifice.

The question that survived the settlement of 1921 was at all earlier
times, even in the years 1912–14, subordinate to the main problem of
Anglo-Irish relations. This is something that deserves restatement, if
only because survival is apt to lend retrospective, and unhistorical,
significance to that which has survived. The future of Ulster, of 'the
third party' in fact derived its importance, which at certain critical
moments was undoubtedly great, from its association with the major
question of the future of Anglo-Irish relations. Or to present the issue
in more general terms—arising from and subsidiary to a national-
imperial conflict there was in this, as in many other cases, a conflict of
more limited dimensions between an indigenous majority and a settler
minority community at the last enjoying the support, albeit at times
equivocal, of the outgoing imperial power.

It was with the fundamental question of Ireland's relations with
Britain and the Empire that English governments and Irish leaders
were chiefly preoccupied between 1800 and 1921. And because it was
fundamental the considerations that were uppermost in men's minds,
when Union was about to be enacted, were not without their continuing relevance, when it was about to be repealed. Charles James Fox,
opposed to Union in any case, because the state of representation in the
Irish Parliament and the state of Ireland at the time combined to make
it in practice 'the most monstrous proposition that ever was made' also,
and at a deeper level, objected to it because 'my general principle in
politics is very much against the one and indivisible'.[1] William Pitt was
otherwise predisposed and after listing the advantages to Ireland of
Union with Great Britain, as he conceived them, he enquired of
members of the House of Commons whether Union 'under such circumstances, by free consent, and on just and equal terms', deserved 'to be
branded as a proposal for subjecting Ireland to a foreign yoke.'[2] The
Irish answer—and they were best placed to give one—was in the
affirmative, though, curiously enough, Pitt's reputation has suffered
little from his misconceptions and miscalculations on so large an issue.

---

[1] J. L. Hammond, *Charles James Fox. A Political Study* (London, 1903), pp. 197–8.
[2] In the House of Commons on January 31, 1799. Reprinted in Curtis and McDowell,
Irish Historical Documents, p. 231. The 'free consent' may be thought a euphemistic
use, or abuse, of language.

At that time it was the chief Unionist contention that the existing two independent legislatures 'in the one empire' were 'as absurd and monstrous as two heads on one pair of shoulders'.[1] But after the lapse of a century and more had it not been conclusively shown, to continue in the not altogether fruitful field of natural, or unnatural, analogy, that it was more absurd and even more monstrous to conceive of two pairs of shoulders with only one head?

[1] R. B. McDowell, *Irish Public Opinion 1750-1800* (London, 1944), p. 248. See also Chap. XIII generally. and J. C. Beckett, *Anglo-Irish Constitutional relations in the later eighteenth century*. I.H.S. Vol. XIV, 1964, pp. 20-38.

BIBLIOGRAPHY

The title and other particulars of all works referred to in the text are set out in the footnotes and the selected bibliography printed below lists, for convenience, the more important of these publications arranged in relation to that part of the book to which they principally refer. A note on the unpublished papers which have been consulted appears in the Introduction. Parliamentary debates, a valuable and often underestimated source of historical information in the period, newspapers, notably *The Freeman's Journal* and *United Ireland*, as well as articles in periodicals or facts contemporarily recorded in *The Annual Register* are annotated in the text but do not reappear in the bibliography. On the other hand in the case of State papers, the titles of those that are most relevant are recorded at the end of each part of the bibliographical list. E. Curtis and R. B. McDowell, *Irish Historical Documents 1172–1922*, contains a necessarily brief but useful selection of some of the more important documents of the period.

Part I

Sir Jonah Barrington: *Historic Memoirs of Ireland.* London, 1833.

Gustave de la Bonninière de Beaumont: *L'Irelande Sociale, Politique et Réligieuse.* Paris, 1839; revised edition 1963.

R. D. Collison Black: *Economic Thought and The Irish Question 1817–1870:* Cambridge, 1960.

Elizabeth Bowen: *Bowen's Court. The story of an Anglo-Irish family from the time of Cromwell to the present day.* London, 1942.

John Bright: *The Diaries of John Bright.* Edited by R. A. J. Walling, London, 1930.

Count Cavour: *Thoughts on Ireland: Its Present and its Future.* Translated by W. Hodgson, London, 1868.

K. H. Connell: *The Population of Ireland 1750–1845.* Oxford, 1950.

E. Curtis: *A History of Ireland.* London, 1936. 6th ed. rev. 1964.

H. W. C. Davis: *The Age of Grey and Peel.* London, 1929.

R. Dudley Edwards and T. Desmond Williams (Editors): *The Great Famine.* Dublin, 1956.

Norman Gash: *Mr Secretary Peel: The Life of Sir Robert Peel to 1830.* London, 1961.

James Grant: *Impressions of Ireland and the Irish.* 2 Vols. London, 1844.

D. Gwynn: *Daniel O'Connell.* London, 1930.

J. L. Hammond: *Gladstone and the Irish Nation.* London, 1938. New Ed. 1964.

Bolton King: *Mazzini.* London, 1902.

J. G. Kohl: *England, Scotland and Ireland.* London, 1844.

G. Mazzini: *The Duties of Man and other Essays.* London, 1907.

G. Mazzini: *The Life and Writings of Joseph Mazzini.* 6 Vols. London, 1891.

R. B. McDowell: *Public Opinion and Government Policy in Ireland, 1801–46.* London, 1952.

R. B. McDowell: *The Irish Administration 1801–1867*. London, 1964.

Karl Marx: *Letters to Dr Kugelmann*. English edition. London, 1934.

Marx–Engels: *Selected Correspondence, 1846–95*. English edition. London, 1934.

Constantia Maxwell: *Dublin Under the Georges*. Revised edition. London, 1956.

Gustav Mayer: *Friedrich Engels:* a Biography. London, 1936.

J. S. Mill: *England and Ireland*. London, 1868.

J. S. Mill: *Chapters and Speeches on the Irish Land Question*. London, 1870.

John Mitchel: *Jail Journal*. Edited by Arthur Griffith. Dublin, 1913.

W. F. Moneypenney and G. E. Buckle: *The Life of Benjamin Disraeli*. 6 Vols. London, 1910–20.

John Morley: *The Life of Richard Cobden*. 2 Vols. London, 1881.

E. R. Norman: *The Catholic Church and Ireland in the Age of Rebellion, 1859–73*. London, 1965.

K. B. Nowlan: *The Politics of Repeal*. 1841–50. London, 1965.

George O'Brien: *The Economic History of Ireland from the Union to the Famine*. Dublin, 1921.

S. O'Faolain: *King of the Beggars: a life of Daniel O'Connell*. London, 1938.

P. S. O'Hegarty: *A History of Ireland under the Union:* London, 1952.

The Works and Correspondence of David Ricardo edited by P. Sraffa: 10 Vols. Cambridge, 1951–55.

Bertrand Russell: *Freedom and Organization*. London, 1937.

R. N. Salaman: *The Influence of the Potato on the Course of Irish History*. Dublin, 1943.

G. Salvemini: *Mazzini*. London, 1936.

Nassau Senior: *Journals, Conversations and Essays relating to Ireland*. 2 Vols. London, 1868.

D. Thornley: *Isaac Butt and Home Rule*. London, 1964.

Alexis de Tocqueville: *Journeys to England and Ireland*. Edited by J. P. Mayer, London, 1958.

Alexis de Tocqueville: *The Recollections of Alexis de Tocqueville*. Edited by J. P. Mayer, London, 1948.

W. S. Trench: *Realities of Irish Life*. London, 1868.

T. de V. White: *The Road of Excess*. Dublin, 1946.

A. J. Whyte: *The Early Life and Letters of Cavour, 1810–48*. Oxford, 1925.

A. J. Whyte: *The Political Life and Letters of Cavour, 1848–61*. London, 1930.

J. H. Whyte: *The Independent Irish Party 1850–9*. Oxford, 1958.

E. L. Woodward: *The Age of Reform*. Oxford, 1938. New edition 1962.

Arthur Young: *A Tour in Ireland*, edited by C. Maxwell. Cambridge, 1925.

Report from H.M. Commissioners of Inquiry into the State of the Law and Practice in Respect of the Occupation of the Land in Ireland. Parl. Papers 1845, Vols. XIX–XXII.

Report of the Commissioners appointed to take the Census of Ireland for the year 1841. Parl. Papers 1843, Vol. XXIV.

Part II

W. S. Armour: *Armour of Ballymoney*. London, 1934.

Robert Blake: *The Unknown Prime Minister*. London, 1955.

Lady Gwendolen Cecil: *Life of Robert, 3rd Marquess of Salisbury.* 4 Vols. London, 1921–32.
Joseph Chamberlain: *A Political Memoir 1880–92.* Edited by C. H. D. Howard. London, 1953.
W. S. Churchill: *Lord Randolph Churchill.* 2 Vols. London, 1906.
W. S. Churchill: *The World Crisis 1911–1918.* Revised edition. London, 1951.
W. S. Churchill: *The World Crisis.* The Aftermath. London, 1929.
Lord Crewe: *Lord Rosebery.* 2 Vols. London, 1931.
L. P. Curtis: *Coercion and Conciliation in Ireland 1880–1892.* Princeton, 1963.
Reginald, Viscount Esher: *Journals and Letters.* 4 Vols. London, 1934–38.
R. C. K. Ensor: *England 1870–1914.* Oxford, 1936.
St J. Ervine: *Parnell.* London, 1925..
H. A. L. Fisher: *James Bryce.* 2 Vols. London, 1927.
Lord Fitzmaurice: *The Life of the Second Earl Granville.* 2 Vols. London, 1908.
J. L. Garvin: *The Life of Joseph Chamberlain.* 3 Vols. London, 1932–34.
Lord Gladstone: *After Thirty Years.* London, 1928.
A. M. Gollin: *Proconsul in Politics.* London, 1964.
J. W. Good: *Ulster and Ireland.* Dublin, 1919.
Lord Grey of Fallodon: *Twenty-Five Years 1892–1916.* 8th edition. 3 Vols. London, 1935.
D. R. Gwynn: *The Life of John Redmond.* London, 1932.
J. L. Hammond: *C. P. Scott of the Manchester Guardian.* London, 1934.
Bernard Holland: *The Life of Spencer Compton, Eighth Duke of Devonshire.* 2 Vols. London, 1911.
M. C. Hurst: *Joseph Chamberlain and West Midland Politics 1886–1895.* (Dugdale Society Occasional Papers No. 15). Oxford, 1962.
R. R. James: *Lord Randolph Churchill.* London, 1959.
R. R. James: *Rosebery.* London, 1963.
Roy Jenkins: *Asquith.* London, 1963.
Thomas Jones: *Lloyd George.* London, 1951.
F. S. L. Lyons: *The Fall of Parnell.* London, 1960.
R. B. McCallum: *Asquith.* London, 1936.
Ronald McNeill: *Ulster's Stand for Union.* London, 1922.
Sir Philip Magnus: *Gladstone. A Biography.* London, 1954.
N. Mansergh: *The Government of Northern Ireland.* London, 1936.
E. Marjoribanks and Ian Colvin: *The Life of Lord Carson.* 3 Vols. London, 1932–36.
Earl of Midleton: *Ireland. Dupe or Heroine.* London, 1932.
John Morley: *The Life of William Ewart Gladstone.* 3 Vols. London, 1903.
John, Viscount Morley: *Recollections.* 2 Vols. London, 1917.
H. Nicolson: *Life of King George V.* London, 1952.
C. C. O'Brien: *Parnell and his party.* Oxford, 1957.
C. C. O'Brien (Editor): *The Shaping of Modern Ireland.* London, 1960.
T. P. O'Connor: *Memoirs of an Old Parliamentarian.* 2 Vols. London, 1929.
Agatha Ramm: *The Political Correspondence of Mr Gladstone and Lord Granville 1868–1876.* London, RHS, 1952.
Agatha Ramm: *The Political Correspondence of Mr Gladstone and Lord Granville 1876–1886.* 2 Vols. Oxford, 1962.

Thorold Rogers: *Speeches by the Right Hon. John Bright M.P.* London, 1869.
Lord Rosebery: *Lord Randolph Churchill.* London, 1906.
J. A. Spender and C. Asquith: *Life of Lord Oxford and Asquith.* 2 Vols. London, 1932.
J. A. Spender: *Great Britain, Empire and Commonwealth.* London, 1937.
Lytton Strachey: *Eminent Victorians.* London, 1918.
E. Strauss: *Irish Nationalism and British Democracy.* London, 1951.
G. M. Trevelyan: *John Bright.* London, 1925.
P. J. P. Tynan: *The Irish National Invincibles and Their Times.* London, 1894.
Kenneth Young: *Arthur James Balfour.* London, 1963.
G. M. Young: *Victorian England. The Portrait of an Age.* Oxford, 1936.
Correspondence between H.M.G. and the Prime Minister of Northern Ireland 1921. Cmd 1561.

Part III

AE: *The Living Torch.* Edited by Monk Gibbon, London, 1937,
AE: *Collected Poems.* London, 1928.
Piaras Beaslai: *Michael Collins.* Dublin, 1937.
James Connolly: *Labour in Ireland.* Dublin and London, 1917.
Nora Connolly O'Brien: *Portrait of a Rebel Father.* Dublin, 1935.
D. Corkery: *Synge and Anglo-Irish Literature.* Cork, 1931.
M. Digby: *Horace Plunkett: An Anglo-American Irishman.* Oxford, 1949.
John Eglinton (W. K. Magee): *Irish Literary Portraits.* London, 1935.
John Eglington: *A Memoir of A.E.* London, 1937.
U. Ellis-Fermor: *The Irish Democratic Movement.* London, 1939.
Sir J. Fergusson: *The Curragh Incident.* London, 1963.
R. M. Fox. *Green Banners.* London, 1938.
R. M. Fox: *James Connolly: The Forerunner.* Tralee, 1946.
O. St J. Gogarty: *As I Was Walking down Sackville Street.* London, 1937.
Arthur Griffith: *The Resurrection of Hungary. A Parallel for Ireland.* First published Dublin, 1904. 3rd edition 1918.
S. G. Gwynn (Editor): *The Letters and Friendships of Sir Cecil Spring Rice. A Record.* 2 Vols. London, 1929.
J. Hendrick: *Life of Walter H. Page.* 2 Vols. London, 1924.
R. M. Henry: *The Evolution of Sinn Féin.* Dublin, 1920.
Douglas Hyde: *The Revival of Irish Literature and other Addresses.* London, 1894.
V. I. Lenin: *Collected Works.* New Edition. Moscow, 1960 (in progress, 21 Vols. published). Vols. 19 and 20.
V. I. Lenin: *Lenin on Britain.* New Edition. Moscow, 1959.
F. S. L. Lyons: *The Irish Parliamentary Party, 1890–1910.* London, 1951.
D. Macardle: *The Irish Republic.* New edition. London, 1951.
F. X. Martin (Editor): *The Irish Volunteers 1913–1915. Recollections and Documents.* Dublin, 1963.
George Moore: *Confessions of a Young Man.* Reprinted. London, 1929.
George Moore: *Hail and Farewell.* 3 Vols. Ebury Edition. London, 1937.
P. S. O'Hegarty: *The Victory of Sinn Fein.* Dublin, 1924.
John O'Leary: *Recollections of Fenians and Fenianism.* 2 Vols. London, 1896.

P. H. Pearse: Political Writings and Speeches. Dublin, 1922.
Sir H. Plunkett: *Ireland in the New Century*. London, 1904.
J. E. Pomfret: *The Struggle for Land in Ireland*. Princeton, 1930.
A. Rivoallan: *L'Irlande*. Paris, 1934.
A. Rivoallan: *La Littérature Irlandaise Contemporaine*. Paris, 1940.
Louis N. Le Roux: *Tom Clarke and the Irish Freedom Movement* (Translation). Dublin, 1926.
A. P. Ryan: *Mutiny at the Curragh*. London, 1956.
W. B. Yeats: *The Trembling of the Veil*. London, 1922.
W. B. Yeats: *Essays*. London, 1924.
W. B. Yeats: *Collected Poems*. London, 1934.
W. B. Yeats: *Last Poems and Plays*. London, 1940.
W. B. Yeats: *Tribute to Thomas Davis*. Cork, 1947.
Report of the Commissioners appointed to inquire into the Financial Relations between Great Britain and Ireland. C. 8262. Parl. Papers 1896., Vol. XXXIII.
Minutes of Evidence taken before the Committee appointed to inquire into the Public Health of the City of Dublin. Cd 244. Parl. Papers 1900, Vol. XXXIX.
Census of Ireland, 1911. General Report. Cd 6663. Parl. Papers 1913, Vol. CXVIII.
Report of the Proceedings of the Irish Convention 1917–18. Cd 9019.

INDEX

GEORGE ALLEN & UNWIN LTD
London: 40 Museum Street, W.C.1

Auckland: 24 Wyndham Street
Bombay: 15 Graham Road, Ballard Estate, Bombay 1
Bridgetown: P.O. Box 222
Buenos Aires: Escritorio 454-459, Florida 165
Calcutta: 17 Chittaranjan Avenue, Calcutta 14
Cape Town: 68 Shortmarket Street
Hong Kong: 44 Mody Road, Kowloon
Ibadan: P.O. Box 62
Karachi: Karachi Chambers, McLeod Road
Madras: Mohan Mansions, 38c Mount Road, Madras 6
Mexico: Villalongin 32-10, Piso, Mexico 5, D.F.
Nairobi: P.O. Box 4536
New Delhi: 13-15 Asaf Ali Road, New Delhi 1
Ontario: 81 Curlew Drive, Don Mills
Philippines: 7 Waling-Wuling Street, Roxas District, Quezon City
São Paulo: Caixa Postal 8675
Singapore: 36c Prinsep Street, Singapore 7
Sydney, N.S.W.: Bradbury House, 55 York Street
Tokyo: 10 Kanda-Ogawamachi, 3-Chome, Chiyoda-Ku

NICHOLAS MANSERGH

SOUTH AFRICA 1906–1961
THE PRICE OF MAGNANIMITY

cr. 8vo.   *9s. 6d. net*

In 1906, four years after the ending of the Boer War, the Liberal Government restored self-government to the Transvaal and in so doing opened the way to Union in South Africa. Their magnanimous gesture had far-reaching consequences not only in South Africa but also, by force of example, in the shaping of the future British Commonwealth of Nations. The purpose of this study is to re-examine, in the light of documentary evidence recently made available, the aims of Liberal policy, the considerations which determined it, and the more important consequences that flowed from it in the broader perspective of history.

Magnanimous gestures customarily exact a price but it is not always those who make them who are called upon to pay it. How carefully did the Liberal government consider the possible consequences for others of their actions? To what extent can it be said that English-speaking South Africans, or to what far greater extent that non-Europeans in South Africa paid the price of Liberal magnanimity in succeeding years? These are the questions with which this book is principally concerned. Its aim is to provide a brief historical and political analysis of the very complex but little changing problems which have confronted British and Commonwealth statesmen in their relations with South Africa from the time of the restoration of self-government to the defeated Boer republics in 1906-7 and the inauguration of the Union on May 31 1910 to the secession of the Republic of South Africa from the Commonwealth on May 31 1961.

W. A. ROBSON

THE GOVERNORS AND
THE GOVERNED

cr. 8vo.   *12s. 6d. net cloth, 7s. 6d. net paper*

The relations between the rulers of a nation and those over whom
they exercise authority are by far the most important feature of
every political system. Yet surprisingly little attention has been
given to the subject in its modern setting. In this short book Professor
W. A. Robson sets out to explore the matter from some new and
unusual angles.

Three main themes are dealt with. The first is a consideration of
bureaucracy as it exists today. The author contends that we must
accept a great expansion of executive power as the necessary and
inevitable concomitant of welfare and planning policies; but that we
must also recognize the need for more and better remedies in cases
of maladministration than those which now exist in this country.

The second theme is the need to evolve new methods of bridging
the gulf of aloofness and misunderstanding which so often separates
the governors from the governed. Professor Robson shows the need
for a continuous process of two-way communication between public
authorities and the public; and considers the methods, the institutions
and the spirit which should inspire the intelligence, information
and public relations services.

The third theme is the attitude of the citizens to politics. Here the
author considers the interaction between the home, the school and
the State; and he also looks at some of the fundamental psychological
forces which influence political behaviour. The effect on politics of
the modern media of mass communication and the deliberate use by
political parties of techniques which exploit the subconscious drives
and emotions of men and women for vote-winning purposes are
examined with unrelenting rigour and devastating frankness.

This is an arresting little book which throws much light on dark
places. Neither the governors nor the governed can afford to ignore
it.

BERTRAND RUSSELL

GERMAN SOCIAL DEMOCRACY

la. cr. 8vo.   21*s. net*

This book is the first that Earl Russell ever wrote, and was based
upon a series of lectures delivered at the London School of Economics
in 1896. Since then much has happened and much has changed.
When the book was first produced the Kaiser was in his glory: he,
and his government were bitterly hostile to the Social Democrats,
who returned the hostility with interest. They were, at that time
completely orthodox Marxists and they hoped for a revolution in
Germany which would turn the country into a socialist republic.
The book was written from the viewpoint of an orthodox Liberal
of the period, and although the author's own politics changed later,
he has made no attempt to modify this book, which is an important
historical document in which, as he himself expresses it, 'a former
writer comments on a former world'.

The purpose of this book was not to supply a full history of Social
Democracy in Germany, but rather to bring into relief those aspects
of its history which seemed to the author to have been the most
important in producing the existing (1896) political situation. Two
chapters are devoted to a study of Marx and Lassalle and their influence on Socialistic opinion in Germany. Two further chapters are
devoted to the history of German Socialism, first during the period
preceding the passing of the law against the party in 1878, and second
during the application of that law until its expiry in 1890. An examination is then made of the tactics of the party following the end of
the persecutions and of its condition towards the end of the century.
It is still a most important document for all students of European
political history.

GEORGE ALLEN AND UNWIN LTD

3 3226 00144 4134